COLLECTED ESSAYS

Charles R. Lanham
Collected Essays

Colloquī
Volume I—2016-2017

Deacon's Corner Publishing

RENO, NEVADA

Deacon's Corner Publishing
Reno, Nevada
www.deaconscorner.org

Collected Essays: Colloquī, Volume I—2016-2017/ Charles R. Lanham. -- 1st ed.
Copyright © 2020 **Charles R. Lanham**
All rights reserved. Published 2020
Printed in the United States of America

ISBN 978-0-9905582-8-6

Restless hearts

You have made us for yourself, O Lord,
and our heart is restless until it rests in you.

—SAINT AUGUSTINE OF HIPPO
Confessions (Lib 1,1-2,2.5,5: CSEL 33, 1-5)

TRUTH

*The truth of life is the truth whereby a thing is true,
not whereby a person says what is true.*

—SAINT THOMAS AQUINAS,
Summa Theologica, II-I q.109 a.2 ad 3.

It is only by believing in God that we can ever criticise the Government. Once abolish the God, and the Government becomes the God. That fact is written all across human history; … The truth is that Irreligion is the opium of the people. Wherever the people do not believe in something beyond the world, they will worship the world. But, above all, they will worship the strongest thing in the world. And, by the very nature of … modern systems, as well as by the practical working of almost any system, the State will be the strongest thing in the world. The whole tendency of men is to treat the solitary State as the solitary standard. That men may protest against law, it is necessary that they should believe in justice; that they may believe in a justice beyond law, it is necessary that they should believe in a justice beyond the land of living men. … You can even make its subjects contented, as opium would make them contented. But if you are to have anything like divine discontent, then it must really be divine. Anything that really comes from below must really come from above.

– G. K. Chesterton, *Christendom in Dublin*, 1932.

It is a characteristic of any decaying civilization that the great masses of the people are unconscious of the tragedy. Humanity in a crisis is generally insensitive to the gravity of the times in which it lives. Men do not want to believe their own times are wicked, partly because it involves too much self-accusation and principally because they have no standards outside of themselves by which to measure their times. If there is no fixed concept of justice how shall men know it is violated? Only those who live by faith really know what is happening in the world; the great masses without faith are unconscious of the destructive processes going on, because they have lost the vision of the heights from which they have fallen. The tragedy is not that the hairs of our civilization are gray; it is rather that we fail to see that they are.

– Fulton J. Sheen, *Communism and the Conscience of the West*, 1948.

CONTENTS

FOREWORD   i

PREFACE   iii

INTRODUCTION   vi

June 2, 2016   1
A Restless Heart
An Insatiable Curiosity
To See Through All Things
A Lexiconic High Jacking

June 9, 2016   6
Running Away
A Hospital for Sinners
Angelic Stubbornness
Enriching the Mind
On Becoming a Cat

June 16, 2016   14
Falling Down
Contemplating Truth
Richer for Poorer

June 23, 2016   20
Considered Thoughts
Heaven and Hell
Encountering God

June 30,2016   25
The Tragedy
Memories and History
Render unto Caesar

July 01, 2016   30
What's New?
Homegrown Saints
Idle Thoughts

July 08, 2016   37
A Reason to Think
On Moral Ground

July 15, 2016   41

    Love Never Ending
    Dialogue or Diatribe

July 22, 2016   45

    Beacons of Hope
    The Joy of Love

July 29, 2016   49

    On That Day
    Unlocking the Chains
    To Lose a Mind
    Unselfish Devotion

August 05, 2016   55

    The Science of Art
    In Name Only
    What Matters Most
    Counter Witness

August 12, 2016   60

    Sunday Rising
    Enslaving the Mind
    You Shall Not Kill

August 19, 2016   66

    What Love is This
    A Ten O'clock Scholar
    Called to a Life

August 26, 2016   72

    What Grand Illusion
    Long Past Dark
    Just Practicing

September 02, 2016   77

    Carrying Their Cross
    When Will We Learn?

September 09, 2016   83

    Catholic Tradition
    What's in Your Mind?

September 16, 2016   88

    Remember the Past
    Instituted by Christ

September 23, 2016   91

    Let Me Entertain You

Ecumenism Run Amok
Tradition: To The East

September 30, 2016   97
To Err is Human
Without Conviction
Ad Orientem

October 07, 2016   103
Through a Glass, Dimly
Private Judgment
Pulpit Politics

October 14, 2016   111
O Mystery, Divine
The Angelic Doctor
Sticks and Stones

October 21, 2016   117
Masking the Taste
A Polemic Unwinding

October 28, 2016   119
A Life Loved
A History Redeemed

November 04, 2016   122
The Measure of Life
From a Distance

November 11, 2016   125
A Silent Salute
Coming Up for Air

November 18, 2016   129
Technological Hubris

November 25, 2016   132
For What We Have
Divine Enters Time

December 02, 2016   135
For the Love of All
What's This Tradition?

December 09, 2016   138
Failure is Not an Option

December 16, 2016   144
A Saint for Geeks?
Sticks and Stones …

December 23, 2016   147
    God Descends to Man
    Angels We Have Heard
    Your Journey of Faith

December 30, 2016   151
    Doctrine of Progress
    Futile Reform

January 06, 2017   157
    Christ's Final Command
    The Word of the Lord

January 13, 2017   163
    A Time of Conversion
    Once Upon a Dream

January 20, 2017   166
    Doing the Right Thing
    How Big Is My Church?

January 27, 2017   169
    For What it is Worth
    Playing God

February 03, 2017   175
    Food for the Soul
    On Holy Ground

February 10, 2017   178
    The Genius of a Mind
    The Spirit Denied
    Objections Noted

February 17, 2017   186
    The KISS Principle
    A Shell of Christianity

February 24, 2017   192
    What Love is This
    Rude Awakening

March 03, 2017   198
    Walking Away
    Keep Them from Idols

March 10, 2017   201
    Under Construction

March 17, 2017   205
    The Rising Son

March 24, 2017   **211**
    Turn Down the Lights
    A Ship of Fools Redux

March 31, 2017   **216**
    The Essence of Being
    Ad Hominem

April 07, 2017   **219**
    On the Transcendent
    Dead or Alive

April 14, 2017   **225**
    In Shadowed Footsteps
    No Act Condemned

April 21, 2017   **233**
    The Cross We Bear
    For Want of Argument
    The Power of Silence

April 28, 2017   **239**
    For Better or Worse
    Wanting More
    Source and Summit

May 05, 2017   **245**
    From a Mirror
    Falling Silent

May 12, 2017   **251**
    Loved into Being

May 26, 2017   **252**
    A Right Order to Love
    Mirror, Mirror …

ABOUT THE AUTHOR   **263**

"Think." My wife and her sisters still recall from their youth the innumerable times my astute and loving father-in-law would implore them to stop, collect themselves, and do this very thing as soon as they had reached their destination. To think about where they were; to think about who they were with; to think about the choices they were going to make. All with the hope they would choose well their next steps and act accordingly.

I was reminded of this wonderful lesson numerous times while reading through these thought-provoking essays penned by my friend of a decade, Deacon Charles (Chuck) Lanham. Clearly, he has challenged me and anyone else who chooses the adventurous path of reading his insightful prose to do just that—to think and then act.

As a cradle Catholic, the viewpoints shared herein remind me that I am not here on earth to merely take up space. Rather, that our Lord continually invites me to nurture my faith and then act accordingly in the world. More specifically, to push myself daily to answer a question of significant importance—when people see me, are they seeing Jesus? All of Him?

Unquestionably a well-researched work born of tedious labor and love, this impressive work is no surprise to me. His love of reading, research, analysis and writing so as to share what he has learned with others in a spirit of love he came by honestly. His mother, Nellie Ann Lanham, was a multi-award-winning journalist and author. A product of the extreme lessons learned while surviving the Great Depression, her appreciation for the less fortunate was noted by many. Her toughness and love for continual learning did not fall on deaf ears—her son, Deacon Chuck, is gifted with both. I encourage you to read more about this remarkable woman in the February 21, 2020 issue of Colloqui, Volume 04, Number 28 which can be found on Deacon Chuck's website, deaconscorner.org, should you have a desire to do so.

Reviewing this collection of essays has galvanized me to use well and often the gifts God has given me. By God's grace I pray the same for you. As to who else may turn these pages and be positively impacted, that, of course, only our Good Lord knows for certain.

Raoul Plus, S. J. states this point well in his enlightening book Radiating Christ: An Appeal to Roman Catholics (p. 135):

> "Put into the foundations of the work all the effort you can, intelligent and detached effort: 'Never give up until you have tried everything,' Foch used to say. But when you have

done that, acknowledge that you have done nothing, and that grace alone can bring the work to fruition."

Deacon Chuck continues to steadfastly put forth his best efforts by his free will and God's loving grace; his light is not remaining under a bushel. May we do the same and do so in haste.

Ron Reigle

The heavens declare the glory of God, and the firmament proclaims his handiwork (Psalm 19:1). There is a beauty in all which God has made, a majesty so breathtaking, so wondrous, so magnificent; words dare not express, for such words would most assuredly fail in their defect and imprecision.

The summers of my youth were generally spent in the rural Midwest, working for any one of several uncles; farmers who tilled the soil, planted corn, soybeans, wheat, and oats in the main; each crop requiring careful tending from seed to maturity; always praying for just the right amount of rain and sunshine to produce a bountiful harvest. The days were long and hot and hard, most often beginning before the sun peeked over the Eastern horizon and ending long after it had said goodnight. And when your head at long last hit the pillow, you did not remember it, for sleep always won the race.

Yet there were nights when boyhood friends would camp beside an indolent pond, an artificial reservoir of still water, alien to the plainness of the earth; the miles and miles of emptiness, no intrusions of manmade stuff; just boys on the cusp of becoming men, in the darkness looking up recognizing the awesome power of God.

We would lay there on our backs – the smell of clover wafting on the night wind – just staring into that vast and endless sea of stars; each alone in contemplation of the wonder of it all.

And we would listen to the silence of that universe which God had made and hear his voice speak to each of us. And we would dream of it. We never wondered why, because we knew the reason. God made it all for us. Why? Because he loves us. Imagine that.

As a young Catholic growing up in the fifties and sixties I can recall – with a longing in my soul – the reverence and the awe I felt when in His Presence. It was a sacred time and you knew it; you were on holy ground and you felt it; you were in His house and you trembled at the very thought of it.

The church was old but filled of marvelous statues and images, beautiful stained-glass windows and ornate light fixtures suspended from high above, and a large wooden altar painted white, with its spires and spindles reaching toward heaven tipped with gold. The altar railing stood low, guarding the sanctuary, in silent testimony to the sacred presence residing beyond its gates.

God was there and so we prayed and worshipped and adored. We knelt in humble supplication when we received our Lord upon the tongue. There was no question what and who we received: it was the Body and Blood of our Lord, so sacred and holy that only the priest could hold or touch His Preciousness.

From the moment you entered the church you knew you were in the presence of God, in His house, on sacred ground. You dressed as if you were in the presence of someone very important – because you were. You left the world behind when you walked through the doors. You behaved as if you were in the presence of a King – because you were.

Many say, "Those days are gone" and I must agree with deep regret for we have lost our sense of the sacred, the mystery and the majesty of God. We receive our Lord now, not with reverence and awe due our Lord, but like a handout. Too many no longer believe we are receiving the Body and Blood of Jesus Christ; it is merely a piece of bread and ordinary wine – symbols. They are mistaken.

I miss the Sacred and the Holy. I miss the trembling before the majesty of God.

On the sixty-ninth anniversary of my birth, which now seems far distant, the first issue of Colloqui was published. I had previously written some 230 essays for the parish bulletin under the guise of *Conversations at Table*.[1] Though well-received, budget constraints resulted in a number of cost-cutting measures, including further continuation of *Conversations at Table*. Thus, Colloqui was born. Now, four years and some two-hundred issues later, it remains a labor of love.

Some number of readers have asked whether I should consider binding these weekly musings into a book. As Chesterton noted introducing his marvelous book *Orthodoxy*: "It was perhaps an incautious suggestion to make to a person only too ready to write books upon the feeblest provocation" and so, in order to satisfy those who have made such an "incautious suggestion," in late January 2020 I began the tedious process of doing just that.

Now, as Colloqui is but a toddler, a mere four-and-a half years of age, I thought there might be enough for a small book or four (one for each volume). But, like many a guileless parent, I was caught completely unawares at my child's prodigiousness. The fifty-two issues of Volume 1 (June 2, 2016 — May 19, 2017) soon filled well over 500 pages, well beyond my poor expectations, and more than the small book or four which I had thought to bring up into adulthood. It became appallingly clear that some corrective discipline would be necessary. As I bent to the onerous task of reexamining old annoying habits, I discovered inattention to trifles a problem most in need of disciplinary action and serious remedy.

I have tried my best to remove some "nonessential" pages without cutting the heart out of it and for the most part I am satisfied with the results. What is missing from the first volume of Colloqui has not been permanently lost but merely moved to another book which needs only another "incautious suggestion."

While every issue can still be found on my website (deaconscorner.org) I sincerely hope this book will find a place on more bookshelves and enjoy a wider audience. As

---

[1] All essays can be found at https://deaconscorner.org/topics/reflections.

you will quickly discover—at least I hope that to be the case—I have a bias toward objective truth and a severe prejudice against deliberate ignorance. As I have noted in every issue:

> Colloqui is a Deacon's Corner weekly journal. Its mission and purpose: to encourage serious discussion, to promote reasoned debate, and to provide serious content for those who hope to find their own pathway to God.
>
> Each week Colloqui will contain articles on theology, philosophy, faith, religion, Catholicism, and much more.
>
> Be forewarned! Articles may and often will contain fuel for controversy, but always with the express intent to seek the Truth, the whole truth, and nothing but the truth, so help us God.

As you will quickly discover, or perhaps not, the essays are a motley lot, often akin to strangers met for an instant or of distant cousins far removed. It is the nature of my wandering mind to question and to ponder but more than mere mental exercise, I blame the Holy Spirit for my rambling muse. There are threads throughout which weave a tale, a tapestry bearing witness to the Divine and the profane. Each thread unique, every note a song unto itself and, yet, by themselves, a symphony incomplete.

I must warn you that some essays have indeed generated unsettling controversy to which I have been quite rightly taken to task. I have not, however, nor will I keep them from seeing the light of day. I wrote them, they were my words and thoughts, and I published them. Others have read and commented on them and I have responded; in other words, we discussed our differences. You, dear reader, must judge for yourself the truth.

Deacon Charles (Chuck) R. Lanham

Whether one is willing to acknowledge it – or not – everyone is a philosopher; it is to our nature as fully as thought and reason, for everyone owns a philosophy unique unto one's self. In a sense, philosophy defines our nature, delineates our humanity, and proves the measure of our soul. Every voluntary human action is predicated upon a set of guiding principles, a philosophy developed through personal experience, shaped and tempered by social mores and the cultural milieu; yet it is the religious, moral and ethical tutelage – or lack thereof – received during one's formative years which often impact the foundations of one's philosophy more than any other. Few are those who are willing or able to consciously articulate the philosophy which guides their actions; fewer still are willing to admit to its inescapable and absolute necessity. In and of itself, a philosophy can be either good or bad, just or unjust, objective or subjective, rational or irrational, for a philosophy is simply a set of beliefs, principles which lead one to act in a certain way. One can embrace a philosophy which holds to no objective reality, no constituent morality, or ethical constraints; despots and tyrants, genocidal maniacs, radicals, terrorists, even the devil himself holds to a philosophy, as evil and devoid of their humanity as they are. There is a commonality among such distorted philosophies, a descent into darkness which pervades the soul.

Into every being there comes that defining moment when what did not exist before now does with unmistakable clarity and purpose. One moment there is simply nothing and then within the brief span of a fleeting thought a new life comes into existence, into being. While there are ongoing questions and serious debate concerning when exactly life does begin, there are two fundamental premises concerning life that should be accepted by everyone: the irreversibility of existence and the unknowable longevity of life.

The first premise states that the threshold that lies between the nothingness of non-existence and existence can be traversed in only one direction; that existence cannot be turned to non-existence. Existence is permanent, existence is forever. Whether a life once lived is remembered or forgotten does not negate the fact that a life once existed. There is a somewhat subtle corollary to this premise that should be made and that is while existence cannot be undone, there is absolutely nothing that one can do about it. Once in existence you cannot wish or cause the cessation of your existence.

The second premise tells us that the length of any life is unknown and unknowable to the created. Whether a life lasts but for a brief moment or for many years cannot be determined by anyone but God. A corollary to this is that to God the value of any life is not measured by its temporal longevity; we are all children of God and loved equally no matter how long or short a time we have on this earth.

It is a false equivalence to equate darkness with light; light exists, darkness is but its absence. Light is energy, it is measurable, it exists; it knows no existential antipode[2], no antithesis[3]. Light is or it is not. All that exists owes its existence to a cause; that is to say, no object can be the cause of its own existence. Existence, just as light, is measurable; it knows no antipode, no antithesis. A thing exists or it does not. Once upon a time there was no time, no light, no matter, no space, no existence, nothing but an Uncaused Cause which can be inadequately but arguably best described using the ternion of "being," "consciousness," and "bliss," what most would identify as God.[4] Logic and reason can explain why there must be an Uncaused Cause. As Thomas Aquinas observed, things move, something must cause a thing to move, and whatever caused it to move must be caused by something else, and so forth and so on – but not forever. This causal chain must have a beginning, there must be an Unmoved Mover, an Uncaused Cause to cause the first domino to fall. Another way of explaining this is to consider that everything that has a beginning must logically have a cause. Nothing can come from nothing, so reason demands there be an Uncaused Cause, a Prime Mover – to make the first move; without a First Cause there cannot be a second cause, or anything at all. If there is no Uncreated Creator to start the chain moving nothing would still be nothing.

Every argument for an Uncaused Cause, and there are many, begins with a set of premises, often a major and one or more minor premises upon which one argues for the conclusion that God exists. The conclusion is the same but the premises for the different arguments are different. The arguments for the existence of an Uncaused Cause, a Prime Mover, a Universal Designer – all different ways of describing the transcendental – that is, God, would fill a library, thus there is little need to expand or defend what others, far more capable, have so ably written. I will, however, offer one brief argument to illustrate.

The argument starts with the major premise, that all design implies a designer. The minor premise is the existence of design through the universe. The conclusion is that there must be a universal designer. Why must we believe the major premise, that all design implies a designer? Because everyone admits this principle in practice. For instance, suppose you came upon a deserted island and found "S.O.S." written in the sand on the beach. You would not think the wind or the waves had written it by mere chance but that someone had been there, someone intelligent enough to design and write the message. If you found a stone hut on the island with windows, doors, and a fireplace, you would not think a hurricane had piled up the stones that way by chance. You immediately infer a designer when you see design.[5]

---

[2] Antipode: *the direct opposite of something*.
[3] Antithesis: *a contrast or opposition between two things*.
[4] David Bentley Hart, *The Experience of God: Being, Consciousness, Bliss*, (New Haven: Yale University Press, 2013), 44.
[5] Peter Kreeft, *Fundamentals of the Faith: Essays in Christian Apologetics*, (San Francisco: Ignatius, 1988), 25.

The existence of God is of utmost importance when it comes to forming one's philosophy; especially when moral precepts are considered. How can one "know" what is good or bad? Science can offer measurable data, "scientific facts" to prove observable phenomena (e.g. the earth is round,) but what facts are there to prove moral behavior? Without God, there can be no moral facts; in a society *sans* God there can be only opinion, yet, whether personal or societal, morality without God can only be opinion and therefore subjective. Even the most ardent atheist philosophers have acknowledged that without God, there can be no objective morality. To put this into perspective, only if there is a God to tell us "Thou shalt not kill" is murder a moral wrong, a moral fact; without God, all morality is but an opinion.

Whether one is a good person, or the devil incarnate has nothing to do with whether one believes in God. There are and have been plenty of good atheists, just as there are and have been plenty of people who believed in God who committed evil acts. Without God, morality is necessarily subject to whatever one chooses as the good. This is known as moral relativism: morality is not an absolute, but relative to the individual or society. Without God, the words "good" and "evil" are just another way of saying "I like" and "I don't like." If there is no God, the statement "Murder is evil" is the same as the statement "I don't like murder." Moral relativism, by rejecting God and his divine moral code – with its concomitant values and moral absolutes – has led to a world of moral confusion. As one professor of philosophy inquired in an article for the New York Times "What would you say if you found out that our public schools were teaching children that it is not true that it's wrong to kill people for fun? Would you be surprised? I was". He then added, "The overwhelming majority of college freshmen view moral claims as mere opinions." The fact is that without a Divine source of morality, morality is just a matter of opinion. And anyone who would choose to base their principle beliefs, their philosophy of life, on mere opinion is "like a foolish man who built his house on sand" (Mt 7:26). Only if God exists can there be objective morality; without God, morality is subjective and relative, nothing more than mere opinion. God is eternal reality whose nature is unconditional love; without God, reality is yours for the choosing and love is but a vagrant feeling, a chemically and neurologically induced emotional response.

Should there be no God, there can be no eternity, no reality outside of time and space, no immortality, nothing beyond this brief existence; death is finality, oblivion, nothingness; life holds no meaning, no value, "all is vanity" (Eccl. 1:2), nothing more. All of creation evidences God's existence. Without God there could be nothing. We are his children, each a child of God made in his image and likeness and therefore of inestimable value.

There are those who would argue that man is inherently good by nature, that is, we are born predisposed toward the good. Those who believe this are likely to ascribe some outside force as the root cause of evil; they will impute poverty or bigotry or some other external influence for the evil that men do. This must be true, they argue, because man is by birth basically good; therefore, some outside force must have driven them to commit evil. Thus, the criminal, the evildoer is exculpated of any blame; something outside is the cause of the evil act: alcohol, not the drunk driver; drugs, not the pusher; guns, not the killer; etc., etc.

> People do not drift toward holiness. Apart from grace-driven effort, people do not gravitate toward godliness, prayer, obedience to scripture, faith and delight in the Lord. We drift toward compromise and call it tolerance; we drift toward disobedience and call it freedom; we drift toward superstition and call it faith. We cherish the indiscipline of lost self-control and call it relaxation; we slouch toward prayerlessness and delude ourselves into thinking we have escaped legalism; we slide toward godlessness and convince ourselves we have been liberated.[6]

The truth is human nature is neither inherently good nor bad. We are all born with the potential to do good, but we are not inherently good. To understand this, consider babies. Although babies are cute, lovable, and innocent, they are not born good. Babies are inherently self-centered, demanding to be fed, held, cleaned, clothed, and comforted – all on their schedule and with immediate effect. History bears stark evidence to man's inhumanity toward man; a quick review of the last century and the current one offers enough proof of man's disposition toward evil. If man is inherently good, how can one explain such atrocities? If man is basically good, why so many laws to control human behavior? Why do people do evil things? Because it is often easier than the alternative and in general it is more tempting; it also accords with human nature, our concupiscence. I would further suggest that those who admit no reverence for God, whose core principles are founded on self-conceit, whose moral precepts are but houses built on sand will be all too easily tempted to dwell in darkness, uncomfortable with the light.

As with philosophies, each of us owns an ideology, a comprehensive set of beliefs built upon conscious and unconscious ideas. Yet, there are those who would argue otherwise, claiming ideologues – those who have an ideology – are necessarily extremists, dogmatists, bigots, and lunatics. Translation: those who disagree have been infected with a mind-warping ideology. Pioneered by Napoleon Bonaparte to demonize his critics as besotted ideologues, Karl Marx would later employ the same technique to silence those who disagreed with him. To Marx, the desirability and inevitability of socialism was a scientific fact, and anyone who disagreed with scientific fact must be either an idiot or a fool. In the twentieth century, American progressives following in the same or similar socialist footsteps, created a whole philosophical school – Pragmatism – which as a matter of principle rejected philosophical principles. One of the leading founders of Pragmatism, William James, argued that ideas should be measured not by whether they were right or wrong, but rather by whether they have "cash value," whether they "work." Herbert Croly wrote of progressive liberal principles: "If there are any abstract liberal principles, we do not know how to formulate them. Nor if they are formulated by others do we recognize their authority. Liberalism, as we understand

---

[6] D. A. Carson, *For the Love of God*, Volume 2, Crossway Books, 1999.

it, is an activity."[7] Contemporary American liberalism has inherited this pose, denigrating opposing viewpoints not as competing ideas or positions but as the products of a warped, "ideological" worldview. There is nothing wrong with ideological principles for they are no different from principles in general. Just as with philosophies, there are good ideologies and bad ideologies, good ideas and bad ideas. Absent light, darkness attends.

As much as we would like to believe in our own self-sufficiency, sooner or later, each of us will come face-to-face with a thing which we are incapable of accomplishing on our own. For some, it may be something so profound as to leave one completely breathless; for others, merely a trigger for an awakening to one's own limitations. For myself, I experienced such a breathtaking profundity some years ago while scuba diving off the coast of Southern California. Exploring a sunken vessel some sixty feet below the surface, my fascination quite literally left me breathless. As I began my prescribed ascent to my first safety stop, I took a breath only to discover I was out of air. Try taking a breath while pinching your nose and keeping your mouth tightly shut. Now, imagine that panicked feeling with some forty feet of seawater above you and an ocean surrounding you. Suddenly, nothing else matters but to reach the surface, to be able to breathe air again.

After years of caring for others and enduring countless dangers, a woman wrote of facing a deep darkness within, a crisis of meaning, of feeling horribly maimed inside. "And all around me the relentless pressure of everyone else's pain, making my own seem so trivial. … I come to this time in life gasping for God as if for air, needing desperately some tangible sense of God's presence with and in me. My life only makes sense if God is alive at the center of me." Like the air which we breathe and take for granted, so also do we frequently take God for granted. It is only then, in our despair, when we acknowledge our brokenness, when we find ourselves desperately gasping for meaning, for healing, for love, it is only then that we find the need for God and acknowledge his presence. Yet, the more we take for granted, the further we accept the absence; what we do not appreciate, we ignore; what we cannot own, we misappropriate; what we are not, we claim as our own.

> The future of the Church can and will issue from those whose roots are deep and who live from the pure fullness of their faith. It will not issue from those who accommodate themselves merely to the passing moment or from those who merely criticize others and assume that they themselves are infallible measuring rods; nor will it issue from those who take the easier road, who sidestep the passion of faith, declaring false and obsolete, tyrannous and legalistic, all that makes demands upon men, that hurts them and compels them to sacrifice themselves. To put this more positively: The future of the Church, once again as always, will be reshaped by saints, by men, that is, whose minds probe deeper than the slogans of the day, who see more than others see because their lives embrace a wider reality. Unselfishness, which makes men free, is attained only through the patience of small

---

[7] Herbert David Croly was an intellectual leader of the progressive movement as an editor, political philosopher and a co-founder of the magazine *The New Republic* in early twentieth-century America.

daily acts of self-denial. By this daily passion, which alone reveals to a man in how many ways he is enslaved by his own ego, by this daily passion and by it alone, a man's eyes are slowly opened. He sees only to the extent that he has lived and suffered. If today we are scarcely able any longer to become aware of God, that is because we find it so easy to evade ourselves, to flee from the depths of our being by means of the narcotic of some pleasure or other. Thus our own interior depths remain closed to us. If it is true that a man can see only with his heart, then how blind we are![8]

We have become blind to the Truth and in our blindness, we have lost sight of who and what we are. We have reimagined God, recreated him in our image and likeness, made ourselves to "be like God" (Gen 3:5).

---

[8] Josef Ratzinger (Pope Emeritus Benedict XVI), excerpted from a 1969 radio broadcast.

A Restless Heart
Searching for truth

Saint Augustine began his Confessions acknowledging the greatness of God. Further on he wrote: "You stir us so that praising you may bring us joy, because you have made us for yourself, and our heart is restless, until it rests in you." Augustine had a restless mind and was ever searching for truth, remarking at a later point: "O Truth, Truth, how the deepest marrow of my mind ached for you!"

Socrates also taught of a restless mind, a mind so restless that it would question and examine the self, thus laying the foundation for scientific and spiritual advancement. Augustine went further by stating that "If you would attain to what you are not yet, you must always be displeased by what you are. For where you are pleased with yourself there you have remained. Keep adding, keep walking, keep advancing."

Sadly, we have become all too pleased with where we are—we have ceased adding, walking, or advancing. Our minds have become moribund masses of mindless mediocrity, all too easily pleased with ourselves, satisfied with what we think we know, not at all restless to question or examine the truth or fullness of it.

Indeed, we have been heavily sedated, conditioned to not think of matters that carry any weight at all. Matters such as objective truth, reason, morality, sanctity, love, chastity, and God have been so denigrated and disparaged it is easy to come to the realization that we have lost the ability to think at all.

Colloquī is the present infinitive of *colloquor*, Latin for *to talk, to discuss*, or *to converse*. Colloquī is for restless minds, minds that ache for the truth, the objective truth. As the name implies, each issue will offer food for thought, for discussion, and conversation. As it is written, "Come now, let us reason together" (Is 1:18) so together let us journey toward the One Source that is all Truth.

An Insatiable Curiosity
Turning back, looking forward

Curiosity is a curious thing or as Alice cried "curiouser and curiouser". To some degree everyone has come across a thing or two that intrigues, that tickles the mind to understand, although curiously no one is ever so curious as to determine the source of their curiosity. Most of us I suppose just aren't curious enough to expend any significant amount of effort in pursuing why they find themselves with an itch they feel the need to scratch. Age and time of course do tend to alter our perspective and change the degree to which we are curious about a great many things. Along the continuum that we call life we see the world through different lenses, lenses that color the mind with an ever-changing kaleidoscope of images and visions of what is real and objectively true. Looking at the world through the unknowing but awestruck eyes of a child is quite different from seeing through cataracts, lenses now become cloudy and poor yet still seeing all that has come from a lifetime of experiences and memories that are indelibly etched upon the soul.

Each of us suffers various forms of mental vision impairment. At times we find ourselves intellectually myopic, living only for the moment, unable or unwilling to see beyond what stands before us, to anticipate the future and what may or may not be; at other times we develop mental hyperopia, losing sight of the now while living beyond this time and place, living a dream but only within the confines of the mind. Somewhere along the way many find themselves suffering from absent-minded presbyopia, finding it increasingly difficult to focus, lost and uncomfortable with what they have or don't have, with what they have accomplished or have failed to obtain.

As with most of what ails us there are remedies for each dysfunction: simply provide corrective lenses for the mind's eyes. Carefully nurtured by an appetite for objective truth and fed by an insatiable curiosity we can turn back the hands of time, defy the ravages of age, while looking forward to what is yet to be. The decline in mental acuity has been intentionally inculcated, with objective truth the primary target. Without question—with no obvious curiosity on our part—we have bought into the skeptic's declaration that there can be no objective truth, a statement so easily refuted yet bought into hook, line, and sinker by those who should know better. Simply ask yourself whether it is true there is no truth and you will realize the inherent fallacy promulgated by those who tell you otherwise. If objective truth is unknowable then all that is left for us is our feelings, leaving objective reality and truth to individual subjective rationalization.

Where has our natural curiosity flown? Peter Kreeft suggests that it hasn't gone anywhere, rather we have simply turned into passive couch potatoes.

> Watching TV and movies is replacing reading books in our lives, and as this happens, images replace words and passivity replaces active thinking. When we read words, we have to actively create the images with our own imagination. But when we watch a movie we are more like a baby in a womb. (Indeed, the comfortable, darkened theater is very like a womb.) Life has become a spectator sport, a large TV screen. Life and TV have become inverted: instead of TV being in life, life is on TV.[9]

---

[9] Peter Kreeft, *Making Choices: Practical Wisdom for Everyday Moral Decisions* (Cincinnati, OH: St. Anthony Messenger Press, Servant Books, July 7, 2011), 129.

Objective truth has been replaced by ideology, a system of ideas created not by God but by man, subjective rather than objective, invented rather than discovered. If we cannot know objective truth, then how can we know moral truths? If morality is just subjective feelings and not objective truths, then anything goes. God gifted us with free will, the ability to make choices, but he also gifted us with the ability to know the truth, the objective truth, so that we might love him. God wants us to know him and to love him, not as fawning sycophants but as those who thirst and hunger for him because they long for him.

To See Through All Things
Is the same as not to see

A reader recently took me to task for not delivering on a promise to complete the discussion concerning the conquest of Nature and C.S. Lewis' prophetic warning of the dangers such conquests will inevitably bring. To that reader I must offer my sincere gratitude for reminding me of that promise for I confess it had slipped my mind.

In his reply to a letter writer concerning an opinion piece on Marquette University[10], Mickey Mattox wrote:

> Without doubt the retreat from Catholic realism as reflected in the natural-law tradition has wreaked havoc in Western, Catholic universities. If nothing is given, not even ourselves, then nature itself becomes merely the inchoate "matter" we shape to serve ends determined solely by desire and techne[11]. The logic that undergirds the movement for "marriage equality" is itself post-natural in this sense. It leads inevitably toward the unreason of transgender "rights," and from there to a trans-humanist movement that promises self-transcendence without the transcendent God. [12]

What Mattox says serves to support and validate exactly what Lewis so prophetically wrote nearly three-quarters of a century ago:

> The real objection is that if man chooses to treat himself as raw material, raw material he will be: not raw material to be manipulated, as he fondly imagined, by himself, but by mere appetite, that is, mere Nature, in the person of his de-humanized Conditioners.

> We have been trying, like Lear, to have it both ways: to lay down our human prerogative and yet at the same time to retain it. It is impossible.

> Traditional values are to be "debunked" and mankind to be cut out into some fresh shape at the will (which must, by hypothesis, be an arbitrary will) of some lucky few people in one lucky generation which has learned how to do it. The belief that we can invent

---

[10] Mickey L. Mattox, Professor of Theology at Marquette University; *Marquette's Gender Regime*, First Things (April 2016): 17.
[11] Philosophical term often translated as craftsmanship, craft, or art.
[12] Mickey L. Mattox, in response to a letter from Christopher Wolfe, University of Dallas, First Things (June/July 2016): 8-9.

"ideologies" at pleasure, and the consequent treatment of mankind as mere … specimens, preparations, begins to affect our very language. Once we killed bad men: now we liquidate unsocial elements. Virtue has become integration and diligence dynamism…. Most wonderful of all, the virtues of thrift and temperance, and even of ordinary intelligence, are sales-resistance.[13]

What Lewis prophesied and what Mattox has confirmed ought to be alarming to us all, but tragically it barely gets a ho-hum response or even a "whatever". Perhaps it is too late to halt the progress, to stop the madness that lives by the credo, "What God intends man amends." We can only hope such is not the case. Lewis concludes:

…you cannot go on "explaining away" forever: you will find that you have explained explanation itself away. You cannot go on "seeing through" things forever. The whole point of seeing through something is to see something through it. It is good that the window should be transparent, because the street or garden beyond it is opaque. How if you saw through the garden too? It is no use trying to "see through" first principles. If you see through everything, then everything is transparent. But a wholly transparent world is an invisible world. To "see through" all things is the same as not to see.

Another observation

If someone from a mere 10 years in the past, let alone 50, were dropped forward into our time, he would conclude that we as a world population had lost our minds or become delusional, denying the obvious reality right before our very eyes.

Our time traveler, unaffected by recent errors in thinking, would make the (once) commonsense assessment that an obviously male person who thinks he is actually a female needs psychological help and healing. He needs our sympathy and offer of help, not our encouragement of his delusion. Our time traveler would marvel at the shocking and collective delusion of a culture that so widely approves of, and even celebrates, such sad confusion.[14]

A Lexiconic High Jacking
In the beginning was the Word

Ancient tradition held that language was more than sterile words, more than utile utterances. Peter Kreeft finds that ancient peoples "thought words were more than artificial, more than pragmatic, more than labels. They thought words were natural, for one thing; that although languages are man-made, *language* was not. Second, they thought of language as a sacred power, not just as a practical human tool. And third, they thought of words not as labels but as presences, incantations."[15] What is key here is to recognize the distinction between language and languages. As Kreeft points out,

---

[13] C. S. Lewis, The Abolition of Man, 1943.

[14] Msgr. Charles Pope, National Catholic Register, May 15-28, 2016.

[15] Peter Kreeft, *Making Choices: Practical Wisdom for Everyday Moral Decisions*, (Cincinnati, OH: St. Anthony Press, 1990): 137-38.

languages are man-made; whether one's native tongue is English, French, Spanish, Mandarin, Italian, Arabic, Hebrew, Swahili, or any one of the estimated 7,000 different languages spoken around the world, each has been constructed and developed by people over time through custom and by usage. Languages are the means by which people communicate with one another; they have form, meaning, and context. While the singular for *languages* is *language*, such as the English language, that meaning is not what concerns Kreeft in this instance. Language has become secularized, high-jacked to subjective, amoral ends, disconnected from morality and its sacred purpose. Martin Heidegger, a twentieth century German philosopher wrote that "Language speaks, it acquires a voice. Words and language are not wrappings for the commerce of those who write and speak. Rather, it is in words and language that things first come into being and are. It is for this reason that a misrelation to language, in the form of slogans or idle talk, must mean a misrelation to being."[16] Kreeft reminds us that "language is not just a part of the world, a thing in the world; rather, the world is in it. It is older than the world: "In the beginning was the Word."

There is an old nursery rhyme that goes "Sticks and stones may break my bones, but words will never hurt me"[17] which feels extraordinarily appropriate here. Originally intended to persuade children to ignore name-calling and other hurtful taunts, to refrain from physical retaliation, and to remain calm and good-natured, its persuasive effectiveness is certainly suspect to say the least. Likewise, it would seem, is the efficacy of the command enjoined by Christ to "love your neighbor as yourself" (Mk 12:31; Mt 22:39). If there is one virtue conspicuously absent in this world today it is love while sadly what appears to be in promiscuous overabundance is quite the opposite. Reasoned discourse, good manners, consideration for the views of others, moderation, a willingness to compromise, respect, a genuine fondness or love for neighbors are virtues no longer held in high regard, especially in the public square. There is little if any consideration to dialogue, for dialogue requires an honest attempt to reach common ground, to depolarize the intransigent, and to accept the unacceptable. It would require recognizing that every issue ought not to be a question of an irresistible force meeting an immovable object. What is perhaps most distressing is the deliberate and malicious high jacking of the lexicon by those who wish to confuse, obfuscate, and distort in order to hide their true purpose.

Mathematicians enjoy the exacting detail upon which all mathematics depends. Two plus two must equal four under any and all conditions and circumstances. It can never equal any other value, no matter how much one might wish or desire it to be so. Linguistics, like mathematics, has defined rules and definitions, but unlike mathematics, its most important rule would seem to be that all rules are meant to be broken. Take the word *"discrimination"* which is defined as an act or instance of making a

---

[16] Martin Heidegger, *Poetry, Language, Thought*, Harper Perennial Modern Classics, Dec 3, 2013.
[17] Mrs. George Cupples, *Tappy's Chicks and Other Links Between Nature and Human Nature*, 1872.

distinction, the ability to see fine distinctions and differences, subtle appreciation in matters of taste, or discriminating judgment. The original meaning which was first defined in the 1640s was *"the making of distinctions"* and from 1814 it meant *"discernment."* Now here is the rub. Based on these definitions no one, absolutely no one, is immune for we all discriminate in some form or fashion, from choosing what color to paint a room to which car to buy or what wine to drink. We all make distinctions and choices based on our own personal preferences and tastes. Quite simply, we discriminate every day and all the time. Somewhere along the way "discrimination" has been high-jacked, conflating bigotry with discernment and obfuscating its true meaning. Discrimination has now become a derogatory, sufficiently opaque to blur and confuse even those most learned among us. And there are so many other high-jacked words, words such as "fundamental", "religion", "faith", "rights", "values", "love", "life", "freedom", "choice", "entitled" and "justice". Our language has been skewered and betrayed, altered to give argument to those whose sole purpose is complete acquiescence and subjugation to their myopic point of view. It is an ethic based on and supported by hate, never by or for the love of God.

Kreeft contends "that our use of language determines our relation to reality, how much reality we know, how deeply we know it and how truly" to which I am in complete agreement. Too much of language has been trivialized, homogenized, and distorted. The word "awesome" used to recognize something that merited our awe but in today's argot it is whatever turns you on. There used to be a clear understanding of the meaning of "good" and "bad" but today those lines have been blurred by those who say, "I'm so bad" meaning "I'm so good". Kreeft adds "Euphemisms blind us to reality. Death becomes merely 'passing away.' Killing unborn babies becomes 'terminating a pregnancy.' Copulation becomes 'going to bed with' or Genocide becomes 'population control.' Sin becomes 'antisocial behavior.' Change the language, and you change people's perception of reality." Should we argue that all this is nothing more than semantics; that what difference does it make? Read George Orwell's novel 1984. When language loses its sacredness, it loses its power to hold us accountable for our actions and we lose the moral high ground.

June 9, 2016

Running Away
Going nowhere

Once long ago I ran away, and like the fictional character Forest Gump, I kept on running for a very, very long time. From what precisely I cannot say nor why, just that

I was running away from something. What is equally unfathomable was whether I was running toward something or somewhere or quite simply going nowhere at all. If I am to be perfectly honest with myself, I must admit it was definitely the latter. Unfortunately, it would appear, going nowhere was then and remains now a very popular destination. Not that anyone going nowhere would admit to such a blear observation, far from it. Let's face it, we all have plenty of places we need to go, things we have to do, and no time to go or do everything that simply, absolutely must be watched, attended, traveled, achieved, participated, gathered, received, played, driven, moved, built, designed, destroyed, etc., etc. Anywhere but God that is, he's optional. And for what?

Where are we going? Are we going somewhere or are we just riding a stationary bicycle or running on a treadmill, going nowhere at all? It seems to me that many have or are behaving much like the prodigal son, running away, just wasting away in Margaritaville searching for our lost shaker of salt. We have lost our souls, lost any concern or fear for what awaits us after death comes calling, for we have indulged in the chimera that we are already heading in the right direction: going nowhere.

Unlike the prodigal son who eventually came to his senses and returned home begging his father for mercy and forgiveness, we have yet to wake up knowing that there is somewhere much better than nowhere. Hopefully we will before it is too late, before we get to nowhere.

A Hospital for Sinners
Desperately hoping for a cure

Christianity is for sinners. There is no room for those who believe they are above the fray, capable of reaching for and taking the moral high ground, no place for those who believe they are capable of attaining moral ideals on their own. Jesus said as much when he told this parable to those who were convinced of their own righteousness and despised everyone else:

> Two people went up to the temple area to pray; one was a Pharisee and the other was a tax collector. The Pharisee took up his position and spoke this prayer to himself, "O God, I thank you that I am not like the rest of humanity—greedy, dishonest, adulterous—or even like this tax collector. I fast twice a week, and I pay tithes on my whole income." But the tax collector stood off at a distance and would not even raise his eyes to heaven but beat his breast and prayed, "O God, be merciful to me a sinner." I tell you, the latter went home justified, not the former; for everyone who exalts himself will be humbled, and the one who humbles himself will be exalted (Lk 18:9-14).

We are all sinners whether we wish to admit it to ourselves or not. In some ways we are as Peter Kreeft describes it, *sinaholics*, in desperate need of a cure, a cure that comes only from God, the physician with every cure for the soul. While God is always willing to make house calls, the church is where sinners are best attended.

> The church is not a museum for saints but a hospital for sinners. To publicly profess to the world that you are a Christian, by going to church every Sunday, is not to say to the world that you are better than they are but that you are desperately ill.

> The church is a lot like *Alcoholics Anonymous*. The very first thing you have to admit and never forget in AA is that "I am an alcoholic" A Christian is one who knows he is a *sinaholic*, and he has accepted God's cure. The stupidest of all reasons for not going to church is one of the commonest ones: "I'm not good enough." The only qualification is to be bad enough. Does anyone refuse to go to the hospital because they're not healthy enough?[18]

The parable of the Pharisee and the Tax Collector adds yet another dimension to our view of church as the hospital for sinners. We cannot help but wonder why: Why would someone so self-righteous and full of self, feel compelled to come to the hospital for sinners? After all, he wasn't like those patients who knew they were broken and were there hoping for a cure. He did not believe he was in the slightest way suffering from any illness (sin.) So why was he there? It is difficult to surmise precisely why those of such self-righteous estate would feel the need to enter the temple of God, the hospital for sinners, yet they do. Although I suspect more find themselves moving to the other side of the street while averting their eyes lest they suddenly feel the need to enter such a den of iniquity and admit their failures. We know why the tax collector came to the temple. He knew and admitted that he was broken, a sinner in need of a cure, a dose of mercy and forgiveness from God. He knew he was a sinaholic and desperately needed to be forgiven. He knew that the best hope for mercy and forgiveness was to place his trust in the most qualified physician at the best hospital for sinners: God and his church.

We still have Pharisees living among us, those who believe they are better than everyone else, those who know more, have more, and think more highly of their selves, who have no need or time for God. There are tax collectors in abundance although we may not call them such these days. Tax collectors were once considered the worst of sinners. Now we know that we don't have to be a tax collector to be a sinner for we know we are all sinners whether we admit it to ourselves or not. Once I heard a voice cry out "Go to church you fool!" and now I know why. Do you?

---

[18] Peter Kreeft, *Making Choices*, 208-09.

Angelic Stubbornness
A voice of one crying out

Robert Cardinal Sarah, Prefect of the Congregation for Divine Worship and the Discipline of the Sacraments, was ordained to the priesthood at the age of 24, appointed Metropolitan Archbishop of Conakry in December 1979 at the age of 34, the youngest ever elevated to the Episcopacy. Pope Saint John Paul II at the end of his three day visit to Guinea in 2001 appointed him Secretary for the Evangelization of Peoples. Pope Benedict XVI appointed him Cardinal in 2010.

His is a remarkable story of faith, hope and love and he has much to teach us of the love of God, unshakable faith, the importance of prayer, and the necessity to speak out forcefully and with conviction against evil no matter the personal cost.

Reading *God or Nothing*, a marvelous book styled as an interview between Nicolas Diat and Cardinal Sarah, you quickly come to understand just how central prayer is and has been in his life. A humble servant of God, Sarah speaks with a refreshing candor. "In my life", he says, "God has done everything; for my part, I just wanted to pray."[19]

In his farewell speech at a state banquet given in his honor upon his appointment to Rome in 2001, Sarah spoke out harshly against the existing regime:

> I am worried about Guinean society, which is built on the oppression of the insignificant by the powerful, on contempt for the poor and the weak, on the cleverness of poor stewards of the public good, on the bribery and corruption of the administration and the institutions of the republic…I am speaking to you, Mister President of the Republic, even though you are not here. Endowed by the Lord with all sorts of natural and culture resources, Guinea, paradoxically, stagnates in poverty. … I am concerned about the young people; they have no future because they are paralyzed by chronic unemployment. I am also concerned about national unity, cohesion, and harmony, which are greatly compromised by the lack of political dialogue and the refusal to accept differences. In Guinea, the law, justice, ethics, and human values no longer provide a frame of reference and a safeguard to regulate social, economic, and political life. Democratic freedoms are taken hostage by ideological trends that can lead to intolerance and dictatorship. In the past, giving your word was something sacred. It is true that a person's merit is measured by his ability to be faithful to his word. Today, the media, demagoguery, mind conditioning, and all sorts of other methods are used to sway public opinion and manipulate minds, giving the impression of a collective rape of consciences and a serious confiscation of freedoms and of thought.[20]

If one were to simply replace references to "Guinea" with "America" Cardinal Sarah's words ring as frighteningly true here as they did for his beloved country of

---

[19] Bianca Czaderna, *Reviews: Angelic Stubbornness*. First Things (June/July 2016): 56-57.

[20] Robert Cardinal Sarah interviewed by Nicolas Diat, *God or Nothing: A Conversation on Faith* (Ignatius Press, August 1, 2015}.

Guinea. Not one for pious evasions, he speaks equally as frank on public issues such as gender theory, abortion, and euthanasia. From his perspective these issues stem from a Western culture that has chosen to "live as though God did not exist" allowing our feelings, experience, and personal desires—rather than moral principles and re-vealed truths—to rule the day.

Just Saying

...for several decades, scholars have taught their students to politicize and relativize knowledge. ...

When it comes to sexuality and gender, the only claim that matters is the sexes are inter-changeable and gender is fluid. Scholars seek accounts of historical processes that reveal how anything that appears to contradict such claims is historically false.

In other words, the claims function as premises, not hypotheses or conclusions. Truth isn't something to be pursued or discussed. The only applicable universal, absolute truth—the truth of equality—is beyond question. No one need ask what is true, because truth is either assumed, if it is politically desirable, or relativized, if it is not.[21]

Enriching the Mind
Where's the fun in that

Technological advances are much like a double-edged sword: while there are gen-erally benefits to be derived from every new or improved thing, there are ___always___ (please note the emphasis here) ___downsides___, unintended consequences that tend to ne-gate or even leave us worse off than before.

Not that I am proposing a complete and utter moratorium on new and improved technology, far from it. What I am suggesting however is that perhaps we have become far too enthralled in adopting every new widget, gadget, toy, or cure-for-what-ails-you that we seldom if ever consider the consequences.

It doesn't take much to see how great a deleterious impact technology—and here I am focusing on media and entertainment technology—has had on the acquisition and understanding of knowledge, particularly knowledge that has been known for millen-nia. On the one hand it is difficult to fathom how we have become so ignorant of the past and yet on the other hand we invite the technological gods to strut before us, preening and gloating with their enticing immediacy and alluring mindless gratifica-tion.

In a nutshell, we no longer read, ponder, or cogitate on weightier matters or con-sider entertaining a quiet moment in silent reflection with God. Truth is, video games

[21] Molly Oshatz, *Opinions: College Without Truth*, First Things (May 2016): 15-17.

await, with all their noise and mayhem to desensitize and dull the mind and heart and soul. Saint Augustine once observed:

> Our Lord Jesus Christ wished us to understand that what he did for people's bodies he also did for their souls. He did not work miracles merely for miracles' sake; his object was that his deeds might arouse wonder in the beholders and reveal the truth to those capable of understanding.
>
> A person who sees the letters in a beautifully written book without being able to read them will praise the skill of the copyist because he admires the graceful shape of the letters, but the purpose and meaning of these letters he does not grasp. What he sees with his eyes prompts him to praise, but his mind is not enriched with knowledge. Another, praising the artistry, will also grasp the meaning; one, that is, who is able not only to see what everyone else sees but also to read it, which is a skill that has to be learned. So too, those who observed Christ's miracles without grasping their purpose and the meaning they had for those able to understand, simply admired the deeds. Others went further: they admired the deeds and also grasped the meaning. As pupils in the school of Christ, we must be such as these.[22]

But I wonder if we have not become less than the "person who sees the letters in a beautifully written book without being able to read them" in that we have lost more than the desire to admire, we have lost the desire to see. Knowledge is no longer a desirable acquisition for where's the fun in that.

On Becoming a Cat
Artificial Intelligence?

What in the world is the world coming to?[23] Or to be more precise, are we now sinking so low as to be heading toward the dogs, or should I say cats?

Pope Benedict XVI once spoke of the dangers that surround the growing tide of relativism, what he called the *dictatorship of relativism.*

> How many winds of doctrine have we known in recent decades, how many ideological currents, how many ways of thinking. The small boat of the thought of many Christians has often been tossed about by these waves—flung from one extreme to another: from Marxism to liberalism, even to libertinism; from collectivism to radical individualism; from atheism to a vague religious mysticism; from agnosticism to syncretism and so forth. Every day new sects spring up, and what St Paul says about human deception and the trickery that strives to entice people into error (cf. Eph 4: 14) comes true.
>
> Today, having a clear faith based on the Creed of the Church is often labeled as funda-mentalism. Whereas relativism, that is, letting oneself be "tossed here and there, carried about by every wind of doctrine", seems the only attitude that can cope with modern

[22] Saint Augustine, *Sermon 98, 1-3: PL 38, 591-592*
[23] Oh, how Sister Ann Maureen would cringe at the dangling participle! My apologies, Sister.

times. We are building a dictatorship of relativism that does not recognize anything as definitive and whose ultimate goal consists solely of one's own ego and desires.[24]

In his book styled as a conversation between Peter Seewald and then Pope Benedict, he explains his remarks made in his homily.

Seewald: In his futuristic novel *Brave New World*, the British author Aldous Huxley had predicted in 1932 that falsification would be the decisive element of modernity. In a false reality with its false truth – or the absence of truth altogether – nothing, in the final analysis, is important any more. There is no truth, there is no standpoint. Today, in fact, truth is regarded as far too subjective a concept for us to find therein a universally valid standard. The distinction between genuine and fake seems to have been abolished. Everything is to some extent negotiable. Is that the relativism against which you were warning so urgently?

Pope Benedict: It is obvious that the concept of truth has become suspect. Of course it is correct that it has been much abused. Intolerance and cruelty have occurred in the name of truth. To that extent people are afraid when someone says, "This is the truth", or even "I have the truth." We never have it; at best it has us. No one will dispute that one must be careful and cautious in claiming the truth. But simply to dismiss it as unattainable is really destructive.

A large proportion of contemporary philosophies, in fact, consist of saying that man is not capable of truth. But viewed in that way, man would not be capable of ethical values, either. Then he would have no standards. Then he would only have to consider how he arranged things reasonably for himself, and then at any rate the opinion of the majority would be the only criterion that counted. History, however, has sufficiently demonstrated how destructive majorities can be, for instance, in systems such as Nazism and Marxism, all of which also stood against truth in particular."[25]

There are far too many who read Benedict's response and quickly walk away with the attitude "why should I care, he is talking egghead stuff, philosophies, nothing that really pertains to me" but they would be wrong to so cavalierly dismiss his insights.

Palpably it feels as though we are all breathing in "dead air." While there are many other voices much like Benedict "crying out in the desert" (Jn 1:23)—Robert Cardinal Sarah immediately comes to mind—it seems as though no one is listening, as if no one really cares. And that should sound an alarm heard everywhere and to everyone.

What so shocks the soul is what no longer bothers. We have become, in a real sense, zombies, the walking dead, mindlessly absorbing the philosophical claptrap that the "more enlightened" are wont to feed us. We have better things to do than walk among the living, searching like Diogenes for an "honest man" or objective truth.

---

[24] Homily of his eminence Joseph Cardinal Ratzinger, Dean of the College of Cardinals, delivered at the Vatican Basilica, Monday, April 18, 2005.
[25] Pope Benedict XVI, *Light of the World: The Pope, The Church and The Signs of The Times* (San Francisco, CA: Ignatius Press, 2010).

We have ceased caring to know of such things as universal truths and unalienable rights. We even doubt our own existence, believing that nothing is real, it is all just a simulation, our own virtual reality.

If you doubt this you might listen to what Elon Musk, the founder of Tesla and SpaceX believes. When asked if he has considered whether advances in video games have been so great that our existence actually takes place within a simulation created by a future civilization, Musk answered, "A lot. Even in hot tubs, so much so I had to be banned from a hot tub." Musk referenced the evolution of video games from Pong more than 40 years ago to nearly lifelike graphics and the rise of virtual reality. "If you assume any rate of improvement at all, then games will become indistinguishable from reality," he says.

Artificial intelligence, such as Amazon's Alexa or Google Assistant, sound useful, but what happens when it gets smarter than humans? Musk says advances in AI could progress to the point where humans would be nothing more than a house pet. "I don't love the idea of being a house cat," he said. His solution: neural lace, a mesh that fits on your brain to give it digital computing capabilities.

Musk said this will be key to avoiding a future as domesticated "cats." He said he sees neural lace as an "AI layer" working symbiotically with your brain that would allow humans to stay on pace with AI. "It will be sort of a direct cortical interface." he said.[26]

Now I would point out here that while I am in complete agreement with Musk on having no real desire of becoming a domesticated house cat, neither do I have any desire to be cortically enhanced with his "neural lace". I like myself just as God created me, thank you very much, Elon.

What Musk envisions for the future is both frightening and symptomatic of the degree to which we have accepted the inevitability of so-called scientific advances. Not all such "advances" are necessarily beneficial; neither should we subscribe to the ideology which touts science and social engineering as all good and all knowing. It would be good to remind ourselves at times of what Joyce Kilmer wrote:

> *Poems are made by fools like me,*
> *But only God can make a tree.*

---

[26] Brett Molina, *Tesla's Elon Musk wants to die on Mars. Really*, Reno Gazette Journal/USA Today, June 3, 2016.

Falling Down
Becoming whole again

Perhaps one of the best-known nursery rhymes in the English-speaking world is with little doubt *Humpty Dumpty*. While there are numerous versions and an equal number of conjectures as to its origin and meaning, its four lines continue to be enjoyed by children everywhere, despite his rather unfortunate demise. The fact that all the king's horses and all the king's men couldn't put Humpty together again has never seemed to dampen the youthful delight in its recital.

There is a moral to this tragic tale, applicable to everyone. Like Humpty, each of us has fallen down at some point in our lives and have been broken. It is in our nature, it is that thing we call concupiscence, the inclination to sin. No one is immune, no one is unbroken. We are all sinners, the best and the worst of us.

Like Humpty Dumpty, all the king's horses and all the king's men can't put us back together again, no matter how many horses and men there are or how hard they may try. Nope! It simply cannot be done.

Except … God can. "For human beings this is impossible, but for God all things are possible" (Mt 19:26). Of course, there does remain one thing necessary in order for the broken to become unbroken, for us to become whole again and that is to repent. We must ask for God's mercy and forgiveness and promise to avoid climbing up on that wall anymore.

Of course, God knows we will almost certainly forget what we promise for it is in our nature to do so. He knows we are fallible, yet, no matter how often we climb that wall he will never stop loving us and forgiving us when we fall, over and over again. Neither will he ever prevent us from climbing that wall.

Contemplating Truth
The spirit rising

Pope Saint John Paul II began his encyclical *Fides et Ratio* by stating "Faith and reason are like two wings on which the human spirit rises to the contemplation of truth."

John Paul was primarily concerned with how certain fundamental truths of Catholic Doctrine which he had spoken of in his Encyclical Letter *Veritatis Splendor* were at risk of being distorted and denied, especially by the younger generation and so hoped to offer further reflection upon the relationship between truth and faith.

In the present Letter, I wish to pursue that reflection by concentrating on the theme of truth itself and on its foundation in relation to faith. For it is undeniable that this time of rapid and complex change can leave especially the younger generation, to whom the future belongs and on whom it depends, with a sense that they have no valid points of reference. The need for a foundation for personal and communal life becomes all the more pressing at a time when we are faced with the patent inadequacy of perspectives in which the ephemeral is affirmed as a value and the possibility of discovering the real meaning of life is cast into doubt. This is why many people stumble through life to the very edge of the abyss without knowing where they are going. At times, this happens because those whose vocation it is to give cultural expression to their thinking no longer look to truth, preferring quick success to the toil of patient enquiry into what makes life worth living.

Increasingly we encounter those who care little or nothing for truth and reason; it goes beyond simple annoyance; it chills the soul. For when we look into the eyes what reflects is dark and empty, void of beauty, love, and hope.

R. R. Reno wrote recently "When reality impinges on our self-image, our conceits, and our cherished assumptions, we tend to falsify things so that we're not challenged, contradicted, or inconvenienced. We want reality to suit us."[27]

We see this literally every day, this empty satisfaction with knowing a bit of this and a taste of that, absent any desire or drive to know more, to understand little more beyond the barest of facts. The sad fact is we are satisfied with the little we believe we know and thus find no need to look further, to seek a coherent, overall picture of reality, to recognize and know what is real and true.

This is nothing new of course, this selective blindness to the truth. Hans Christian Anderson imagined such self-inflicted blindness nearly two centuries past with his short tale "*The Emperor's New Clothes*" a tale of two disreputable weavers who promise an emperor a new suit of clothes so constructed as to be invisible to those who are unfit for their positions, stupid, or incompetent. The emperor's vanity forbids him from admitting the truth and so he vaingloriously parades before his subjects in his new clothes. No one dares to admit to being unfit, stupid, or incompetent by stating the obvious, until a small child shouts "But he isn't wearing anything at all!" Cardinal Ratzinger said:

> We are building a dictatorship of relativism that does not recognize anything as definitive and whose ultimate goal consists solely of one's own ego and desires....An "adult" faith is not a faith that follows the trends of fashion and the latest novelty; a mature adult faith is deeply rooted in friendship with Christ. It is this friendship that opens us up to distinguish the true from the false, and deceit from truth. We must develop this adult faith; we must guide the flock of Christ to this faith. And it is this faith—only faith—that creates unity and is fulfilled in love.[28]

---

[27] R. R. Reno, *The Loving Intellect*, First Things (March 2016) 41-46.
[28] Joseph Cardinal Ratzinger a few hours before his election to the throne of Peter, April 18, 2005.

As adults, we have lost a thing so precious, something essential: the innocence and faith of a child. A child sees the world as once it was, a garden full of delightful things, just waiting to be explored, touched and tasted, filled with the presence of God. What they see and touch and taste is real and true and good.

Such faith in the goodness of God fades all too quickly. What was once seen as fresh and new and filled with incredible beauty becomes cloaked and covered by the sober weight of adulthood. Where once there was no fear, no hesitation, no reluctance to explore, to learn, to discover all there is and what might be has now been constrained and subdued by new realities, realities which can only lead us away from the beauty and love that is God.

The desire to know more than we know, to learn beyond our expertise, to see the whole of things has been drummed out of us by the exigencies of the daily grind. Our world offers a cornucopia of alluring enticements and simple pleasures guaranteed to provide us with immediate gratification. Slowly we succumb to that easy chair, unwilling to advance another step, irresistibly drawn to the false realities and titillating imagery projected before our eyes.

We have been seduced to the dark side, bit by bit, unwitting and unknowing of our ever-increasing addiction even as looming shadows cast a veil upon our memories of the one transcendent God. "In abandoning God, man loses his reason and becomes blind." We turn inward to a place where god is "I", where only "I" adores and is adored by "I".

> A Godless society, which considers any spiritual questions a dead letter, masks the emptiness of its materialism by killing time so as better to forget eternity. The farther material things extend their influence, the more man takes pleasure in sophisticated, narcissistic, and perverse amusements; the more man forgets God, the more he observes himself. In looking at himself, he sees the deformations and the ugliness that his debauchery has encrusted on his face. Then, to delude himself that he still shines with the original splendor of a creature of God, he puts on his make-up. But the hidden evil is like the glowing coal beneath the ashes.[29]

In his *Pensées* Blaise Pascal observed that since man could not remedy death, misery, and ignorance man therefore had decided that what was necessary in order to be happy was to not think of such things at all.[30]

Elsewhere, mention is made of material destitution (See Richer For Poorer) but as Pope Francis observed in his Lenten message in 2014:

> No less a concern is moral destitution, which consists in slavery to vice and sin. How much pain is caused in families because one of their members—often a young person—is in thrall to alcohol, drugs, gambling, or pornography! How many people no longer see

[29] Robert Cardinal Sarah, *God or Nothing: A Conversation on Faith with Nicolas Diat*, Ignatius Press, August 31, 2015
[30] Blaise Pascal, *Thoughts*, trans. W. F. Trotter, Harvard Classics 48, Collier & Son, 1910, p. 54.

meaning in life or prospects for the future, how many have lost hope! And how many are plunged into this destitution by unjust social conditions, by unemployment, which takes away their dignity as breadwinners, and by lack of equal access to education and health care. In such cases, moral destitution can be considered impending suicide. This type of destitution, which also causes financial ruin, is invariably linked to the spiritual destitution which we experience when we turn away from God and reject his love. If we think we don't need God who reaches out to us through Christ, because we believe we can make do on our own, we are headed for a fall.

What worries is the deafening silence from far too many Christians, often promoted by self-inflicted ignorance of faith and a lack of will to form a closer more intimate relationship with God. Silence in the face of evil lends tacit consent and acceptance of it. To live and to act as if God does not exist is perhaps the greatest tragedy of our time.

Cardinal Sarah calls those who remain silent guilty of silent apostasy. It would certainly appear a valid argument, one far too close for comfort.

> The circumstances and developments in the world surely do not help us to give God his proper place. Western societies are organized and live as though God did not exist. Christians themselves, on many occasions, have settled down to a silent apostasy. If the concerns of contemporary man are centered almost exclusively on the economy, technology, and the immediacy of material happiness that has been wrongly sentimentalized, God becomes distant;…

What is needed is a wake up call. We need to be shaken from our complacency and satisfaction with the status quo, to learn more about our faith, to contemplate the truth, and refocus our hearts, minds, and souls on God.

Richer for Poorer
The virtue of poverty

What ought we to think of poverty? The common vision of it fails to lead to understanding for as with so much of what we perceive these days to be true what rolls off the tongue is too often unrelated to reality.

While this may sound reminiscent of a Gershwin tune[31], there is an important distinction to be made within a specific context when one speaks of poverty and its constituents. What lies at the heart of the matter, as often is the case when considering the depths of human suffering and the plight of those living in unimaginable destitution, is precisely how to corrupt the hearts of those who have abundant means to care for those who are in such desperate need.

To this end, seemingly endless programs have been implemented and literally thousands of organizations have been instituted, all with well-intentioned goals and

---

[31] George and Ira Gershwin, "*Let's Call the Whole Thing Off*", 1937.

objectives, with catchy slogans and heart-rending marketing campaigns, to solve an intractable human condition which only becomes more dire with each passing day.

That there are those who are destitute, lacking in nearly every basic necessity for life, can be neither denied nor ignored, especially by anyone who hopes to be placed on the right side of the King come judgment day. However, with the means to do so, anyone who feeds the hungry, gives drink to the thirsty, clothes the naked, provides care for the ill, welcomes the stranger, and visits the prisoner, will be abundantly blessed by God (Mt 25:31-46).

Jesus said, "Blessed are the poor in spirit, for theirs is the kingdom of heaven" (Mt 5:3) and we fail to comprehend. He tells us "The poor you will always have with you; but you will not always have me" (Mt 26:11) and we miss his point completely. He says "Toe-may-toe" and we hear "Toe-mah-toe" and our inclination is to just "call the whole thing off." Likewise, those who would call for the eradication of poverty are guilty of calling Jesus, the Son of God, a liar. It is they who are mistaken and lying.

Why do we not get it? As with so much of what bombards and pummels our minds these days it boils down to a poor choice of words, coupled with a desire to avoid as much as possible any unpleasantness which would threaten our personal utopian worldview.

Those who are in most need are not poor, they are destitute, possessing none of the basic necessities of life. The destitute lack in virtually everything upon which to survive. Destitution is a social condition created soberly and deliberatively through the godless actions of some over others; it is the direct result of man's inhumanity toward man. Destitution rests upon the willful and deliberate actions of those who care only for themselves and who place no value on human life. It will be those who will be placed on the left of the King, to whom he will say, "Depart from me, you accursed, into the eternal fire prepared for the devil and his angels" (Mt 26:11).

We most often consider poverty and the poor in economic or financial terms — those who have little financial resources or material possessions are poor, those whose incomes fall below a certain point, the so-called poverty line — and to a limited extent it is accurate to say this is so, but only to a point. For poverty is much more and encompasses far more than the emptiness of one's wallet.

Poverty is both a biblical and a Christian value. We seldom consider it to be so, but it is as confirmed by no less than Jesus Christ. As Saint Paul tells us "our Lord Jesus Christ, that for your sake he became poor although he was rich, so that by his poverty you might become rich" (2 Cor 8:9).

Clearly Jesus had little material possessions so how could he be rich if not through nonmaterial means? God was the source and substance of his wealth and as God no one could be richer than the Son of the Father. By becoming man, through his incarnation, he who was rich became poor, reduced to the meanest poverty in order to bring the richness of salvation to all.

> A poor person feels dependent on God; this bond is the foundation of his spirituality. The world has not favored him, but all his hope, his sole light, is in God.

> The poor person is someone who knows that, by himself, he cannot live. He needs God and other people in order to be, flourish, and grow. On the contrary, rich people expect nothing of anyone. They can provide for their needs without calling either on their neighbors or on God. In this sense, wealth can lead to great sadness and true human loneliness or to terrible spiritual poverty.[32]

Most religious take a vow of poverty, a solemn declaration of forbearance to worldly possessions. Saint Francis of Assisi asked those who would follow him to wear poor habits, work to support their community, and to acquire no material goods. Such a penurious vow sits sourly on the stomach; cultural and social norms would prove quite the opposite to be the case for we have been brainwashed to believe the measure of our success in life rests solely upon all we may acquire and possess. It is not the sanctity of our souls but the size and quantity of our toys which has become our abiding creed.

So why do some deliberately eschew all the toys for a life of poverty? It is quite simple: they do so in order to be closer to God.

Saint Francis of Assisi wanted to be poor because Jesus chose to be poor, because to Jesus poverty was a virtue not a fault or failure. Jesus became poor to show us the best possible way for us to know God and to find our way back to him.

> The Son of God loves the poor; others intend to eradicate them. What a lying, unrealistic, almost tyrannical utopia! I always marvel when *Gaudium et spes* declares: "The spirit of poverty and charity is the glory and witness of the Church of Christ" (*GS* 88).

> We must be precise in our choice of words. The language of the UN and of its agencies, who want to suppress poverty, which they confuse with destitution, is not that of the Church of Christ. The Son of God did not come to speak to the poor in ideological slogans! The Church must banish these slogans from her language. For they have stupefied and destroyed peoples who were trying to remain free in conscience.[33]

---

[32] Robert Cardinal Sarah, *God or Nothing:: A Conversation on Faith with Nicolas Diat*, Ignatius Press, August 31, 2015.
[33] Robert Cardinal Sarah, *God or Nothing*.

Considered Thoughts
From where do you speak

During a recent conversation that tended to be mainly a critique on my particular style of writing a friend said he thought of me as cerebral. Now my initial reaction was to take his comment as a compliment but after thinking about it, I'm not quite so sure. Whether it was intended as a compliment or if I should have been offended will simply have to be left as a question unanswered.

According to one source "if you are a cerebral person, no one would ever call you a drama queen." As I am definitively male and blissfully unaware of royal lineage, I can readily agree the probability of being anointed a drama queen is indeed remote. However, the same source further claims, "You make decisions using your intelligence and cold, hard facts, instead of your emotions." To a point I must plead "guilty as charged" although implied here is a certain absence of emotion, suggesting a lack of compassion, empathy, or feeling for others and to that I must declare unequivocally "not guilty".

Someone once told me it seemed I was much more comfortable writing (or texting) than I was in personal conversation and here again resides an element of truth. While I am not necessarily uncomfortable in speaking directly and in person, the fact is I long ago recognized the inherent danger in directly engaging in any serious conversation without preparation. In much the same way and at the same time I came to the realization there was no small amount of comfort and considerable safety to be garnered in retiring behind a keyboard to cogitate before expressing my thoughts and ideas.

The simple truth is the mouth often declares independence of the mind and is a bit too eager to utter a word without any consideration or thought. When we speak off-the-cuff there is little or no time in which to consider or deliberate what we will say and therein rests the danger. Far too many of us, especially those of us who have a tendency to viscerally react to certain topics, find ourselves guilty of "open mouth, insert foot" syndrome. This syndrome is not entirely restricted to oral utterances; denizens of social media are often equally guilty, if not more so, since there is a certain degree of anonymity associated with social media and no real impetus to deliberate and think about what one is posting.

We have become "quick-draw" artists, spitting words out faster than a speeding bullet, too often without a moment's thought. Quite bluntly, we do not think before we leap. We have taken Yoda's admonition to heart "Do. Or do not. There is no try" and we unthinkingly blurt out or post what sits so tenderly upon the heart, wrapped up nicely with our feelings and emotions.

It is much different when one sits down to put thoughts to paper, assuming the writer wishes to be taken seriously, for a careful, thoughtful writer will suffer and worry over every word, every phrase, every thought expressed. Here is where one's intelligence and cold, hard facts are essential, where one's emotions and feelings must give sway to the truth. To do otherwise would be dishonest and irresponsible.

The writer should never hide or deny his feelings of compassion and empathy for the misfortunes of others or for any tragedy inflicted upon mankind and the human spirit. Yet the truth, tempered and steeled by cold, hard facts, must always, always rise above one's emotional response; to do otherwise would be to lie, compounding the distress or pain or suffering others may be experiencing.

Not too long ago I was texting with a dear friend and our conversation had traveled down a path upon which I found myself becoming increasingly distressed. It came to a point where I felt a visceral, unreasoned urge to lash out, to respond with a quick sarcastic retort.

As I began tapping my response, I found myself over several long minutes erasing what I had just typed and then beginning again. Back and forth I went as I agonized over what and how I should respond until I realized what I most wanted to do was to not respond at all.

And so, I wrote: "You know, I've been sitting here thinking how to respond … and I think the best thing to say is nothing at all." And I did just that. It may not have been the kindest or best response, but it was an honest one and, in my mind, it forestalled greater unpleasantness and reduced the risk of further offending a friend.

Often that is what should be said: nothing at all. But we seldom exhibit such restraint and as a result our conversations rapidly deteriorate into incoherent argument that only serve to make us look foolish.

It would behoove us all to take a moment to rediscover how to stop, look, listen, and think before we speak for as the Roman lyric poet Horace wrote several thousand years ago: "A word once uttered can never be recalled." It may be ancient advice, but it still rings true today.

We must stop opening our mouths and inserting a very large boot in there. We need to think first, reason first, and then consider carefully what we ought to say before we spit out that next speeding bullet.

Heaven and Hell
Just one breath away

Some years ago, I was introduced to a small book with a rather odd title: *The Great Divorce*. Written by the marvelous English author C. S. Lewis, it is an extraordinary meditation upon good and evil, grace and judgment, a beautifully woven allegorical tale of a bus ride from hell to heaven.

In the preface, Lewis begins with mention of William Blake's book *The Marriage of Heaven and Hell* and thus explains his own rather odd title.

> Even on the biological level life is not like a river but like a tree. It does not move towards unity but away from it and the creatures grow further apart as they increase in perfection.

> I do not think that all who choose wrong roads perish; but their rescue consists in being put back on the right road. A sum can be put right: but only by going back till you find the error and working it afresh from that point, never by simply going on. Evil can be undone, but it cannot "develop" into good. Time does not heal it. The spell must be unwound, bit by bit, "with backward mutters of dissevering power" — or else not. It is still "either-or". If we insist on keeping hell (or even Earth) we shall not see heaven: if we accept Heaven, we shall not be able to retain even the smallest and most intimate souvenirs of Hell.

What resonates in the reading of this book is how well Lewis captures human nature with its insatiable appetite for all that is not good for the soul.

Anyone can catch the bus from hell to heaven. When you get there you even have a choice to stay or return to hell. As Lewis tells it many choose to return to hell. That in and of itself begs the question: why? Why would anyone choose hell over heaven? Here again, Lewis suggests a possible hypothesis.

Those who find little use for God or who for their own purposes make themselves to be god, have little fear of what would follow death. Their lives are filled with the here and now and they live as if there is no tomorrow for in truth that is what they so ardently want to believe. Nothing changes upon their entry into hell. In his allegorical tale, Lewis describes how whenever a denizen of hell moves to a new place all one must do is think of a house and it is instantly constructed. Of course, not surprisingly the houses they think into existence are rather insubstantial as they are mere figments of their imagination. They are no more real than their self-proclaimed godhood, which is to mean, not real at all.

Mother Teresa of Calcutta once said, "Even God could do nothing for someone already full. You have to be completely empty to let Him in to do what He will." The more self-satisfied one becomes, the more desirous of earthly pleasures and possessions, the more self-important the less room there will be for God.

Why would anyone prefer hell over heaven? Because in heaven their delusions of grandeur and all they have come to hold dear are laid bare, stripped of all substance, nothing but transparent shadows; "They were in fact ghosts: man-shaped stains on the brightness of that air. One could attend to them or ignore them at will as you do with the dirt on a windowpane." Only in hell can they hold onto the false realities which they have self-created.

George MacDonald once wrote "No, there is no escape. There is no heaven with a little hell in it—no plan to retain this or that of the devil in our hearts or our pockets. Out Satan must go, every hair and feather." For many that is very difficult to accept, for to rid one's self of the devil one must empty one's self of the obsession for earthly things, those pleasures and possessions which possess us and fill our soul of all that is not God.

Jesus said to the young man who asked what he lacked in order to gain eternal life "If you wish to be perfect, go, sell what you have and give to the poor, and you will have treasure in heaven. Then come, follow me." This was the one thing the young man was unwilling to do, "for he had many possessions" (Mt 19:21-22).

The young man, in many ways, is emblematic of many who express the desire to live a good and virtuous life and obey God's commandments but are unwilling to let go of all that precludes them from becoming perfect in the eyes of God. We have many possessions and are possessed by far too many things, unwilling to let go or to be exorcised of all that will lead us away from God.

The world is like a candy store, stocked floor to ceiling, wall to wall with sweet delightful things and like children we are easily beguiled, we want to satisfy our need for pleasure and possessions. But it only leaves us hungry for more.

When they arrived in heaven, those who took the bus from hell could not bear the thought of losing all they had, even for eternity with God. They had for too long gorged themselves on devil's food and simply had no room left for God. Are you already full or have you left room for God?

Encountering God
Where will you find him?

We have all been told at some point in our lives we should look to find Jesus in everyone we meet but I cannot help but wonder how many of us ever bother to try. We simply hold on too tight to the many prejudices and unreasoned fears that deny us the freedom to see beyond the surface or to ignore what offends in order to share a moment with a stranger.

Not too long ago I came across a small story that reminded me of this simple truth: if you never look for God chances are you will never find him.

> There once was a little boy who wanted to meet God. He knew it was a long trip to where God lived, so he packed his suitcase with Twinkies and a six-pack of root beer, and he started his journey.
>
> When he had gone about three blocks, he met an old woman sitting in the park just staring at some pigeons. The little boy sat down next to her and opened his suitcase. He was about to take a drink from his root beer when he noticed the old woman looked hungry,

so he offered her a Twinkie. She gratefully accepted it and smiled at him. Her smile was so pretty the little boy wanted to see it again, so he offered her a root beer. Once again, she smiled at him. The little boy was delighted! They sat there all afternoon eating and smiling, but they never said a word. As it grew dark, the little boy realized how tired he was and he got up to leave but before he had gone more than a few steps; he turned around, ran back to the old woman, and gave her a hug. She gave him her biggest smile ever.

When the little boy opened the door to his own house a short time later his mother was surprised by the look of joy on his face. She asked him, "What did you do today that made you so happy?" He replied, "I had lunch with God." But before his mother could respond, he added, "You know what? She has the most beautiful smile I've ever seen!"

Meanwhile, the old woman, also radiant with joy, returned to her home. Her son was stunned by the look of peace on her face and he asked, "Mother, what did you do today that made you so happy?" She replied, "I ate Twinkies in the park with God." But before her son responded, she added, "You know, he's much younger than I expected."

Too often we underestimate the power of a touch, a smile, a kind word, a listening ear, an honest compliment, or the smallest act of caring, all of which have the potential to turn a life around.

People come into our lives for a reason, a season, or a lifetime. Through them we can and will encounter God, but only if we look for him, see him in the eyes of a stranger and say hello.

The truth is God is always present wanting nothing more than to share a smile. The problem, we insist, is we are too busy, we cannot seem to find the time, or we do not know where to look for him. He has one word for you: Balderdash!

How much time does it take to offer a kind word or a smile to someone who could use it? How much effort does it take to look a stranger in the eye instead of ignoring their presence?

We forget we will be judged not by our achievements and successes but by how we encountered God in the stranger and the prisoner, the hungry and the thirsty, the ill and the naked.

As long as we look only at ourselves, we will never encounter God.

June 30, 2016

The Tragedy
Silent Acquiescence

Living in the high desert comes with its own unique challenges; perhaps the most challenging is the regular occurrence of wildfire, almost invariably accompanied by high winds sweeping over difficult terrain. Twice in the past six years the community where I live has seen homes threatened and wildlands charred by wildfire. It never fails to raise the level of fear and anxiety.

Six years ago, outside our door the nightscape was reminiscent of the fires of hell: angry flames racing up the mountainside before us, fueled by the dry cheat grass and fanned by high gusting winds. With the most recent wildfire there was smoke, lots of it, but far less visible flame. As darkness fell, instead of descending into a hellish nightmare there was a sense of complacency, not quite a feeling of normalcy and yet not so far removed from it. In short, most simply tried to ignore it as if it were no big thing.

Venerable Archbishop Fulton J. Sheen once remarked "The refusal to take sides on great moral issues is itself a decision. It is a silent acquiescence to evil. The Tragedy of our time is that those who still believe in honesty lack fire and conviction, while those who believe in dishonesty are full of passionate conviction."

All this is to say we live at a time when our religious liberties are more threatened than ever by the flames of religious intolerance fueled by those who find God an impediment. We are confronted on a daily basis with grave moral issues, some burning like the fires of hell, so evil they threaten to consume everything and anyone in their destructive path; while others like smoldering smoke raise brief but complacent alarms even as they slowly choke the life from our very souls.

Silence in the face of evil is acquiescence but it is much more, for it grants voice to those who would destroy all that is good and holy, all that is of God. Speak out! Let your voice cry out with fire and conviction. Let freedom ring!

Memories and History
Think while you still can

Memories are often like unwelcome guests, arriving unannounced; generally disrupting an otherwise normal routine. One must always be prepared to admit to moments when an unexpected memory comes calling and is most gratefully welcome.

A long time ago, much longer than I care to cipher, during study hall one day Sister Ann Maureen stood towering above my desk glaring with grim disapproval at the book held firmly in my fourteen years-old hands. "Does your mother know you are reading that book?" she demanded. To which, as I clearly recall, I smiled and said, "Oh yes, we are reading it together. See, this is her bookmark."

The book my mother and I were reading together was John Steinbeck's *The Winter of Our Discontent*, his last novel, published in 1961, the year in which I was "caught" reading it by the good Dominican Sister.

Two brief side notes to this memory: This book awoke in me the nascent desire to write. I remember after finishing it I sat down and wrote a short story along a similar vein (typed on a manual typewriter of course; as to where the story is now, I have no recollection.) I also find myself ever grateful to my mother for encouraging me to read and to always appreciate great literature. She taught me to never fear the truth but to avidly seek it, for she believed and lived as Jesus taught "and you will know the truth, and the truth will set you free" (Jn 8:32).

Steinbeck's novel was at the time controversial, for it touched on issues which were seldom discussed in polite company. Sadly, times have changed; the issues for the most part have grown ever more malignant and metastasized.

At the heart of the novel is the human struggle between good and evil. In a very real sense, it is a morality play where social and economic status wage battle with the values of honesty and integrity.

The protagonist, Ethan Allen Hawley, was born into Long Island aristocracy, but through family misfortune, finds himself working as a grocery store clerk. Surrounded by temptation and corruption, Hawley struggles to hold onto his inherent integrity even while trying to reclaim his former status and wealth.

Although *The Winter of Our Discontent* was published fifty-six years ago, the story still reads as current today as it did when it first found its way to print. It speaks to many of the most important social and moral issues encountered today: illegal immigration, bribery, corruption, moral decay, ruthlessness, social status, power, wealth, alcoholism, drugs, depression, and suicide. Yet Steinbeck never glorifies, nor does he pasteurize, the evil; neither does he paint Hawley as a saint. It is a story of one man's struggle to hold onto what is good amid the temptations presented to him by his family, friends, and society.

All this came knocking at the door of my mind when I came across an article written by Randy Boyagoda in which he warns against the institutionalization of creativity.[34] Boyagoda rightfully bemoans the current trend toward academic efforts to mechanize a heretofore creative art form—writing—and to conform those who would indulge— writers—to ideological zombies.

---

[34] Randy Boyagoda, Ph.D, *Write Away*, First Things, August/September 2015, pp.33-37.

He relays some counsel he received from Richard John Neuhaus prior to his death: "If you want to write, then write." And he goes on to write how Neuhaus would be highly skeptical of the explosion of creative writing programs at American universities, programs designed to teach writers how to write—and what to write about.

Boyagoda points out the danger posed by the American contemporary secular academia to the health and future of American literary culture:

> We know how contemporary secular academia often constrains the mind, turning deeper questions of life and belief into objects of expertise. There is no reason to think that literature can maintain a catholic and diverse approach to the Big Questions if its producers first pass through five or six years of formal instruction in an ideological setting that tends to constrain ambition and concern.

> One especially bad effect of the academic institutionalization of creative writing, he [David Foster Wallace] observed, is the reigning secular progressive ethic that comes to rule over emergent literary imaginations. Focused on current concerns and topical matters, secular progressivism treats history and tradition less as right storehouses for new writers to explore, learn from, and plunder, than as musty prisons from which to escape into the bright bare present: "Way too many students are being 'certified' to go out there and try to do meaningful work on the cutting edge of an artistic discipline of whose underpinnings, history, and greatest achievements they are largely ignorant." Would be writers are taught to pass over "Homer and Milton, Cervantes and Shakespeare, Maupassant and Gogol, to say nothing of the Testaments."

At this juncture there may be some question as to exactly how Steinbeck and Boyagoda should be connected and precisely where this is heading. I promise they are and we will get there straightaway.

Memories are important for they remind us of our past and the wisdom gained from our experiences, our successes and our failures, of all that has formed and shaped our lives. Similarly, cultures and societies are built upon the foundation and work of all that has come before.

Memories and history are the records upon which we must rely lest we find ourselves beginning each new day as if it were the first. When either becomes clouded or distorted we must of necessity become newborn, placing our unquestioning trust in an ever malleable and fluid truth which no one has the ability to confirm or deny. We become dependent upon something other than our own intellect to tell us what or why we should remember anything at all.

Steinbeck wrote of the truth as he saw it then and Boyagoda writes of just how far we have succumbed to the mind-numbing incessant chatter of a gaggle of geese having been saved from the chopping block.

On the back cover of Ray Bradbury's masterpiece *Fahrenheit 451* is this inscription:

> Fahrenheit 451 is a masterpiece that stands with George Orwell's "1984" and Aldous Huxley's "Brave New World." This is no rocket story or trip to the moon, but a

frightening forecast of the world as it might be in the next few generations...when a powerful government has given people every physical comfort but denied them the right to think![35]

While we may not have yet reached the time when firemen burn books, we have certainly traveled well down the road toward a future when government provides every physical comfort. We have yet to be denied the right to think although the less we seek the truth on our own accord, the more we place our complete trust and reliance on what we are told rather than on our own minds, the sooner the day will come when we will deny ourselves the right to think. Think about it while you still can.

Render unto Caesar
To whom do you serve?

From where does the notion of a separation of church and state derive? For most Americans I suppose their immediate response might be from the First Amendment to the Constitution but that would be dreadfully incorrect.

The idea of a distinct separation of church and state goes much further back, over a millennia before the birth of Christ, to the time when Samuel anointed Saul to be the King of Israel.

> In his old age Samuel appointed his sons judges over Israel. His sons did not follow his example but sought illicit gain and accepted bribes, perverting justice. Therefore, all the elders of Israel came in a body to Samuel at Ramah and said to him, "Now that you are old, and your sons do not follow your example, appoint a king over us, as other nations have, to judge us."

> Samuel was displeased when they asked for a king to judge them. He prayed to the Lord, however, who said in answer: "Grant the people's every request. It is not you they reject; they are rejecting me as their king. ... Now grant their request; but at the same time, warn them solemnly and inform them of the rights of the king who will rule them" (1 Sm 8:1-7, 9).

Samuel, the prophet, priest and judge, reluctantly anoints Saul by pouring oil on his head, thus raising him up to the stature of king, Yahweh's anointed one. In doing so, Samuel relinquishes his role as judge and becomes solely a priest and prophet.

This is the beginning of the distinction between the sacred (church) and the political (state.) A principle is established that delineates and defines the roles of priest and king:

> A priest is not a king, and a king is not a priest. ...

---

[35] Ray Bradbury, *Fahrenheit 451*, Ballantine Books, 1953.

Moreover, the two functions are not equal. Implicit in this very act of anointing we can see that the prophet is really higher than the king. Saul receives his royal stature from a prophet, a man of God, and a priest. If there is any doubt in that regard, when King Saul takes it upon himself to offer a sacrifice as if he were a priest, Samuel accuses him of violating "the commandment of Yahweh your god," and so declares that the kingship is to be taken from him, and given to another.[36]

Here we see the beginnings of a moral and theological basis for the separation of church and state. The people of Israel, including their king, were to be judged by the Law. The word of the king was not law unless it conformed to the Law (Yahweh's commandments.) If the king's law did not conform to the Law, the people were not bound to obey it.

Fast forward 1400 years to the time of Saint Augustine, who wrote in *City Of God*:

While the homes of unbelieving men are intent upon acquiring temporal peace out of the possessions and comforts of this temporal life, the families which live according to faith look ahead to the good things of heaven promised as imperishable, not as snares or obstructions to block their way to God, but simply as helps to ease and never to increase the burdens of this corruptible body which weighs down the soul. Both types of homes and their masters have this in common, that they must use things essential to this mortal life. But the respective purposes to which they put them are characteristics and very different.

So, too, the earthly city which does not live by faith seeks only an earthly peace, and limits the goal of its peace, of its harmony of authority and obedience among its citizens, to the voluntary and collective attainment of objectives necessary to mortal existence. The heavenly city, meanwhile—or, rather, that part that is on pilgrimage in mortal life and lives by faith—must use this earthly peace until such time as our mortality which needs such peace has passed away. As a consequence, so long as her life in the earthly city is that of a captive and an alien (although she has the promise of ultimate delivery and the gift of the Spirit as a pledge), she has no hesitation about keeping in step with the civil law which governs matters pertaining to our existence here below. For, as mortal life is the same for all, there ought to be common cause between the two cities in what concerns our purely human living. ...

So long, then, as the heavenly City is wayfaring on earth, she invites citizens from all nations and all tongues, and unites them into a single pilgrim band. She takes no issue with that diversity of customs, laws, and traditions whereby human peace is sought and maintained. Instead of nullifying or tearing down, she preserves and appropriates whatever in the diversities of divers races is aimed at one and the same objective of human peace, provided only that they do not stand in the way of the faith and worship of the one supreme and true God. ... Of course, though, the City of God subordinates this earthly peace to that of heaven. For this is not merely true peace, but, strictly speaking, for any rational creature, the only real peace, since it is, as I said, "the perfectly ordered

---

[36] Benjamin Wiker, Worshipping the State: How Liberalism Became Our State Religion, Regnery Publishing, March 25, 2013.

and harmonious communion of those who find their joy in God and in one another in God."[37]

Augustine affirms there ought not be any conflict between the state (earthly city) and the church (heavenly City) so long as the state limits its concerns to earthly things and subordinates itself to the heavenly City. He makes clear while there ought to be a separation between the earthly city and the heavenly one, the state must always stand in judgment to the Law of God.

> The distinction between church and state, religious and political power is peculiar to Christianity, and the church invented it. ...

> We cannot comprehend how the distinction between church and state ever arose until we grasp the fundamental fact: Christians believed that the Bible really was the revealed truth of God, and so they treated what it said as the authoritative guiding source for their approach to everything, including the relationship of the church to political power. The distinction between church and state arose within Christianity, and nowhere else, because of the accepted authority of the Bible.

The Christianization of the Roman Empire, contrary to legend, did not result in the fusion of church and state but their separation. "The church insisted that it must be independent of the state for two very good reasons: so that the church would not corrupt itself by becoming worldly, and so that the state would not corrupt the church by bending the Christian religion to serve political ends." What differs today is the absence of any stricture upon the state to be subordinate to the will of God. It no longer holds that the church has the higher authority, rather it acts as if precisely the opposite were true.

July 01, 2016

What's New?
Nothing under the sun

One thing holds true of every age—true since God first created man and woman—where good resides, evil is its neighbor.

> From the Fall of Adam, there was never a time when evil was not working with fury, spite and cunning. Since Eden, always and everywhere has vice warred against virtue, tyranny against justice, lies against truth, lust against purity, blasphemy against sanctity, the grisly against beauty. When we are horrified and repulsed by the darkness we see around us and within us, we should be alarmed—but not surprised. Darkness has always raged against the Light. What is different about our time is perhaps the swiftness and

---

[37] Saint Augustine, *City of God, Book XIX, Chapter 17.*

reach of evil. Where can anyone hide from the powers of seduction or destruction? Whether these are the best or worst of times does not matter. What matters is that these are our times, or better said, the times in which Divine Providence calls upon us to serve, testify and love."[38]

Scripture reminds us of the inevitability of this endless stalemate: "What has been, that will be; what has been done, that will be done. Nothing is new under the sun" (Eccl 1:9). As does literature:

> It was the best of times, it was the worst of times, it was the age of wisdom, it was the age of foolishness, it was the epoch of belief, it was the epoch of incredulity, it was the season of Light, it was the season of Darkness, it was the spring of hope, it was the winter of despair, we had everything before us, we had nothing before us, we were all going direct to heaven, we were all going direct the other way.[39]

We ought to remind ourselves while we may believe the darkest hour is just before dawn, that our time is the worst of times, darker times have come before. We must remind ourselves God does not change nor does human nature, yet we are still called to do good and to remain faithful to God.

Homegrown Saints
All are one in Christ Jesus

Two men, born in the nineteenth century in small Midwestern towns less than 200 miles apart are currently being considered for canonization. Both were Catholic priests.

One was born into slavery, the son of slaves, in the tiny farming community of Brush Creek, located some 12 miles southeast of my childhood home, Monroe City, Missouri. The other was born in the small town of El Paso, Illinois, the eldest of four children.

Augustus Tolton (1854-1897)

His parents, Peter Paul and Martha Tolton, were slaves belonging to Mr. and Mrs. Stephen Elliot who brought them from Kentucky when they migrated to Missouri. Augustus was baptized in St. Peter's Church at Brush Creek along with his older brother after receiving religious instruction from Mrs. Elliot.

Augustus was seven years old when the Civil War broke out and while different versions of what actually happened at that time remain, what is known is that the Toltons were granted their freedom. Mr. Tolton left for St. Louis to join the Union Army but while there died of dysentery.

---

[38] Father Robert McTeigue, SJ, *Was Fulton Sheen a prophet?*, Aleteia, June 29, 2016.
[39] Charles Dickens, *A Tale of Two Cities*, 1859.

Martha, with her nine- and seven-year-old sons and a 20-month-old daughter fled across the Mississippi River into Illinois which was a free state and settled in Quincy, Illinois.

Although only seven years old, Augustus found work in a tobacco factory, later in a saddlery, and then as a factory hand. He also was employed as custodian of St. Peter's Church in Quincy.

He began his formal education but due to the extreme prejudice that existed at the time attended two schools for only brief periods before being admitted, along with his siblings, to St. Lawrence Catholic school where he graduated with distinction and was confirmed.

Privately tutored by some of the local priests he eventually expressed his desire to become a priest.

But his efforts to enter a seminary were thwarted by the same old enemy, prejudice. He was even denied entry into a seminary whose white priests were being trained to serve the American Negro.

Ironically, the prejudice that prevented this brilliant young man from studying for the priesthood in his own land was the cause of his being sent to the foremost college of the Catholic Church. Finding that he could not pursue his studies here, some of his priest benefactors found channels through which he might be sent to the College of Sacred Propaganda at Rome.

There, after six years of study, Father Augustus Tolton was ordained a Catholic priest. Receiving his priesthood from Cardinal Parochia in St. John Lateran in Rome, the young prelate was informed that his mission was to be the Negroes of the United States.

Returning to Quincy, Father Tolton celebrated his first Solemn High Mass at St. Boniface where he had served as an altar boy years before. He was appointed pastor of St. Joseph Negro Church and soon became quite well known in Quincy for his excellent sermons, his splendid education, and his eloquent voice.

But although the young priest succeeded in attracting many whites as well as his own people to his services, the ugly face of prejudice soon appeared again. The large number of people who sought his classes of inquiry, the crowded Sunday Masses, the coming together of people of both races in his church brought down on him not only the jealousy and scorn of some white priests, but also the envy of some Protestant Negro ministers.

The combination was too much. He bowed to prejudice and left Quincy, accepting the invitation to found a Negro Church in Chicago.

He began his ministry there in the basement of "Old St. Mary's," while laboriously building up a parish among the entire Negro community. Four years after his arrival there, Mrs. Anna O'Neil donated $10,000 for the building of a Negro church, which was to be named St. Monica's.

Success of a sort appeared to be within the reach of this young man, only 43 years old, after a lifetime of frustration caused exclusively by the color of his skin. He had been invited to preach in the Cathedral of Baltimore and had been sought by bishops and cardinals who wanted him to establish Negro churches in their dioceses.

But on July 9, 1897, with Chicago in the grip of an intense heat wave, Father Tolton suffered a heat stroke. … Father Tolton's remains were brought back to Quincy as he requested. He is buried there in a circular plot in the center of St. Peter's Cemetery."[40]

In 2010 the late Francis Cardinal George initiated a cause for sainthood for Father Tolton with these words:

Many Catholics might not ever have heard of Fr. Augustus Tolton; but black Catholics most probably have. He was the first American diocesan priest of African descent, the son of slaves. After studying in Rome, because no American seminary would accept him, he was ordained for the Diocese of Quincy, in southern Illinois, and later came to Chicago to start a parish for black Catholics. He died young, at only 43 years of age; but most priests in the nineteenth century died before their fiftieth birthday. Visiting the sick on a daily basis was risky in an age before antibiotics. Many priests sickened sometime in their forties and died after a period of ill health.

Fr. Tolton's cause for sainthood is being introduced in the Archdiocese of Chicago, and during this year for priests it would be good to pray to him and to ask the Lord to send us many more priests like him."[41]

Fulton J. Sheen (1895-1979)

The firstborn son of Newton and Delia Sheen, Peter John Sheen, better known as Fulton, his mother's maiden name, grew up in Peoria, Illinois, where he graduated from Spalding Institute with valedictorian honors in 1913. He was ordained September 20, 1919 in St. Paul, Minnesota, attended the Catholic University of America in Washington, D.C. and earned a doctorate in philosophy at the Catholic University of Leuven in Belgium in 1923, winning the Cardinal Mercier award for the best philosophical treatise. In 1924 he continued his studies in Rome earning a Sacred Theology Doctorate at the *Pontificium Collegium Internationale Angelicum*.

He was consecrated a bishop on June 11, 1951, serving as an Auxiliary Bishop of the Archdiocese of New York from 1951 to 1965.

Beginning in 1925 Fulton J. Sheen authored 73 books and in 1930 began a weekly Sunday night radio broadcast, *The Catholic Hour*, which by 1950 had an audience of four million listeners and received 3,000-6,000 letters each and every week. In 1951, he began a weekly television program *Life Is Worth Living* which consisted of him speaking unscripted in front of a live audience. In 1952 he won an Emmy which he accepted by saying: "I feel it is time I pay tribute to my four writers—Matthew, Mark, Luke and

---

[40] This account of Father Augustus Tolton's life was taken from portions of a feature article written for the Monroe City News by my mother, Nellie Ann Lanham, published February 6, 1973 under the headline: *Brush Creek's Illustrious Son Recognized Only After Death.*
[41] Francis Cardinal George, OMI, Archbishop Emeritus of Chicago, *Cause for Sainthood of Fr. Augustus Tolton*, March 1, 2010.

John." The show ran until 1957, drawing as many as 39 million people each week. Archbishop Sheen died of heart disease after having open-heart surgery on December 9, 1979.

In 2002, Bishop Daniel R. Jenky, C.S.C., Bishop of the Diocese of Peoria initiated Sheen's *Cause for Canonization*. Due to a disagreement with the Archdiocese of New York, the cause was paused in November of 2010. On June 28, 2012, the Vatican announced officially that it had recognized Sheen's life as one of "heroic virtue" which elevated his stature to "Venerable Servant of God." To date, one miracle attributed to Sheen has been examined and officially recognized by a panel of medical experts to have no determinable natural cause, subsequently agreed to by a panel of theologians, and approved by the Bishops and Cardinals who are members of the Congregation for the Causes of Saints.

Since November 2014, the cause has been suspended due to a disagreement with the Archdiocese of New York to move his remains to Peoria. In order for the cause to move forward the body must be closely examined, and first-class relics taken in the initiating Diocese. Recently however, a niece and oldest living relative, Joan Sheen Cunningham has petitioned the Supreme Court of New York to allow his remains to be transferred to Peoria. There is now hope the cause may now proceed and his Beatification may be approved.[42]

Idle Thoughts
Too tired to think

Few could or would argue that the Venerable Fulton J. Sheen was a superb communicator, both as an author and orator.

His 73 books written over a span of 54 years stands as testament to his intellect and his talents. In one of his first books *Old Errors and New Labels* first published in 1930 he decries the decline in the art of controversy and places such decline on two underlying causes: religious and philosophical. But he begins with a rather astute observation concerning the difficult task of thinking:

> The hardest thing to find in the world today is an argument. Because so few are thinking, naturally there are found but few to argue. Prejudice here is in abundance and sentiment too, for these things are born of enthusiasms without pain of labor. Thinking, on the contrary, is a difficult task; it is the hardest work a man can do — that is perhaps why so few indulge in it. Thought-saving devices have been invented that rival labor-saving devices in their ingenuity. Fine-sounding phrases like "Life is bigger than logic," or "Progress is

---

[42] Update: Venerable Fulton Sheen's beatification was originally scheduled for December 2019 but was delayed weeks before at the request of the Bishop of Rochester, NY. No date has been rescheduled as of this printing.

the spirit of the age," go rattling by us like express trains, carrying the burden of those who are too lazy to think for themselves.

Not even philosophers argue today; they only explain away. A book full of bad logic, advocating all manner of moral laxity, is not refuted by critics; it is merely called "bold, honest, and fearless." Even those periodicals which pride themselves upon their open-mindedness on all questions are far from practicing the lost art of controversy. Their pages contain no controversies, but only presentations of points of view; these never rise to the level of abstract thought in which argument clashes with argument like steel with steel, but rather they content themselves with the personal reflections of one who has lost his faith, writing against the sanctity of marriage, and of another who has kept his faith, writing in favor of it. Both sides are shooting off firecrackers, making all the noise of an intellectual warfare and creating the illusion of conflict, but it is only a sham battle in which there are no casualties; there are plenty of explosions, but never an exploded argument.

As you read your mind cannot readily disassociate his words from the prevailing social and cultural norms of today even with the clear understanding they were written over 86 years ago. Either the times have not changed as much as we might suppose or the norms have been slowly deteriorating over the ensuing years, or both; whichever it may prove to be, the reality appears to be things have not improved in the slightest.

Sheen goes on to explain the religious and philosophical causes for the decline in the art of controversy.

Creeds and confessions of faith are no longer the fashion; religious leaders have agreed not to disagree and those beliefs for which some of our ancestors would have died they have melted into a spineless Humanism. Like other Pilates they have turned their backs on the uniqueness of truth and have opened their arms wide to all the moods and fancies the hour might dictate. The passing of creeds and dogmas means the passing of controversies. Creeds and dogmas are social; prejudices are private. Believers bump into one another at a thousand different angles, but bigots keep out of one another's way, because prejudice is antisocial.

The second cause, which is philosophical, bases itself on that peculiar American philosophy called "Pragmatism," the aim of which is to prove that all proofs are useless. ... As a result, there has sprung up a disturbing indifference to truth, and a tendency to regard the useful as the true, and the impractical as the false. The man who can make up his mind when proofs are presented to him is looked upon as a bigot, and the man who ignores proofs and the search for truth is looked upon as broadminded and tolerant.

Another evidence of this same disrespect for rational foundations is the general readiness of the modern mind to accept a statement because of the literary way in which it is couched, or because of the popularity of the one who says it, rather than for the reasons behind the statement. In this sense, it is unfortunate that some men who think poorly can write so well. ... To some minds, of course, the startling will always appear to be the profound. It is easier to get the attention of the press when one says, as Ibsen did, that "two and two make five," than to be orthodox and say that two and two make four.

He reasoned the Catholic Church was then impoverished for want of good sound intellectual opposition; the fact the Church then did not appear to be producing great chunks of thought was because she had not been challenged to do so.

"The Church loves controversy, and loves it for two reasons: because intellectual conflict is informing, and because she is madly in love with rationalism. The great structure of the Catholic Church has been built up through controversy. It was the attacks of the Docetists and the Monophysites in the early centuries of the Church that made her clear on the doctrine concerning the nature of Christ; it was the controversy with the Reformers that clarified her teaching on justification. And if today there are not nearly so many dogmas defined as in the early ages of the Church, it is because there is less controversy — and less thinking. One must think to be a heretic, even though it be wrong thinking.

The fact is that there is now less intellectual opposition to the Church and more prejudice, which, being interpreted, means less thinking, even less bad thinking.

The Church is accused of being the enemy of reason; as a matter of fact, she is the only one who believes in it.

The Church asks her children to think hard and think clean. Then she asks them to do two things with their thoughts. First, she asks them to externalize them in the concrete world of economics, government, commerce, and education, and by this externalization of beautiful, clean thoughts to produce a beautiful and clean civilization. The quality of any civilization depends upon the nature of the thoughts its great minds bequeath to it. If the thoughts that are externalized in the press, in the senate chamber, on the public platform, are base, civilization itself will take on their base character with the same readiness with which a chameleon takes on the color of the object upon which it is placed. But if the thoughts that are vocalized and articulated are high and lofty, civilization will be filled, like a crucible, with the gold of the things worthwhile. ...

But no thought is born without silence and contemplation. It is in the stillness and quiet of one's own intellectual pastures, wherein man meditates on the purpose of life and its goal, that real and true character is developed. A character is made by the kind of thoughts a man thinks when alone, and a civilization is made by the kind of thoughts a man speaks to his neighbor.

Fulton Sheen certainly offers us some timely food for thought—and this was only the first chapter.

A Reason to Think
Why bother?

There are moments when a memory collides with a current thought and a new insight begins to form in the mind, moiling at first, then gradually becoming a vortex, inexorably pulling all thought toward a central point.

A recent 3-panel comic strip initiated just such a vortex. The first panel showed three men climbing a steep hill. The next panel depicted a fork off to the right and down from the path they were traveling with two signs: one pointed straight up and read "Truth and Enlightenment" while the other pointed to the right and down and read "Celebs Without Makeup". The third panel displayed an old bearded guru sitting on the top of the hill saying, "It's sure been lonely up here lately."

This brought to mind an uneasy realization of the casualness to which truth and enlightenment have been tossed aside, replaced by banal trivia and crude nonsense for no other reason than the latter requires no effort or thought.

It is enough to make one think or cause one to kneel in supplication—or at the very least it should.

What coincidental memory came to mind was of a song from years ago, which sang of a silly old ram who thought he'd punch a hole in a dam.

> *But he's got high hopes,*
> *he's got high hopes.*
> *He's got high apple pie,*
> *in the sky hopes.*
>
> *So any time your feelin' bad*
> *'stead of feelin' sad*
> *Just remember that ram*
> *Oops there goes*
> *a billion kilowatt dam.*

God made us in his image and likeness; he gave us free will and the ability to reason and to think beyond the instinctual habits of all other living things. We are free to choose to do nothing, know nothing, think nothing, be nothing—but that isn't what God had in mind. If that were the case, why would he have bothered to make us at all? Think about it.

On Moral Ground
Sailing against the wind

Two-hundred forty years ago a new nation was born. A nation expressly created under the aegis of Almighty God, in whom those who founded it pledged their lives, their fortunes, and their sacred honor.

Some would argue this country is no longer and never has been a Christian nation and to those who would so argue I must, to a limited degree, stand in agreement. While our fundamental documents unequivocally declare allegiance to and a belief in a Creator God there is nothing in them which so boldly claims the nation to be a Christian one.

The First Amendment to the Constitution forbids the establishment of a state religion and grants all citizens the right to freely exercise their own religious beliefs. Whether Christian, Deist, Jew, Hindu, Buddhist, Muslim, Pagan, or of another faith or a non-believer, the state (government) can neither interfere with, mandate nor legislate adherence to a particular religion. The First Amendment does not restrict or deny individual citizens the right to live and act in according to their conscience and their religious beliefs.

In *Christianity and the Constitution: The Faith of Our Founding Fathers*, John Eidsmoe contends "that at least 51 of the 55 delegates to the Constitutional Convention were members of Christian churches, and that leading American political figures in the founding era quoted the Bible far more than any other source."

> The ideals on which they framed the Declaration of Independence and the Constitution — that man is subject to the laws of nature and of nature's God, that God created man equal and endowed him with basic unalienable rights, that human nature is sinful and therefore government power must be carefully restrained by the Constitution—are ideals that they derived, directly or indirectly, from the Bible. Some of these ideals may be shared by those of other religious traditions. But the Founding Fathers, with few exceptions, did not read the Koran, or the Upanishads, or the Bagavigita. They read the Bible, and they heard the Bible preached on Sunday mornings.

Thus, while it may be true our nation is not a Christian nation, it remains true it was framed and constituted upon a deep and abiding devotion to the one God, the author of the Christian and Jewish Bible.

George Washington, our nation's first president noted "It is the duty of all nations to acknowledge the providence of Almighty God, to obey His will, to be grateful for His benefits, and humbly to implore His protection and favor."

John Adams, the second president of the United States went so far as to firmly state our constitution was conditioned on the necessity for a moral and a religious devotion; it could not effectively govern without God. "We have no government armed with power capable of contending with human passions unbridled by morality and religion. Our Constitution was made only for a moral and religious people. It is wholly inadequate to the government of any other."

Our third president, Thomas Jefferson wrote "and can the liberties of a nation be thought secure when we have removed their only firm basis, a conviction in the minds of the people that these liberties are a gift of God? That they are not to be violated but with His wrath? Indeed, I tremble for my country when I reflect that God is just; that His justice cannot sleep forever."

When the Constitutional Convention became deadlocked over congressional representation, Benjamin Franklin, who was eighty-one at the time, addressed the delegates with a plea for daily prayer.

> I've lived, sir, a long time, and the longer I live, the more convincing proofs I see of this truth—That God governs in the affairs of men. And if a sparrow cannot fall to the ground without his notice, is it probable that an empire can rise without his aid? We have been assured, Sir, in the Sacred Writings, that, "except the Lord build the house they labor in vain who build it." I firmly believe this, —and I also believe that without His concurring aid, we shall succeed in this political building no better than the builders of Babel.

The United States Supreme Court in their unanimous decision in the case of *Vidal v. Girard's Executors 43 U.S. 2 How. 127* (1844) wrote:

> Why may not the Bible, and especially the New Testament, without note or comment, be read and taught as a divine revelation in the college [a public school for orphans] — its general precepts expounded, its evidences explained, and its glorious principles of morality inculcated? What is there to prevent a work, not sectarian, upon the general evidences of Christianity, from being read and taught in the college by lay teachers?

> Now it may well be asked what is there in all this which is positively enjoined, inconsistent with the spirit or truths of Christianity? Are not these truths all taught by Christianity, although it teaches much more? Where can the purest principles of morality be learned so clearly or so perfectly as from the New Testament? Where are benevolence, the love of truth, sobriety, and industry, so powerfully and irresistibly inculcated as in the sacred volume?

In *Church of the Holy Trinity v. United States, 143 U.S. 457* (1892) the U.S. Supreme Court in another unanimous decision held:

> If we pass beyond these matters to a view of American life, as expressed by its laws, its business, its customs, and its society, we find everywhere a clear recognition of the same truth. Among other matters, note the following: the form of oath universally prevailing, concluding with an appeal to the Almighty; the custom of opening sessions of all deliberative bodies and most conventions with prayer; the prefatory words of all wills, "In the name of God, amen;" the laws respecting the observance of the Sabbath, with the general cessation of all secular business, and the closing of courts, legislatures, and other similar public assemblies on that day; the churches and church organizations which abound in every city, town, and hamlet; the multitude of charitable organizations existing

everywhere under Christian auspices; the gigantic missionary associations, with general support, and aiming to establish Christian missions in every quarter of the globe. These, and many other matters which might be noticed, add a volume of unofficial declarations to the mass of organic utterances that this is a Christian nation. In the face of all these, shall it be believed that a Congress of the United States intended to make it a misdemeanor for a church of this country to contract for the services of a Christian minister residing in another nation?

There is no dissonance in these declarations. There is a universal language pervading them all, having one meaning. They affirm and reaffirm that this is a religious nation. These are not individual sayings, declarations of private persons. They are organic utterances. They speak the voice of the entire people.

This case is famous for the statement made by Justice Brewer that "These, and many other matters which might be noticed, add a volume of unofficial declarations to the mass of organic utterances that this is a Christian nation." Justice Brewer would later explain in his 1905 book, *The United States: A Christian Nation*:

But in what sense can it be called a Christian nation? Not in the sense that Christianity is the established religion or that people are in any matter compelled to support it. On the contrary, the Constitution specifically provides that "Congress shall make no law respecting an establishment of religion, or prohibiting the free exercise thereof." Neither is it Christian in the sense that all of its citizens are either in fact or name Christian. On the contrary, all religions have free scope within our borders. Numbers of our people profess other religions, and many reject all. Nor is it Christian in the sense that a profession of Christianity is a condition of holding office or otherwise engaging in public service, or essential to recognition either politically or socially. In fact, the government as a legal organization is independent of all religions. Nevertheless, we constantly speak of this republic as a Christian Nation — in fact, as the leading Christian Nation of the world. This popular use of the term certainly has significance. It is not a mere creation of the imagination. It is not a term of derision but has substantial basis — one which justifies its use."

Significantly, while the 1892 court cited dozens of court rulings and legal documents as precedents in arriving at their unanimous decision, no such precedent was used in 1962 when the U.S. Supreme Court struck down voluntary prayer in public schools.

Clearly, the political winds have blown far astray from what was conceived as a new nation under God. John Adams warned us of the Achilles heel inherent within the Constitution. *We, the People*, have lost sight of the weaknesses inherent in the Constitution: that it was made only for a moral and religious people. *We, the People*, have allowed, with often careless disregard, those who are neither moral nor religious to circumvent the intent of the founders and the will of the people to take unwanted liberties and unwarranted advantage of the inherent inadequacies of the Constitution. God help us.

Love Never Ending
There is nothing more to say

Whenever I chance to recall that moment when I first held her in my arms; it is the eyes I remember with such deep and lasting memory. Those dark brown eyes stole my heart with such promise of never-ending love and so it has been these past fifteen years.

There is a special bond and a love that never wavers, never falters, but only strengthens over the years between two companions who find themselves bound together on the road of life. Where there is love, there is really nothing else, nothing more to say. It is for the eyes to express far more than words for the eyes are but tiny windows into love.

CJ was and has been my canine companion for nearly fifteen years, born on September 7, 2001 in Fallon, NV. She was my first and only, as was I, hers. We lived a quiet life together, for she seldom made a sound, although she communicated far more clearly than many humans are seemingly capable of doing these days.

Loving her was far too easy for she never asked for anything in return for her unconditional love. She knew no strangers and was always eager to give of herself to everyone she met—especially her abundant white fur and lots of licks. She taught me what it is to love without reserve, to live only for the joy which comes from loving another so completely.

We are taught that God is Love and I know the truth of this. In my heart and soul I do believe G-O-D made a mirror image of himself, which he lovingly called D-O-G, to be a companion and an outward expression of his unconditional, everlasting love for those he made in his image and likeness, M-A-N.

My beloved companion has passed away. She lived far longer than most and I believe she loved more than most. She loved me, what more is there to say.

Dialogue or Diatribe
An argument in search of reason

Long ago, we, who still enjoy calling this great nation our home, were very familiar with a song—personally I first remember hearing it sung by Gene Autry—whose refrain included these lyrics:

Home, home on the range,
where the deer and the antelope play,
where seldom is heard a discouraging word,
and the skies are not cloudy all day.

At some point, and it is difficult or perhaps impossible to now recall, we as a nation quit singing that tune. All I know, with unpleasant and discouraging certainty, is seldom do we hear an encouraging word these days, and I find myself more often than not wondering why all the bitterness, anger, resentment, hatred, vitriol, confrontation, shouting, ranting, blaming, and name-calling? Need I add more?

Where and when precisely did we lose the ability to engage in reasoned dialogue on issues without resorting to diatribe—a forceful and bitter verbal attack against someone or something? Of equal or more important weight, why must every comment, tweet, post, or utterance we make be devoid of any semblance of decency or respect for others. When did the bully pulpit become a pulpit for bullying?

This goes well beyond the body politic—where diatribe has been elevated to a level that defies imagination. Regrettably, verbal abuse has become the only acceptable form of speech for the preponderant population of this great nation as well as beyond our borders.

Name a subject and within less than a heartbeat you will find yourself on the defensive, castigated for either your ignorance, stupidity, incompetence, bigotry, hatred, or simply for having the temerity to utter a simple cogent thought. Never mind the thought—that never was of any importance—merely the fact you dared express one.

Yet beyond the growling and the mindless, thoughtless assault to any particular point of view, one will find—if one were only to make any effort at all to look—an unwillingness, disinclination, and a complete indifference to determining objective truth.

Truth, for most, has become subjective and relative, that is, whatever is true rests within one's own mind. Your truth is of no consequence to my truth unless it is by chance in complete agreement with mine—which is of course impossible or well beyond improbable.

Prevailing progressive instruction has long imposed the notion truth is derived from our emotions, our feelings and our personal reality, thus, subjective and relative; and because they are subjective and relative, they are therefore as solid and as changeable as the wind.

Reality, thus, has become entirely one's own point of view, unless of course you subscribe to the quite common novelty life is but an illusion. Likewise, morality. Right and wrong are what each wish to make of them. And if either reality or morality is mine to determine as I will, it follows I may choose to alter or abandon either as I am wont to do.

How often have you heard someone say, "Don't impose your values on me because they aren't my values?" This condemnation comes from a subjective and relativistic ideology that holds society is merely a man-made construct, not based on God or natural law; that all values come from man, so a society is then nothing but some imposing their values on others—majorities on minorities, or rulers on ruled, or teachers on students, or media mind molders on the ignorant, traditionalist masses.[43]

The measure to which we have succumbed is readily discerned: all we have to do is ask ourselves "To what degree do I fear the Lord?" Seriously, it is an honest question. Many, if not most, to some degree or another, no longer retain much or any fear of God—that is to say, few hold God in such high regard or awe as to worry in the least for the consequences of disobedience to his commandments or to the natural law which he endowed us.

The laws of God and of nature are clear, absolute and apply equally to all, as are the penalties for failure to comply; we ignore them at our own peril. It is perhaps God's intransigence and man's transigence which has turned the hearts and minds of so many away from the righteousness of God.

Without objective truth, which can only come from God, there can be no objective and absolute morality, reality or law. What is left is a truth which is no truth at all—it is whatever we wish it to be. There is no right or wrong, good or bad, truth or falsity, real or unreal. There is only what I feel to be right, good, true, or real. And when your right, good, truth, or reality comes into conflict with mine—which they inevitably will—then it is obvious you are either too stupid to live, a racist, hate-monger, misogynist, dimwit, imbecile, lunatic, etc., etc., etc.

Since truth is subjective and relative to every individual, facts that contradict such truth are irrelevant, immaterial, and unworthy of consideration. It should be obvious to anyone with half a brain there is no need for discussion or reasoned dialogue. After all, 97% of those who know anything at all agree the matter is settled, so shut up, you loser.

When Archbishop Charles Chaput issued pastoral guidelines for clergy and Philadelphia archdiocesan leaders on implementing *Amoris Laetitia*, "The Joy of Love" the clamor of dissenting voices was deafening but quite telling. According to the guidelines, divorced and civilly remarried Catholics, as well as cohabiting unmarried couples, must "refrain from sexual intimacy" in order to receive Holy Communion. The guidelines further stated Catholics in same-sex partnerships, those remarried without an annulment, and cohabiting persons may not serve on parish councils, instruct the faithful, serve as lectors or Extraordinary Ministers of Holy Communion. Archbishop Chaput correctly recognized the moral confusion that would ensue.

---

[43] Peter Kreeft, *A Refutation of Moral Relativism,* Ignatius Press, 2009.

Allowing persons in such irregular relationships, no matter how sincere, to hold positions of responsibility would offer a serious counter-witness to Catholic belief, which can only produce moral confusion in the community.

Among the first to denounce Archbishop Chaput was Mayor Jim Kenney of Philadelphia, a "catholic" and frequent critic of the Archbishop's conservative stances on matters of faith. Mayor Kenney quickly tweeted "Jesus gave us gift of Holy Communion because he so loved us. All of us. Chaput's actions are not Christian." One unhappy commenter wrote:

So Chaput gets to decide ... The sheer arrogance and un-Christian attitude of Chaput continues to stun. I, for one, will continue to receive Communion unless the one distributing it is obliged to ask each communicant, 'Are you divorced, gay, cohabiting, or remarried but chaste?' Perhaps the archbishop could issue identification tags.

Another wrote,

Archbishop Charles Chaput should focus on policing his priests, who take a vow of celibacy, instead of his flock. Protecting innocent victims of sexual abuse by his employees seems to be a much more important problem than the sex lives of lay Catholics.

There were many more who objected to the Archbishop's pastoral guidelines as well as many who spoke in support. What is missing in virtually all of those who wrote in opposition is any reasoned argument.

Yes, Jesus gave us the Eucharist as his gift of love. But throughout his public ministry he consistently admonished the sinner to "go and sin no more." He also commissioned the eleven apostles to "Go, therefore, and make disciples of all nations, baptizing them in the name of the Father, and of the Son, and of the holy Spirit, teaching them to observe all that I have commanded you" (Mt 28:19-20).

Those offended by Archbishop Chaput's teaching would like to ignore that Jesus himself ordered the apostles and their successors—bishops (including the Pope, bishop of Rome)—to teach us to *observe **all*** that Jesus commanded and Jesus commanded us to go and sin no more. Those who choose to live in a state of habitual sin would like to ignore that uncomfortable fact, but it remains true no matter how much they may wish it otherwise.

July 22, 2016

Beacons of Hope
Standing alone above the fray

For those of us with more years behind us than remain, the future is often a dark and foreboding place. Our memories of the past are of brighter days, filled with rainbows and laughter, light winds and calm seas, and enduring hope for the future. Dark days and fearful nights have been swept away, long forgotten for their unpleasant memory.

With all the ugliness and hate which surrounds us it would be easy to succumb to the dark side, to lose hope. At times it feels as if we are lost on a vast storm-tossed sea with no light to guide us safely home.

And yet among the darkness there stand beacons of hope willing to keep the flames of faith and love alive if only we would follow where their light would lead.

This week over a million youth will begin converging on Krakow, Poland for World Youth Day 2016. This past Monday forty-two youth from the Diocese of Reno embarked on their journey to Krakow, including Robert Hamon from St. Albert the Great Catholic Church.

Robert stands out as a beacon of hope for us all. At 20, he serves as a helicopter crew chief with the National Guard, is a member of the Knights of Columbus and the parish youth ministry, assists with after school care, is an altar server, Extraordinary Minister of Holy Communion, Lector, Choir member, and Sacristan.

As Catholics and disciples of Jesus Christ we are called to bring the Good News to everyone we meet. At times it seems far too many light the lamp of faith and then place it beneath a basket, reluctant to let it shine for all to see.

Pope Francis, who will celebrate Mass at WYD 2016 once said, "Love is shown by little things, by attention to small daily signs which make us feel at home. Faith grows when it is lived and shaped by love." Look into the eyes of our youth and you will see the light of faith shining bright.

The Joy of Love
Please state your intentions

Pope Francis certainly has a way with words—at times with great compassion and mercy and upon occasion with seemingly little thought as to how his words will be construed. In the first chapter of *Amoris Laetitia* he beautifully writes:

The majestic early chapters of Genesis present the human couple in its deepest reality. Those first pages of the Bible make a number of very clear statements. The first, which Jesus paraphrases, says that "God created man in his own image, in the image of God he created them; male and female he created them" (1:27). It is striking that the "image of God" here refers to the couple, "male and female". … God's transcendence is preserved, yet inasmuch as he is also the Creator, the fruitfulness of the human couple is a living and effective "image", a visible sign of his creative act. … The couple that loves and begets life is a true, living icon … capable of revealing God the Creator and Saviour.[44]

Not long ago, in an unscripted response to a question, Pope Francis commented "a great majority of our sacramental marriages are null," setting off an immediate media firestorm and raising questions among many in the church as to whether what he said was really what he intended to say. To that point, "a great majority" was quickly amended to "some" or "a portion".

As several Catholic writers have since opined, the point Pope Francis was making was not that most marriages were invalid but that in our contemporary culture of impermanence where prevailing attitudes concerning love and marriage disparage making intentional life-long commitments, there can be little doubt some sacramental marriages were entered into under false pretenses and are thereby sacramentally suspect.

Any time either or both parties enters into a marriage without the full and complete intention to take as their husband or wife "until death do us part" but only until it is not fun anymore or something better comes along, then the marriage necessarily begins on the wrong foot because it is missing an essential element within the sacramental marriage vows: *intention*.

Once during a marriage preparation session, a couple quite openly and emphatically stated they had no intention of staying in their marriage if "things didn't work out." Among the things that would cause their marriage to not work out were unfaithfulness, falling out of love, sexual dysfunction, and unhappiness. When informed such attitudes displayed a serious lack of commitment on their part as well as a misunderstanding of the permanence of the sacrament of matrimony, they were outwardly offended and left without further comment or question.

At the 12th annual National Catholic Prayer Breakfast in Washington, D.C. Robert Cardinal Sarah in his keynote address spoke of the beauty of the Catholic Church's teaching on marriage and the family. In his remarks he stated "God is being eroded, eclipsed, liquidated" in the United States.

Advanced societies, including, I regret, this nation, have done and continue to do everything possible to legalize such situations [as cohabitation and same-sex relationships].

---

[44] Pope Francis, Post-Synodal Apostolic Exhortation: Amoris Laetitia, March 19, 2016, pp 8-9, par 10-11.

But this can never be a truthful solution. It is like putting bandages on the infected wound. It will continue to poison the body until antibiotics are taken.

All manner of immorality is not only accepted and tolerated today in advanced societies, but even promoted as a social good. The result is hostility to Christians, and increasingly, religious persecution. Nowhere is this clearer than in the threat that societies are visiting on the family through a demonic "gender ideology," a deadly impulse that is being experienced in a world increasingly cut off from God through ideological colonialism.

This is not an ideological war between competing ideas. This is about defending ourselves, children and future generations from the demonic idolatry that says children do not need mothers and fathers. It denies human nature and wants to cut off an entire generation from God.

Every human being, like the Persons of the Trinity, has the capacity to be united with other persons in communion through the ... bond of charity of the Holy Spirit. The family is a natural preparation and anticipation of the communion that is possible when we are united with God. ... This is why the devil is so intent on destroying the family. If the family is destroyed, we lose our God-given anthropological foundations and so find it more difficult to welcome the saving good news of Jesus Christ: self-giving fruitful love.

The rupture of the foundational relationships of someone's life — through separation, divorce or distorted impositions of the family, such as cohabitation or same-sex unions — is a deep wound that closes the heart to self-giving love unto death, and even leads to cynicism and despair.

These situations cause damage to little children through inflicting upon them a deep existential doubt about love. They are a scandal — a stumbling block — that prevents the most vulnerable from believing in such love, and a crushing burden that can prevent them from opening to the healing power of the Gospel.

Considerable controversy has been raised concerning a footnote (351) in Chapter Eight of *Amoris Laetitia*—a footnote which I will write of shortly. *Chapter Eight: Accompanying, Discerning and Integrating Weakness* begins with:

> The Synod Fathers stated that, although the Church realizes that any breach of the marriage bond "is against the will of God", she is also "conscious of the frailty of many of her children". Illumined by the gaze of Jesus Christ, "she turns with love to those who participate in her life in an incomplete manner, recognizing that the grace of God works also in their lives by giving them the courage to do good, to care for one another in love and to be of service to the community in which they live and work."[45]

Throughout the 264 pages of his Apostolic Exhortation Pope Francis focuses on the essentiality of marriage between a man and a woman and the necessity of a self-giving procreative love that is the basis of such a union.

On his return flight from Lesbos on April 16th he expressed concerns that young people increasingly renounce marriage altogether, that ever fewer children are born

---

[45] Pope Francis, Post-Synodal Apostolic Exhortation: *Amoris Laetitia*, 291.

and the children who are born very often have to grow up without their parents. The principle problem is the family is no longer perceived as good news. Thus, the primary focus and concern of the document is on love and the importance of the family.

> No one can think that the weakening of the family as that natural society founded on marriage will prove beneficial to society as a whole. The contrary is true: it poses a threat to the mature growth of individuals, the cultivation of community values and the moral progress of cities and countries. There is a failure to realize that only the exclusive and indissoluble union between a man and a woman has a plenary role to play in society as a stable commitment that bears fruit in new life. We need to acknowledge the great variety of family situations that can offer a certain stability, but defacto or same-sex unions, for example, may not simply be equated with marriage. No union that is temporary or closed to the transmission of life can ensure the future of society.[46]

As for the controversy surrounding footnote 351, the Catholic view seems to be one of confusion, not so much for what is stated or implied but for its ambiguity. Referenced within paragraph 305 which reads in part:

> Because of forms of conditioning and mitigating factors, it is possible that in an objective situation of sin — which may not be subjectively culpable, or full such — a person can be living in God's grace, can love and can also grow in the life of grace and charity, while receiving the Church's help to this end.

Footnote 351 then states:

> In certain cases, this can include the help of the sacraments. Hence, "I want to remind priests that the confessional must not be a torture chamber, but rather an encounter with the Lord's mercy." I would also point out that the Eucharist "is not a prize for the perfect, but a powerful medicine and nourishment for the weak."[47]

Those who had been hoping for a change in the Church's position with respect to the reception of Holy Communion by those in irregular relationships (primarily divorced and remarried) have interpreted this as a change in church doctrine. That is simply not the case here. It is unfortunate while Pope Francis was quite clear everywhere else in *Amoris Laetitia*, he chose at this point to be ambiguous.

---

[46] Pope Francis, Post-Synodal Apostolic Exhortation: *Amoris Laetitia*, 52.
[47] Pope Francis, Post-Synodal Apostolic Exhortation: *Amoris Laetitia*, 305, footnote 351.

J u l y   2 9 ,   2 0 1 6

On That Day
Al-tirah ki imekha-ani

That lowly worm, I have no doubt, carries no dreams of gossamer wings that float upon warm uplifting currents to lofty heights and unimagined vistas yet revealed. It only knows the ever present need to eat and grow and crawl upon the ground and then to shroud its body within a tomb of its own making; it knows not its fate and thus no fear of death or thought of future glories.

 Like that worm, we have no true and certain knowledge of what we will become beyond this brief, brief moment, but we know there is more, much more: an eternity in truth awaits. And for all its promised glories and the assurance of an eternity in the loving arms of God, we resist, unwilling to embrace eternity, to accept angelic wings and fly beyond this mortal coil.

Yet, it is not our fears that hold us here but love's reluctance to letting go. Those who have yet to be invited into eternity want no part of it for the pain of loss and emptiness that will, with certitude, scar the soul and stab the heart enter in; unwanted guests who then refuse to leave.

There is no cure or care which can ameliorate the grief that follows any death, yet we who grieve should rejoice in the knowing of what the dying have attained. For Jesus often said, *"al-tirah ki imekha-ani"* "Fear not for I am with you." And in the truest sense those whom we love are with us even more than before, for they, like the Father, Son and Holy Spirit, are with us always.

What beauty would be lost were not the worm to become the butterfly. How bleak and dreary would life be if there was nothing more, no greater beauty, no angelic wings to soar beyond the gates of heaven into the loving arms of God.

Unlocking the Chains
Using the key in our hand

It requires no genius nor high degree to recognize the deep divisions that have fractured our spirit, sorely wounded our collective pride, and weakened our will and our resolve. And while the recognition of it comes easy enough, any resolution of it will, with near certainty, prove as irresolvable as the Gordian knot.

"It is", as Winston Churchill once famously quipped, "a riddle, wrapped in a mystery, inside an enigma;" yet as with the Gordian knot and as Churchill would then suggest: "perhaps there is a key." Churchill was speaking of the difficulty in forecasting what action Russia might take in 1939 yet what he perceived as the key offers a possible means of addressing the current public schizophrenia that hangs before us now, threatening us with ever maddening madness. To paraphrase his response: "That key is America's national interest."

This past weekend I attended the 31st annual reunion of the descendants of Bob and Nellie Ann Lanham, my parents. This annual event has been held every year in northeast Missouri, since their untimely deaths in 1985, on the weekend closest to July 21st, the anniversary of their happy union in 1946, seventy years ago.

For those unfamiliar with Missouri in July, the weather is generally overwhelmingly hot, with humidity generally described as swampy without the crocodiles, and almost always interrupted by thunderstorms that do little to lower the thermostat. To anyone accustomed to breathing thin air at higher elevations, it is much the same as trying to breathe soup through a tiny swizzle straw: thick with a heavy helping of sludge.

Yet year after year my siblings and their spouses, their children, grandchildren, great-grandchildren, boyfriends, girlfriends, occasionally relatives and friends, and frequently a fetal freeloader (this year there were three, expected to arrive next February) who come together to enjoy one another's company, reminisce on the past, and make new memories to be retold and embellished in the years to follow.

What is most amazing is that year after year increasingly more than sixty people come together and spend three days with nary a discouraging word: no anger, little argument, no bitterness or vitriol. Four generations spanning nearly seventy years; rich and poor; married, unmarried, divorced, and single; Catholic, protestant, atheist, and agnostic; straight and gay; liberal and conservative; white, yellow, and brown genuinely enjoying the company of one another.

While there may be and are as many divergent viewpoints and areas of serious disagreement as the numbers in attendance, there is among those an unspoken but well-understood tacit agreement to agree to disagree without rancor or bitterness, to find common ground upon which we can have civil and friendly discourse. What binds us together is family and that is of greater and far more importance than what would divide us.

We are, in every sense of the word, a microcosm of our nation—with at least one significant difference—we genuinely love one another and accept one another without condition or pause. And it is in recognizing that value in which the unique individual contributions of each member add to the *corpus familia* which we welcome with open arms. We recognize it is in the best interests of the family to accept and embrace our differences and focus on what is truly important to the strength and welfare of the family.

We play together, we laugh together, we cry together, we eat together, and we pray together. Chasms that could divide us are but opportunities to build bridges in order to span what separates.

There have been disagreements just as there have been good times and bad times, glad days and sad days, yet never, never, never has there been unreasoned bitterness and hate. When one is hurting, we feel their pain and do what we can to salve the wound and mend the brokenness. Those who have less find no comfort or will in making demands of those who have more. The welfare and well-being of one is as important as another for we are each a member of the family and know the value and importance of it.

Our nation once was "One nation, under God, indivisible, with liberty and justice for all." It once was a nation whose motto *E Pluribus Unum* "Out of many, one" held great truth. It was once a country filled with those who stood tall, silent and still, with hand over heart, while the nation's anthem played tribute to a flag so revered. It once was the "land of the free and the home of the brave."

Our nation was once created by those who stated with firm resolve "We hold these truths to be self-evident, that all men are created equal, that they are endowed by their Creator with certain unalienable Rights, that among these are Life, Liberty and the pursuit of Happiness."

And this nation came into existence founded upon these hallowed words:

We the People of the United States, in Order to form a more perfect Union, establish Justice, insure domestic Tranquility, provide for the common defense, promote the general Welfare, and secure the Blessings of Liberty to ourselves and our Posterity, do ordain and establish this Constitution for the United States of America.

From the beginning there have been disagreements and differences in direction and purpose. And yes, there was once that moment when such division and hatred became so severe as to sorely test the bonds of our blessed union. For one brief but violent moment our nation was torn and divided, statesmanship and civil discourse lost to the irrational violence of bigotry and hate. Too many died, far too many, yet our nation survived and began anew, much as it had first begun.

Through it all we have faithfully recognized and given due praise and thanksgiving to Almighty God for his providential care and blessings bestowed upon this great land we call home. Yet somewhere in the not too distant past we have turned away from God, our families, our friends, our neighbors, our communities, and our country. We have turned inward, looking only to ourselves.

In his inaugural address on January 20, 1961, newly elected Democratic President John F. Kennedy spoke to the citizens of this great nation and said, "And so, my fellow Americans: Ask not what your country can do for you—ask what you can do for your country." Sadly, for this nation, his words have been tortured and strained by far too many to precisely the opposite effect: "Ask not what you can do for your country—ask what your country can do for you."

We have lost the ability and the will to respect others, seek common ground, look out for one another, and to acknowledge that we must depend on each other.

Benjamin Franklin, at the signing of the Declaration of Independence, is known to have said "we must all hang together or most assuredly we will all hang separately" which should give us pause to consider how little we can do or accomplish on our own. Nearly eighty years later, on June 16, 1858, Abraham Lincoln in his acceptance speech at the Republican State Convention upon being nominated the Republican candidate from Illinois for the U. S. Senate said, "A house divided against itself cannot stand. "

We are now once again a house divided against itself, and indeed we are all hanging separately for we most assuredly are no longer hanging together.

There is perhaps a key that, even at such a late hour as now, can yet unlock the chains upon which we now hang separately. Each of us holds a key but it is not our own. Unaided we cannot unlock the chains from which we now hang. The key that will unlock my lock is in my neighbor's hand as his resides in mine. As long as we each look to our own self-interest and not to our neighbor's neither will ever be free. There is no master key with which any man or woman can unchain us all; to believe so is but false hope. Only God holds such a key but first we must use the one we hold in our hand.

To Lose a Mind
No critical thought required

Each year begins anew the annual rite of letting go, entrusting such young minds which have been planted, carefully nurtured on Catholic values, morals, ethics, and truth and showered with all the love and tenderness one could muster into the arms of strangers.

Every summer begins a new exodus of our young Catholic men and women, now free from the ever vigilant eyes of those who by the blessings of Almighty God and through their procreative love for one another gave them life and raised them to believe in the one who made us all.

And then they are gone, blithely dancing to a different tune, adults if only by the measure of years now lived. And we let them go because we must, but seldom is it easy or welcome. We want so desperately to hold on just a moment more, to know with certainty they are safe and they love us as much as we love them.

There is a disquietude that rests within the heart, an uncomfortable uneasiness, a feeling of missing and of loss. Mothers attempting to hold back the tears, seeing yet a newborn, so softly wrapped, held close in her loving arms. Fathers braving smiles while deep within the heart is pounding with both pride and trepidation. And all the while their child laughs and dances in anticipation of such great adventure now awaiting.

We cannot help but wonder what they will find beyond hearth and home, but we have heard the tales and they leave us cold and uncertain of what they will encounter away from us. There is no doubt what awaits will reshape their malleable minds but to what ends or purposes they will be molded is perhaps what worries most.

We taught them how to use their minds to think, to reason, and to value all God has made. We gave them love and faith and understanding of what is good and right and true. And yet we harbor nagging doubts, wondering will it be enough or will it all be forgotten, discarded and abandoned as quickly as their parting.

From orientation to graduation some number of years from now our nation's colleges and universities will fill their minds with new ideas, indoctrinating them with a vision of reality vastly different from values so carefully inculcated and instilled. Those impressionable young minds, especially those who have not the skills necessary to detect and question with a critical eye, will find themselves succulent prey to the sophistry of the intellectual elite whose ideologies are largely anti-church, anti-faith, and anti-God.

Our young deserve better; they need the tools to think critically and to defend themselves against an educational system that opposes reason, truth, faith, and God. Thankfully there is at least one such tool which should be required reading for anyone and everyone preparing to enter those hallowed halls of our colleges and universities. It is a small book with a rather lengthy title: *Disorientation: How to go to college without losing your mind*. Written by fourteen of the top Catholic writers in America—professors, priests, journalists, philosophers, and theologians—through a series of essays they dissect the trendy ideas that most often lead young Catholic minds astray. The book provides intellectual ammunition for every college student and parent, breaking down the history, analyzing the appeal, and debunking the empty promises of such popular ideological errors as: Sentimentalism, Hedonism, Relativism, Progressivism, Modernism, Scientism, Fundamentalism, Feminism, Multiculturalism, Anti-Catholicism, Utilitarianism, Consumerism, Cynicism, Americanism, and Marxism. It is well worth the price, for what price would you pay to save a mind?

Unselfish Devotion
Where poppies blow

Touring the National WWI Museum and Memorial in Kansas City served as a stark reminder of a dark time in world history and yet there were souls, bright with the lights of courage, honor, duty, and love, who would not allow the darkness to prevail. It was to those souls and their unselfish devotion to their fellow man with whom I felt a gravitational pull.

Florence Edith Hemphill was born in 1887 in Wilson County, Kansas, the sixth of nine children. Trained as a nurse, when America entered the war, she immediately volunteered for the U. S. Army Nurse Corps and volunteered to serve on the front lines.

Eleanor E. Washburn from Pine Grove, Illinois read a YMCA proclamation calling for volunteers to support the troops and she seized the opportunity. She and 35,000 other artists went anywhere and everywhere to entertain the troops. One observer noted they brought the gospel of laughter while the shells burst over their heads. Even after the armistice, they stayed on to ease the homesickness that afflicted the young troops.

After the United States entered the war, the government turned the American Red Cross into a branch of the US military. Subsequently, the ARC went from 238,000 to 6.4 million members by mid-1917, raised over 100 million dollars for relief services and provided all Americans with opportunities for loyal national service.

American women volunteers served in all duties except combat. They were doctors and nurses, founded and ran hospitals, drove heavy trucks and ambulances, sang, entertained, and translated. One observer wrote "they do anything they were given to do; that their hours are long; that their task is hard; that for them there is small hope of medals and citations and glittering homecoming parades."

Beneath a glass bridge we saw a field of poppies which reminded us of the poem written by Canadian physician Lieutenant-Colonel John McCrae during the First World War:

> *In Flanders fields the poppies blow*
> *Between the crosses, row on row,*
> *That mark our place; and in the sky*
> *The larks, still bravely singing, fly*
> *Scarce heard amid the guns below.*
>
> *We are the Dead. Short days ago*
> *We lived, felt dawn, saw sunset glow,*

Loved and were loved, and now we lie
in Flanders fields.

Take up our quarrel with the foe:
To you from failing hands we throw
The torch; be yours to hold it high.
If ye break faith with us who die
We shall not sleep, though poppies grow
In Flanders fields.

To those with the courage and the honor enough to serve when country calls: God bless you.

The Science of Art
Discovering the art works of God

Within the mind of man resides an insatiable desire to discover truth, to acquire knowledge, to know what precisely makes a thing tick or tock, whichever the case might be. Saint Thomas Aquinas wrote, "Natural things are midway between the knowledge of God and our knowledge; for we receive knowledge from natural things, of which God is the cause by His knowledge. Hence, as the natural objects of knowledge are prior to our knowledge, and are its measure, so the knowledge of God is prior to natural things and is the measure of them."[48]

Aquinas saw knowledge (Truth) from two different perspectives: man's and God's. Man discovers truth by observing what exists prior to acquiring knowledge of it; God creates truth so man can observe it and come to know it. "Truth in science is discovered; truth in art is created. God is an artist, not a scientist; He designed and created the world, which is first of all the product of His art and then becomes the object of our science. ... And since all art reveals something about its artist, the knowledge of creatures, by its very nature, leads us in the direction of the knowledge of the Creator, if we are only fair and honest and open-minded toward it."[49]

Following a similar train of thought perhaps we should consider precisely how great the distance sits between "knowing God" and "knowing of God." Those who

---

[48] Saint Thomas Aquinas, *Summa Theologicae*, I,14,8.
[49] Peter Kreeft, *Practical Theology: Spiritual Direction from St. Thomas Aquinas, 17*, (San Francisco, CA: Ignatius Press, Dec 16, 2014).

claim to "know God" claim the impossible for no one who has not seen God can lay claim to such a truth, yet by truth discovered through reason and common sense all men may "know of God."

In Name Only
Self-defined Catholicism

There appears to be no end to the parade of political know-it-alls and wannabes along with other prominent public figures, be they policy wonks, advisors of every ilk and kind, or talking heads who are eager and willing to proclaim they are strong, faithful, practicing Catholics. It is enough to make we less-than-well-known Catholics dive for cover, ashamed and embarrassed by the company suddenly forced upon us.

Do not get me wrong. I applaud those who stand up, unafraid and unapologetic, witnesses to their faith and faith in God, no matter to what church or religion they may ascribe or follow. What abrades are those who pompously claim membership in the Catholic faith while publicly rejecting and/or renouncing fundamental church doctrine, even well-established dogma, either for the sake of political or personal expediency or because they find it too difficult to comply.

That is not to say disagreement with Church teaching doesn't exist. It does. To be perfectly frank, the odds of finding but one Catholic who doesn't find something that bends the nose one way or the other are so high as to be impossible to calculate. We all can find something that doesn't set right, that we question or that we accept but only reluctantly. And thankfully most of what we find disagreeable or question falls well short of heresy and the threat of excommunication. And again, thankfully most disagreements are kept private or at least at a level to where reason and dialogue have a chance to satisfactorily remove or mollify the disagreement. Most disagreements arise out of misunderstanding or miscommunication. Few rise to the level of being antithetical to Church doctrine and dogma and fewer still are laid bare before the ravenous anti-Christian secular media and the public to chew on.

What truly rankles are the public figures who profess to be Catholic but by their own admission have publicly smeared and splattered their anti-Catholic positions in bold headlines across the front pages of every tabloid and scandal sheet unworthy of print. The most recent example of this inexplicable public disagreement with Catholic Church doctrine is none other than Democratic Vice-presidential nominee, Tim Kaine. Before the balloons had hit the floor at the recent convention the Most Reverend Thomas J. Tobin, Bishop of Providence, Rhode Island, posted a sharp critique of Kaine's Catholicism and anti-Catholic positions:

Democratic VP choice, Tim Kaine, has been widely identified as a Roman Catholic. It is also reported that he publicly supports "freedom of choice" for abortion, same-sex marriage, gay adoptions, and the ordination of women as priests. All these positions are clearly contrary to well-established Catholic teachings; all of them have been opposed by Pope Francis as well.

Senator Kaine has said, "My faith is central to everything I do." But apparently, and unfortunately, his faith isn't central to his public, political life.

Kaine's support for abortion rights certainly breaks no new ground. John Kerry was told by then Archbishop Raymond Burke of St. Louis in 2004 he would deny him communion for his pro-choice advocacy. Vice President Joe Biden and Former Speaker of the House Nancy Pelosi have likewise come under increasing scrutiny for their pro-choice views, votes, and advocacy.

As a Catholic I try my utmost to faithfully follow Jesus Christ. That includes following and obeying all his Church teaches. It is what I must do in order to call myself a faithful Catholic.

When we as Catholics come in conflict with some aspect of Church teaching, there are questions you should ask and steps you can take to narrow the gap between your personal views and what the Church teaches. You can begin by asking yourself: "Do I agree with everything the Catholic Church teaches?" Not likely. As with most Catholics you will disagree with something the Church teaches. Where there is disagreement, make a concerted effort to discern the why and the what regarding the Church's position. Study and research the issue. Ask questions of those who are better acquainted with the issue. In short, become informed. In the end you may still disagree, but you will have a better understanding of the Church's position.

As Catholics we have every right to disagree but *no right to disobey*. The Church teaches what Jesus commanded of the members of his church. Willful disobedience to the magisterial teachings and doctrine of the Catholic Church is disobedience to what Jesus commanded of us. Moreover, it is hard to argue with two-thousand years of tradition and teachings from the likes of Augustine, Aquinas, John Paul II, saints and doctors of the church. Am I obligated to follow what the Church teaches even when I disagree? *Always!* Remember, the Church is the voice of Christ on earth. She speaks authoritatively for him. Whether we agree or disagree, as disciples of Jesus Christ we must follow where he commands us to go. If for no other reason we must obey what his Church commands. Jesus told the apostles, his Church "All power in heaven and on earth has been given to me. Go, therefore, and make disciples of all nations, baptizing them in the name of the Father, and of the Son, and of the holy Spirit, teaching them to observe all that I have commanded of you" (Mt 28:18-20). I find no latitude, no equivocation in this. We are to observe all, not some or only those with which we agree, but all he commands. While we may object or disagree with some of what Jesus, through the apostles and their successors, teaches, we must, as Catholics, obey all he commands, including what his Church teaches.

Do I make public my disagreements? *Never!* Of what business is it to anyone else? To publicly bare disagreement serves no good purpose; it is self-serving; it is the cause for scandal, from which no good can result for either you or the Church. Martin Luther disagreed with certain actions of the Church and because of his public display he was branded a heretic and excommunicated. Whether his disagreements were valid or invalid did not alter or remove the scandal that resulted from his public declaration. No doubt Jesus had much to disagree with the Romans especially with regard to the cruel nature of his crucifixion. If he could bear his disagreements in silence, even more so, should we.

What is most troubling with those politicians and other public figures who admit so publicly to their fundamental break with Church teachings is the impression they leave with the unsuspecting public. In the minds of the public they are perceived as good, faithful Catholics who just happen to have some disagreement with the Catholic Church. It's no big deal, right? Sadly, nothing could be further from the truth. They are catholic in name only and have chosen to self-define what Catholicism and being Catholic means. Like Thomas Jefferson, they cut out those sections of faith which they find objectionable and follow whatever they feel like following. The result of their self-defined, self-proclaimed catholicity is nothing short of heretical. It leads others to the false conclusion they too may self-define their own Catholicism and still call themselves faithful Catholics. Too many Catholics have fallen for the false narrative and the snake oil Tim Kaine and others public figures are selling. Catholicism is not, never has been, and never will be up for debate or self-definition. It is all or nothing, there can be no in-between.

For those who believe the Catholic Church is out of touch with the modern world and believe it needs to change, to modernize, to get with the program: sorry to disappoint. Jesus said "I am the way and the truth and the life. No one comes to the Father except through me." Jesus said this. I believe him and will do what he asks of me. I may not like it but faithful I will be.

What Matters Most
Oblivious to the obvious

Last week our pastor introduced his homily with a bit of humor. Now often humor within a homily runs the risk of falling flat, either because the delivery is off, or it simply isn't a very good joke. But in most cases the humor fails simply because it doesn't fit well enough with the message one intended to convey.

But this time the humor was spot on. Not only was it thoroughly enjoyed by the congregation (based solely upon my own personal laugh-o-meter) but it was perfectly suited for and germane to the readings and the gospel that had just been read.

There once was this yuppie (short for Young Urban Professional for those too young to remember) who enjoyed a high degree of wealth. Among his possessions was a perfectly maintained and very expensive BMW. It was his pride and joy and he loved to drive it and to be seen in it.

One day he drove his beautiful automobile downtown to go to the bank. Parking near the curb he opened the door only to have a large truck pass by tearing the door from its hinges, leaving the yuppie in tears. Angry and upset, he cried at the injustice, the tragedy, the destruction and mutilation of his marvelously beautiful automobile.

When a policeman arrived on the scene, the yuppie kept going on and on about what had befallen him, loudly and angrily bemoaning how unjust and incomprehensible that such a great tragedy could happen to him and his beautiful automobile.

The policeman stood by quietly listening and as soon as he could get a word in asked "Sir, aren't you the least bit concerned that you are missing your left arm?" To which the yuppie exclaimed in abject horror: "Oh no, my Rolex!"

While humorous the parable hits solidly on point. It should make us pause; it should make us think, it should. But, will it? Or will we gently nod our heads even as we remain oblivious to the obvious: the wooden beam protruding from our own eye? It is far too easy to blind ourselves, to ignore what should be obvious. Here is another parable, although this one is true.

At the age of thirty-six, on the verge of completing a decade's worth of training as a neurosurgeon, Paul Kalanithi was diagnosed with stage IV lung cancer. Both he and his wife Lucy, also a physician, were the first to review the scans and understand what they meant. *When Breath Becomes Air* chronicles the transformation of a naïve medical student possessed by the question of what makes a virtuous and meaningful life into a young neurosurgeon at Stanford, guiding patients toward a deeper understanding of death and illness, and finally into a patient and a new father to a baby girl, confronting his own mortality.

That wooden beam lodged in my eye? It is a reminder of our own mortality, for while we know neither the day nor the hour, we can be certain death will come to us all and when it does it will come like a thief in the night. Equally as certain is all our dreams and our desires, all we possess—houses, cars, watches, rings, money, power, or fame—will no longer be of any importance. Standing before God no one will feel compelled to shout, "Oh no, my Rolex!"

Counter Witness
The USCCB responds

From the USCCB website, a post written by Archbishop Joseph E. Kurtz, Bishop Richard J. Malone and Archbishop Thomas G. Wenski in response to Vice-president Joe Biden, a Catholic, presiding at a same-sex union:

When a prominent Catholic politician publicly and voluntarily officiates at a ceremony to solemnize the relationship of two people of the same-sex, confusion arises regarding Catholic teaching on marriage and the corresponding moral obligations of Catholics. What we see is a counter witness, instead of a faithful one founded in the truth.

Pope Francis has been very clear in affirming the truth and constant teaching of the Church that same-sex relationships cannot be considered "in any way similar or even remotely analogous to God's plan for marriage and family." Laws that redefine marriage to deny its essential meaning are among those that Catholics must oppose, including in their application after they are passed. Such witness is always for the sake of the common good.

During our Holy Father's remarkable visit to us last year, he reminded us that all politicians "are called to defend and preserve the dignity of [their] fellow citizens in the tireless and demanding pursuit of the common good, for this is the chief aim of all politics." Catholic politicians in particular are called to "a heroic commitment" on behalf of the common good and to "recognize their grave responsibility in society to support laws shaped by these fundamental human values and oppose laws and policies that violate [them]."

Faithful witness can be challenging—and it will only grow more challenging in the years to come—but it is also the joy and responsibility of all Catholics, especially those who have embraced positions of leadership and public service. Let us pray for our Catholic leaders in public life, that they may fulfill the responsibilities entrusted to them with grace and courage and offer a faithful witness that will bring much needed light to the world. And may all of us as Catholics help each other be faithful and joyful witnesses wherever we are called.

The Bishops' response, while clearly articulating the challenges Catholic politicians face in their responsibility to faithful witness, nevertheless falls well short of confronting the ever-menacing gorilla standing directly in front of them. In their view, Biden acted as a counter witness to the truth, yet they are either reluctant or afraid to take him (and other Catholic politicians of similar suasion) to task for their egregious behavior and blatant disregard for Church teachings. The bishops' reaction is something akin to "see no evil, hear no evil, speak no evil." Actions have consequences, except and unless you are a Catholic politician. Obviously, that grants you a free pass.

August 12, 2016

Sunday Rising
Out of sight, out of mind

There is a certain truth in the proverb: "Out of sight, out of mind" which speaks implicitly of our relationship with God. Although we know of him, we cannot know him for we do not see him and thus what we do not see is, by our nature, relegated to those things which obtain little of our attention. What inevitably follows is a bit of slight-of-hand logic that generally goes something like this: "I know God is every-where and he is always with me. Since he is always with me, I can pray to him whenever and wherever I want; like when I'm walking through the woods, or in the desert, or on the beach, at a game, anywhere and anytime. So, there really isn't any reason or purpose for me to go to church. Church is boring and I don't get anything out of it anyway, so why bother. I'd just as soon talk to God on my own, in my own time and place."

What a marvelous idea! And to a point, I'm sure God would welcome the conver-sation. After all, how would you feel if the only time anyone paid you any mind at all was one hour a week on Sunday. So, pray and talk to God wherever and whenever you have the opportunity to do so. But ... talking yourself out of going to church would be a huge mistake. Here's why: The reason we go to church has nothing to do with us. Church isn't entertainment, we don't go to be entertained or to watch as we do a foot-ball or baseball game. We go to do homage and to worship God. We go to give God our prayers and petitions, our hope and fidelity, our promises and above all else, our love.

What we so often forget is that, as in life, the more we give the more we will receive. The more we give to God, the more we will receive from him. We may not see God, but we ought not forget God or give him little more than an occasional passing thought. Give him your all.

Enslaving the Mind
In mindless pursuit of Pokémon

Seldom will you, dear reader, find within these few pages anything that should or ought to be construed as political partisanship. That is a personal admission of neither indifference nor ignorance of the body politic; for *au contraire*, I hold grave concerns for where the winds should blow across our fair and blessed land. Which side of the divide I gravitate some may assume, but only God and I know what others may merely presume.

The reason for my abstinence rests solely with my firm belief nothing good may come of partisan persuasion; only grief and the bitter bite of anger will be the result of it, which will with little doubt, carve wounds far too deep and ragged to quickly heal. What will be written from time to time in this brief mention will be some issue which has perhaps for want of diligence or indifference been left unattended or found want-ing in its characterization or importance. Grave issues are before us; issues which should alarm us, both for now and when. Yet we act as if we care not or dare not care to look beyond the surface for fear of what dark terror awaits us there. We would rather take our cue from someone else for that requires no thought or effort to discern what may be the truer measure of it.

It is a fearsome thing to lose one's mind, but it would be worse by far, if by total disregard, we were to simply give the mind away. Yet give it away is precisely what we have, with eagerness and aplomb, accomplished. We have become a people far too complacent, content to leave unpleasant things for others to digest and summarize while we but while away the hours in mindless pursuit of Pokémon. We have become addicted to the pursuit of happiness without concern nor hope of ever acquiring it. Collectively, we have offered up our minds, demanding our minds be filled with what? Whatever those who tell us they know far more than we choose for us to know. We dare not look behind the curtain for we might find the truth reclining there.

Dare I say it, yet I must, for it must be said, now before the hour has left us beyond redemption. We do not know the truth, we have no want to know of it, and thus we enslave ourselves by our deliberate ignorance of what truth would reveal. Jesus said to those who believed in him, "If you remain in my word, you will truly be my disciples, and you will know the truth, and the truth will set you free" (Jn 8:31-3). We cry for freedom's sake even as we secure the chains of slavery upon our minds.

In my youth I was keenly aware of the truth as I knew it. Everything was black or white; there were no shades of gray. My brother, ten and a half months my junior, was much of the same mind although invariably some 180 degrees from my own and thus quite obviously not of the right mind. Rightness or wrongness were never at issue for each believed in the absolute verity of his position, while truly neither had a leg upon which to stand. Truth, objective truth, never had the opportunity to appear or prevail for we were equally as stubborn and determined in what we knew to be "the truth." Most common, the matter was settled by the intervention of our father who could stop words in mid-air with nothing more than a stare (we knew it as the evil eye.) Words that had been outward bound were instantly sucked like a vacuum back into the offending orifice, never to be uttered.

Time and retrospection ought to have a profound effect upon childish minds. St. Paul tells us: "When I was a child, I used to talk as a child, think as a child, reason as a child; when I became a man, I put aside childish things" (1 Cor 13:11) but too often we simply refuse to grow beyond our childhood. We enjoy the childish games, the nonchalance of having never to think of tomorrow, of living in the moment, and chasing endlessly after rainbows and moonbeams. We want to live forever in Neverland with Peter Pan and the lost boys, unwilling or incapable of ever growing up.

What offends the reasoned adult mind is the incessant whining and temper tantrums that are on constant display by those long past their childhood. Age, it would appear, is not a factor; we are confronted by this childish behavior from toddler all the way to well beyond knowing better. There is neither rhyme nor reason for such childishness; whether purpose or accident has caused this incapacity to think beyond want or need is but a question left unanswered. And it is annoying, lacking for any possibility of resolution or cessation. One cannot reason with the irrational or unreasonable. The current popularity of timeout notwithstanding, sometimes a good spanking is what should prove both appropriate and necessary.

What is perhaps most perplexing is how so many in possession of more than a modicum of brain cells and education have developed PPS (Peter Pan Syndrome.) Similar in many ways to the various forms of dementia, those with PPS live far from reality in a constant state of denial, completely unaware of what is going on around them. They neither care nor bother to be informed—they can, however, recite with intricate detail meaningless minutiae on any team or player for whom they have come to idolize, or watch endless hours of mind-numbing drivel masquerading as entertainment. Never do they desire to know of more serious matters because that would disturb their finely tuned feelings of equanimity and awaken them to the harsher realities of truth. Stupefied, they stumble through each day alternatively mumbling and shouting thoughtless nothings to no one in particular—in truth no one cares to discover what nonsense they may at any given moment regurgitate. It matters not what cause or side they would support—even as they lean heavily on one another to stay upright and conscious—for they seldom possess a mind sufficient to understand what they suppose to propose, oppose and dispose.

Great minds are fading fast away; we are diminished by the absence of the reasoned mind and what could yet be born of it. It is a loss too grievous to contemplate. What Mind must be that we exist, and yet we laugh such thought away. For God and man are but imagined and thus inconsequential to the play before us.

We have succumbed to a pathos of hopelessness and despair and like Macbeth, we are wont to desperately declare:

> Tomorrow, and tomorrow, and tomorrow, creeps in this petty pace from day to day to the last syllable of recorded time, and all our yesterdays have lighted fools the way to dusty death. Out, out, brief candle! Life's but a walking shadow, a poor player that struts and frets his hour upon the stage and then is heard no more: it is a tale told by an idiot, full of sound and fury, signifying nothing."[50]

Those who live but for the day who care for nothing but their want will wound us with their vacant vote but a brief moment more and then will quickly learn of their conviction at the hand which they did choose to favor without mental exercise. Holding fast to what they know—no matter the size of it—they will not yield to reason or to truth, for they know what they know not, and that is assuredly all but the end of it.

It is the effort we oppose, the necessity to consume and then digest what fuels the mind beyond mere sustenance. Therein lies the gravest sin: the abdication of the soul to mental laxity and moral decrepitude. What remains within us seldom borrows from

---

[50] William Shakespeare, *Macbeth, Act V, Scene V.*

the good for "The evil that men do lives after them; the good is oft interred with their bones."[51] Sadly, we no longer subscribe to the premise "whatever the mind can conceive and believe, it can achieve"[52]for beyond all doubt we have lost our minds.

Perhaps the current battle is in question, yet the war rages unabated for whom would win the mind of man. It is a contest of the will, fought, not with weapons made of steel, but with far stronger substance, wrought not by the hands of man but forged by the hand of God.

You Shall Not Kill
Ignoring the fifth

Reading an article concerning the legacy of Justice Antonin Scalia and the ramifications that will inevitably ensue from whomever is chosen to replace him caused serious reflection on my part these past few weeks, specifically with respect to the current and future direction of jurisprudence in America. I am neither an attorney nor jurist—although I did manage to take Business Law three times in college—so I will offer no legal advice or counsel here.

Justice Antonin Scalia was by all measures a legal force of nature: A deeply religious Catholic whose principles of jurisprudence have inspired countless others to follow the law as he did so magnificently. One of the chief principles upon which he based his decisions was "that the law, whether statutes or the Constitution itself, must be applied according to its text."

> In other words, judges should not apply the law based on what is good policy or what they suppose Congress may have intended (but did not express) in passing legislation. In addition, Justice Scalia believed that the words of the law should be understood as they were understood by the people when the law was enacted…. There are some who believe that the meanings of words change over time, untethered from any objective measure.

> [Justice Scalia had an] unwavering respect for the idea of popular government. Laws, including the Constitution, receive their legitimacy from the people. The Constitution is not an autonomously evolving document that spins out new "rights" and obligations to which the people have not given their consent. Rather than discovering new rights in the Constitution, judges should respect the constitutional prerogative of the people to pass laws through their representative legislatures, limited by the restraints imposed by the Constitution—which was itself ratified by popular means.

> [He also firmly held to the] conviction that the rights actually guaranteed in the Constitution should be tenaciously defended, from the right of free speech to the rights of criminal defendants. … In short, Justice Scalia rejected the judicial activism of inventing

---

[51] William Shakespeare, *Julius Caesar*.
[52] Napoleon Hill, *Think and Grow Rich*.

law while embracing judicial engagement by ensuring that the limits on government are strictly enforced.[53]

I deeply admired Justice Scalia for his deep Catholic faith and the principles of law for which he so brilliantly championed.

I could not help but think of Justice Scalia upon recalling a recent conversation I had with someone very close to me. What initiated the conversation was my mention of the public admonishment by the bishop of Roanoke, Virginia directed to Democratic Vice-presidential nominee Tim Kaine, who claims to be a faithful Catholic while being an outspoken advocate for a woman's right to choose abortion, same-sex marriage, and other positions clearly at odds with Church teaching.

The response I received was two-fold: The Catholic Church needs to change and become more current with the times and "while I personally oppose abortion, I have no right to deny others their right to have an abortion." Without engaging further debate on current Church teachings, I asked whether abortion should be considered killing of an unborn human being and received an equivocal "maybe" in response. "If abortion is, as in fact it is, killing of an unborn human life," I then asked, "how can you support such murder?" to which the response was to completely ignore my question and repeat "I have no right to deny others their right to have an abortion." Obviously, this conversation was effectively over before it began.

What is tragic is the false innocence assumed by those who do not condone abortion for themselves yet refuse to argue against it. It is more than tragic; it is criminal. Refusing to oppose abortion or euthanasia or any other form of killing of another human being is nothing less than the aiding and abetting in the killing of innocent human life. Unfortunately, our current judicial system disagrees, at least in some significant ways.

Be that as it may, there is a higher court which holds a decidedly different view: The Supreme Court of God. His fifth (sixth for non-Catholics) commandment states without equivocation "You shall not kill." The Ten Commandments were given to Moses by God with the explicit instructions that these were carved in stone and all men (and women) were to diligently observe them. They applied to all human beings, all those living creatures created in the image and likeness of God. God did not add an "except" in the case of the unborn or the elderly or the sick or the weak or the stupid or the lame. He kept it simple and to the point: YOU SHALL NOT KILL—period, end of commandment.

Yet, much as the judicial activists who sit on the U. S. Supreme Court, Catholics and non-Catholics alike have made themselves quite comfortable with ignoring the fifth (or sixth) commandment—whether it is out of mere convenience or to soothe their consciences, I dare not venture a guess. Now to be perfectly fair, they do not completely

---

[53] Scott Pruitt, Attorney General, State of Oklahoma, *The Next Supreme Court Justice*, Imprimus, Hillsdale College, July/August 2016, Volume 45, Number 7/8.

ignore it, they simply modify or update it, adding words that are not and never have been a part of God's commandment. And they do this to bend the law rather than to break it. It is easier on the conscience that way.

Here I will return to the principles of law which Justice Scalia held so dear: the law must be applied according to its text and the law must be understood as it was understood by the people when the law was enacted. The law consists of four words: You shall not kill. Clear, concise, unambiguous, and its meaning remains precisely the same today as it did when God carved them in stone. If this law were the product of men, then the people would have the right to amend it by appending exceptions to it. But God is the author of this law and no man or woman has either the right or the authority to alter or abolish it. Only God can change his law and there is absolutely no evidence he is or has been inclined to do so. Which means the law as written must stand, unabridged and unchanged. There are no exceptions. Those who would ignore it or add exceptions to it do so at the peril of their immortal soul. Whether considering the laws and the Constitution of the U.S. or the Laws written by God, we owe it to ourselves and those who will come after us to live by the rule of law laid down by man and those ordained by God. Abortion kills. We simply cannot turn a blind eye to that.

August 19, 2016

What Love is This
Dining on nothing but appetizers

What we call love seldom plays a happy song, for in truth we want little more than the smallest taste of it; an appetizer: nothing more. I wonder at the question: why do so many choose to dine on appetizers and not enjoy the meal? What love is this that seeks the bed, but all too soon tires of it? What love is this that tastes only what sits sweet and pleasant upon the tongue? What love is this that hears a single tune and cares for nothing more? What love is this that sees and sees more than enough?

How jaded we have become to any thoughts of love. Listen to someone who has no idea of what love is:

> I'm 35; I've never been married. My parents have both been married three times, so I no longer believe in the fairy tale. In my mind it's so great, whatever, but statistically I can't shake the facts. I'm a romantic person but I'm a realist. So, I'm not like, "We did it! Now we are going to be together forever!" I think there's a chance we'll be together for a long time—or not. Sometimes I'm like, "Yeah we're going to be together!" And sometimes I'm like, "This is doomed."

Appetizers. Nothing of any substance to be consumed. What love is this? We have bought into living on snack food because it is quick and easy. When we tire of potato chips, we pick up a bag of Doritos. When they grow stale, we settle for corn chips. And when we run out of corn chips, we look for popcorn beneath the seat cushions. What love is this?

Love cannot be taken, only given. Love is never quick or easy. Perhaps that is why we have little patience for it. We want what we want, and we want it now! Those unwilling to spend the time and effort to know love will neither know it nor have it. They will never be filled or satisfied for they do not know what love is.

A Ten O'clock Scholar
No time for scholarship

University comes from the Latin *universitas magistrorum et scholarium* which loosely translated describes a community of teachers and scholars. Central to its purpose, the university was instituted with a sharp focus on academia, higher education and scholarship requiring students to engage in serious study and abstract thought.

While few universities today acknowledge their unmistakable Catholic roots, the truth is the earliest universities were developed under the aegis of the Roman Catholic Church by papal bull dating as far back as the 6th century and for centuries were taught by monks and nuns. By the twelfth century with the rediscovery of works by Aristotle, universities had become centers of scholasticism where teachers focused on applying Aristotelian logic and thoughts about natural processes to biblical passages, while attempting to prove the viability of those passages through reason. Astonishing as this may sound to the modern university attendee, this was precisely the expectation of the students of the time. The acquisition of knowledge from the masters was what drove students to the universities. In short, students came to learn from scholars, teachers who had studied the philosophies of the Greeks, Aristotle and Plato, or the theology and metaphysics of saints such as Augustine and Aquinas. Students also came to study the masters of mathematics, science, law and business.

Sadly, what once drove students toward the university—the study and acquisition of knowledge—no longer compels them to attend. What purpose drives them there is neither clear nor understood. Students no longer attend universities to learn, to discuss or to debate weighty issues. To do so runs the risk of offending another's delicate sensibilities. Rather than acquiring an education, students today are focused on building safe spaces and on tackling such manufactured and imagined problems as engagement, diversity, and inclusion, as a recent blog post suggests.

"Today, universities all across the nation are tackling problems of engagement, diversity, and inclusion (or a lack thereof). As much as we wish that those issues didn't exist, they do. And sweeping them under the rug will not solve anything. But you know what will solve them? Engaging faculty, professors, students, and alumni to collaborate and bring new ideas into the mix.

This same post makes note of how Harvard was recently confronted by a student group called Reclaim Harvard Law who demanded the official school shield be changed to be more inclusive and less racially offensive. Why? Because it displayed the crest of a plantation owner and slave trader. One can only wonder as to the pertinence of such a fact to the actual study of the law. The writer further suggests universities should establish a "Brave Space," similar to a "Safe Space" but differing in that participants "should be comfortable in opening up and sharing their opinions without fear of judgment. ... everyone should be encouraged to speak their truth, even if it is different than someone else's.[54]

Herein rests the lie upon which the modern university contends: the idea that truth is relative, that your truth may differ from mine and yet inexplicably both remain true. The fallacy of relative truth should be obvious but apparently it fails to find fault within academia, both with faculty and student. Should I claim as true $1 + 1 = 2$ and you claim $1 + 1 = 3$, the truth must rest with either one or neither of us. We both cannot simultaneously possess the truth. Yet, that is precisely the philosophical casuistry that has been and continues to be impressed upon far too many impressionable young minds in attendance at our colleges and universities. The state of higher education is dire and sinking ever faster into the mire and muck of *feel good* relativism, where the core curriculum has turned away from a search for objective truth toward bland mediocrity and the salving of emotional scar tissue. If it wasn't so ridiculous it would most assuredly be laughable.

What academia simply cannot stomach is the insistence by those—primarily the Catholic Church—who dogmatically "claim we can have knowledge, real knowledge, even certain knowledge, and not just opinion or belief, about objective reality—about any objective reality, much less about God.

> If all we know are our own concepts, we are like prisoners in a cave staring at images on the wall. (Does that sound familiar?) Or like people who watch only TV and media, not the real world. (Does that sound eerily familiar?) And even though we do not usually believe that about the things our senses perceive, if we believe that about the things our mind believes, including religion, then all we can do is to believe in ourselves, hope in ourselves, love ourselves, pray to ourselves, obey ourselves, and trust ourselves for our own salvation. That is a perfect definition of the philosophy of Hell.

> Philosophy is important because a really bad philosophy, like subjectivism, can endanger our salvation.[55]

---

[54] Author Unknown, Uncovering University Diversity and Inclusion Issues Before They Escalate, July 20, 2016, popinnow.com.
[55] Peter Kreeft, Practical Theology: Spiritual Direction from St. Thomas Aquinas.

What is especially dangerous to minds yet fully formed, still malleable is how prevalent philosophies such as subjectivism and relativism have become, not only inside the ivy-covered walls of the university but throughout our entire society and culture. Here is what one recent horoscope purported to predict: "You understand that your truth is not the only truth, and you respect the rights of others."[56] One can readily discern what those who have a mind to believe such astrological gibberish must themselves believe. What the writer would have you believe is whatever you and others believe to be true (whether true or not) is somehow a right which must be respected. Poppycock and balderdash! While anyone may believe or think whatever they may, there is no right for it be true. A lie is still a lie, still a falsehood, no matter how many times or how stridently one claims it their truth.

While the price of higher education has escalated well beyond affordability, the quality of the product delivered has declined precipitously even as the knowledge imparted has become terrifyingly suspect. Universities are no longer the wellsprings of grand and glorious intellectual pursuits to which they were once so dedicated. The search for truth—that is objective truth and objective reality—have been unceremoniously discarded, replaced by much more important studies such as basket weaving, tree hugging, gender identification, alternative lifestyles, ethnic culture, and social reorientation. Almost always described as studies, these so-called courses offer nothing pursuant to objective truth or reality, but rather, are seldom more than the subjective beliefs of someone with an emotion-laden agenda and a need to lay guilt-trips on unsuspecting, naïve young minds. In truth they are nothing more than propaganda disguised as truth and indoctrination served up as education.

While admittedly not all colleges and universities have fallen sway to the constant secular and political pressures; more have acquiesced to the false philosophies of subjectivism and relativism than have resisted. Sadly, far too many recognizably Catholic Universities have bent and folded under the relentless pressures of modern social and political will. Well-known and respected Catholic institutions have been far from immune to the demands for engagement, diversity, and inclusion. It is especially difficult to resist whenever an institution is dependent upon public largesse for significant portions of their ongoing funding needs. Our colleges and universities would do well to take a lesson, a lesson that states "when you lie down with dogs, you will likely get up with fleas."

---

[56] Holiday Mathis, *Horoscope: Gemini*, Reno Gazette Journal, p 5-C, August 16, 2016.

Called to a Life
Ordained to service

Ask any Catholic to list the sacraments and most would know there are seven and would be able to list most if not all of the seven: Baptism, Confirmation, Holy Communion, Confession, Marriage, Holy Orders, and Anointing of the Sick.

The first three sacraments—Baptism, Confirmation, and Holy Communion—are referred to as the Sacraments of Initiation by which one becomes a full member in the body of Christ and his Church. While not considered a Sacrament of Initiation, Confession normally precedes reception of First Holy Communion.

The sacrament of Anointing of the sick can be received by any Catholic, usually under threat of a serious medical condition or death. The two remaining sacraments—Marriage and Holy Orders differ from the other sacraments by virtue of their restrictive covenants—not every Catholic can be validly and licitly married in the Catholic Church and only men can receive Holy Orders.

It is to the last—the Sacrament of Holy Orders—which this essay will address for it is the rarest of the sacraments and thus the least experienced or understood. I suggest it is the rarest only quantitatively because it has by far the fewest participants.

The Sacrament of Holy Orders is received by men at ordination, who are called to a life of service to God, the Church, and his fellow man. While there is one sacrament within it there are three degrees: Deacon, Priest, and Bishop. These degrees are commonly described in order of deacon, priest, and bishop.

While this is in many ways correct, it offers but a single dimensional view of the ordained ministry and often results in confusion and misunderstandings. Although not perfectly analogous, one might gain a better understanding of Holy Orders by considering a simple cup of coffee. Consider the ingredients necessary: water, coffee grounds, sugar, and cream. Water represents mankind, the coffee grounds represents ordination to the diaconate, sugar represents ordination to the priesthood, and cream represents ordination to the episcopacy. To make coffee only the first two ingredients are required. Brewing coffee grounds with water results in a new, indivisible liquid we call coffee. Once brewed you cannot unbrew it, return to its original two ingredients. The same can be said for diaconal ordination. The man that was, is now a new man, with an indelible mark on his soul. It cannot be removed. Add a spoonful of sugar and it dissolves, melting into the coffee. The coffee has been changed and its ingredients are permanently bonded. It is still coffee but now more than it was before. This is similar to what occurs at the ordination of a priest. Previously ordained to the diaconate, a priest, like the coffee with sugar is still coffee, is still a deacon, only more, different, changed, with another indelible mark on his soul which can never be removed. Not to belabor the point for I believe it should be obvious where I am going with this: add cream and once again you still have coffee, but it is once again changed, yet inseparable. Likewise, a bishop becomes a new person, yet remains a deacon and a priest.

Five years ago, next month, eight men from the Diocese of Reno were ordained to the permanent diaconate. A few months ago, two men from the Diocese of Reno, currently attending seminary were ordained to the transitional diaconate. All ten men were ordained Deacon; all ten received the Sacrament of Holy Orders; all ten are now and will forever be members of the hierarchy of Clergy in the Roman Catholic Church.

The differences that distinguish transitional from permanent are largely superficial and in the minds of many subject to misunderstanding. A transitional deacon at some future date will most likely be ordained to the priesthood while a permanent deacon will not. A permanent deacon may be married while a transitional deacon must be unmarried and celibate. A permanent deacon who is married prior to ordination cannot remarry should his spouse die after his ordination. A single person may be ordained as a permanent deacon but cannot marry after ordination. With either form, transitional or permanent, ordination to the diaconate is permanent, placing an indelible mark on the soul which once received can never be wiped away. Once a deacon, always a deacon. As an ordained minister, deacons are members of the clergy, united to the bishop in service. At ordination they promise to obey the bishop and his successors. They assist the bishop and priests in celebrating the sacraments, as well as other duties and ministries. Deacons are granted faculties by the bishop to celebrate baptisms, marriages, and funerals but cannot consecrate the Eucharist, hear confessions, or anoint the sick. The deacon is an ordinary minister of Holy communion and the proclaimer of the Gospel.

Priests are co-workers with the bishops. They assist and obey the orders of the bishop, care for the communities of the faithful, administer the sacraments (priests can confirm only with permission of the bishop and they cannot ordain.) The highest act of the office of the priesthood is the celebration of divine worship, the Mass.

The bishop is the third and final degree of ordination. The Pope selects priests who have been recommended for ordination to the episcopacy and through his ordination the bishop receives the fullness of the Sacrament of Holy Orders. He is Christ's representative and given the power to sanctify, teach and to lead. He becomes a member of the college of bishops. Bishops have the power to ordain.

Archbishops, Cardinals, and the Pope are conferred or elected and are not additional degrees of the Sacrament of Holy Orders. What is important to remember, however, is they remain ordained: deacon, priest, *and* bishop, indelibly marked by virtue of their ordinations to the diaconate, priesthood, and episcopacy.

An archbishop is a bishop who is assigned to a province of bishops.

A priest can be appointed a Cardinal, but current Canon Law stipulates any priest must first receive episcopal consecration before their appointment. There are three orders of Cardinals: Cardinal Bishops, Cardinal Priests, and Cardinal Deacons. These are not degrees of Holy Orders.

August 26, 2016

What Grand Illusion
Admiration of reflected grace

The problem we face this November can well be illustrated perhaps by a brief conversation between two elderly gentlemen. One asks the other, "Have you decided who you're going to vote for?" And the second replies, "No. I can't say I care for either one of them. I'm thinking maybe I'll just cast a write-in vote for God instead." To which the first responds: "Bad idea. Both candidates would claim you voted for them." And I should add, "and so would the majority of the population."

We have a serious problem in this country which isn't limited to those seeking political office or positions of authority; the problem is within each of us to some degree or another. It is our arrogance and our conceit which serves to prevent us from seeing our god delusion for what it is: a lie. Lucifer suffered from such a delusion and we know the price demanded, yet we follow the devil just the same, still believing we are capable of being gods ourselves.

What grand illusion it is in which we convince ourselves of our divine necessity. We are but fools believing we exist by our own countenance. And yet we do persist in standing before the mirror in admiration of reflected grace and admire the view as if it were reality. If but the universe was so inconsequential as to contain but only the god of me!

Now God, in his goodness, created all that is by thinking it into being, by knowing it into existence. He wills us into being by knowing us into being. The best we can do is to know something before we will it. Poor gods that we are, we are incapable of causing a single atom into existence out of nothing. God, however, has been doing infinitely more, long before the beginning of time. It might be well to consider abdicating to the one true God before we find ourselves kneeling before the devil.

Long Past Dark
Persecution? Forget about it!

The attitude for a growing number of Catholics is the Church—especially its leadership—has lost both currency and relevancy. More are coming to believe, with growing consternation, the Church is living in the past, evidenced by its steadfast refusal to adapt to modern cultural mores. As Monsignor Charles Pope points out in a recent post for the National Catholic Register:

> It is long past dark in our culture, but in most parishes and dioceses it is business as usual and there is anything but the sober alarm that is really necessary in times like these.

> It is zero-dark-thirty in our post-Christian culture. And while we may wish to blame any number of factors for the collapse, we cannot exclude ourselves. We who are supposed to be the light of the world, with Christ shining in us, have preferred to hide our light under a basket and lay low. The ruins of our families and culture are testimony to the triumph of error and the suppression of the truth."[57]

What Msgr. Pope writes is alarmingly true, Catholics—he is especially critical of Church leadership in this regard—in our desire to make ourselves acceptable to the culture have lost or eliminated what was once distinctively Catholic. In his essay *The Papal "Apology"* Joseph Sobran on March 14, 2000 wrote:

> So faithful Catholics are entitled to wonder whether Pope John Paul II's recent "apology" for the historical sins of the Church was really a wise idea.

> His Holiness made two basic distinctions: he was speaking of sins pertaining to the human part of the Church—her "sons and daughters"—which don't touch the divine essence of the Church as the Mystical Body of Christ; and he was asking forgiveness of God, not of non-Catholics.

> The reaction showed that these distinctions didn't register with most people. Non-Catholics (including plenty of nominal Catholics, many theologians among them) don't distinguish between the human and divine aspects of the Catholic Church, because they regard the Church as a purely human institution; after all, if they believed the Church was of divine origin they would be Catholics.

> An editorial in the New York Times lamented the Pope's "continued opposition to" abortion, contraception, and the ordination of women, adding this priceless observation: "Regrettably, he made no mention of discrimination against homosexuals" In other words, the Pope failed to repudiate Catholicism. God may forgive this, but the Times isn't about to.

> There is no bigotry like the blank-eyed liberal bigotry that demands that the Pope reach liberal conclusions from Catholic premises. The Pope's "continued opposition" to abortion, et cetera, is not just the stubborn attitude of one old priest; it derives from the most

---

[57] Msgr. Charles Pope, *Comfort Catholicism Has to Go; It is Time to Prepare for Persecution*, National Catholic Register Online, posted August 21, 2016.

fundamental teaching and principles of Catholicism itself, which differ in certain respects from the editorial positions of the Times.

But what might Catholics of the past (or the future) condemn in the Church today?

They certainly wouldn't accuse us of excessive zeal. They might be shocked by our luke-warmness, our cowardice masquerading as tolerance, our laxity, our willingness to countenance heresy, sacrilege, blasphemy, and immorality within the Church itself, our eagerness to ingratiate ourselves with the secular world—of which the papal statement itself is a symptom.

Nearly a century ago, the French Catholic poet Charles Peguy remarked: "We will never know how many acts of cowardice have been motivated by the fear of appearing not sufficiently progressive."[58]

What most comes to mind is this: far, far too many of us who claim to be Catholic—and here I must include Church leadership as well—have lost the courage demanded of faithful discipleship. Jesus did not say for us to sit back and let the world come to us; neither did he say discipleship would be easy or painless, rather he commanded us to go tell the world all he taught us and in doing so we would be persecuted. Yes, he did. Jesus said very clearly, "Blessed are they who are persecuted for the sake of right-eousness, for theirs is the kingdom of heaven. Blessed are you when they insult you and persecute you and utter every kind of evil against you falsely because of me. Re-joice and be glad, for your reward will be great in heaven. Thus they persecuted the prophets who were before you" (Mt 5:10-12). Persecuted? Forget about it! We have become too sanitized and weak in our faith; we no longer want to harbor such disturb-ing thoughts. Yet persecution and martyrdom are very much a part of our Catholic faith and not just in the far distant past.

On July 26, 2016 just as Father Jacques Hamel, 85, was finishing Mass at Église St.-Étienne in Normandy, France, two ISIS terrorists forced the elderly priest to kneel and when he resisted they slit his throat. Christians throughout the middle east have been persecuted and martyred so consistently in recent years, almost to the point of com-plete annihilation. What stands out is how, when given a choice between denouncing their faith and living or standing firm and dying, they had the courage to choose the latter without hesitation.

From St. Peter to Constantine there were 33 Popes. Thirty of them were martyred and two died in exile. Countless clergy and lay people too were martyred. It is hard to imag-ine the Church in the decadent West being willing to suffer so. Surely our brethren in much less affluent parts of the world are dying in large numbers. But I wonder: After all these years of "Comfort Catholicism", would the average American parishioner or cler-gyman be willing or able to endure such loss?[59]

---

[58] Joseph Sobran, Subtracting Christianity: Essays on American Culture and Society, pp 267-268, FGF Books, June 20, 2016.

[59] Msgr. Charles Pope, Comfort Catholicism Has to Go; It is Time to Prepare for Persecution, National Catholic Register Online, posted August 21, 2016.

I cannot help but wonder for myself whether I would have the strength of will and the courage of faith to refuse to yield when confronted by such evil. It is more than unpleasant to contemplate, but I believe we must, for we have lived far too long in quiet comfort, far removed from the dark and looming threat of evil which so many have and are facing still. For the sake of cultural acceptance, we have spent the last half-century compromising our Catholic faith, our Catholic identity, and our Catholic values. We have, in the interests of communal uniformity, tolerance, and equanimity chosen to forego our unique Catholic heritage. We have been tamed into submission and taught to sit quietly and behave for the sake of the common good, much to the detriment of our immortal souls.

Persecution has come upon us whether we wish to acknowledge it or not. Like a growing cancer slowly metastasizing all that is good inside, the forces of evil have been steadily eating away at our fundamental religious liberties—all in the name of toler-ance—by force of compulsory compliance and criminalization. And for the most part we Catholics have permitted this malignancy to grow without complaint; and when it has suited our purposes, we have even welcomed it. Above all else we have become too complacent, afraid to address controversial issues for fear of causing offense or causing a ripple in the force. Yet, that is not what Jesus demands of his disciples. Jesus knew the persecution that awaited him in Jerusalem, yet he journeyed there unafraid and with a certain joy in what was to come. He never hesitated or demurred when confronted by evil but stood firm in his righteousness. It is "long past dark" for we to do the same.

Msgr. Pope asks when will the Church say to the bureaucrats who demand we comply with evil laws, "We will not comply. If you seek to confiscate our buildings, we will turn maximum publicity against you, but we still will not comply. If you arrest us, off to jail we go! But we will simply not comply with evil laws or cooperate with evil."

Just Practicing
Be or be not, there is no try

Whenever I meet with a couple preparing for marriage there is one question—asked of those who identify themselves as Catholic—which always gives me pause. Not due to any doubt as to the sincerity or honesty of the response but because I won-der whether the couple have any clear understanding of what they are affirming. Unfortunately, I believe few Catholics do.

The question: "Are you a practicing Catholic?" begs the question as to whether one understands precisely what is meant by the question. Personally, I have serious objec-tions to this terminology for it implies one's catholicity may be improved or increased with practice; that one can somehow acquire catholic virtuosity should one practice long enough or with enough perseverance and constancy. Conversely, it would seem no matter how minimal the practice, one may still lay claim to being: a "practicing Catholic." And then if one is not a "practicing Catholic" but a "Catholic" by virtue of being baptized "Catholic" is there any discernible difference? What about a "non-practicing Catholic" whatever that might mean? Do protestants have similar terminology? Have you ever heard of a "practicing Protestant" or a "practicing Buddhist" or even a "practicing atheist"? I think not.

The question is subjective and therefore subject to interpretation. It is easy to understand what was intended but only under an objective lens sans personal whim or desire. But few are wont to so restrict their options when it comes to faithfully following what Catholicism requires. In short, too many believe they can have their cake and eat it too. But it simply and practically does not work that way. Simply put, Catholicism is not a sport or a skill that demands endless hours of practice to achieve any measure of expertise. Nor does it require any special talents, physical prowess, or mental ability. It does however require an unshakable faith in God, an unconditional acceptance and unwavering devotion to the teachings, doctrines, and dogma of the Catholic Church, the church instituted directly by Jesus Christ. And that is where the rubber meets the road for many who identify themselves as Catholic. Cultural attitudes have left the impression in many minds there are no absolutes, only personal preferences. What defines "Catholic" is left to personal whimsy.

> Catholics may recall the high hopes for liturgical reform in the wake of the Second Vatican Council of 1962-65. The vernacular Mass and the relaxation of old disciplines were supposed to inspire a new piety in the laity, who were given a larger role in the rites, including the freedom to receive the Eucharist in their hands—traditionally regarded as a desecration. The upshot, as such observers as James Hitchcock and Michael Davies noted many years ago, was precisely the reverse of what the liberals predicted and far worse than the reactionaries feared: Mass attendance immediately plummeted and tens of millions of Catholics in the United States alone have fallen away from the Church. Those who remain formally within the Church feel free to defy Catholic teaching on such matters as contraception and abortion; most no longer believe the Eucharist is the true Body of Christ; and young Catholics are stunningly ignorant of Catholic doctrine.

> The general liberalization of religion has failed in the same way. The attempt to keep Christianity and Judaism *au courant* with contemporary fads has merely enfeebled the sense of the sacred, turning worship into thinly disguised self-indulgence. A "nonjudgmental" God is not God at all and, precisely because he needn't be obeyed, can't be adored. "If God does not exist," says Dostoyevsky's Ivan Karamazov, "everything is permitted." And a God who permits everything doesn't really exist. What's the point of calling such an entity "God"?[60]

---

[60] Joseph Sobran, Subtracting Christianity: Essays on American Culture and Society, FGF Books, June 20, 2016.

And therein lies the true issue: those who call themselves "Catholic" have lost any understanding of the sacred, and as Sobran so clearly points out, a God who need not be obeyed cannot be adored and a God who permits everything and denies nothing really doesn't exist at all.

Returning to the question posed earlier, there are two questions asked prior to it. They are: "What is your religion?" and "What parish are you a member?" The question left unasked—but certainly ought to be—is "Do you regularly attend Mass every week?" It cannot be found anywhere on the form, but I ask it anyway. The responses vary from "occasionally" to "seldom", with "every week" rarely noted. Individually, they are asked for the mundane but important information to include their name, address, and phone number. Nine out of ten engaged couples will admit to the same address, a clear indication of cohabitation, a high probability of pre-marital sex and the use of some form of contraception. All are clearly contra to long established Church teaching and all are in direct disobedience to the will of God. And yet moments later they will state without hesitation "Yes" to being a "practicing Catholic".

By no means is this overt disobedience to God's will limited only to those who wish to be married in the Church. The attitude that holds God no longer needs to be obeyed has reached pandemic levels. "Fear of the Lord" has been replaced by the more palatable "Ignore the Lord". Examples of this attitude can be readily observed in many public figures across this country who openly claim to be "practicing Catholics" but their talk simply doesn't walk the straight and narrow. Those who insist on being labeled Catholic but are in public opposition to Church teachings, doctrine, and dogma are a scandal to their faith and to those who remain in faithful devotion to the Church. Those who once were Catholic but left to join another faith and no longer call themselves Catholic at least have shown the courage of their convictions and left without causing further scandal to the Church.

It isn't enough to say, "I am a practicing Catholic." To be Catholic one must live Catholic, believe Catholic in all things, not just in what you prefer. Practice makes perfect may work for the piano, but it doesn't work for God. Be or be not, there is no try.

September 02, 2016

Carrying Their Cross
Even Jesus had help

Grief is excruciatingly painful and timeless. No one welcomes grief, yet uninvited it enters in without surcease. Grief's dark shadow descends upon the soul far more than the cold kiss of death would allow, for life presents other crosses as difficult to bear.

But what of those who look upon such pain and sorrow and see love grieving so? What acts of kindness, gifts of love, or thoughts expressed might ease the suffering, salve the dark despairing pain that salts ragged wounds too soon to heal? The greatest gift for the grieving is such a simple thing, yet for most, far too difficult to gracefully deliver. Give the gift of Silent Presence; be there, nothing more. Lift their cross and walk with them for "some things in life cannot be fixed. They can only be carried."[61] Their grief is theirs and theirs alone. You cannot take any part of it or accept it as your own. You cannot fix it. You can only help them carry it.

Even Jesus needed help to carry his cross. What good would have come of platitudes and encouragement shouted at him along the way to Calvary? Imagine how Jesus would have felt to hear "Go Jesus Go! You can make it!" or "It will all be better soon." or "Something good will surely come from all of this." or best of all, "Everything's going to be alright." If these would not have worked for Jesus how then can they possibly be alright for those who are grieving? Obviously, they can't, yet we still want to say something, generally without thinking.

Let those who grieve, grieve; be a silent presence; there, when and if, through the anguish and the pain, they realize they don't have to carry their cross alone.

When Will We Learn?
Where have all the children gone?

Let me address this head on: I have a sincere disaffection for polls, polls of any kind. My animus for polls runs deep; any lawmaker who would propose legislation to proscribe them would have my full, though admittedly completely inconsequential, support. At the heart of my opposition to polls is the reliance on the statistical pseudo-science so ardently supported, it appears to me, by charlatans selling pure unadulterated snake-oil. Some of course are easier on the palate, but all are much too difficult to swallow and seldom benefit anyone except to line said charlatan's pockets. Polls are like sots, incapable of standing upright or walking a straight line; they either lean one way or slant another, preconditioned to generate predetermined results from preselected respondents—fodder for those whose sole function is to convince the emperor is fully clothed.

Disregarding the political swill fed into the public trough on a daily basis, the results of two national studies (polls) conducted by the Center for Applied Research in the Apostolate (CARA) have recently been released for further indigestion. Keep the

---

[61] Megan Devine, *Refuge In Grief*, http://refugeingrief.com.

Alka-Seltzer handy. These two studies/polls were conducted to determine why young Catholics are leaving the faith. The first study surveyed a random, national sample of young people, ages 15 to 25, who had been raised Catholic but no longer self-identified as such. The second surveyed a random sample of self-identified Catholics, ages 18 and older, focusing on matters of religion and science. The conclusions derived from both studies were made and reported in a 4-page article in *Our Sunday Visitor* by Mark Gray.[62]

As I previously noted, the studies/polls are textbook examples of how to turn stuporous assumptions into besotted results with pickled conclusions. The report begins with an introduction which should be read with great care.

> Young Catholics are leaving the Faith. Multiple national surveys indicate that only about two-thirds or fewer millennials (those born in 1982 or later) who were raised Catholic remain Catholic as adults.

Note how this introduction leads the reader toward a false understanding and a probable misreading. The first sentence sets the unwary reader up for the bad news sure to follow. The next raises the level of concern stating "multiple national surveys indicate"—leading the reader to assume certainly more than two surveys which undoubtedly surveyed a large number (a number never provided.) Then the kicker which gives the reader the distinct impression it must be really bad news: only about two-thirds or fewer millennials who were raised Catholic—OMG, that is absolutely terrible news! Dare I read more? But wait! What is this: "*remain* Catholic"? Two-thirds *remain* Catholic? But...but... In other words, Mark, what you are really telling us is only about one-third leave the faith. True, that is far too high but why the deliberate scam? It leaves the rest of the article highly suspect, and after reading the entire article several times with highlighter in hand, this reader remains highly skeptical.

Perhaps most problematic are the conclusions derived from the scant data provided in the report. There is however sufficient information to determine the conclusions that were made failed to identify the root causes for the increasing number of young people leaving the faith. To be fair to CARA, the OSV report fails to provide access to the full results from either study further reducing confidence in the conclusions reported. The results OSV did report are both informative and worrying, notwithstanding the inadequate and misleading conclusions derived. Perhaps the most relevant information provided comes from a single paragraph.

> The interviews with youth and young adults who had left the Catholic Faith revealed that the typical age for this decision to leave was made at 13. Nearly two-thirds of those surveyed, 63 percent, said they stopped being Catholic between the ages of 10 and 17. Another 23 percent say they left the faith before the age of 10. Those who leave are just

---

[62] Mark M. Gray, *Young People Are Leaving The Faith: Here's Why*, Our Sunday Visitor, August 28, 2016, pp 9-12.

as likely to be male as they are female, and their demographics generally mirror those of all young Catholics their age. So why are they leaving?"

A reporter once asked Willie Sutton, an infamous bank robber, why he robbed banks and he replied, "because that's where the money is." Asking Sutton why he did what he did was puerile and provided no insight as to the root causes of his criminal behavior. It did sell magazines, however. And here is where the CARA studies leave orbit. Asking those who have left the faith why they left is equally fatuous and fails to lead us to the why. It does make for some mildly annoying juvenile responses which I suppose some, like the author, find somehow informative. CARA interviewed former Catholics and asked them an open-ended question "What are the reasons that explain why you are no longer Catholic?" The responses reveal a level of ignorance but little more.

"Because I grew up realized it was a story like Santa or the Easter Bunny."

"Catholic beliefs aren't based on fact. Everything is hearsay from back before anything could be documented, so nothing can be disproved, but it certainly shouldn't be taken seriously."

"I realized that religion is in complete contradiction with the rational and scientific world, and to continue to subscribe to a religion would be hypocritical."

In another study conducted by the Pew Research Center, they report a variety of reasons why young people are leaving Christianity, including:

- Learning about evolution when I went away to college
- Religion is the opiate of the people
- Rational thought makes religion go out the window
- Lack of any sort of scientific or specific evidence of a creator
- I just realized somewhere along the line that I didn't really believe it

There are many more but no need to belabor the point. It all comes down to a level of understanding that is painfully absent in our youth and young people concerning God and his Church. But the question remains unanswered: why are they leaving? OSV's Mark Gray provides an observation, laying the primary reason for the increasing exodus of young people from the faith on a decline in Catholic school attendance. While this might certainly be a factor, Gray wastes far too much space on the declining numbers receiving a Catholic education and the increasing numbers of those who see no relationship between faith and reason or compatibility between science and religion. While important, the decline in attendance is a symptom rather than the cause of the infection. "I don't doubt for a moment the sincerity of those who responded to the survey, but the reasons they offer for abandoning Christianity are just so uncompelling. This is to say, any theologian, apologist, or evangelist worth his salt should be able easily to answer them. And this has led me to the conclusion that 'we have met the enemy and it is us.'"[63] While I agree with Bishop Barron that the reasons are un-compelling I respectfully disagree with who he holds responsible for rectifying the growing problem of our children leaving the faith. He says in closing, "My *cri de coeur* is that teachers, catechists, theologians, apologists, and evangelists might wake up to this crisis and do something about it." I hold Bishop Barron in the highest regard but his passionate appeal is misdirected, aiming at those who can and should be actively involved in any solution but teachers, catechists, theologians, apologists, and evange-lists are secondary, not primary to any corrective remedy.

The question as to why so many are leaving is important no doubt but before we can hope to discover the why we must first know the when and the who. The problem didn't begin with millennials (those born in 1982 or later.) They are but the most cur-rent to be infected with a disease first contracted nearly sixty years ago. The genesis of the infection first arose in the 1960s with the confluence of two events: the convening of the Second Vatican Council and the launch of the Great Society. While neither prom-ised to effect great and lasting change, the unexpected and unintended consequences that occurred as a result of these two seminal events were nothing short of catastrophic. On the face of it, the objectives of the two events, to most observers, seem to be unre-lated in nearly every possible way: one considered traditionally conservative and the other progressively liberal, one religious and the other secular, one global in scope, the other geographically limited. But it was not the onset of these two separate and distinct events that created the pandemic but the confluence of their output which, like co-reactant epoxy resin, altered the course of human history, resulting in the moral desu-etude that exists today. There is far more to be said on this subject but far more than need or can be written here.

For all the good, necessary changes for the Catholic Church resulting from the Sec-ond Vatican Council, there were serious unintended consequences. From many quarters and especially in America there was an overwhelming sense of release from the rigid, hard-bound strictures long-held by the Church and demanded of its mem-bers. Finally! The Church was moving into the modern age—despite and in spite of Pope Paul VI and *Humanae Vitae*—and Catholics were quick to take advantage of this apparent relaxation of the strict rules of conduct imposed on them for two millennia. The complete failure of the magisterium to address these misperceptions directly and with the necessary seriousness required resulted in the false belief (heresy) Catholicism was now self-defining. Catholics could now decide for themselves what it meant to be catholic. Catholics were now free to accept or ignore what had heretofore been doctri-nally and dogmatically imposed. The Commandments were now suggestions, the moral law optional, and natural law suspect. Free at last, free at last, thank Vatican II, we are free at last! Those who came of age then (of which I am one) quickly saw this as an opportunity to define their own relationship with God if they wanted to do so;

---

[63] Bishop Robert Barron, *Apologists, catechists, theologians: Wake up!*, September 1, 2016.

many chose to simply ignore God because there were no longer any serious conse-quences—falsely believing there was no heaven or hell—of much concern. Like religion, God was now self-defining as were his laws. It was indeed a heady time for young Catholics.

Yet the changes that came about within the Catholic Church as a result of the Sec-ond Vatican Council would most likely have been far less reaching had it not been for the launching of the liberal and progressive policies of Lyndon Johnson's Great Soci-ety. The growing sense of entitlement and secular progressive attitudes engendered and encouraged the sexual revolution of the sixties resulting in a near total moral col-lapse within American society. The landmark and disastrous 1973 decision by the U.S. Supreme Court legalizing abortion precipitated an even faster rate of decline in com-pliance and acceptance of moral and natural law, respect for the sacredness of the human person made in the image and likeness of God, and the belief every life, from conception to natural death should be valued and protected.

That generation, my generation, as a result became ever more distracted by the sec-ular and less attracted to the holy. Even if one continued to believe in God, no one really cared because there didn't seem to be any reason to be seriously concerned. What was happening during the sixties and seventies was a steady erosion in faith and a turning inward to the self. As Joseph Sobran accurately describes, "Being self-cen-tered leads inevitably to hating others who are obstacles to selfish desires. What is 'natural' in fallen human nature easily descends to the diabolical. And our modern, post-Christian, liberal culture treats the self-centered life as normal, rejecting abortion laws as tyrannical impositions on what has been called 'the imperial self.'"[64]

Even as the general population was turning away from God and inward toward themselves, many clergy were following, or in some cases, leading the charge toward this new moral order. For the most part, however, the clergy in American churches simply fell silent, and their congregations quickly became unchurched. Catholic clergy, never admirers of "fire and brimstone" preaching, picked up the liberal mantra of tol-erance and acceptance of immorality. Thus, as a result, we are witness to the leadership of the USCCB euphemistically dancing around the serious issue of same-sex unions officiated by the second highest office holder in America who sardonically calls himself a Catholic. Rather than publicly denouncing Vice-president Biden for his insolence and obvious disdain for the church he professes to be a member (sounds like a raspberry to me) they proffered neither punishment nor absolution. For Catholics the clear mes-sage is (with apologies to Barry Goldwater), "intolerance in defense of righteousness is no virtue. And tolerance in the pursuit of immorality is no vice."

Most of us who aged into adulthood in the sixties and seventies eventually found ourselves with families. Having been infected with a virulent distaste for authority and

---

[64] Joseph Sobran, *Subtracting Christianity*, FGF Books, June 20, 2016.

authoritarian rules, we consciously or unconsciously readily infected our progeny. I, for one, must admit to rarely darkening the entrance to any church and giving little notice to God. Religious education was never a priority, to the point there was none. Although baptized Catholic, that was much the extent of my children's religious upbringing. While they eventually and completely on their own received the Sacraments and were married in the Catholic Church, they have over time walked away from active participation in their faith. Their children have fared worse with little or no knowledge of God, faith, the Catholic Church, and all that Catholics should and ought to know and believe.

So why are young people leaving the faith? Don't ask them because they really have no idea of what that means. If you really wish to know why young people are leaving, don't look to a poll for answers, look in a mirror. The answer will be staring back at you.

September 09, 2016

Catholic Tradition
Knowing what is demanded

One distinct advantage to living a long life—beyond the mere satisfaction of outlasting more than a few unpleasant acquaintances and perhaps an annoying neighbor or two—is in having had the opportunity to dine upon a larger slice of the historical pie. Far better it is to dine on knowledge obtained through lived experience than from second-rate peddlers pushing third-hand watered-down politically correct left-overs to the naïve, comatose, or intransigently dumb-founded.

Catholicism is an ancient faith, the only faith founded directly by Jesus Christ; all other "Christian" faiths are recent (no older than 500 years) heretical knock-offs absent the authenticity and authority of the Catholic Church which Christ instituted. This is neither my opinion nor is it based on direct personal knowledge—I'm old but not that old—but the product of two millennia of irrefutable scholarship and a matter of empirical historical record. Through apostolic succession, the magisterium (bishops) of the Catholic Church affirm the doctrines of the Church are authoritative: taught by Christ to his apostles, "Go, therefore, and make disciples of all nations, baptizing them in the name of the Father, and of the Son, and of the holy Spirit, teaching them to observe all that I have commanded you" (Mt 28:19-20). Under the guidance of the Holy Spirit the Church is protected from doctrinal error. Thus, to deny one or more doctrines is to deny what Christ taught us.

Saint Thomas Aquinas defined heresy as "a species of infidelity in men who, having professed the faith of Christ, corrupt its dogmas." Heresy is both the non-orthodox belief itself, and the act of holding to that belief. The Catholic Church makes several distinctions as to the seriousness of an individual heterodoxy and its closeness to true heresy. Only a belief that directly contravenes an Article of Faith, or that has been explicitly rejected by the Church, is labelled as actual "heresy." The Code of Canon Law defines what Catholics must believe and what constitutes heresy:

> Canon 750 §1. A person must believe with divine and Catholic faith all those things contained in the word of God, written or handed on, that is, in the one deposit of faith entrusted to the Church, and at the same time proposed as divinely revealed either by the solemn magisterium of the Church or by its ordinary and universal magisterium which is manifested by the common adherence of the Christian faithful under the leadership of the sacred magisterium; therefore all are bound to avoid any doctrines whatsoever contrary to them.

> §2. Each and every thing which is proposed definitively by the magisterium of the Church concerning the doctrine of faith and morals, that is, each and every thing which is required to safeguard reverently and to expound faithfully the same deposit of faith, is also to be firmly embraced and retained; therefore, one who rejects those propositions which are to be held definitively is opposed to the doctrine of the Catholic Church.

> Canon 751. Heresy is the obstinate denial or obstinate doubt after the reception of baptism of some truth which is to be believed by divine and Catholic faith; apostasy is the total repudiation of the Christian faith; schism is the refusal of submission to the Supreme Pontiff or of communion with the members of the Church subject to him.

The essential elements of heresy are therefore, 1) obstinacy, or continued denial; 2) denial (a proposition contrary or contradictory in formal logic to a dogma) or doubt (a posited opinion, not being a firm denial, of the contrary or contradictory proposition to a dogma); 3) after reception of valid baptism; 4) of a truth categorized as being of "Divine and Catholic Faith," that is truth declared within either Sacred Scripture or Sacred Tradition.

What is of utmost is that pesky verb *must*, which proffers absolutely no wiggle room for any Catholic. A Catholic *must* believe all those things contained in Sacred Scripture (written) or Sacred Tradition—the Deposit of Faith as proposed to be divinely revealed either by the solemn magisterium of the Church or by its ordinary and universal magisterium— (handed on.) To be perfectly clear: Catholics *must* obey and believe all doctrine and dogma as proposed definitively by the magisterium of the Catholic Church. To obstinately deny or obstinately doubt any doctrine or dogma is heresy; there simply is no other word for it although since the conclusion of the Second Vatican Council, there has arisen a new vocabulary which sadly and frustratingly too often mirrors the broader secular vocabulary in its ambiguity and imprecision. The Church, since the Council, has produced a bewildering collection of neologisms[65]

---

[65] Neologism: a relatively new or isolated term, word, or phrase.

lacking any of the classical precision of Catholic doctrine: "collegiality," "dialogue," "dialogue with the world," "interreligious dialogue," "ecumenism," "ecumenical venture," "ecumenical dialogue," "partial communion," "imperfect communion," "reconciled diversity," "the Church of the new Advent," "the new springtime of Vatican II," "the new Pentecost," "the new Evangelization," "the civilization of love," "the purification of memory," "responsible parenthood," "solidarity," "the globalization of solidarity," "the Spirit of Assisi," "what unites us is greater than what divides us," and so on. Although these words and phrases evade any precise definition, they have become the watchwords of post-conciliar thinking. "Never before in Church history has the activity of the Church come to be governed by slogans and buzzwords that appear nowhere in the perennial Magisterium. In consequence, never has the Church's message been so uncertain."[66] As a result of this new vocabulary, Catholics—especially those born post-council—are largely incapable of discerning precisely what it means to be Catholic and what Catholics must believe. Why should this be so? Simply put, it has become increasingly difficult to "know the truth" because truth has become relative, history has been radically and frequently adjusted to erase or alter whatever might be considered objectionable, and rational thought has been highly discouraged.

To be preconciliar Catholic meant no ambiguity in what was demanded by Sacred Tradition. Postconciliar Catholics were left confused by the lack of clarity in what was required of them. One example should suffice to illustrate the radical nature of the Second Vatican Council which although it did not repudiate any article of divine and Catholic faith often materially opposed Catholic tradition.

> The preconciliar Popes uniformly condemned the contention that the received and approved rite of Mass had fallen into obscurity and ought to be "simplified," but Paul VI approved an entirely new and simplified rite which Cardinals Bacci and Ottaviani were constrained to protest as "a striking departure from the Catholic theology of the Mass as it was formulated in Session XXII of the Council of Trent."

> The preconciliar Popes taught that the Latin liturgy must be preserved as a barrier against heresy and a bond of unity in the Church, but Paul VI taught that it must be abandoned because "understanding of prayer is more important than the silken garments in which it is royally dressed" — thus contradicting even the teaching of his own immediate predecessor, Pope John XXIII.

The imposition of the new rite of Mass had an immediate impact: drastic declines in Mass attendance, emptying of seminaries, and drastic declines in protestant conversions. As a Catholic who grew up in the preconciliar Church I was taught and thus knew what every Catholic was required to believe as matters of faith. Doctrine and dogma were understood and well-attended because we knew what was at stake: the

---

[66] Ferrara, Christopher; Woods Jr., Thomas. The Great Facade: The Regime of Novelty in the Catholic Church from Vatican II to the Francis Revolution (Second Edition), Angelico Press.

sanctity and salvation of our immortal soul. As I have written elsewhere[67] Catholics today often hold no concern for what is at stake should they ignore or deny Church teaching. This *a la carte* attitude is the direct result of the confusing and ambiguous output promulgated by the Council and the near total absence of clear, precise, unambiguous teaching provided by the leadership of the Church since. Let us pray for clarity and for the Catholic Church.

What's in Your Mind?
Can you hear me now?

The precipitous descent of the Catholic mind into the abyss of blithe obliviousness and bland indifference ought to be of great concern yet by all indications it barely produces a yawn from Church leadership and Catholic public figures. As noted in the October edition of First Things (R. R. Reno, While We're At It, p. 67) this past July, Archbishop Charles Chaput of the Archdiocese of Philadelphia issued a set of guidelines for implementing Pope Francis's apostolic exhortation on marriage and family, *Amoris Laetitia*. "The document urges the Church's pastors to recognize Catholics today are often profoundly misled by the prevailing culture, making it very difficult for them to accept the truth of the Church's teaching on the permanence of marriage and the moral meaning of sexual acts. … It's not uncommon for Catholics to think divorce and remarriage are fine, and gay unions should be blessed." Both the Archbishop and Reno are correct in their recognition of the alarming trend toward vacuity of the Catholic mind, yet their recommended correctives fall vapidly short of useful. "These people should not be pushed away, but instead drawn into a close engagement with the Church's teaching and communal life. This means pastors must be willing to be present to them to explain what the Church actually teaches. The greatest work of mercy, therefore, isn't to bend rules. It is to form consciences according to the truth."

One might reasonably ask what is meant precisely by the statement: "These people should be … drawn into a closer engagement with the Church's teaching and communal life?" Small wonder our minds are turning to mush. As for pastors explaining what the Church teaches, good luck with that. This presupposes every pastor is well-versed and in complete agreement with Church teaching—at best questionable in either regard—and assumes those in "irregular situations" are willing to listen and accept what the Church teaches and are prepared to "go and sin no more." Honest, straightforward conversation is essential, of course, but seldom of any permanent or serious consequence. Just as the question "Can you hear me now?" presupposes someone listening, the guidelines assume the same. But how often will that be the case, I wonder? Reno continues, "Which, as the guidelines state with exemplary clarity, is why it's not

---

[67] Deacon's Corner Commentaries: *Catholicism A La Carte: choosing what to believe*, April 12, 2016, http://deaconscorner.org/catholicism-a-la-carte.

merciful to tell a divorced and remarried couple who live as husband and wife that it's fine for them to receive Communion. Nor is it merciful for a pastor preparing a couple for marriage to act as if their cohabitation presents no serious impediment. And it's certainly not merciful to pretend that same-sex couple who insist on public affirmation of their sexual union can simply become normal members of a parish community."

From personal experience in preparing couples for marriage, nine out of ten couples are in a cohabitating relationship. No matter how well-informed they may become after I have explained clearly and precisely what the Church teaches and why cohabitation is sinful and immoral, and as firmly as they assent to cease cohabitating, I harbor no illusions as to how many actually follow through with their promise. The divine truth of the Church's teaching—of Christ's teaching—is lost, beyond their ability to comprehend any more than a three-year old is capable of comprehending nuclear physics. What is needed is clear, unambiguous speech— something seldom heard these days—reminiscent of the old adage: "Say what you mean, mean what you say, and do what you say you will do." Instead, what we hear is most often what someone thinks we want or expect to hear rather than the unvarnished truth. Or ... we hear spin, with speech couched in "politically correct" terminology with the explicit intent to obfuscate and misdirect. Or ... we are bombarded with neologisms—slogans and buzzwords—so imprecise and ambiguous as to convey nothing of any import.

> Isn't it better to hear what was meant rather than what the speaker thinks you want to hear? How can people expect to make informed decisions if the person speaking to them isn't saying what he/she means? By really saying what you mean, you cut through the clutter and present the facts or your direct opinion so that things can be discussed meaningfully without going through a kabuki dance. While this direct approach of saying what you mean may startle, surprise, or discomfort others, you're really better off knowing directly what was meant rather than having to interpret, often incorrectly. This doesn't mean you should be insulting, just direct.[68]

Of course, speaking clearly and saying what you mean carries with it the risk of condemnation for being so forthright and honest. It also requires certain knowledge of the facts upon which you speak to ensure you are free from the dreaded "foot in mouth" disease, of which politicians are frequently infected but blissfully ignorant. A few days after Archbishop Chaput issued his guidelines, the mayor of Philadelphia, Jim Kenney, a professed Catholic and liberal Democrat publicly offered this sarcastic commentary on Twitter: "Jesus gave us the gift of Holy Communion because he so loved us. All of us. Chaput's actions are not Christian." As Reno makes clear, "The mayor demonstrates theological illiteracy."

> His logic leads to the conclusion that the unbaptized should receive Communion. To deny it to them would be unchristian. But let's leave that aside. More striking is the abuse of public office. It's chilling to see a person exercising secular authority pronounce on the

---

[68] Tom Dennis, Workplace Insanity, September 29, 2010.

theological legitimacy of an archbishop's statements and policies. It appears that liberals insist on the separation of Church and state—except when they don't.

The pattern is common. Liberals insist on tolerance—except when political correctness dictates otherwise. They champion inclusion—except when they ruthlessly exclude anyone who dissents from their "inclusive" views. They chastise those who are judgmental, a self-contradiction that would be amusing were it not so punitive. Thus Kenney: Jesus loves all of us—except for Archbishop of Philadelphia Charles Chaput, who holds supposedly unchristian views."[69]

Archbishop Charles Chaput is, in this Catholic's mind, a breath of fresh air in a room filled with stale smoke. I can only hope it is contagious.

September 16, 2016

Remember the Past
The future depends upon it

Growing up I found little use for history, a common enough sentiment, I suppose, for those who have created so little of it themselves. For myself I found it rather tedious: remembering all those names, dates, and places—which is how history was generally taught in those days. I suspect the pedagogy hasn't changed much since, although, I fear the content has been so tortured as to bear little resemblance to the truth. In any case, I imagine the low regard for history remains much the same to the youth of any age. Given my antipathy for the past, earning a BA in History now seems quite ironic and historic (pun intended.)

Nowadays I find myself hoping others will discover the importance of and necessity for remembering the past. Confucius wrote you must study the past if you would define the future, something few seldom consider, especially those who are wont to change it or to install progress. Progressives are wont to define change as progress; removing all traces of what was, all the while claiming new and improved—what? It is like "throwing the baby out with the bath water." George Santayana wrote "Progress, far from consisting in change, depends on retentiveness. When change is absolute there remains no being to improve and no direction is set for possible improvement: and when experience is not retained, as among savages, infancy is perpetual. Those who cannot remember the past are condemned to repeat it."[70] Too many accept without question the present mindset: what is must have been, made better and improved. Few questions what once was, it matters not to them. The truth is of

---

[69] R. R. Reno, *While We're At It*, First Things, October 2016, pg. 67.
[70] George Santayana, *The Life of Reason, Vol I, Reason in Common Sense*, 1905.

no consequence, the past vacuously forgotten. They care not to know what has been deliberately constrained by those who would enslave them for their profit. May God help us all.

Instituted by Christ
Making disciples of all nations

Were it not for opinion, the silence would be deafening. Facts are impediments, too often dispelling myth and tale upon which we are wont to hold dear. What we believe (opinion) and what is truth (fact) are in rare sympathy for it is easier to opine than to bear witness to what is objectively and historically true. A few issues ago (*When Will We Learn?*) I raised the argument that the "genesis of the infection" — the disease causing many of our young to leave the Catholic faith — "first arose in the 1960s with the confluence of two events: The convening of the Second Vatican Council and the launch of the Great Society." While no doubt some may have read this as little more than opinion, there is a plethora of well-documented evidence (facts) to advance it far beyond opinion into well-founded argument.

A reader provided thoughtful comment on the article and as much as I always appreciate comments — positive or negative — I was left with the disturbing sense the article was somehow misread or misunderstood.

> I read with interest about your concern for why young people are leaving the faith. I am not of the opinion that Vatican 2 or LBJ have anything to do with it. Unintended consequences are part of every decision in human history and it might be that the good that came out of those instances in history far outweigh the bad. I invite you to not get discouraged by them but to consider how many people might be drawn to the church by acts of inclusiveness such as Vatican 2. I know many priest (sic) who cite it as a pivotal point in their decision to enter the priesthood.

Allow me to state as firmly as I may that I was in no way discouraged. I was merely attempting to offer a reasoned argument based upon the multitude of unintended consequences that occurred by the confluence of the two events, and which I posited, three successive generations were subsequently negatively compromised.

One thing the writer makes clear: it is personal opinion; opinion based on supposition rather than argument substantiated by fact. In truth, there are no facts or sources cited, beyond suggestion, to support the conclusions drawn. Sadly, the opinions expressed are all too commonly held — by Church leaders and laity alike — especially the false hope that "many people might be drawn to the church by acts of inclusiveness such as Vatican 2." The facts prove otherwise. The facts are quite the contrary to the illusory desires expressed. In a book first published in 2001, *The Great Façade*, authors Christopher Ferrara and Thomas Woods Jr. provide clear and irrefutable evidence that illustrate the disastrous effects brought upon the Catholic Church since the Second

Vatican Council. The facts speak for themselves and the sources are undeniable for they come directly from the Vatican's own reports.

> It is an empirical fact, demonstrated by every available statistic, that the Postconciliar liturgical reform and the commencement of programmatic "ecumenism" and "dialogue" were followed immediately by precipitous declines in the number of priests, the number of new ordinations, the number of conversions and baptisms, and the percentage of Catholics attending Mass. In the immediate aftermath of the Council, an astounding 50,000 priests defected, and today there remain approximately 50,000 fewer Catholic priests than there were thirty-one years ago. In 1997 there were fewer baptisms in the United States than there were in 1970! See, e.g., statistical analysis of the priesthood in L'Osservatore Romano, 13/20 August 1997, and 'The Index of Leading Catholic Indicators,' The Latin Mass, Winter 2000, presenting extensive data from the Vatican's Statistical Yearbook of the Church and other standard reference works.[71]

While there were clearly unintended consequences such as previously outlined, the Council deliberately abrogated two millennia of Sacred Tradition and chose to ignore the Church's perennial counsel against the embrace of substantial ecclesial novelties of any kind. Perhaps the most disastrous novelty embraced by the Council has been the new ecumenism which effectively reduced Catholicism to an equivalency with all other religions. Preconciliar Church teaching had been consistent and clear: The Catholic Church was the one true Church divinely instituted by Christ outside of which there is neither Church nor salvation (*extra ecclesiam nulla salus*—the dogma that there is no salvation outside the Church.) The 1917 Code of Canon Law 2, cc. 1258 and 2316, explicitly forbade any active participation by Catholics in worship with Protestants; *Mortalium Animos* by Pope Pius IX and the 1949 Instruction of the Holy Office on the "ecumenical movement," forbade any form of common worship at discussion groups authorized by the local bishop, and required the "Catholic truth" on "the return of the dissidents to the one true Church" be presented. In *Mortalium Animos*, Pius XI taught pan-denominational congresses "can nowise be approved by Catholics, founded as they are on that false opinion which considers all religions to be more or less good and praiseworthy, since they all in different ways manifest and signify that sense which is inborn in us all, and by which we are led to God and to the obedient acknowledgment of His rule. Not only are those who hold this opinion in error and deceived, but also in distorting the idea of true religion they reject it, and little by little turn aside to naturalism and atheism, as it is called; from which it clearly follows that one who supports those who hold these theories and attempt to realize them, is altogether abandoning the divinely revealed religion." The preconciliar Popes condemned any common worship with Protestants as a danger to the Faith, but the Council opened the door to it and Pope Saint John Paul II (expressly and by example) taught that common prayer and joint liturgies with Protestant ministers (who condone abortion, contraception and divorce) is essential to the search for Christian unity. John Paul subsequently doubled

---

[71] Ferrara, Christopher; Woods Jr., Thomas. *The Great Facade: The Regime of Novelty in the Catholic Church from Vatican II to the Francis Revolution* (Second Edition), Angelico Press.

down on this position when he held joint Catholic-Lutheran Vespers at the Vatican as it was then reported by CWNews.com on November 13, 1999:

> Archbishops G.H. Hammar and Jukka Paarma—the Lutheran primates of Sweden and Finland, respectively—and Bishops Anders Arborelius of Stockholm and Czeslaw Kozon of Copenhagen joined with the Holy Father for the Vespers service. Several other Lutheran bishops from the Scandinavian countries were present for the ceremony, including two female bishops.

The Council and Pope Paul VI intentionally and deliberately broke with Sacred Tradition, while ignoring and dismissing the consistent condemnations of the preconciliar Popes in this regard. Post-council the Catholic Church was no longer the one true Church divinely instituted by Jesus Christ for the salvation of the world but simply one among many. Logic would clearly suggest this has played a significant role in the ever-increasing mass exodus of Catholics from the Church. If Catholicism is merely one religion among many as the Council and post-conciliar Popes have consistently proselytized, then there is no longer a compelling reason to remain Catholic. This is especially evident with those who hold any disagreement with Catholic doctrine and dogma.

Why then are young Catholics leaving their faith? The answer should be blatantly obvious, but it apparently is either too bitter a pill to swallow or too difficult to contemplate for many Catholics, especially those who were raised Catholic before the Second Vatican Council. Actions have consequences and nowhere is this more apparent than the *kumbaya* ecumenical movement engendered by the progressive mindset of the Council and the post-conciliar Popes.

September 23, 2016

Let Me Entertain You
We'll have a real good time

Believe it or not, there once was a time before television. While difficult as it may seem to many to think such an unthinkable thought, life did exist and even thrived quite nicely without constantly being connected.

A question often asked of those born in the dark ages is "What did you do for entertainment?" As I can clearly recall we were seldom bored because we found ways to entertain ourselves. I can clearly recall performing the Mass with my brother when we were 8 or 9. This was conducted with great solemnity and in Latin no less. The altar was generally a box with a sheet to cover it along with a crucifix and candles, carefully shaped flattened bread for hosts, and a sheet for the chasuble. While it was play it was serious worship in its own way for, we knew even then what the Mass meant: the worship of God.

It is difficult to imagine youth of any age today engaging in such faithful play for most have no clear idea of why they are asked to attend Mass. There is a common belief worship must be entertaining; that in order to attract youth to worship we must use worldly methods to beat the world at its own game. We are kidding ourselves if we believe we can ever compete with pop concerts and video games. Worship is not a competition. A.W. Tozer wrote: "Every great spiritual work from Paul to this hour has sprung out of spiritual experiences that made worshipers. Unless we are worshipers, we are simply religious dancing mice moving around in a circle getting nowhere.... God wants worshipers first."

A young man recently asked why we didn't offer Adoration at our parish. Having just attended an OnFire Catholic Youth Day he described how those who attended Adoration were greatly moved by the spiritual experience. The lesson to take from this: Worship is a spiritual experience with God; it is not entertainment.

Ecumenism Run Amok
That which defines us

In a web exclusive article (firstthings.com, 9.19.16, *Lund and the Quest for Christian Unity,*) Timothy George, founding dean of Beeson Divinity School of Samford University wrote:

> Next month, on October 31, the eve of All Saints Day, Pope Francis will visit Lund, Sweden, to participate with Lutheran church leaders in a joint ecumenical commemoration of the Reformation. October 31 is Reformation Day on Protestant church calendars, and this year it will mark the 499th anniversary of Martin Luther's posting of the 95 Theses on the Castle Church door at Wittenberg. The Pope's presence at the prayer service in Lund Cathedral (Domkyrka), a church where Christians have worshiped for more than one thousand years, will be followed by a larger gathering at nearby Malmö. This historic occasion, which will launch a full year of Reformation remembrances, will doubtless be the most talked about ecumenical event of 2016.

When I read this my heart stopped; I couldn't breathe; my mind screamed with unfathomable violence and horror. For the Supreme Pontiff of the Holy Catholic Church to celebrate a heresy seems beyond the pale, yet there it was in black and white. Not willing to accept such a travesty from a single source, I proceeded to search for others to confirm it. It didn't take long to find other sources. A post by John Vennari (Catholic Family News, Celebrating an Apocalyptic Plague: Pope Francis to Lead "Common worship service" to Commemorate 5th Centenary of Lutheran Revolt, January 25, 2016) reported:

It is now official what many of us expected. Pope Francis will participate in ceremony commemorating the 500th anniversary of the Reformation. The January 25 *Vatican Bolitano* announces: "The Holy Father Francis in Lund, Sweden, to commemorate the 500th anniversary of the Reformation. His Holiness Francis intends to participate in a joint ceremony of the Catholic Church and the World Lutheran Federation to commemorate the 500th anniversary of the Reformation, scheduled to take place in Lund, Sweden on Monday, October 31, 2016." The Pope will lead the "common worship service" along with two Lutheran leaders: Lutheran World Federation (LWF) President Bishop Dr. Munib A. Younan and LWF General Secretary Rev. Dr. Martin Junge.

What so roils is the madness of Catholic leaders celebrating the 500th anniversary of a man who spent his life debasing Christian revelation. Yet it is not the first time. Pope St. John Paul II in 1983 praised Luther for his "deep religiousness,"[72] voicing the highest public esteem for a man whose warped religious views led him to reject the true Church, deny his priesthood, and teach the Mass was an abomination worse than the most loathsome brothel.[73]

Forgotten in this ecumenical maelstrom is the fact that Protestantism is heresy, and heresy is a sin. In the objective order, it is a mortal sin against Faith that sends souls to hell for eternity. The revered Father Frederick Faber explained that heresy is "the sin of sins, the very loathsomest of things which God looks down upon in this malignant world. ... It is the polluting of God's truth, which is the worst of all impurities."

Thus, Father Faber observed, "where there is no hatred of heresy, there is no holiness."[74]

Likewise, Saint Alphonsus Liguori spoke of the duty to fight heresy because it kills our souls and the souls of others: "Heresy has been called a canker: 'It spreadeth like a canker.' (2 Tim. 2:17) As a canker infects the whole body, so heresy infects the whole soul — the mind, the heart, the intellect and the will. It is also called a plague; for it not only infects the one contaminated with it, but others who associate with him. Truly the spread of this plague in the world has injured the Church more than idolatry."[75]

Blessed Pope Pius IX recognized Protestantism as "a revolt against God, it being an attempt to substitute a human for a divine authority, a declaration of the creature's independence from God." The Catholic historian Hilaire Belloc wrote heresy not only affects the individual, but has a negative impact on society; man must live his life according to a Creed, a system of beliefs, but when it is distorted away from God's truth, life will become distorted as well. Thus, when large masses of people fall into heresy, and live accordingly, it will change the entire structure of their society away from the

---

[72] New York Times, Pope Praises Luther in an Appeal for Unity on Protestant Anniversary, Nov. 6, 1983.
[73] Of the Holy Sacrifice of the Mass, Luther said that no sin of immorality, nay not even "manslaughter, theft, murder and adultery is so harmful as this abomination of the Popish Mass." He said further that he would have "rather kept a bawdy house or been a robber than to have blasphemed and traduced Christ for fifteen years by saying the Masses." *Luther*, by Hartman Grisar, S.J. (English translation, Herder), Vol. 2, p. 166; Vol 4. p. 525.
[74] Father Frederick Faber, D.D., *The Precious Blood: The Price of Our Salvation*, 1860.
[75] St. Alphonsus Liguori, *The History of Heresies*, English translation taken from the No. 1-2, 2000 edition of Christ to the World (Rome) in its first installment of serializing the book.

Divine Program of Our Lord. It will create an environment not conducive to living a life of sanctifying grace but rather a society where evil is institutionalized.[76]

Thanks to the Protestant heresy, we now have legalized divorce, contraception, abortion, and the inordinate rise in the power of the State. This last because Protestants do not look at their "church" as an authority established by Christ to teach and govern all men. According to Protestants, Christ never founded such a Church. Thus, the highest authority on earth is the State. Protestants do not hold to a Divine Faith received from Heaven through a teaching Church established by Our Lord. For the Protestant, there is no visible Church, there is only the individual and his Bible, subject to individual interpretation. Father Michael Müller said as much: "The main spirit of Protestantism, then, has always been to declare every man independent of the divine authority of the Roman Catholic Church and to substitute for his divine authority a human authority."[77] But apparently for many of today's Catholic leaders (including recent popes,) the heresy of Protestantism no longer presents a problem. "Have these leaders no love of Catholic doctrine? If they did, they would publicly oppose the Protestant heresies that disfigure it. Have they no love of souls? If they did, they would not pretend that a Protestant can be saved by remaining in his own man-made religion that teems with errors against the express teaching of Our Lord Jesus Christ." Saint Teresa of Avila called Lutheranism "that wretched sect." She established her first Carmelite foundation of nuns at Avila to help "cure this terrible evil" by bringing "some comfort to our Lord…. Thus, being all of us employed in interceding for the champions of the Church and the preachers and theologians who defend her, we might, to our utmost, aid this Lord of mine Who is attacked with such cruelty …"[78]

As a Catholic I was taught Martin Luther was a Catholic priest who dissented against the abuse of indulgences. That was the sum of my knowledge of the man. I suspect most Catholics own much the same understanding. The Orthodox writer Rod Dreher expressed his befuddlement at the anticipated Catholic-Lutheran rapprochement in Lund: "How can this or any pope do this, or approve of it? It makes no sense to me. It's as if a man and a wife got together to commemorate the occasion of their divorce!" Dreher is far too easy on the Pope. Perhaps a more accurate portrait of the seriousness of the betrayal to our beloved Catholic Church and to our faith by the Supreme Pontiff would be of Pope Francis standing next to Martin Luther as he hammers his 95 theses onto the door of All Saints' Church in Wittenburg. It is Ecumenism run amok—aiding and abetting a heresy. Jesus said, "you are Peter, and upon this rock I will build my church, and the gates of the netherworld shall not prevail against it" (Mt

---

[76] Hilaire Belloc, *The Great Heresies*, 1936.

[77] Father Michael Müller,C.SS.R., *The Catholic Dogma* New York: Benzinger Brothers, 1888.

[78] Saint Teresa of Avila, *The Way of Perfection*, English Translation by the Benedictines of Stanbrook, [First published in 1911. Republished by Tan Books, 1997.

16:18). One can only wonder for how much longer Christ's Church can prevail against such ecumenical rapprochement. One can only ask: "Is the Pope still a Catholic?"[79]

Tradition: To The East
Praying with, not prayed at

The great Broadway musical *Fiddler on the Roof*, with music by Bock and Harnick, begins with Tevye, the father of five daughters, singing of *Tradition*, a lament for the vanishing Jewish religious and cultural traditions he has always known.

In the *Introduction to The Meaning of Tradition*, Yves Congar wrote "for many, tradition is simply a collection of time-honored customs, accepted, not on critical grounds, but merely because things have always been so, because 'it has always been done'."[80] He contended attempts to innovate were often opposed in the name of tradition, generally by conservative forces as a safeguard against novelty; tradition was favored because it prevented change. According to Avery Cardinal Dulles, S. J. who penned the foreword:

> Regarded in some circles as a dangerous innovator, he was treated with suspicion and had to endure suspension from teaching and occasional banishment from France during the 1950s.

> In 1959 Pope John XXIII restored Congar's good name by appointing him a theological consultant to the preparatory commission for the Second Vatican Council. At the Council itself, Congar's influence was equal to, and perhaps greater than, that of any other Catholic theologian. His influence is manifest in the Council's teaching on Revelation, on the Church, on the laity, on ecumenism, on missiology and on many other topics.

> "Tradition is memory, and memory enriches experience. If we remembered nothing it would be impossible to advance; the same would be true if we were bound to a slavish imitation of the past. True tradition is not servility but fidelity."

Tradition comes from the Latin *traditio*, the noun of the verb *tradere*, which means to transmit or to deliver. *Tradere, traditio* meant to hand over an object with the intention, on the one hand, of parting with it, and, on the other, of acquiring it. *Tradere* implied giving over and surrendering something to someone, like passing a torch in a relay race.

---

[79] This essay, as one might expect, given the ecumenical climate and the veracity of some of the sources referenced, was the subject of no small amount of controversy. In retrospect, I firmly believe the final sentence inflammatory and unnecessarily provocative. Since I wrote this essay, I have discovered other statements—though basically true in fact—to be unnecessarily biased, cruel and vitriolic. For these as well as for the acerbic tone presented, I sincerely and deeply apologize. In the October 07, 2016 issue 20, I respond to several readers who took umbrage with what I have written here. I further responded to my bishop, but, as to our communications, that will remain between us.

[80] Yves Congar, O.P., *The Meaning of Tradition*, Translated from the French by A. N. Woodrow, Ignatius Press, 2004.

Protestants claim the Bible is the only rule of faith, meaning it contains all of the material one needs for theology and this material is sufficiently clear one does not need apostolic Tradition or the Church's magisterium (teaching authority) to help one understand it. According to the Protestant view, the whole of Christian truth is contained within the pages of the Bible. Anything not found within the Bible is simply non-authoritative, unnecessary or wrong—and may in fact hinder one's relationship with God. Catholics, however, hold a different view; one in which the Protestant view is rejected, contending it is neither endorsed nor validated in Scripture. The true "rule of faith"—as expressed in the Bible itself—is Scripture plus apostolic tradition, as manifested in the living teaching authority of the Catholic Church, to which were entrusted the oral teaching of Jesus and the apostles, along with the authority to interpret Scripture correctly. Sacred Tradition differs from the normal understanding of tradition. Congar wrote, "Usually, when it is a question of handing over a material object, the donor loses possession of it and can no longer enjoy it. But this is no longer true when it is a question of spiritual riches—when a teacher transmits a doctrine, he commits it into the keeping of another, to be enjoyed by him, without losing any of it himself."

I will expound more on Sacred Tradition in future issues but wish to address a current controversy that has been the topic of some debate over the past few months. Robert Cardinal Sarah, the prefect of the Congregation for Divine Worship wrote in an essay in the June 12 edition of *L'Osservatore Romano*, "The liturgy is essentially the action of Christ".

> If this vital principle is not received in faith, it is likely to make the liturgy a human work, a self-celebration of the community. … To speak of a "celebrating community" is not without ambiguity and requires real caution. The *participatio actuosa* [active participation] should not therefore be understood as the need to do something. On this point the teaching of the Council has often been distorted. It is instead to let Christ take us and associate us with his sacrifice.

> It is entirely consistent with the conciliar constitution, it is indeed opportune that, during the rite of penance, the singing of the Gloria, the orations, and the Eucharistic prayer, everyone, priest and faithful, should turn together towards the East, to express their will to participate in the work of worship and of redemption accomplished by Christ. This manner of doing things could opportunely be put into place in cathedrals, where liturgical life must be exemplary.

What the Cardinal was speaking of is *Ad Orientem*, Latin for "to the east" which, simply put, has traditionally been the direction Catholic churches were built. It also refers to the traditional way the priest faced during the Mass. The priest facing the altar is also referred to as *Ad Deum*, which is Latin for "to God" rather than the current direction, which is referred to as *Versus Populum*, that is "facing the people". While ancient liturgies did speak of the priest turning and "facing the people" during certain parts of the mass, celebrating the entire mass *Versus Populum* is a novelty of the 1970's, a novelty that stands in direct contradistinction to the Church's ancient traditions.

There is much confusion as to precisely what *Ad Orientem* means in today's liturgical environment.

> It is as if *Ad Orientem* and *Versus Populum* were matter and anti-matter, so antithetical that disaster would result from their combination.... In reality, of course, the celebrant...faces the people much, if not most of the time—specifically (1) at the greeting, (2) during the readings, (3) during the homily, (4) to introduce the intercessions, (5) at 'Pray, brothers and sisters,' (6) at the exchange of peace, (7) at 'Behold, the Lamb of God,' (8) at Communion, (9) to introduce the prayer after Communion, and (10) at the final blessing and dismissal.[81]

As one priest reflects "After five years of offering Holy Mass *Ad Orientem*, I can say that I never want to have to return to the *Versus Populum* position." He lists ten advantages to *Ad Orientem* on his blog, *Vultus Christi*[82], which are both compelling and instructive. I will list them next week along with further commentary on *Ad Orientem*.

To Err is Human
Fallible and peccable every one

No one is perfect except for God, in whom all perfection is manifest. We human creatures are by our nature both fallible and peccable, which is to say, we are quite capable of making considerable mistakes, errors in judgment, and sinning. There are those who would deny this of course, either for themselves or for another. This only serves to prove within each of us is an innate desire—more so for some than for others—to filter what might add tarnish to the perfected image we have constructed of our own self or another.

We quite simply want to believe somewhere in this world there is someone who is above the fray, supernormal, and perfectly holy, a living saint. We think of Saint Teresa of Calcutta and imagine her as such a person. After all, she has been canonized and by all measures she certainly fits within our image: being above the fray, supernormal, and perfectly holy. Yet, if that is our perfected image of her, are we not guilty of granting her equality with God? A saint, yes. God, no. She, like all of humanity, was fallible and peccable, an imperfect being created with concupiscence which is as much a part of us as are hearts and minds. How great or small were her sins I leave for God's mercy, yet to believe she never sinned would be to deny her, her great humanity.

---

[81] Charles Shonk, *Ad Orientem And Absolutism*, First Things, September 20, 2016.
[82] Fr. Mark Kirby, Silverstream Priory, Stamullen, County Meath, Ireland, *Vultus Christi*.

Whenever we blind ourselves to the faults and failures of anyone, including our-selves, we deny the essential nature of our humanity: no one is perfect. This is true whether rich or poor, large or small, famous or unknown. To err is human, even should you find yourself sitting on the throne of Saint Peter. We ought to remind ourselves of this every day.

Without Conviction
Does anyone care anymore?

The great English writer and Catholic convert G. K. Chesterton loved to take pop-ular sayings, proverbs, and allegories and turn them inside out. As a political thinker he once observed, "The whole modern world has divided itself into Conservatives and Progressives. The business of Progressives is to go on making mistakes. The business of Conservatives is to prevent the mistakes from being corrected." Time Magazine said of Chesterton "He was a man of colossal genius."

In the introduction to Heretics, he wrote of *Orthodoxy*—another marvelous book.

Nothing more strangely indicates an enormous and silent evil of modern society than the extraordinary use which is made nowadays of the word "orthodox."' In former days the heretic was proud of not being a heretic. It was the kingdoms of the world and the police and the judges who were heretics. He was orthodox. He had no pride in having rebelled against them; they had rebelled against him.... The man was proud of being orthodox, was proud of being right. If he stood alone in a howling wilderness he was more than a man; he was a church. He was the centre of the universe; it was round him that the stars swung. All the tortures torn out of forgotten hells could not make him admit that he was heretical. But a few modern phrases have made him boast of it. He says, with a conscious laugh, "I suppose I am very heretical," and looks round for applause. The word "heresy" not only means no longer being wrong; it practically means being clear-headed and cou-rageous. The word "orthodoxy" not only no longer means being right; it practically means being wrong. All this can mean one thing, and one thing only. It means that people care less for whether they are philosophically right. For obviously a man ought to confess himself crazy before he confesses himself heretical.[83]

Hilaire Belloc, an orthodox Catholic writer whose Catholicism was uncompromis-ing, decried the modern diminishing concern for heresy.

Today, with most people (of those who use the English language), the word "Heresy"' connotes bygone and forgotten quarrels, an old prejudice against rational examination. Heresy is therefore thought to be of no contemporary interest. Interest in it is dead, be-cause it deals with matter no one now takes seriously. It is understood that a man may interest himself in a heresy from archaeological curiosity, but if he affirms that it has been

---

[83] G. K. Chesterton, *Heretics*, John Lane Company, 1905.

of great effect on history and still is, today, of living contemporary moment, he will be hardly understood.[84]

What precisely then is heresy? How should we define it?

Heresy is the dislocation of some complete and self-supporting scheme by the introduction of a novel denial of some essential part therein....

Heresy means, then, the warping of a system by "Exception": by "Picking out" one part of the structure and implies that the scheme is marred by taking away one part of it, denying one part of it, and either leaving the void unfilled or filling it with some new affirmation.

The denial of a scheme wholesale is not heresy, and has not the creative power of a heresy. It is of the essence of heresy that it leaves standing a great part of the structure it attacks. On this account it can appeal to believers and continues to affect their lives through deflecting them from their original characters. Wherefore, it is said of heresies that "they survive by the truths they retain."

The word heresy is derived from the Greek αἵρεσις *hairetikos* (to choose) and was used by many of the early Church Fathers to describe those who promoted dissension. In his second century tract *Contra Haereses* (Against Heresies) Irenaeus wrote of the heretical teachings of the Gnostics while describing a community's beliefs and doctrines as orthodox (from the Greek ὀρθός, *orthos* "straight" + δόξα, *doxa* "belief"). Canon 751 states: "Heresy is the obstinate post-baptismal denial of some truth which must be believed with divine and catholic faith, or it is likewise an obstinate doubt concerning the same; ..." The Catholic Church has consistently held obstinate and willful manifest heresy is considered to spiritually cut one off from the Church, even before excommunication is incurred. The *Codex Justinianus* (1:5:12) defines "everyone who is not devoted to the Catholic Church and to our Orthodox holy Faith" a heretic.

Over two millennia, from the early days of the Church to the present time, literally thousands of heresies have arisen to challenge the orthodoxy of Church teaching. Most have been short-lived and have had negligible impact, yet there have been a few — five according to Belloc — which have had both lasting and serious effect upon the Church and her members. In *The Great Heresies*, Belloc identified five heresies which have formed the main and longest-lasting assaults upon the Church, her teaching, and the Catholic faith: Arian, Mohammedan, Albigensian, Protestant, and Modernity.

Today, the Catholic Church is faced with a host of new heretical threats, different in many ways from the past, yet strikingly similar. What differs the most from the past is the attitudes concerning these threats. The modern *heresiarch*[85] and heretic holds to the belief, previously expressed by Chesterton, that up is the new down and right and wrong are mere words which carry no cost or penalty. Much of current Church

---

[84] Hilaire Belloc, *The Great Heresies*, 1938.
[85] A heresiarch is the founder of a heresy or the leader of a heretical sect, e.g. Arius was the heresiarch of the Arian heresy and the leader of the Arian movement.

leadership seems to have adopted the attitude expressed by Belloc where any interest in heresy is now a dead issue because no one no longer takes it seriously. Above and beyond these attitudes is the near universal condescension of anything which might be considered as intolerance. Venerable Archbishop Fulton J. Sheen once said of those who believed America suffered from intolerance (and here I would dare include the better part of the entire world), "America, it is said, is suffering from intolerance—it is not. It is suffering from tolerance. Tolerance of right and wrong, truth and error, virtue and evil, Christ and chaos. Our country is not nearly so overrun with the bigoted as it is with the broadminded." Thus, we are presented with the current tolerance for heterodoxy by the supposed defenders of orthodoxy. Heterodox Catholics, those who obstinately refuse to conform to doctrinal orthodoxy on such issues as contraception, abortion, euthanasia, cohabitation, marriage, and divorce, are by definition and Canon Law, heretics, no less so than those who accepted and believed in any of the multitude of heresies for two millennia. Today, those whose duty it is to confront and anathematize (condemn) such heresies and to show the heretic the error or errors upon which such heresies are founded are conspicuously silent, complicit in ignoring the philosophical necessity for strident condemnation; they do thus, so as to appear tolerant. Baruch Spinoza asserted, "government inculcates into its citizens the belief that the chief of all virtues is tolerance—the affirmation of everyone's right to believe anything he wants as long as he behaves himself in public. To put the principle in a form that's familiar to us, dogma is subjective. What people believe is entirely a personal matter. What matters is whether they disturb the peace or physically hurt someone else."[86] Likewise Chesterton noted: "Tolerance is the virtue of the man without convictions." Pope Emeritus Benedict XVI warned of the evil nature of the *Dictatorship of Relativism,*" whose signature virtue is one of tolerance, tolerance for what others believe as long as it doesn't infringe one's own. Relativism—the philosophical ideology that we have the right to believe whatever we want to believe, that there is no wrong or evil because we believe only what is good—is heretical in both form and function for it disallows any orthodoxy except one's own. It denies there is any power beyond the self which can command strict obedience and adherence to objective truth. What we are seeing today from Church leadership is quite clearly an intolerance for orthodoxy and a tolerance for heresy. It is little more than that vapid question: "Can't we all just get along?" The toleration of evil is evil, in and of itself. But then does anyone even care anymore?

---

[86] Benjamin WIker, Ph.D., Worshipping The State: How Liberalism Became Our State Religion, March 25, 2013, Regnery Publishing.

Ad Orientem
It's not what you may think

Traditionally, Catholic churches have been built facing the East, because, as then Cardinal Ratzinger taught, this direction reflects the "cosmic sign of the rising sun which symbolizes the universality of God."[87] As mentioned previously[88], the priest facing the altar is also referred to as *Ad Deum*, which is Latin for "to God" rather than the current way, which is referred to as *Versus Populum*, facing the people. The phrase *Ad Deum* sidesteps problems that arise if the priest is facing the altar in a Church that has not been built facing the East. In addition — as previously stated — while ancient liturgies did speak of the priest turning and facing the people during certain parts of the mass, celebrating the entire mass *Versus Populum* is a novelty of the 1970's, a novelty that stands in direct contradistinction to the Church's ancient traditions.

Father Mark Kirby who has been offering Holy Mass for five years lists ten advantages to *Ad Orientem*. As promised, I will list them and then make further comment on what they mean:

1) The Holy Sacrifice of the Mass is experienced as having a theocentric direction and focus.

2) The faithful are spared the tiresome clerocentrism that has so overtaken the celebration of Holy Mass in the past forty years.

3) It has once again become evident the Canon of the Mass (*Prex Eucharistica*) is addressed to the Father, by the priest, in the name of all.

4) The sacrificial character of the Mass is wonderfully expressed and affirmed.

5) Almost imperceptibly one discovers the rightness of praying silently at certain moments, of reciting certain parts of the Mass softly, and of cantillating others.

6) It affords the priest celebrant the boon of a holy modesty.

7) I find myself more and more identified with Christ, Eternal High Priest and *Hostia perpetua*, in the liturgy of the heavenly sanctuary, beyond the veil, before the Face of the Father.

8) During the Canon of the Mass I am graced with a profound recollection.

9) The people have become more reverent in their demeanor.

---

[87] Joseph Cardinal Ratzinger, *The Spirit of the Liturgy*, Ad Solem, 2006, p. 64.
[88] *Tradition: To The East*, Colloqui, Volume 1, No. 18, September 23, 2016/

10) The entire celebration of Holy Mass has gained in reverence, attention, and devotion.

In contrast, he also speaks of the disadvantage of occasionally having to celebrate *Versus Populum*. He laments, "I suffer from what I can only describe as a lack of sacred *pudeur*, or modesty in the face of the Holy Mysteries. When obliged to celebrate *Versus Populum*, I feel viscerally, as it were, that there is something very wrong — theologically, spiritually, and anthropologically — with offering the Holy Sacrifice turned toward the congregation."

Father Kirby is not the only advocate of *Ad Orientem* in the Tulsa Diocese. His Excellency Bishop Edward Slattery returned to the practice of celebrating the Eucharistic liturgy *Ad Orientem / Ad Deum* in his cathedral and has been a vocal critic of *Versus Populum*. In his own words, he states, "Unfortunately this change (*Versus Populum*) had a number of unforeseen and largely negative effects. First of all, it was a serious rupture with the Church's ancient tradition. Secondly, it can give the appearance that the priest and the people were engaged in a conversation about God, rather than the worship of God. Thirdly, it places an inordinate importance on the personality of the celebrant by placing him on a kind of liturgical stage."[89] What, from a personal point of view, is most revealing and appreciated is the comment made by Bishop Slattery, "it can give the appearance that the priest and the people were engaged in a conversation about God, rather than the worship of God." Elsewhere it was similarly explained *Ad Orientem* allowed all, both the congregation and the celebrant to pray with each other *to* God rather than the congregation being prayed at by the celebrant. Celebrating the Holy Mass in its entirety *Versus Populum* has, as Bishop Slattery stated, "had a number of unforeseen and largely negative effects." One, which has shown to be quite obvious since the 70's, is the radical and precipitous loss of reverence, attention and devotion which the Holy Mass deserves, as Father Kirby makes note of this in advantages 9 and 10, observing the discernible change in the people's demeanor with the shift to *Ad Orientem*. Another negative effect of *Versus Populum* has been the people's experience of the Mass has been shifted from its proper theocentric direction and focus—the worship and adoration of Almighty God—to a clerocentric one, with all eyes on the celebrant priest and not on God. This has been especially true whenever the priest is or has been particularly charismatic. In many cases those who attend are there expecting to be entertained than to worship and give thanks to God. As Father Kirby observes with advantage 3: "It has once again become evident the Canon of the Mass (*Prex Eucharistica*) is addressed to the Father, by the priest, in the name of all." Can I hear an Amen to that? Too many of us come to mass rather than to Holy Mass. We forget or have forgotten why we are there, of whom we are in the presence, and what we are supposed to be doing while in his presence: pray.

---

[89] Bishop Edward Slattery, Diocese of Tulsa Oklahoma, Catholic World News, August 18, 2009.

Two common and enduring objections to *Ad Orientem* (and the Tridentine (Latin) Mass have been 1) the priest turns his back to the people and 2) the people don't understand Latin and thus have no reason to continue coming to Mass. The problem with these objections is they miss the mark for neither admits to the reason and purpose of Holy Mass, the worship due God through the sacrifice of his only Son, Jesus Christ. We understand the words, we heard them many times before, and they have become mundane, banal, and meaningless because of their familiarity. We come to Mass, no longer in thanksgiving, but for entertainment and to socialize. Holy Mass was and always has been a sacred time for worship and prayer to our Father in heaven. It has never had as its purpose to entertain. It honestly feels long-past due to bring reverence, attention and devotion back into our lives, especially when in the real presence of Almighty God.

October 07, 2016

Through a Glass, Dimly
Non quod scriptum est

Saint Paul wrote of many things yet perhaps his discourses on love and our imperfect nature are what offers us the greatest food for thought, words for us to mull over and consider.

Several readers took umbrage with a recent article (*Ecumenism Run Amok*, Sep 23, 2016), expressing their deep disappointment and anger, in personal letters, to what they clearly perceived to be an effort to denigrate Pope Francis, as well as Lutherans and non-Catholics, in general. As I have made clear on several occasions in the past, whether reader comments are appreciative or not, I always welcome what they have to say, and these latest letters offer no exception. I thank those who wrote for their thoughts and will respond to their concerns with the utmost respect and love.

As Saint Paul wrote "At present we see indistinctly, as in a mirror, … At present I know partially, ..." (1 Cor 13:12). and that is perhaps truer than we imperfect creatures are wont to admit at times. We often see, or in this instance, read indistinctly and know but partially, and in such instances, we see what we are inclined to see while blinded to what we perceive to be irrelevant or of little import. We impart meaning without understanding and see phantoms where none exist. Such, it would appear, is the case in this instance.

One reader wrote: "Saying Lutherans and Protestants are heretics and we should not show mercy or have anything to do with them is not what Jesus came for." Had I written such a statement I most certainly would have to agree with the reader, but nowhere in that article did I make such a statement, either directly or by implication. That is simply *non quod scriptum est*—not what was written. What I did write, backed up by reputable and verifiable sources, was "Protestantism" is a heresy, one clearly established and acknowledged as such by the Catholic Church and every pope from the Council of Trent up to and including the *present* Pope. Catholics have been proscribed from attending "protestant services" since the Council of Trent; nothing however precludes Catholics from any non-religious association with non-Catholics. We are called by Jesus to love our neighbor as ourselves, that means everyone, not just Catholics. While the Second Vatican Council called for "dialogue" with all faiths, it neither altered or abolished any long-standing doctrine nor did it promulgate any new doctrine. What precisely was meant by "dialogue"—within any council documents— was not and never has been clearly defined. Whether dialogue is clearly defined is of little consequence with respect to the proscription banning Catholics from attending non-Catholic worship services. That proscription remains in force.

I stand by the statement that for the Pope to celebrate the 500th anniversary of one of the grave and most consequential heresies by presiding in common worship with Lutheran Bishops is wrong. It is wrong to do so because of the public celebratory statement it makes concerning an event that did grave and long-lasting harm to the Church. It is wrong because it ignores the ugly truth concerning the actions of the heresiarch Martin Luther who hated the Catholic Church and all she represented. The Catholic Church excommunicated Luther and anathematized the heresy which he developed and supported. No mercy is owed Luther for the damage he inflicted upon Holy Mother Church; to celebrate the anniversary of his heresy and excommunication is simply unconscionable.

Frequently mentioned was the Year of Mercy. I firmly believe we must be merciful as Jesus taught us. As disciples of Jesus Christ we must show mercy to the less fortunate, the hungry, the poor, those falsely imprisoned, and to all who share in our common humanity. We should show mercy to those who are not members of the one true Catholic faith and ask God the Father to help them find their way home to the Church instituted by his Son, Jesus Christ—the Catholic Church. However, it is not mercy to give false hope of rapprochement by conceding theological principles. It is not mercy to imply grave doctrinal issues are somehow inconsequential or of little consequence in the search for future unity. It is not mercy to imply through ecumenism and dialogue the Catholic Church will alter fundamental doctrine and dogma to meet somewhere in the middle. It is not mercy to imply acceptance of beliefs antithetical to the Catholic faith (e.g. true presence of Christ in the Eucharist, papal authority, apostolic succession, the sanctity of marriage, the inestimable value of every human life, etc.) which are not subject to papal or magisterial revision. It is not mercy to deny, through word or deed, there is only one true church, the Catholic Church.

The same reader continued: "You sound like we should go back to the Dark Ages and forget about the Vatican II Council. A number of popes worked on it and approved it." I have no desire to return to the dark ages although I readily admit to a deep and abiding hope one day the *radical consequences* of the Second Vatican Council may be forgotten much as the Church has forgotten the Second Council of Constantinople, held in 553. What? You have never heard of such a council? There is a reason why you have not. It has been purposely and effectively erased, forgotten because it was so disastrous. A number of popes worked on that council and approved of it as well but that doesn't change the fact it was later decided to let it languish in the dusty forgotten annals of irredeemable Church history. And yes, I personally would love to see the Church return to pre-council form, to return the Mass to its former regal beauty and remove the decidedly protestant influence of the current rite. And before you decide to write angry letters, it would do well for us to remember the stated intention of Pope Paul VI, the author of the current liturgy, to turn the traditional Catholic Holy Mass into a more collegial protestant service:

> The intention of Pope Paul VI with regard to what is called the Mass, was to reform the Catholic liturgy in such a way that it should almost coincide with the Protestant liturgy…. There was with Paul VI an ecumenical intention to remove, or at least to correct, or at least to relax, what was too Catholic in the traditional sense, in the Mass, and, I repeat, to get the Catholic Mass closer to the Calvinist mass."[90]

This position contradicted every pope from the very beginnings of the Catholic Church up to and including his predecessor, Pope John XXIII. We should also remember popes are not of themselves infallible. They are men, subject to the weaknesses which plague all men, and are capable of making mistakes, errors in judgment, and yes even sin. Pope Saint John Paul II received the Sacrament of Reconciliation every week. We ought not place the pope, any pope, on too high a pedestal or canonize him before he leaves this mortal coil. The first and only duty of any pope is to defend and protect the Catholic Church and her doctrinal and dogmatic teaching, the faith which all Catholics are to believe.

Another reader quoted Pope Francis: "We are called to be one in Jesus Christ and to avoid putting disharmony and divisions between the baptized first, because what unites us is much more than what divides us." While I admire the sentiment, I cannot agree to the minimization of what divides us, for what separates us are truly grave and serious matters, not so easily diminished or dismissed. The reader continues: "Pope Francis reaches out to all people, showing us that we're all one human family. Why would you want to judge his living the message of Christ?" Here is perhaps the crucial point. There is nothing wrong with Pope Francis reaching out to all people, to show us we are all one human family (that in itself should be obvious) but in reaching out he should be asking all to come into the loving arms of Christ's Church, not walking into theirs. Jesus said, "Go, therefore, and make disciples of all nations, baptizing them in the name of the Father, and of the Son, and of the holy Spirit, teaching them to observe

---

[90] Apropos, #17, pp. 8f.

all that I have commanded you" (Mt 28:19-20). Notice what he did not say: he did not say go out to all the nations and worship and believe as they worship and believe. Nor did he say to incorporate their beliefs into our own. He said go, teach them to observe all that he had commanded. Jesus consistently said, whenever he encountered a sinner, to "go and sin no more." Yes, he forgave sinners and he showed love and mercy to those willing to hear his voice, but he showed no mercy to those who refused to change their sinful ways. The reader continued: "They have been and continue to be examples of seeing Our Lord in each and every person regardless of religious affiliation and status and wealth. We must live by their examples of reconciliation, dialogue and forgiveness and not by shortsightedness and/or pharisaical views. ... This means showing loving concern for all people, caring for one another and respecting one another." Seeing Our Lord in each and every person is true and right and just. Loving, caring, and respecting one another are what Jesus says we are to do. We are called to love everyone because we are all created by God, but we are not called to accept what they believe. We are called to evangelize. Living by the recent pope's examples is problematic due to the ambivalence with the words: *reconciliation* and *dialogue*. To reconcile differences implies acceptance, in some measure, with the heretical views that caused the original separation. If it was heretical 500 years ago, precisely how is it no longer heretical? Acceptance of any part of a heresy is heresy. There can be forgiveness but no dialogue between right and wrong or truth and heresy.

Private Judgment
In whom is your faith?

There is certitude in divine faith which transcends faith of a more general nature. In general, faith, which includes human faith, is a firm assent of the mind to things unseen. We frequently choose to act, relying on the witness of other people who have seen what we have not. All education begins with human faith in our parents and teachers. We learn primarily by human faith, trusting in the authority of teachers, books, the media, public opinion, and friends.

> The essence of faith is that one does not directly see the intrinsic reason for the truth of a given proposition. In this sense, it is like opinion. However, faith differs from opinion in its certitude. In the act of faith, one sees clearly that the proposition merits firm assent on account of the authority of those who teach it, though not on account of its own intrinsic evidence. It is held as certain, and so mere opinion or deliberate doubt cannot coexist with faith, for they are mutually exclusive. A religious opinion is distinct from an act of religious faith, for the former is held to be uncertain or without sufficient foundation."[91]

[91] Lawrence Feingold, *Faith Comes from What is Heard: An Introduction to Fundamental Theology*, Emmaus Academic, July 8, 2016.

Divine faith is much the same as human faith, but concerns unseen objects such as God, the Trinity, the Incarnation, heaven, etc. "The act of divine faith is made possible when one grasps that God, who is the First Truth who can neither deceive nor be deceived, has indeed revealed Himself. This is the source of the firmness of divine faith and the grounds for the moral duty of believing." The First Vatican Council defined divine faith as a "supernatural virtue whereby, inspired by the grace of God, we believe that what he has revealed is true, not because the intrinsic truth of things is recognized by the natural light of reason, but because of the authority of God himself who reveals them, who can neither err nor deceive."[92] The Second Vatican Council in *Dei Verbum* adds to Vatican I's definition by speaking of faith as the "obedience by which man commits his whole self freely to God, offering 'the full submission of intellect and will to God who reveals,' and freely assenting to the truth revealed by Him."[93]

> The light of divine faith, unlike human faith, is not subject to error, for faith is properly divine or supernatural only insofar as it is belief in what has actually been revealed by God. For this reason, divine faith is strong enough to be described as "the substance of things hoped for." Divine faith has a certainty that comes from its divine source that enables it to be a sufficient foundation for man's journey to his supernatural end.

> However, it sometimes happens that a believer is mistaken in thinking that something has been revealed by God that has not in fact been revealed. When someone believes something false in matters of religion, the error should not be attributed to the virtue of divine faith, but rather to human faith in some heresy or false interpretation or insight that is mistaken for divine Revelation. Something has been believed out of ignorance or negligence that ought not to have been believed.

Martin Luther radically altered the definition of divine faith by disconnecting it from the witness of the Church and her Magisterium. In a dispute with Johann Eck, a Catholic theologian, Luther explicitly stated ecumenical councils could err. Eck responded if ecumenical councils were subject to error, then there could no longer be any certainty on any point of faith. The denial of the infallibility of ecumenical councils and popes undermines the faith of the Church for how does the believer know what truths God has revealed if there is not infallible authority to interpret Revelation?

The result of Luther's disconnection was the Protestant principle of *private judgment*. Used by Luther, Zwingli, and Calvin, it inevitably led to the division of the churches and the multiplication of sects. The nineteenth-century Spanish writer, Jaime Balmes wrote: "If there be anything constant in Protestantism, it is undoubtedly the substitution of private judgment for public and lawful authority."[94] As Feingold notes, "In consequence of the multiplication of Christian denominations, faith has increasingly become identified with mere religious sentiment or opinion. At first, such a view

---

[92] First Vatican Council, Dogmatic Constitution on the Catholic Faith *Dei Filius* (1870), ch. 3 (DS, 3008)

[93] Second Vatican Council, Dogmatic Constitution on Divine Revelation *Dei Verbum*, ch. 1, 5.

[94] Jaime Balmes, *Protestantism and Catholicity Compared in Their Effects on the Civilization of Europe* (Baltimore: J. Murphy, 1851), 26-27.

was characteristic of liberal Protestantism of the nineteenth century. It has since come to be shared by many Catholics as well, aptly referred to as 'cafeteria Catholics'."

Saint John Henry Cardinal Newman wrote of what he called the dogmatic principle and of private judgement. First, dogmatic principle and then, the principle of private judgment.

> That there is truth then; that there is one truth; that religious error is in itself of an immoral nature; that its maintainers, unless involuntarily such, are guilty of maintaining it; that it is to be dreaded; that the search for truth is not the gratification of curiosity; that its attainment has nothing of the excitement of a discovery; that the mind is below truth, not above it, and is bound not to descant upon it, but to venerate it; that truth and falsehood are set before us for the trial of our hearts; that our choice is an awful giving forth of lots on which salvation or rejection is inscribed; that "before all things it is necessary to hold the Catholic faith"; that "he that would be saved must thus think," and not otherwise; that "if thou criest after knowledge, and liftest up thy voice for understanding, if though seeketh her as silver, and searchest for her as for hid treasure, then shalt thou understand the fear of the Lord, and find the knowledge of God," — this is the dogmatic principle, which has strength.

> That truth and falsehood in religion are but matter of opinion; that one doctrine is as good as another; that the Governor of the world does not intend that we should gain the truth; that there is no truth; that we are not more acceptable to God by believing this than by believing that; that no one is answerable for his opinions; that they are a matter of necessity or accident; that it is enough if we sincerely hold what we profess; that our merit lies in seeking, not in possessing; that it is a duty to follow what seems to us true, without a fear lest it should not be true; that it may be a gain to succeed, and can be no harm to fail; that we may take up and lay down opinions at pleasure; that belief belongs to the mere intellect, not to the heart also; that we may safely trust to ourselves in matters of Faith, and need no other guide, — this is the principle of philosophies and heresies, which is very weakness.[95]

Feingold concludes, "The notion of private judgment, ... is weakness because it attacks the very possibility of making the total gift of one's mind to God. Divine faith is the supernatural submission of the intellect to God, the divine Teacher. This submission is actually a great liberation, freeing the mind from ignorance. But this submission will never be total if one retains the prerogative of private judgment."[96]

While recent writings within these pages have dwelt upon the issue of heresy — which to some may appear to be much to do about nothing — it is, on the contrary, the very real presence of heresy held by so many and our inability or unwillingness to admit to it that makes it of particular relevance to us all. Let us remind ourselves of what heresy means and who is a heretic:

---

[95] Saint John Henry Cardinal Newman, *An Essay on the Development of Christian Doctrine*, 6th ed. (Notre Dame: University of Notre Dame Press, 1989), 357-358.
[96] Lawrence Feingold, *Faith Comes From What Is Heard*, 46.

Heresy is a particular kind of disbelief by which someone who believes in Christ obstinately rejects the authority of the Church to define doctrine and corrupts or denies some truths of faith. They "choose" and obstinately hold their tenets of faith according to their own reason and will, which they put above the authority of the Church. Interestingly, the word "heresy" comes from the Greek for election or choice. Every heresy involves a kind of picking and choosing of the faith according to one's own personal (or group) criteria. This is the same spirit that leads to "cafeteria Catholicism."[97]

While we must love everyone as God loves us, that does not preclude us from recognizing, either in ourselves or others, those actions and beliefs which are heretical, antithetical to the divine faith and the teachings of the Church and the magisterium on matters revealed by God. Catholics do not have the right to pick and choose what to believe. To do so is heresy, to believe so is heretical, and to be so, a heretic.

Pulpit Politics
We must speak out

There is a palpable sense of urgency and consequence coursing through the veins of citizens of faith these days. Few would deny whoever is elected this year will determine the course of our country for the foreseeable future; few would deny the choices leave much to be desired. But choose we must, or the choice will be made by others who may have a far different and less palatable vision of the direction our nation ought to go.

The United States Conference of Catholic Bishops have spoken out on many of the issues that lay before us, those that threaten our religious freedoms and our right to freely worship God through our Catholic faith. Many bishops have spoken publicly whenever Catholics in public office and those who are seeking office, have through their actions and words expressed beliefs counter to the teachings of the Church and her magisterium. The bishops have been forthright in calling upon all clergy to speak out from the pulpit, if and when necessary, on these issues. It is crucially important we speak up whenever our fundamental freedoms are threatened. It is not only our responsibility and our duty to speak up; as citizens, we have a solemn obligation to do so. To keep silent is to ignore those obligations incumbent upon all free members of society.

There are some who hold the notion the practice of preaching politics from the pulpit is somehow inappropriate, wrong, or forbidden. This is a common assertion, but fortunately an incorrect one. A 1954 amendment to the U.S. tax code states tax-exempt organizations (churches fall into this category) are "absolutely prohibited from directly or indirectly participating in, or intervening in, any political campaign on behalf of (or in opposition to) any candidate for elective public office." An online guide for churches

---

[97] Lawrence Feingold, *Faith Comes From What Is Heard*, 47.

and religious organizations states "Violation of this prohibition may result in denial or revocation of tax-exempt status and the imposition of certain excise tax." Please note what this amendment to the tax code prohibits. It prohibits the promotion of "any candidate for elective public office." It does not prohibit nor preclude, in any form or fashion, the free exercise of speech on any subject or matter that endangers, threatens, or limits our religious freedoms.

The United States Conference of Catholic Bishops (USCCB) have clearly stated:

> That is our American heritage, our most cherished freedom. It is the first freedom because if we are not free in our conscience and our practice of religion, all other freedoms are fragile. If citizens are not free in their own consciences, how can they be free in relation to others, or to the state? If our obligations and duties to God are impeded, or even worse, contradicted by the government, then we can no longer be a land of the free, and a beacon of hope for the world.

> [From the earliest days of our nation,] Catholics in America have been advocates for religious liberty, and the landmark teaching of the Second Vatican Council on religious liberty was influenced by the American experience.... We have been staunch defenders of religious liberty in the past. We have a solemn duty to discharge that duty today.

> We need, therefore, to speak frankly with each other when our freedoms are threatened. Now is such a time. [It is incumbent on every American] to be on guard, for religious liberty is under attack, both at home and abroad.

Those who would believe our religious freedoms remain secure from encroachment by those who find no necessity for them are deluding themselves. The continual erosion of our religious freedoms has been intensifying over the past several decades.

A recent video of Catholic priest, Father Michael Orsi, the host of the pro-life TV show *Action for Life*, warned of the seriousness of the battle that must be fought between those who are for religious liberty and those (the state) who wish to deny or diminish the right to freely worship as one chooses. Father Orsi urged Christian church leaders to speak up about abortion and religious freedom in his message on the National Day of Remembrance for the Unborn on September 10th of this year.

> The churches have to begin to speak out fearlessly. For too long, pastors and churches have been bullied into believing that they can say nothing political from the pulpit. Let me remind you the Bible's a political document. The prophets, including John the Baptist and Jesus, lost their lives because they spoke the truth to those in power.

> Too many of the pastors—too many, practically all—in Germany refused to speak against national socialism...the result: millions of Jews, pastors, priests, homosexuals, gypsies all lost their lives because everyone was afraid. What are you afraid of, a couple of bucks? Your tax-exempt status? What's that going to do to you? Your churches may be closed anyway, because if a certain party gets elected, this certain party said, if the churches do not agree with our interpretation of women's reproductive rights, they'll just have to change their doctrine.

We are in a battle for the soul of America. Somehow, Christians have come to buy the story that you cannot be political in church. Let me tell you right now, oh yes, you can, and oh, yes, you better be. Because you might not have a church to go to if you don't vote the right way in November.

Some consider Father Orsi's view to be nonsense, claiming Christ promised his church would endure forever. There is some merit to that position, at least from a holistic view, because Jesus did say, "For where two or three are gathered together in my name, there am I in the midst of them" (Mt 18:20). But that does not guarantee we will be free to worship as we choose and to live as our faith and our God have called us to live. All we have to do is look at past and present states such as the former Soviet Union, Communist China, and much of the middle East countries to understand how quickly religious freedom can be taken away, eroded, or trampled into the ground. The Church may indeed endure forever but how well and how openly we can proclaim it and live it remains an open question. It is incumbent upon all who cherish their religious freedoms to choose wisely next month. We can do so only if we are well informed.

O Mystery, Divine
Thirsting for truth

How often do we encounter something that intrigues us and beckons us to discover its secrets? We humans have a love/hate relationship with mystery for we naturally yearn to know of that which we cannot comprehend while equally uncomfortable with the unknowing of it.

The truths of Christianity would not stir us as they do, nor would they draw us or hearten us, and they would not be embraced by us with such love and joy, if they contained no mysteries. What makes many a man recoil from the Christian mysteries as from sinister specters is neither the voice of nature nor the inner impulse of the heart nor the yearning for light and truth, but the arrogance of a wanton and overweening pride. When the heart thirsts after truth, when the knowledge of the truth is its purest delight and highest joy, the sublime, the exalted, the extraordinary, the incomprehensible all exercise an especial attraction. A truth that is easily discovered and quickly grasped can neither enchant nor hold. To enchant and hold us it must surprise us by its novelty, it must overpower us with its magnificence; its wealth and profundity must exhibit ever new splendors, ever deeper abysses to the exploring eye. We find but slight stimulation and pleasure in studies whose subject matter is soon exhausted and so leaves nothing further for our wonderment. But how powerfully sciences enthrall us when every glance into them suggests new marvels to divine, and every facet of the object imprisons new and greater splendors.[98]

It is no small wonder we are drawn to the mystery of the Divine for in God rests the unfathomable Truth; the unknowable Divine Mystery. On Psalm 33:9 "O taste and see that the Lord is good" Saint Thomas wrote, "In material things we see first, and then we taste. But in spiritual things we taste first so that we can see, because no one knows who does not taste. And thus he says first taste, and then see." What a marvelous insight on prayer and the Divine Mystery: The Lord says we must first taste (contemplate) so we might see his face.

The Angelic Doctor
On the science of God

Often referred to as the Angelic Doctor, Saint Thomas Aquinas holds no equal in illuminating fundamental Catholic Theology. Indeed, popes, councils, and even the Code of Canon Law have consistently emphasized the importance of teaching the principles of theology and metaphysics developed by the Angelic Doctor. Pope Leo XIII highly recommended the study of Saint Thomas. Of Aquinas, Pope Pius X wrote: "But we warn teachers to bear in mind that a slight departure from the teaching of Aquinas, especially in metaphysics, is very detrimental. As Aquinas himself says, 'a slight error in the beginning is a great error in the end.'" Canon 1366, 2 of the 1918 Code of Canon Law promulgated by Pope Benedict XV says: "Mental philosophy and theology must be taught according to the method, teaching and principles of the Angelic Doctor, to which the professors should religiously adhere." Pope Pius XI reiterated this in promulgating the new law for the doctorate in his Encyclical *Deus scientiarum Dominus*. It would be impossible to minimize the profundity of his prodigious output—*Summa Theologica*, his unfinished theological manuscript, written for beginning theology students exceeds 3500 pages—written in his own hand. As with any work of such magnitude and importance, his work has met with criticism, primarily, although not entirely, concerning his methodology, considered to be too scholastic. While such criticism has varied over time, the general thrust has been "The method and principles by which the old scholastic doctors cultivated theology are not at all suitable to the demands of our times and to the progress of the sciences."

Reginald Garrigou-Lagrange writes where many modern critics frequently departed from Aquinas was in their belief "no system is absolutely true, but each is relatively true, that is, in opposition to another preceding doctrine, or else to some other brief evolutionary period of the past. They say that, for instance, Thomism was relatively true in the thirteenth [century] in opposition to the doctrine of certain

---

[98] Matthias Sheeben, *Mysteries of Christianity* (trans. C. Vollert; St. Louis: B. Herder Book, Co., 1946 [1865/1888]), 4–5.

Augustinians, which it surpassed; but it, too, is not absolutely but relatively false with respect to the subsequent system which, either as an antithesis or as a superior synthesis, is of a higher order in the evolution of ideas. Thus *Scotism*, coming at a later date, would be truer than St. Thomas' doctrine…"[99] What must be clearly understood is that underlying this relativistic view, which is so prevalent today, is the premise, if it is at all true, that nothing can "be absolutely true, not even the principle of contradiction, at least as a law of being and higher reason." Consider if this were so, no definition could be absolutely expressed, such that the true properties of a thing could be deduced. "There would be only relative truth, in its reference to the present state of knowledge, and this rather as regards the already superseded past than the unknown future. Even for knowing the relative truth of any doctrine, it would be necessary to have full knowledge of the preceding periods of evolution, which were the prerequisites for the manifestation of its ultimate development."

This concept of what defines truth is the mantra of the Modernists who said: "Truth is no more immutable, than man himself is, in that it is developed with, in, and by him," which suggests, even presupposes, immanence or absolute evolutionism, condemned by Pope Pius IX. In the *Syllabus of Errors*, Pius IX wrote the Modernist held the notion "In effect God is produced in man and in the world, and all things are God and have the very substance of God, and God is one and same with the world, and, therefore, spirit with matter, necessity with liberty, good with evil, justice with injustice." Accordingly, God is in the process of becoming both in man and in the world, and yet He never will be in any true sense. "Thus, nothing would be absolutely true and nothing absolutely false. There would be only relative truth and relative falsehood. Only relativity would be absolute." Theology is not, nor can it be, relative. It is, quite literally, the science of God, a science that has God as its object. Lawrence Feingold offers a fuller explanation.

> Theology studies not only God, but also all created things insofar as they are related to God as Creator, Legislator, and Final End. Hence, theology also studies creation, by which creatures proceed from God and thus have Him as their final end; ethics, by which rational creatures live according to God; and salvation history, by which God intervenes in history to lead human beings to Himself. The many themes studied in theology all relate to its main subject and unifying principle, which is God Himself.[100]

Now of Aquinas and his methodology, which so many have voiced objection and criticism, we should make note of his manner of first stating the question, followed immediately with three objections. Thus, he followed in the footsteps of Aristotle and most of the early Church Fathers.

---

[99] Reginald Garrigou-Lagrange, *The One God: A Commentary on the First Part of St. Thomas' Theological Summa*, (trans. Dom. Bede Rose. St. Louis: B. Herder, 1943; repr., Lexington KY: Ex Fontibus, 2015), p. 11-12.
[100] Lawrence Feingold, *Faith Comes from What Is Heard: An Introduction to Fundamental Theology* (Steubenville, OH: Emmaus Academic, 2016) p. 118.

Just as he who wishes to free himself from a chain that binds him, must first inspect the chain and the way it binds him, so he who wishes to solve a doubt must first examine all the difficulties and their causes.... Those who wish to search for truth, not taking doubt first into consideration, are like those who do not know where they are going...hence they cannot go by a direct route, unless perhaps they do so by chance...nor can they know when they find the truth sought, and when they do not....Just as in judgments no one can give a decision unless he hears the reasons for and against, so he who has to examine philosophical questions is necessarily in a better position to judge if has informed himself of practically all the reasons for the doubts raised by the adversaries. On account of these reasons it was Aristotle's custom in almost all his works to prepare for the search or determination of the truth by recounting the doubts raised against it."[101]

It is perhaps this willingness, one could even call it eagerness, to confront the skeptics with their doubts and objections which lends the greatest credence to Saint Thomas' theological acumen. And it is likewise his critics greatest challenge. Certainly, there is great reluctance on the part of many modern theologians to follow his methodology for to do so would be to insist on accepting the reality which is objective truth in the absolute. Too many have bitten into the forbidden fruit of relativism, which Pope Benedict XVI called the "dictatorship of relativism," and thus no longer wish to acknowledge God as the absolute truth. Saint Thomas argues theology is indeed a science.

I respond that sacred theology is a science. But it must be recognized that there are two kinds of sciences. One kind is based on principles evident in the light of natural reason, such as arithmetic, geometry, and others of that sort. Another kind is based on principles evident in the light of a higher science, as the art of perspective is based on principles known by geometry, and music is based on principles known by arithmetic. And in this way sacred theology is based on principles known by the light of a higher science, which is the science of God and the blessed. Therefore, as music believes principles transmitted to it by mathematicians, so sacred theology believes principles revealed to it by God."[102]

Saint Thomas recognized theology is not a science based on empirical evidence, but one based on authority. He thus contends theology "has a most sublime dignity because it is a science subordinated to the science that God has of Himself and of His creation. Thus, sacred theology is the most certain of all the sciences, even though it treats of the most sublime questions, for it participates in the certainty of God's own omniscience. ... Despite the borrowed nature of its principles, theology is similar to other sciences in that, from its borrowed principles, it builds a systematic body of knowledge by defining terms, making distinctions, demonstrating conclusions, clarifying through analogy, and defending its conclusions against those who attack them."[103]

---

[101] Saint Thomas Aquinas, *Commentary on Metaphysics, Bk III, chap. I, lect. i.*
[102] Saint Thomas Aquinas, *Summa Theologica I, q. 1, a. 2.*
[103] Lawrence Feingold, Faith Comes from What is Heard, p 117

Sticks and Stones
Lions, tigers and bears, Oh my!

So conditioned are we to what we hear in thirty-second, highly edited, purposely distorted sound bites, there is little wonder as to the state of confusion and the stomach-churning nausea that afflicts much of the electorate these days. And that is long before hearing the candidates themselves as they work diligently and with seeming enthusiasm to destroy one another while simultaneously hoisting themselves on their own petards. What is increasingly evident is the purposed unwillingness or intentional refusal of many to inform themselves of the issues and what precisely is at stake in the upcoming election. The reliance of so many on highly suspect, biased reportage is both appalling and frightening. What is blatantly apparent is we have ceased any and all efforts to understand the issues; rather we have hung ourselves on the cult of personality, selling our vote and our soul, not for what is important or what truly matters, but for who dons the friendliest mask and wears the best costume. The reality of it is, that, for perhaps the first time in the history of our country, we are faced with making a choice between two otherwise totally unelectable and equally despicable caricatures of humanity. Neither is worthy of our vote for neither has come close to earning it. Yet, truth be told, someone will be elected in November, no matter how odoriferous the wind blows. What is an honest citizen to do given such unpleasant choices? The answer, while unpleasant, is to vote, but vote informed, clearly understanding the issues. The answer, at this moment in our country's history, is to hold your nose in voting for the candidate of your choice, but in doing so, consider the larger issues which are clearly at stake. Elsewhere, I offered this advice: forget the candidates—neither is worthy of your vote but that is how our system works—vote on the potential and probable outcomes should one or the other become the next chief executive. There are many possibilities—and at this juncture that is all they should be considered—but we can make a well-educated supposition as to which way the wind will blow by looking at the platforms, policies, and public statements made by both candidates. Another important but often neglected area to consider is, based upon the platform, policies, and statements, who will the candidate appoint to run the bureaucracy and what will their most likely political and policy leanings be.

For Catholics and those who are Christian, in general, this election is a seminal and decisive one. For those who have no further need to know, it would behoove you to stop reading at this point. For those who are open to understanding what is at stake, read on. The current administration has clearly been a disaster for those of deep religious conviction. Never has the assault on faith been so persistent, overt, or pernicious. In a pamphlet produced by CatholicVote *"Our Government's War on America's Catholics"* you will find page after page of anti-Catholic and anti-Christian government assaults on our religious freedoms. Many have been well publicized, such as the Little Sisters of the Poor and the Sweet Cakes bakery in Portland, Oregon. But the reality is there are many more, some presenting far greater danger to our right to worship and follow our faith. And some are, at this juncture, of concern because of what a candidate has publicly stated.

Here, I will only highlight one or two of the most egregious examples. The Mayor of Houston, Texas, as part of her campaign of intimidation against Christians, issued subpoenas to Houston pastors demanding they turn over copies of their sermons. She wanted to see if these pastors might be violating civil rights or hate crime laws by teaching homosexual conduct is sinful—presumably hoping to fine, perhaps even jail these pastors and shut down their churches. The owner of Arlene's Flowers in Richmond, Washington, declined to provide flowers for a same sex wedding for her Christian beliefs. She was found in violation of the state's antidiscrimination law. Offered a settlement: pay a $2,000 fine, a $1 payment for costs and fees, and agree to not discriminate in the future, she refused saying: "You are asking me to walk in the way of a well-known betrayer, one who sold something of infinite worth for 30 pieces of silver. That is something I will not do." Hillary Clinton has publicly stated: "Laws have to be backed up with resources and political will. And deep-seated religious beliefs have to be changed."

Robert P. George, a professor of jurisprudence at Princeton University, and chairman of the U.S. Commission on International Religious Freedom (2013-2014 and 2015-2016) noted the noxious anti-Catholic bigotry contained in the recently published emails exchanged between leading progressives, Democrats and Hillary Clinton operatives. "Many elites, having embraced secular progressivism as not merely a political view but a religion, loathe traditional faiths that refuse to yield to its dogmas."[104] Another email calls for Mr. Podesta, Clinton's campaign chairman and a "Catholic" to support a "Catholic Spring in which Catholics themselves demand the end of a middle ages dictatorship and the beginning of a little democracy and respect for gender equality in the Catholic Church."

Neither candidate has an admirable record with respect to religion. Mr. Trump has demonstrated questionable ethics, intemperance, insensitivity, and a willingness to stretch the truth (a trait well-tuned for any politician) among other unadmirable character flaws. Yet he has not publicly declared war on religion or on those who wished to follow the doctrines of their faith. Nor is there any indication he would pack the government bureaucracy and the Supreme Court with those who would eliminate our first freedom. No matter who is elected, no one will be satisfied or happy with the results, no one. The rotten smell is too overwhelming on either side for anyone to ignore it. In the end we must ask ourselves: Whom do you believe offers the slightest possibility of returning our country, founded on Christian values, to once again be "One nation under God, with liberty and justice for all?"

---

[104] Robert P. George, Non-Catholics for Church 'Reform': Clinton allies mock the faithful and demand they embrace secular dogmas, The Wall Street Journal, October 13, 2016.

Masking the Taste
Or let hunger win the game

There are memories of a time when the world turned topsy-turvy: when rich turned poor in an instant, while the poor, never rich, stood somehow taller; when none owned more than empty pockets and worn out shoes to last a winter, all were equal, just the same.

We who have lived not three score and ten have never known such bleak privation; knowing not where or when but whether there would be some moment, better than the one before. We complain and worry so, of nothing really, no surprise, of words in chalk upon a wall, and wonder how we will survive. Then memories of depressing times flash before us: when what to eat were sliced tomatoes, such vile disgusting things, whether fruit or vegetable matters not. The look, the taste, were simply more than any child should have to stomach ... and yet, the choice was to swallow, or, let hunger win the game.

Necessity bears its stamp on what solutions will resolve, and yet, leave it to childish genius to contrive sweet remedies. Should a teaspoon of sugar make the medicine go down, a cup of sugar, most assuredly, will mask the unpleasantness that awaits the palate. Four score the years have come and gone, yet sliced tomatoes, none the same, still lay covered beneath the sugar, out of habit, nothing more.

Childhood is but a memory, but the memory reminds the soul: life is filled with many choices, which choice we choose is ours to make, yet choose we must lest sliced tomatoes once again be forced upon us. So, it remains until today, for we must choose off the menu, choose between the vile and foul: choose one, choose one, then quickly swallow, or, let hunger win the game.

A Polemic Unwinding
Ego Praesidium

Colloquī is the present infinitive of *colloquor*, Latin for *to talk, to discuss,* or *to converse*. Colloquī is for restless minds, minds that ache for the truth, the objective truth. As the name implies, each issue will offer food for thought, for discussion, and conversation. As it is written, "Come now, let us reason together" (Is 1:18) so together let us journey toward the One Source that is all Truth.

Twenty-two issues ago I closed the first article of the inaugural issue of Colloquī with those words. It was my intent then, as now, to provide positive informed instruction for Catholics to help them grow in their faith and love of God, the Father, Son, and

Holy Spirit, to share and inform accurately and faithfully what the Catholic Church and the Magisterium teaches, and to add fuel to that fire, that unquenchable flame of the Holy Spirit that burns within each of us to spread the Good News. It was and is my diaconal ministry: Colloquī is ministry of service, a means to fulfill a portion of my diaconal promise to serve the people of God.

It was never my intent nor my desire to polemicize or exercise thoughtless controversy, and yet, inexplicably—solely on my part—that is precisely what I have unintentionally now done. Four issues ago, I wrote an article (Ecumenism Run Amok, September 23, 2016)) for which I deeply and with great sorrow regret. I apologize and ask for your mercy and forgiveness as I have asked God for his. Here and now, I will make no attempt to erase or ignore what was written, for it has been written and the damage has been wrought. Nothing I might say or do can undo the pain from such wounds inflicted. I can only hope to salve the wounds and the scars I have so unjustly made. There is both a solemn duty and a corresponding responsibility I owe to those whom I have been called to serve. My duty is to faithfully proclaim, through word and deed, the Gospel of Jesus Christ and my responsibility is to do so with the utmost love, mercy, and compassion so as to never cause scandal to our Lord Jesus Christ, his Church, her apostolic successors, and to God. I take these duties and responsibilities with all due seriousness for they are all in his holy name.

Reus. Ego enim non praesidium defendere (I stand accused. I offer no defense for I cannot defend it.) Although I cannot nor will not make any attempt to defend what I wrote, I must, in all good conscience, offer some reasoned explanation, attempt to unwind the polemic, and correct the errors which I so scandalously promoted. To do so I must begin at the ending, for it was in the ending where the gravest injustice and greatest scandal was pronounced. I asked a question—which I will not repeat—which was intemperate, scandalous, disrespectful, unwarranted, and completely unjustifiable. Had I not asked it, the article would still have been polemical in its content, but scandal would have been reduced or possibly eliminated. I asked it, I was wrong to do so, it was scandalous, it was most assuredly disrespectful of the Supreme Pontiff, and for all that, I sincerely and humbly pray, "O God, be merciful to me a sinner."

As to the article, I most humbly submit to wretched failure on my part to adequately research and understand the situation in its fullness. Perhaps the most important criteria for any writer, but especially for Catholic theological writers and apologists is to always speak and write the truth through the narrow lens of Christ, his Church and her magisterium. That places great and serious demands upon anyone who wishes to inform or instruct or offer witness to the Word of God, demands that must be and can only be honestly met through diligent effort and strict attention to discovering the Truth. In writing the article I must confess I allowed my emotions and distress to override my reason. I knew better, but in my zeal to write the wrong which I then perceived, I lost objectivity and let my heart overrule my head. I believed at the time I was writing from authentic sources, which, as I have subsequently become aware, while perhaps "authentic," were less than objective or honest in their presentation of the facts and the truth. And to be fully and completely honest, I must admit to having been of a mind whereby I had so biased my own thoughts so much as to be incapable and unwilling to attempt any determination of the truth. Such disregard was and is quite plainly irresponsible and again, I humbly submit my regret and sorrow.

The truth, of what I so arrogantly disregarded, is of far greater import and deserves far greater space than current pages can hold, but I will begin this week to bring the truth to light without polemic exercise or undeserved bias.

> In his address at a private audience with the delegation from the United Evangelical Lutheran Church in Germany on 24 January 2011, Pope Benedict emphasized that on this occasion Lutherans and Catholics would have the opportunity "to celebrate throughout the world a common ecumenical commemoration, to grapple at the world level with fundamental issues" and to do this not "in the form of a triumphant celebration, but as a common profession of faith in the One Triune God, in common obedience to Our Lord and to his Word."

The above is but a small part of a much larger speech presented to the Council meeting of the Lutheran World Federation by Cardinal Kurt Koch. In it, Cardinal Koch explains much of the current Lutheran and Catholic progress that has been made, including two extremely important and enlightening documents. *"From Conflict To Communion: Lutheran-Catholic Common Commemoration of the Reformation in 2017"* which provides a well-constructed overview of the past 500 hundred years and the differences, but also the many agreements both share in common. It is a marvelous read and I highly recommend it for those who truly wish to be informed. The second document is fundamental to the first: *"Joint Declaration on the Doctrine of Justification" by the Lutheran World Federation and the Catholic Church.*

October 28, 2016

A Life Loved
You were born—loved

You were born—loved. Of that there can be no dispute. For God loves into existence and with love sustains all that was, is, and ever shall be. Thus, if you are, you are loved and will forever be—loved.

What makes us human is not the mere summation and composition of elemental matter; for if that were so, beyond form and function, what may we say differs us from any animate creature? No, we differ in this way: "The human person, created in the image of God, is a being at once corporeal and spiritual," which is to say we are composed of body and soul as affirmed in Holy Scripture: "the Lord God formed man out of the clay of the ground and blew into his nostrils the breath of life, and so man became a living being."[105] Now the soul, the breath of God, is a gift of love from the One who loves us, and "it is because of its spiritual soul that the body made of matter becomes a living human body; spirit and matter, in man, are not two natures united, but rather their union forms a single nature."[106] As Catholics we are taught and believe "that every spiritual soul is created immediately by God — it is not 'produced' by the parents — and also that it is immortal: it does not perish when it separates from the body at death, and it will be reunited with the body at the final resurrection."[107]

While parents are of necessity participants in the procreative process, love may or may not be witness to the act which may produce a life. Yet if it is God's will, life will come to be, with or without human love, but life can never be without the love of God. Wisdom says, "For you love all things that are and loathe nothing that you have made; for what you hated, you would not have fashioned" (Wis 11:24). Thus, you were born—loved.

A History Redeemed
Reexamining the past

History is immutable; what has gone before is forever beyond the will of man to alter; its course has engraved a mark too deep to permit erasure of its passing. To be sure, time will, in a sense, inevitably erode the clarity of the recorded moment, soften-ing the harsh light of its truth, ultimately leaving an impression not in keeping with objective reality. What will be recorded upon the dusty pages of history—beyond mere fact of some occurrence and the players so employed—must of necessity be penned by such observers whose biased thoughts and discriminating hands provide but a por-tion, a single facet of what it was that once occurred. We live in the present, seldom does the past invade our thoughts, which to our detriment carries forward perceptions gained from past experience without the bother to amend what we believe or under-stand as truth. History is the past, whether but a second gone or a thousand years ago; never is it yet to come, or even now, which quickly turns the page. How well do we remember yesterday or the day before? Not well, to be certain. If we forget so quickly the what and where and why of our own past, what then of those whom we have never known except through dusty tomes written so long ago. All this is preface to a history which has long been taught, yet depending on the circumstance and the magister, told as though looking thru the lens of a kaleidoscope, ever changing shape and color to the eye.

---

[105] Catechism of the Catholic Church §362.
[106] Catechism of the Catholic Church §365.
[107] Catechism of the Catholic Church §366.

Five-hundred years is well beyond the knowing of those now living and thus we must rely on what was recorded long ago by partisans whose views were tempered by time and place and station. Subsequent the Second Vatican Council, an ecumenical dialogue between Lutherans and Catholics has long engaged in achieving a common understanding and hopeful reunification. Much attention has been paid to the historical context and content of the historical record surrounding Martin Luther and the onset of the Protestant Reformation. In the document *"From Conflict to Communion"* the authors write: "What happened in the past cannot be changed, but what is remembered of the past and how it is remembered can, with the passage of time, indeed change. Remembrance makes the past present. While the past itself is unalterable, the presence of the past in the present is alterable. In view of 2017, the point is not to tell a different history, but to tell that history differently."[108]

As I wrote previously, "As a Catholic I was taught Martin Luther was a Catholic priest who dissented against the abuse of indulgences. That was the sum total of my knowledge of the man. I suspect most Catholics own much the same understanding." Of that much of my polemic I can say was true, of the remainder poor interpretation. Twentieth-century Catholic research on Luther offers a redemptive perspective through which Catholics and Lutherans can collegially agree.

> In a new way, Luther was portrayed as an earnest religious person and conscientious man of prayer. Painstaking and detailed historical research has demonstrated that Catholic literature on Luther over the previous four centuries right up through modernity had been significantly shaped by the commentaries of Johannes Cochaleus, a contemporary opponent of Luther and advisor to Duke George of Saxony. Cochaleus had characterized Luther as an apostatized monk, a destroyer of Christendom, a corrupter of morals, and a heretic. The achievement of this first period of critical, but sympathetic, engagement with Luther's character was freeing of Catholic research from the one-sided approach of such polemical works on Luther. Sober historical analyses by other Catholic theologians showed that it was not the core concerns of the Reformation, such as the doctrine of justification, which led to the division of the church but, rather, Luther's criticisms of the condition of the church at his time that sprang from these concerns.[109]

Out of the new evidence it has become increasingly clear Luther never intended to split from the Catholic Church. "Implicit rapprochement with Luther's concerns has led to a new evaluation of his catholicity, which took place in the context of recognizing that his intention was to reform, not to divide, the church. This is evident in the statements of Johannes Cardinal Willebrands and Pope John Paul II. The rediscovery of these two central characteristics of his person and theology led to a new ecumenical understanding of Luther as a 'witness to the gospel.'"[110]

---

[108] From Conflict to Communion, §16.
[109] From Conflict to Communion, §22.
[110] From Conflict to Communion, §29.

Lutheran research on Luther and the Reformation, commensurate with Catholic research, also underwent considerable development. "Dialogue with historians helped to integrate historical and social factors into descriptions of Reformation movements. Lutheran theologians recognized the entanglements of theological insights and political interests not only on the part of Catholics, but also on their own side. Dialogue with Catholic theologians helped them to overcome one-sided confessional approaches and to become more self-critical about aspects of their own traditions."[111] With new insights and greater historical and theological understanding both Lutherans and Catholics felt compelled to move forward together.

> The dialogue partners are committed to the doctrines of their respective churches, which, according to their own convictions, express the truth of the faith. The doctrines demonstrate great commonalities but may differ, or even be opposed, in their formulations. Because of the former, dialogue is possible; because of the latter, dialogue is necessary.

> Dialogue demonstrates that the partners speak different languages and understand the meanings of words differently; they make different distinctions and think in different thought forms. However, what appears to be an opposition in expression is not always an opposition in substance. In order to determine the exact relationship between respective articles of doctrine, texts must be interpreted in the light of the historical context in which they arose. That allows one to see where a difference or opposition truly exists and where it does not.

> Ecumenical dialogue means being converted from patterns of thought that arise from and emphasize the differences between confessions. Instead, in dialogue the partners look first for what they have in common and only then weigh the significance of their differences. These differences, however, are not overlooked or treated casually, for ecumenical dialogue is the common search for the truth of the Christian faith.[112]

November 04, 2016

The Measure of Life
The joy of an angel

How do you measure a life? The thought of placing some certain value, a price or measure upon a life, any life, repels us. Yet inevitably, it would seem, we are wont to gauge, to weigh, to measure ourselves and others in some form or fashion. Why? God only knows. God measures not a single hair or eyelash, for he looks upon each of his children with the same inestimable love. He cares not whether we have achieved greatness or fame, wealth or power nor does he concern himself with such vanities which

---

[111] From Conflict to Communion, §31.
[112] From Conflict to Communion, §32, 33, 34.

we are want to measure ourselves and others, such things as height or weight, intellect or profundity, beauty or wit, longevity or brevity of life.

What is important is often not at all deemed important, for we seldom consider the intangibles, those things in which we have no means to measure. This past week there was a celebration of life for one so briefly among us, a beautiful, vivacious young nine-year old girl, who, though so very young, was truly an angel of God. As was written of her, "Maddie endured and bravely fought aggressive brain cancer for well over a year. She knew no strangers, only friends she had not met yet. She emanated love and compassion and touched everyone she met." She was in every sense of the word an angel of God and she made the world a better place while she was in it.

Maddie may not have achieved what many would dare call greatness or fame or fortune; her time here was too brief for that. But the true measure of her life was, is and will continue to be far greater than our vanities could ever imagine or attain: she gave us joy, love, happiness, she brought sunshine when there was rain, she made us smile despite the pain, she inspired us to look beyond ourselves, to see sunshine and rain-bows. She showed us there is always hope of life eternal in the loving arms of God. The measure of her life is beyond ours to discover.

From a Distance
An uncommon witness

Perhaps in the years to come humanity will grow up and learn how to live with one another in peace and harmony. Perhaps. But then the sceptic would argue either humanity is incapable of growing up or owns no inclination to a deeper understanding of the human condition. It requires no effort of the mind to realize how uncommon we have become, each a subspecies of one, incapable of sharing in our common humanity. We speak but do not communicate; we hear but do not listen; we see without seeing; we think without thinking; we feel without feeling; we know without knowing; we exist without living. Once I wrote of *Bab-ili* and perhaps it should be offered anew as a reminder of what we have or are fast becoming.

There once was a city that lay nestled upon the floor of a broad verdant valley. The first men to come upon the valley were so taken by its beauty that they named the place *Bab-ili*, which meant "gate of the gods" for they thought such beauty must surely be a worthy entrance to the home of the divine.

Alas, over time those who lived in *Bab-ili* lost sight of the beauty that surrounded them; a beauty which they had neither created nor had the power to create. Yet in their arro-gance and pride they convinced themselves that they were gods whose rightful place was in the heavens above the sky. And so, they conceived a stairway that would extend beyond the clouds, a far more perfect entrance to their rightful home among the stars.

They believed solely in their ability to accomplish anything they desired and denied existence to any power greater than their own. They laughed at the very possibility of retribution from the divine for were they not gods themselves and none greater or more powerful than they? If indeed greater gods did exist, then why would those gods not display their greater power and rain destruction down upon such weak pretenders? They laughed and jeered and scoffed at the preposterous notion that in truth they were not gods at all. They refused to admit that they were but mortal creatures whose very lives or those of any other creature were beyond their poor powers to conceive let alone create.

Then one day, a day like all the days that had come before, the gods of *Bab-ili* awoke and discovered they could no longer understand one another; not one word from their neighbor or from anyone else for the matter. Imagine the frustration, the consternation, the irksome irritation that ensued when all those almighty self-important gods could no longer command, demand, or pontificate. Imagine the moment when familiar words were now so strangely unfamiliar, when *yes* was heard as *no* to one and *maybe* to some and *phooey* to others, when *up* sounded a lot like *down*, *in* meant *out*, *over* was *under*, *good* was *bad*, *hello* was spoken but *goodbye* was heard. Imagine the bitterness, the anger, the hatred that resulted from the complete inability to communicate in any way with one another.

It was a tragedy, a disaster, a chaotic mess of epic proportions. Alone with thoughts and words only each could comprehend, the inhabitants of *Bab-ili* could no longer stand to live together and so they quickly dispersed to the far corners of the world, no longer pretending or believing themselves to be gods.

It is an ancient tale, first told at the dawn of time and retold over the millennia hence without any loss in weight as to its importance. But we forget the past or else we simply choose to do so in order to more readily convince ourselves of our own importance, our greatness, and our godhood.

God is watching and has seen it all before. No doubt he knows exactly what to do. If the ancient tale of *Bab-ili* holds true, then we have assuredly arrived at that seminal moment when we realize that we are but human and not gods at all.

Consider for a moment what this tale imputes upon the current state of the affairs of men. No matter what the subject or the topic set before us we find ourselves babbling incoherent nothings to be heard by no one but ourselves. Reasoned debate has been replaced by *ad hominem* assault. Language has become an arcane art, nuanced and crafted so as to articulate nothing of substance with unwarranted gravitas. Whether too close or at too great a distance to clearly discern what is truth is of impractical importance for the wise among us for they know this: we will unconsciously and vacuously submit to their self-proclaimed wisdom. There are questions we should ask and answers we should demand yet the truth is we have little want to be bothered beyond the mundane and inane.

Edward Pentin, Rome Correspondent for the National Catholic Register, reports on the solemn commemoration of 500th anniversary of the Reformation and 50 years of Catholic-Lutheran dialogue, "A lengthy document to coincide with the commemoration, 'From Conflict to Communion,' drawn up by the Lutheran-Catholic Commission for Unity, is meant to serve as the ecumenical basis of the meeting" between Pope Francis and the leaders of the Lutheran Church in Sweden.

> It [the document] notes how the Second Vatican Council led to leaving behind the 'charged polemic atmosphere of the post-Reformation era.' It does not cover all that either church teaches about justification; it does encompass a consensus on basic truths of the doctrine of justification and shows that the remaining differences in its explication are no longer the occasion for doctrinal condemnations." There has been significant progress over the past 50 years toward greater understanding. One Bishop stated that the document and the commemoration "aims to turn past wounds and divisions into an attitude of hope and trust in God's will to bring about the reconciliation of all in Christ's body, the Church." Another, Bishop Anders Arborelius of Stockholm said that the commemoration was "an historic and prophetic sign on the path toward full visible unity that sometimes seems so far away.[113]

But Pentin reports, "not all is rosy behind the scenes, particularly in Sweden, where the scars of the Reformation run deep. Apprehension is growing that the event will be used to gloss over significant Catholic-Lutheran differences."

November 11, 2016

A Silent Salute
To those who served

What sad tribute it must be
which so darkens the soul with animus
for the flag of freedom's toil,
while white stars and stripes,
now stained by blood once warm and red,
cover hearts at silent rest beneath the soil.
Those who served for freedom's gain
seldom care to boast or brag;
they served, served well the call
to proudly wave their nation's flag.

Some are wont to quake in fear,
of what, they will or cannot say,
in voices shrill and quite profane;
they want, they need, they cry, they pray,
they kneel and shake their fists again.
Not with their blood,

---

[113] Edward Pentin, *Scandinavian Sojourn*, National Catholic Register, Oct 30-Nov 12, 2016, pp. 9-10

no, not theirs you see:
to them the price of freedom: free.

The ragged coat of olive green
upon the beggar cold and drear,
speaks of long ago and gallantry,
of duty, honor, country dear,
of battles fought for freedom's gain;
the fear of losing life or limb,
worth any price, strife, or pain.

Raise the flag now, raise the flag.
Hold the torch of freedom high above the dark forbidding throng;
let freedom ring and flag unfurl,
for God and country, faith still strong.

For those who served and gave their all,
a debt still owed, none can repay;
the price, the price of purchased death,
lies cold and still beneath the clay.

To serve without reserve,
to lift the eye in reverent awe,
to stand in silent grace before the deathly pawl;
to know the price which has been paid,
a price too high, yet few there are who would refuse
to serve their God and country yet again.

To those who have and those who now serve
we bow our heads in silent salute for their sacrifice.

Coming Up for Air
Reshaping the wind

Someone inquired a week ago who would win the presidential election. My response was purposefully vague and superficially prescient for I assured them no matter who won some would be happy and others would not. While my prognosticating talents may leave much to be desired, it certainly fared better than most of the pollsters, pundits, and media who were "shocked" by the outcome. What has shocked most since has been the unrelenting vitriol, violence, and hateful rhetoric which has arisen across the country primarily from those most unhappy with the outcome. Last issue I began this column with a few words which now seem so apropos I will simply repeat them here:

Perhaps in the years to come humanity will grow up and learn how to live with one another in peace and harmony. Perhaps. But then the sceptic would argue: either humanity is incapable of growing up or owns no inclination to a deeper understanding of the human condition.

It requires no effort of the mind to realize how uncommon we have become, each a sub-species of one, incapable of sharing in our common humanity. We speak but do not communicate; we hear but do not listen; we see without seeing; we think without think-ing; we feel without feeling; we know without knowing; we exist without living.

It is truly sad to see how unhappy, bitter, and divided we have become as a com-munity, a society, a nation, and a species created by a transcendent, ineffable, and loving God. The question we should be asking ourselves is "Why?" Why is there so much hate? Why is there so much anger and bitterness directed toward others? Why can't we just get along? We have become accustomed, whenever anything fails to please or satisfy, to immediately seek to establish fault, to determine who is to blame for our unhappiness, disappointments, and failures. We seldom if ever look to our-selves for the cause of our discomfiture; the blame always and inevitably lies elsewhere. Our self-importance and our pride permit no weakness or imperfection; we know the truth and the truth has set us free. The predominant views opined post-elec-tion have been from disaffected writers who in the main expressed some measure of unreasoned, indeterminate fear; indeterminate in their fear was never or could not be identified or named. One blogger however posted a well-considered article in which she offered some salient words of wisdom. It is certainly food for thought.

> In less than 24 hours since Donald Trump has been named the President-elect of the greatest nation on this earth, it's become apparent he's being given far more credit than he's due. There are anguished cries of, "How will my children grow up knowing not to discriminate?" or, "How can I look my daughter in the eye and tell her she has purpose?" Really? Really, America? You have given Donald Trump, a mere mortal man, far more credit than he deserves, especially considering the man hasn't even taken office yet. Trump does not have the power to mold our families, that is flat-out our responsibility.

> Your children will learn to love or hate, be respectful or disrespectful, wise or foolish, not by the character of the family in the White House, but by the family in their house. May I submit to you that your sons and daughters will be far, far more influenced by their teachers, coaches, 4-H, FFA, Scouts or church group leaders than they will a man on TV. I don't feel my character was molded by the Bush, Clinton, or Obama families, but I did learn perseverance from my Dad, work ethic from my Mom, and to do my best (and then redo it) from my sister. My college bible study leaders modeled to me how to seek God and my husband leads me in prayer.

> Should those in the public spotlight conduct themselves in a honorable fashion with ut-most integrity? Absolutely. However, it is not the responsibility of Miss America, the NFL, or the President, to set the example of moral conduct. It is not the government's responsibility to ensure American children have a good example. It is our responsibility, as American citizens, to ensure that we lead our youth in showing what is right and good and honorable and true. One good, God-fearing, America respecting football coach can do far more to shape the hearts and minds of teenage boys than Colin Kaepernick. If we

want to make a difference, let's stop worrying about Trump's moral example and take an active role in our classrooms, churches, youth groups, sports team, 4-H and FFA.

Secondly, it is only a lie that one man in Washington can determine another person's value or worth. If you're living and breathing, you have a purpose. Case closed. God fearfully and wonderfully made each one of us, and then continues to work in us for His good pleasure! If I ever, ever seek another man or woman's approval or affirmation to find purpose in my life, I will be sorely disappointed. It does not matter if that individual is a supervisor, friend, husband, or the President himself, no one can provide me with purpose outside of the Lord.

Friends and fellow Americans, "Your success as a family... our success as a nation... depends not on what happens inside the White House, but on what happens inside your house." I pray these wise words of Barbara Bush should resonate with us. Our nation has always and will always depend on the moral fiber of our families, nothing more, nothing less. God bless, America, and America, bless God![114]

There is much to chew on here. One thought, which has been percolating for several years now, has begun to crystalize: we, as Christian families, have abrogated our duties and responsibilities in educating our children; in our busyness and singled-minded focus on careers, we have too often willingly and even eagerly released our progeny to the care and feeding by educators who, more often than not, do not share our values, our morals, or our faith. Indeed, this is multi-generational, for it goes well beyond the current one. We, who have lived well beyond our youth, whose life experiences have tempered the mind, made us less impressionable and more judicial in thought and deed, are now realizing the fruits of our own youthful abnegation of responsibilities toward our children. We are now understandably reaping what we have fatuously sown. Our youth have no faith: in God, country, family, or anyone. They believe—for that is all they have been taught—they are entitled. They are, evidenced by their degrees, highly educated yet woefully ignorant, ill-informed, even misinformed on basic truths. With God's help we can correct what we have wrought, but only if we have the strength of mind and will to do so.

---

[114] Purpose on the Prairie, *Don't give Trump so much credit, America*, November 10, 2016, https://purposeon-theprairie.wordpress.com/2016/11/10/dont-give-trump-so-much-credit-america.

Technological Hubris
Know truth when you find it

Recently I have found reason for serious introspection and reflection which has disturbingly elevated an unspoken question to a quandary. The question is quite simple in form yet virtually impossible to answer either objectively or with precise certitude: What is truth? In earnest search for that priceless quality we inevitably find ourselves increasingly reliant upon technological resources to uncover and discover what is true. Yet when we find it, is it? Or is it something else?

Once upon a time, say before the year 1439, most of the world's population was illiterate and uneducated. The principle reason: books or manuscripts were simply unavailable in sufficient quantities; each requiring laborious time-consuming hand-copying. Such a process necessarily limited what was copied to what was deemed of greatest value. Today anyone can write, publish, and produce anything and nothing at all with the click of a button. We are inundated with tommyrot and folderol all advanced as either reality or truth. We find ourselves increasingly incapable or unaware of anything which hasn't been digitally generated. Reality is nothing but an app and life, but a game downloaded to a computer or a smartphone. We are sustained by sound bites and images taken out of context, twisted and contorted to square with circular reasoning and blatant sophistry. Reality is what someone wants you to believe and there is little if any desire to learn the truth of it. Technology has clouded our minds, hardened our hearts, enshrouded our souls; and we have allowed it, welcomed it, reveled in its fantasies and meaningless delights. Technological hubris has left us empty, devoid of our own humanity. We have blithely enslaved ourselves, no longer capable or knowing truth when we find it. Tragically we have lost even the will to come to know the truth. Why this is so thus alters the question into a quandary for "what is truth" no longer holds relevance for the self-enslaved, now kneeling in complacent submission to their golden calf, their digitized, pixelated god.

The English poet Thomas Gray expressed the current sentiment for truth some two-hundred and seventy years ago, long before the age of the technological advances which we are now so inescapably enslaved:

> *To each his suffering: all are men,*
> *Condemned alike to groan;*
> *The tender for another's pain,*
> *The unfeeling for his own.*
> *Yet ah! Why should they know their fate?*
> *Since sorrow never comes too late,*

and happiness too swiftly flies.
Thought would destroy their paradise.
No more; where ignorance is bliss,
tis folly to be wise.[115]

Perhaps we should not be so prompt to fault the calf upon the spear, for it well and truly does appear, we have not changed so much from yesteryear. So why the will toward ignorance? What drives us toward such obliviousness? Could it be precisely what Gray surmised: thought would destroy their paradise? There is, I believe, no small amount of truth to be discerned from that. What rests upon the minds of those who would refuse to wade the shallow shores of here and now to dive to deeper depths for greater gain fills the soul with hope of life beyond the grave. Those who find their happiness in empty shells and pretty things, such detritus the sea has cast upon the shore, will soon find wanting what has so easily been obtained. Petulancy does not become us well, yet petulant and self-absorbed we have become. John Rosemond, author and family psychologist, suggests the problem is a serious lack of Vitamin N, that is, the word "No." Multiple generations of parents have deprived their children of this essential vitamin by seldom if ever saying no to their children; and parents, their children, and our entire culture is paying the price.

> [A story] of a father who gave his son, age five, pretty much everything the little boy asked for. Like most parents, the father wanted more than anything for his son to be happy.
>
> But he wasn't. Instead he was petulant, moody, and often sullen. He also had problems getting along with others. In addition, he was very demanding and rarely if ever expressed any appreciation, let alone gratitude, for all the things his parents gave him.
>
> His parents were concerned, worried that their son might be suffering from depression, wondering if he might need therapy. The psychologist told them that their son was suffering the predictable ill effects of being over-indulged. What he needed was a healthy and steady dose of Vitamin N.
>
> Over-indulgence—a deficiency of Vitamin N—leads to its own form of addiction. When the point of diminishing returns is passed (and it's passed fairly early on), the receiving of things begins to generate nothing but want for more things.
>
> One terrible effect of this is that our children are becoming accustomed to a material standard that's out of kilter with what they can ever hope to achieve as adults. Consider also that many, if not most, children attain this level of affluence by not working, sacrificing, or doing their best, but by whining, demanding, and manipulating. So, in the process of inflating their material expectations, we also teach children that something can be had for next to nothing. Not only is that a falsehood, it's also one of the most dangerous, destructive attitudes a person can acquire.

---

[115] Thomas Gray, Ode on a Distant Prospect of Eton College, 1747.

This may go a long way toward explaining why the mental health of children in the 1950s—when kids got a lot less—was significantly better than the mental health of today's kids. Since the '50s, and especially in the last few decades, as indulgence has become the parenting norm, the rates of child and teen depression have skyrocketed. Children who grow up believing in the something-for-nothing fairy tale are likely to become emotionally stunted, self-centered adults.

Then, when they themselves become parents, they're likely to overdose their children with material things—the piles of toys, plushies, and gadgets one finds scattered around most households.

In that way, over indulgence—a deficiency of Vitamin N—becomes an inherited disease, an addiction passed from one generation to the next. This also explains why children who get too much of what they want rarely take proper care of anything they have. Why should they? After all, experience tells them that more is always on the way.

Children deserve better. They deserve to have parents attend to their needs for protection, affection, and direction. Beyond that: They deserve to hear their parents say "no" far more often than yes when it comes to their whimsical desires. They deserve to learn the value of constructive, creative effort as opposed to the value of effort expended whining, lying on the floor kicking and screaming, or playing one parent against the other. They deserve to learn that work is the only truly fulfilling way of getting anything of value in life, and that the harder they work, the more ultimately fulfilling the outcome.

In the process of trying to protect children from frustration, parents have turned reality upside down. A child raised in this topsy-turvy fashion may not have the skills needed to stand on his or her own two feet when the time comes to do so.

Rosemond concludes by offering this advice to parents: "Here's a simple rule: Turn your children's world right-side up by giving them all of what they truly need, but no more than twenty-five percent of what they simply want." He calls this the "Principle of Benign Deprivation" and suggests the most character-building two-letter word in the English language is No, Vitamin N. He says, "dispense it frequently. If you do you will be happier in the long run, and so will your child."[116] There can be little doubt of what Rosemond speaks goes a long way to explaining much of what is going on around us, but it is far from the complete picture. What is even more deficient is vitamins F and G, Faith and God. We have forgotten to feed our children daily doses of faith, infused with vitamin G. Without faith in God and the promise of eternal life our children's spiritual life is not fed and their souls suffer from a deficiency of those essential vitamins, F and G. It is often been said the best way to evangelize is to live the gospel every minute of our lives. Someone once said, "we can hardly think like Christians if we do not live like Christians" which seems obvious, yet what should be equally as obvious is "we cannot live like Christians if we do not think like Christians."

We owe everything to God. The measure with which we live for, with, and in God, the depth and frequency of our prayer, the openness to accept all he has planned for

---

116 John Rosemond, *Vitamin N*, Prager U.

us, our every moment behaviors and actions, these all reflect outwardly upon others, especially our children. Children are but mirrors of ourselves and what they reflect is all we do, say, and believe. If we say no to God, why should we expect our children to say anything different? If God is the center of your life, if you are filled with Vitamins F and G, your children will be properly nourished as well.

November 25, 2016

For What We Have
For those who have nothing

Those who have never wanted for anything so mundane as the next meal, warm clothing, or shelter from the weather have great difficulty finding compassion for those who have known nothing but endless want and emptiness. Their lack of compassion is seldom a product of inhumanity or cruel indifference, rather, for most, such poverty is simply inconceivable, beyond their ability to comprehend, beyond their experience.

In many ways, poverty as described in those classic books and films, such as Charles Dickens' *A Christmas Carol*, were of a time long past and no longer relevant in this age of plenty. What salves the conscience is the belief that those who are poor are simply too lazy or unwilling to work because of all the welfare programs. And while there is no doubt the cheat, the charlatan, and the freeloader, none such have ever been restricted to those who have nothing at all. Some would argue, quite correctly, those who have, are equally as apt to attend to such decadent behavior as those who have not.

Jesus told us "… you always have the poor with you, whenever you will, you can do good to them …" which ought to make us remember them in those moments when we give thanks for the bounty we have received. We must remember the poor and do good for them.

Enjoy your bountiful feast if you are so fortunate but do not forget those who have nothing. St. Gregory Nazianzen, 4th century Archbishop of Constantinople wrote "Give something, however small, to the one in need. For it is not small to one who has nothing. Neither is it small to God, if we have given what we could." Good words to remember and act upon.

Divine Enters Time
The Word became flesh

Some two-thousand years ago "the divine entered time in the womb of a virgin, and from that day forward the world was stripped of divinity, political existence was cut down to size, and emperors and kings, powers and potentates, were called to bend the knee before Bethlehem."[117]

This view of a divinity in time was anathema to classical paganism, not because pagan religious thought was opposed to gods existing in time. What rankled was the Christian claim there was only one God, who was outside of time, thus rendering false their multitudinous divinities who died and rose like the phoenix; ethereal and mythological creatures who were to be found in every household, ruling over such mundanities as gardens and household plants. Antiquity was full of religion, but it bent and used religion for its own ends. The Church would not bend or adjust its beliefs to pacify those who believed otherwise and was more than the powers-that-be could approve. Thus, the persecutions and slaughter of Christians ensued. No matter how bitter and vicious the persecutions became, Christians would neither deny nor refuse the reality which was the Incarnation. What differed the Christian from pagan was the truth of their faith. The pagan gods, their rituals and pieties meant much to pagan man, but at its core, the pagan knew it all was a sham, a fiction, an untruth. Even Cicero whispered "there were probably no gods at all, but we must never say so out loud. Without them Rome would collapse, and what counts is the city of Rome: in that we do believe."

Fast forward to modernity, to the heart of American society and culture. The obvious ties to ancient Rome can be seen throughout our neo-classical buildings, on our coins minted with the phrase "In God we trust," at public sessions and court proceedings where we affirm our belief in God by prayers and oaths foresworn, just as we pledge our allegiance to "one nation under God." Yet does this give proof to a Christian nation or something far less orthodox?

> If God became man, was incarnated in the womb of a virgin, then everything man did, has done, and will do, is totally changed. Everything moves forth from and returns to this shattering event. The Christian ethos means something to most Americans, and, even more, it means something to the corporate image that America has of itself. It is highly improbable, though, that this vague Christian sensibility converts itself into an affirmation of the truth of Christianity.

> To say that man by nature is religious is to say that by nature he is a pagan. He feasts on a surplus that must be consumed. He sacrifices solemnly in duly appointed places

---

[117] Frederick D. Wilhelmsen, *Christmas Means What It Is: The Incarnation utterly changed all reality*, Catholic Answers Magazine, November-December 2016, pp. 10-15. This article first appeared in this magazine (under the title *The Rock*) in 1991.

hallowed by tradition. He thus admits his dependence on powers and forces sensed by him to buoy him up in being. He blesses his young and guards his dead in well-kept cemeteries. He sets up statues to his heroes, and he sings songs remembering their deeds.

The Catholic Church has known this and embraced all of it. Thus, many of her enemies have called her pagan. But if this natural religiosity be equated formally with religion, then we would have to admit in all candor that Catholic Christianity is no religion at all. Based as it is not on what man does naturally as a religious being but on what God did freely for man, the faith proclaims the good news that Christ the Savior is born.[118]

Consider what it is we proclaim whenever we recite the Creed at Mass. Were we to pause to seriously contemplate the affirmation "the Word became flesh and dwelt among us" would we ever continue with the sacrifice of the Mass? It is, it was, the most singular event in the long history of man. Of all the religions of the world only Christianity claims to have begun from a single historical event: The Incarnation of the Son of God. Every truth, every doctrine, every dogma of the Christian faith is predicated on this orthodoxy: God the Father, so loved the world that he sent his only begotten Son to save us from our sins and open the gates of heaven to us once again.

The other great religions tend to dissolve in speculations about what their founders meant, upon truths they taught, upon dimensions of the real beyond themselves but discovered in their lives. But our Lord did not say: "I have the truth." He said, "I am the truth (and the way, and the life)." This separates Christ from all myths and mystifications. He stands before all history as the God-Man who says, "Accept me or reject me."

God is. Christ is, first as the eternal Son of the Father, himself God in all his glory, and then as Jesus in a manger, true man born of the Virgin. We affirm all these truths in the creed. To take these propositions literally is to undo everything that previously was in the order of nature. The world is turned upside down, transfigured, altogether itself yet so much more.

The God who names himself "I Am" is the same God who is in the manger on Christmas. The Catholic Faith begins and ends with a God who in every sense is Creator of the world that is, making each and every thing be at this very moment in time. An assertion of the priority of existence runs through the most basic catechism taught youngsters when they are first introduced to the Faith.

The world has seldom admitted to the Incarnation, for in doing so it must necessarily admit to the severe poverty of the creature that is man. Just as in the beginning, man continues to believe gods are what we make of them, they are creatures made in our image and likeness and thus hold no special power over us but exist to do our bidding.

Jesus Christ is God, the Word become flesh, and he was born and lived among us, sharing in our humanity, showing us the way to our heavenly Father. "Theologians tell us that when he hung there those three hours, in which mankind was redeemed,

---

[118] Frederick D. Wilhemsen, *Christmas Means What It is*, p. 13-14.

he summed up all existence—both human and cosmic—in which all time came together in a supreme moment of salvation and the tears of history, from its first beginning to its final end in judgment, were wiped away by the incarnate Author of all that is."[119]

Christmas is the time to acknowledge the power and the glory Christ, our Savior. Let us rejoice and be glad.

For the Love of All
Encountering a life that loved

Two weeks ago, as I was reflecting on the life of a very special human being, what came immediately to mind was the memory of a man who lived to love and loved to live a life of love for the love of life. While this may seem trite or saccharine, nothing could be further from the truth.

Traveling to the Midwest for the Thanksgiving holiday, normally a happy and relaxing time with family and friends, the news of my brother-in-law Dave's passing, while not entirely unanticipated, was nevertheless saddening. Yet, over the ensuing days, in preparing for his funeral, the grief palpable, deep and aching, there was never a disparaging word expressed for a man of seventy-seven years.

At his funeral service I said if we were to see Dave through the eyes of God, here is what I believe we would see, love. It wasn't that Dave loved my sister Elizabeth although he loved her more than life itself. His last words to her were of how much he loved her. It wasn't that Dave loved his family, although he loved them indeed. It wasn't that he loved Elizabeth's family; he loved them as his own. No, Dave loved much more than that. His love was bigger than that. While I had known him but a brief portion of our lives, I have encountered very few who loved so completely, so unreservedly, so fully.

I loved the man. I loved him for the deep devotion and unabashed love he had for my sister. Seldom do we find such love. I loved him for his faith in God, of which we shared much over the years. When diagnosed with cancer he never lost faith, rather he looked to God and prayed "Lord, increase my faith." I loved him for his quiet ways, perhaps it was from his many years on the bench, for he always appeared to be listening in silent contemplation, absorbing all the joy from those around him; he fed on

---

[119] Frederick D. Wilhemsen, *Christmas Means What It is*, p. 15.

their laughter, he drank of their friendship, he grew young through their exuberance. Dave is with God and their love will never die.

What's This Tradition?
The source of truth

The Catholic Church teaches, and we believe the fullness of divine revelation was revealed to the apostles through and in Jesus Christ and that they in turn handed it on to their successors. Jesus commanded the apostles and their successors to teach and preach to all the nations everything that he had taught. In Mark, we read he said to the apostles: "Go into all the world and preach the gospel to the whole creation" (Mk 16:15). Jesus did not tell the apostles to write the Gospel, but to preach it, which means to transmit orally the teaching they received. Likewise, in Matthew, Jesus gave them a missionary commission when he said, "All authority in heaven and on earth has been given to me. Go therefore and make disciples of all nations, baptizing them in the name of the Father and of the Son and of the Holy Spirit, teaching them to observe all that I have commanded you; and lo, I am with you always, to the close of the age" (Mt 28:18-20). This is what the Church refers to as apostolic Tradition. How God has chosen to reveal himself has long been a subject of theological debate and controversy both inside and outside the Church for this is not your typical tradition. Tradition, as generally understood, is the transmission of customs or beliefs from generation to generation. In a limited sense, this remains true, but Tradition, with a capital T, means much more.

God, in his infinite wisdom, has chosen to reveal himself through two complementary forms: oral and written. "Revelation passed on through oral means and through the whole life of the People of God is called divine Tradition, while Sacred Scripture is the inspired communication of God's Word in writing."[120] Through Tradition and Scripture God's Revelation has been and continues to be handed down through the ages. Tradition has been a part of God's plan from the beginning, an essential part of God's salvific Word. Oral Tradition is not a recent innovation but has preceded, even paralleled the written Word. Through Moses, the prophets, and others the Old Testament was passed on orally before it was written down. Likewise, truths revealed by Christ were passed on orally by the apostles and their successors before they were put down in writing. "This transmission will continue until the end of the world because of Jesus's promise that He will remain with them until the end of time. Thus, the Tradition that is imparted by the Apostles and their successors is a living Tradition, bringing each new generation of disciples into vital contact with Christ and His Gospel."[121]

---

[120] Lawrence Feingold, *Faith Comes From What Is Heard: An Introduction to Fundamental Theology*, (Steubenville: Emmaus Academic, 2016), 206.
[121] Lawrence Feingold, *Faith Comes From What Is Heard*, 194.

Tradition was defined as a dogma of faith at the Council of Trent to counter Protestantism's denial of Tradition as a source of Revelation, leaving Scripture (*sola Scriptura*) as the only certain source of faith and morals.

> "The holy, ecumenical and general Council of Trent … clearly perceives that these truths and instruction [of the Gospel] are contained in the written books and in the unwritten traditions, which, received by the Apostles from the mouth of Christ Himself, or from the Apostles themselves, the Holy Spirit dictating, have come down to us, transmitted as it were from hand to hand. Following, then, the examples of the orthodox Fathers, it receives and venerates with piety and reverence all the books both of the Old and New Testaments, since one God is the author of both; also the traditions, whether they relate to faith or to morals, as having been dictated either orally by Christ or by the Holy Spirit, and preserved in the Catholic Church in unbroken succession.[122]

Tradition is necessary for the Church in all times for many reasons. First, oral Tradition is chronologically prior to Sacred Scripture, both in the Old and in the New Testaments.

> God revealed Himself to our first parents, to Noah, to Abraham, Isaac, Jacob, and Joseph, but the Revelation was only written down many centuries later in Genesis. Even the great prophets first taught orally. Their prophecies were put together and written down later. Similarly, in the New Testament, the decisive Revelation is the Person of Jesus and His words and actions, especially the Paschal mystery. This was transmitted orally by the Apostles for the first generation of the Church's life. In both covenants, oral Tradition was present from the beginning and was written down in inspired form only at a later date. This shows that the living and spoken word is the first means chosen by God to reveal Himself.[123]

Second, without Tradition, Scripture is a dead letter, having no key for interpretation.

> Without Tradition, it would be impossible to defend the faith against heretics who cite Scripture against its true meaning. The Fathers and Doctors easily detected the presence of heresy because it clashed with their sense of the living Tradition. The fragmentation of the Protestant world into thousands of branches is a demonstration of what would happen to the Church if she were stripped of her authoritative Tradition.[124]

Third, Tradition contains truths not explicitly found within the pages of Scripture. This is evidenced by the conclusion in the Gospel of John: "But there are also many other things which Jesus did; were every one of them to be written, I suppose that the world itself could not contain the books that would be written" (Jn 21:25). Obviously, John taught many truths that were never written down but handed on orally; truths which were faithfully guarded and transmitted by the first bishops, the successors of the Apostles. "Not all revealed truths are found explicitly in the Bible, and therefore

---

[122] Council of Trent, Session 4 (1546), in DS, 1501.
[123] Lawrence Feingold, *Faith Comes From What Is Heard*, 201.
[124] Lawrence Feingold, *Faith Comes From What Is Heard*, 201.

the Church can define dogmas of faith on the basis of her Tradition and what is only implicit in Scripture. For example, the Assumption of Our Lady is not narrated explicitly in Scripture, but was defined as dogma on the basis of the living Tradition. ... Another example is the canon of Scripture. No text of Scripture teaches which are the true books of the Bible. The canon of Scripture is known by the Church only through Tradition, confirmed by the Magisterium."[125]

Even when a truth of faith is contained directly in Scripture, Tradition is necessary as a witness of the correct interpretation. Thus, truths can be defined solely on the basis of Tradition (although with the aid of what is implicit in Scripture), but never on the basis of Scripture alone without Tradition. The two form an organic unity and together are "like a mirror in which the pilgrim Church on earth looks at God, from whom she has received everything, until she is brought finally to see Him as He is, face to Face. ... For Sacred Scripture is the Word of God inasmuch as it is consigned to writing under the inspiration of the divine Spirit, while Sacred Tradition takes the Word of God entrusted by Christ the Lord and the Holy Spirit to the Apostles, and hands it on to their successors in its full purity, so that led by the light of the Spirit of Truth, they may, in proclaiming it, preserve this word of God faithfully, explain it, and make it more widely known."[126]

December 09, 2016

Failure is Not an Option
It is of absolute necessity

Growing up used to be a necessity, often far sooner than one might wish it, for no other reason than survival. I can still recall being told of a distant relative who, at the age of five, sold matches and wasn't allowed to come home until he had sold all he had. It was not cruelty that compelled his parents to send such a young lad out each day, it was necessity, for everyone had to contribute for there to be enough money to eat.

I can also recall first reading of the adventures of Peter Pan, the boy who would not grow up. It was not that Peter could not grow up. No, Peter simply refused to do so. Peter was a boastful and careless boy, a symbol of the selfishness of childhood, forgetful, self-centered, nonchalant, and fearlessly cocky. The author J. M. Barrie wrote of Peter that when he thought he was going to die on Marooners' Rock, he was scared,

---

[125] Lawrence Feingold, *Faith Comes From What Is Heard*, 203.
[126] Second Vatican Council, *Dei Verbum*, §7, §9.

yet he felt only one shudder. With this blithe attitude Peter says, "To die will be an awfully big adventure." As for Peter's unending youth, Barrie explained Peter must forget his own adventures as well as anything he learns about the realities of the world in order to stay childlike. Somedays it seems as though this country has become Neverland with an ever-increasing number of Peter Pans and lost boys (and girls) flitting around in childish ignorance, ever forgetful, refusing to grow up. Maturation is thus blissfully denied for what fun is there in adulthood? Sadly, too many are well beyond their childhood to the point Neverland is where they do now permanently reside. Reality is but a figment, maturity unsought, reason disdained, repulsive to their childish minds; their only thought: to think not at all. They care not for tomorrow for today is all that matters. Solipsism is their unacknowledged philosophy; their first principle is this: the truth about truth is there is no truth; all truths are mere claims. They believe only in themselves because all else is but a ghost within their minds. G. K. Chesterton describes those who believe in themselves as madmen.

> Shall I tell you where the men are who believe most in themselves? For I can tell you. I know of men who believe in themselves more colossally than Napoleon or Caesar. I know where flames the fixed star of certainty and success. I can guide you to the thrones of the Super-men. The men who really believe in themselves are all in lunatic asylums. … If you consulted your business experience instead of your ugly individualistic philosophy, you would know that believing in himself is one of the commonest signs of a rotter. … It would be much truer to say that a man will certainly fail, because he believes in himself. Complete self-confidence is not merely a sin; complete self-confidence is a weakness. Believing utterly in one's self is a hysterical and superstitious belief.

> Modern masters of science are much impressed with the need of beginning all inquiry with a fact. The ancient masters of religion were quite equally impressed with that necessity. They began with the fact of sin—a fact as practical as potatoes. … But certain religious leaders …, not mere materialists, have begun in our day not to deny the highly disputable water, but to deny the indisputable dirt. Certain new theologians dispute original sin, which is the only part of Christian theology which can really be proved. … The strongest saints and the strongest skeptics alike took positive evil as the starting-point of their argument. If it be true (as it certainly is) that a man can feel exquisite happiness in skinning a cat, then the religious philosopher can only draw one of two deductions. He must either deny the existence of God, as all atheists do; or he must deny the present union between God and man, as all Christians do. The new theologians seem to think it a highly rationalistic solution to deny the cat.

> In this remarkable situation it is plainly not now possible (with any hope of a universal appeal) to start, as our fathers did, with the fact of sin. This very fact which was to them (and is to me) as plain as a pikestaff, is the very fact that has been specially diluted or denied. … I mean that all thoughts and theories were once judged by whether they tended to make a man lose his soul, so for our present purpose all modern thoughts and theories may be judged by whether they tend to make a man lose his wits.

In short, oddities only strike ordinary people. Oddities do not strike odd people. This is why ordinary people have a much more exciting time; while odd people are always complaining of the dullness of life.[127]

Frank Cronin ruefully reports on the demise of orthodoxy. "Orthodoxy doesn't matter. And it hasn't for decades. It has become a word foreign to modern ears, an idea meaningless to modern minds, a body of practical ideas and principles with no real practicality or significance, except as a predictable means of inciting controversy and conflict or fostering intolerance and bigotry."[128] The very nature of "orthodoxy" is one of conclusion, of assertion about the way things are, not as we might prefer them or choose them to be. This of course is radically antithetical to the modern relativistic mind: to believe in a set of ideas and to assert those ideas are objectively and factually true. Such orthodoxy is simply unbelievable, a modern heresy, an act of prejudice. Cronin says it is very easy to test this.

> Just tell any modern person Catholic orthodoxy is true — objectively, factually, rationally and scientifically true. They will either be incredulous that you could be so naïve or stupid to think the Catholic faith is actually true or they will be angry that you could be so arrogant as to believe Catholic orthodoxy is actually true.

> In fact, to moderns, all orthodoxies are acts of bigotry by virtue of the simple act of asserting a claim of objective truth. For actual and factual truth is inherent to the very idea of real orthodoxy. And all that type of thinking and the very content of orthodox thought itself is outside our modern truth paradigm.

> Our modern way of thinking presumes there are no real right answers. Modern minds perceive any and all such orthodoxies as merely claims, beliefs and nothing more.

Logic and reason are no longer relevant to the modern way of thinking; thus, such a mind sees no contradiction in their illogical and nonsensical assertion that: the truth is there is no truth. One can only wonder where such lunacy was first implanted in their never-never-minds. Perhaps it is Chesterton who offers the most plausible cause of modern thinking (or lack thereof). "Poetry is sane because it floats easily in an infinite sea; reason seeks to cross the infinite sea, and so make it finite. The result is mental exhaustion, …. To accept everything is an exercise, to understand everything a strain. The poet only desires exaltation and expansion, a world to stretch himself in. The poet only asks to get his head into the heavens. It is the logician who seeks to get the heavens into his head. And it is his head that splits." Chesterton believed (and rightly so) that the modern mind moves in a perfect but small circle, a circle while quite as infinite as a large one, yet not as large. For instance, a marble is as round as the world, but it is not the world. He writes "we may say that the strongest and most unmistakable mark

[127] G. K. Chesterton, *Orthodoxy*, 1908, 4-5.
[128] Frank Cronin, *Orthodoxy, Heresy and Objective Truth*, National Catholic Register, November 27, 2016, 11-12.

of madness is this combination between a logical completeness and a spiritual contraction." To explain, he speaks of a madman who would call himself Christ.

> If we said what we felt, we should say, "So you are the Creator and Redeemer of the world: but what a small world it must be! What a little heaven you must inhabit, with angels no bigger than butterflies! How sad it must be to be God; and an inadequate God! Is there really no life fuller and no love more marvelous than yours; and is it really in your small and painful pity that all flesh must put its faith? How much happier you would be, how much more of you there would be, if the hammer of a higher God could smash your small cosmos, scattering the stars like spangles, and leave you in the open, free like other men to look up as well as down!"

> If the man is the real God, he is not much of a god. And similarly, if the cosmos of the materialist is the real cosmos, it is not much of a cosmos. The thing has shrunk. The deity is less divine than many men; and the whole of life is something much more grey, narrow, and trivial than many separate aspects of it. The parts seem greater than the whole.

> For we must remember that the materialist philosophy (whether true or not) is certainly much more limiting than any religion. In one sense, of course, all intelligent ideas are narrow. They cannot be broader than themselves. A Christian is only restricted in the same sense that an atheist is restricted. He cannot think Christianity false and continue to be a Christian; and the atheist cannot think atheism false and continue to be an atheist.

The ordinary man Chesterton describes as a mystic, with one foot on earth and the other in fairyland. Such souls are free to doubt their gods and free to believe in them. "If he saw two truths that seemed to contradict each other, he would take the two truths and the contradiction along with them. His spiritual sight is stereoscopic, like his physical sight: he sees two different pictures at once and yet sees all the better for that. ... Thus he believed that children were indeed the kingdom of heaven, but nevertheless ought to be obedient to the kingdom of earth. He admired youth because it was young and age because it was not." Such disturbing insight from a century past remains relevant to our time and place. So much madness, so much insanity. So much anger, hatred and violence. So little peace.

> Mick Jagger is old enough to be the grandfather of a good number of the protestors who have taken to the streets following the major presidential upset. ... Maybe they've never heard of the rock star—or the Rolling Stones for that matter. But it's about time to sit those folks down—along with much of the blatantly biased secular press, a fairly long list of political pundits, and lawmakers who are still in a total meltdown mode now weeks after the election—and inform them, as one of the classic Stones' tunes explains, that guess what? You can't always get what you want.

> It's one thing to peacefully practice our First Amendment rights. There's nothing wrong with marching or rallying to raise awareness about an issue. ... But what we've seen since Nov. 8 has crossed into recklessness and lawlessness by people old enough to know better.

> Not only are adults taking part in the violent acts that have occurred during some of the ... protests, but in many ways, they're adding to the problems by encouraging the

ridiculously bad behavior, keeping silent about it and in some cases even using our tax dollars to coddle those who just can't deal with reality of defeat.[129]

One Iowa State legislator has introduced what he calls the "'Suck it up, Buttercup' bill" which would cut budgets at public colleges and universities that are spending extra money on students upset over the presidential election. This same legislator remarked, "I've seen four or five schools in other states that have established 'cry zones' … staffed by state grief counselors, and kids come and cry out their sensitivity to the election results. This is what a lot of people have been thinking, knowing this is not how life works at all." Where is the mature understanding that hurt, and disappointment are a big part of life? The concern most often expressed: if you are of such a mind, still childishly living in Neverland, then when adversity stares you in the face you will have convinced yourself all you have to do is simply press the reality "pause" button. Unfortunately, at some point there will no longer be someone around to hug and coddle you and provide "safe zones" and surrogates to assure you everything will be ok. One day you will wake up and be hit with a very painful slap to the face. Reality provides no timeouts, no rewinds, no resets, no pauses. There comes a time, call it adulthood, when we must all grow up and leave Neverland. The madness of it all is palpable and real. It also, sadly, is neither a new phenomenon nor is it limited to the young—although young college students seemingly comprise a major portion of the most visible and worst affected. In addition to students, the secular press, political pundits, and lawmakers—and I would add academic elites and Hollywood glitterati— collectively have experienced a total meltdown, refusing to leave their Neverland asylum.

The *zeitgeist* of privilege and entitlement which now permeates our society, from highbrow to low rent, threatens the heart and soul of the nation. Questions abound as to how such a surfeit of angst, anger and irrational fear could have so suddenly and so virulently infested the social fabric of our nation. There are no easy answers; solutions have proven as elusive as the yeti and bigfoot. Yet, it may well be possible to begin to look toward ourselves to ponder and to well-consider what it is we have wrought. We cannot place the burden of blame on nameless, faceless others, although we may well wish to do so, for that only serves to perpetuate and strengthen the infection. Unintentional though it may have been, each of us has become a carrier, unwittingly in most cases, spreading the infection by our words and actions. As parents and adults, we are responsible for preparing our children to become productive adults, to teach them of the world, God, faith and morality, and to show them how to succeed in life. Yet far too many of us have abrogated our responsibilities as parents and guardians of the next generation. And in our failure to treat our children as children and thus guide them toward maturity we have created a monstrous society of self-indulgent, self-

---

[129] Teresa Tomeo, *Eye on Culture: Dose of Reality,* Our Sunday Visitor, December 4, 2016, 17.

centered, unhappy Peter Pans who have not the skills necessary to grow up and leave childhood behind.

Family psychologist John Rosemond describes one aspect of the problem in telling a true story of a 14-year-old girl, an only child, and her parents in a typical white-collar home.

It is the summer of 2016, and said young teen is between eighth grade and her first year of high school. One hot and humid summer day she tells her parents she does not want to go to the high school in her district because her friends, all of who play (as does she) on the same elite athletic squad, are going to go to a high school some twenty miles away in another county. She informs her parents she wants to go to Twenty-Mile High. After much yelling, crying, gnashing of teeth, threats, resentment and guilt, the parents put their home on the market, promptly sell it and move to the Twenty-Mile High district. And everyone lives happily ever after or until said child's next outrageous demand, whichever comes first.

What is it like, wonders a person who was denied such privilege as a child, to be 14 years old and in complete control of one's family, to be able to throw a tantrum and thus cause one's parents to pick up and relocate? What is it like to be a Big Deal at age 14? What sort of adulthood (in the chronological sense of the term only) does this portend?

The answers are, in order: weird, strange and unhappy. Concerning weird and strange, it must be noted the children in question lack a proper frame of reference. They have no way of knowing what a legitimate childhood is like, including being no Big Deal. Therefore, they are (to borrow from their vernacular) clueless. Because the Big Deal child is ubiquitous, they do not know their childhoods are weird and strange from a normal, albeit outmoded, point of view.

But the real problem, not just for them but the rest of us as well, is the strong likelihood they will never experience sustained contentment as adults. … I have long noticed that a good number of children now known as millennials seem to believe a life without drama is a life without meaning. And so, because life is not drama, they manufacture it out of the mundane. Every insult is cause for drama. Every conflict is cause for drama. Every disappointment is cause for drama. Every bump in the road is cause for drama. This is the inevitable consequence of a childhood high on indulgence and short on reality.[130]

Another related aspect comes from a recent article by Katie Coombs who wrote of millennials and how entitled they have become. Stereotypically they are more often than not pictured "sitting in their parents' basement playing Xbox and eating nacho flavored Doritos. They are the first generation truly impacted by the smart phone and its ability to take away social interaction. They were the first to grow up with the trophies-and-ribbons-for-everyone mentality, and they are confused. Some of them have graduated from college and are having difficulty finding jobs. … There are some adults in their twenties struggling from a combination of being handed too much from their

---

[130] John Rosemond, *Avoid 'Big Fish' illusion when parenting*, Reno Gazette Journal, December 7, 2016, 3C.

parents and always being told they were amazing in all of their activities."[131] Coombs writes of the first time she let her daughter fail. Torn between helping her on a school project in order to get an A or allowing her to complete the project on her own and get a C, she chose the latter. She said when her daughter came home with the C she asked her mother why she had let that happen, to which she replied "Why did you let it happen?" Coombs goes on to say, she knows "so many people who would have fixed the project for their children, or even worse, completed the entire project for them."

> We have all seen the science fair projects completed by Mom and Dad. What is the lesson in that? That you can only succeed if someone helps you? That you are better off winning by cheating than you are losing with your own best effort? Isn't the feeling of losing the exact motivation our children need to grow and improve?

> I do not have homework when my children do. It is 100 percent their responsibility, and if they can't complete it, I encourage them to seek out their own solutions. If they expect Mommy or Daddy to be the solution every time, the only result will be a future adult who can't truly function in society. You must let your children fall—hard sometimes. You must let them fail, which means they will feel pain and get an occasional, emotional bruise. These bruises form their conviction and their passion for success.

Failure is not an option. Rather, it is an absolute necessity for success. If we ever hope to stem the madness, we must allow our children to fail.

December 16, 2016

A Saint for Geeks?
Aiming for the infinite

The stereotypical computer geek, the one often depicted in film and books, resides in isolation surrounded by a plethora of computer equipment and almost always depicted as disheveled, hyperactive, suffering from manic paranoia, and completely antisocial. Definitely not the image of a saint. While there are those who would fit the stereotype, they are fortunately few and far between. I say this with a certain degree of confidence having over thirty years of high-technology experience. Recently I came across an article which spoke of a young computer genius who died of leukemia in 2006 at the age of 15. On November 24, 2016, Cardinal Angelo Scola closed the diocesan phase in the canonization process for Italian teenager Carlo Acutis, a gifted computer geek, considered a genius by adults with computer engineering degrees.

---

[131] Katie Coombs, *Our kids must fail to succeed*, Reno Gazette Journal, December 3, 2016, 1-2D.

Yet, as gifted as he was, his brief life was always centered on Christ. He once said, "To always be close to Jesus, that's my life plan." Carlo attended Mass every day, he remained close to Jesus in whatever he did, whether praying in front of the Blessed Sacrament for hours, creating websites, or going to school like every other teenager. His mother said, "His immense generosity made him interested in everyone: the foreigners, the handicapped, children, beggars. To be close to Carlo was to be close to a fountain of fresh water… [he] understood the true value of life as a gift from God, as an effort, an answer to give to the Lord Jesus day by day in simplicity. I should stress that he was a normal boy who was joyful, serene, sincere, and helpful and loving company, he liked having friends." Carlo believed "All people are born as originals but many die as photocopies," for to die as an "original" was to be guided by Christ, and to look at Him constantly.

When Carlo was 11 years old, he began a project of cataloguing all of the Eucharistic miracles of the world. He wrote at the time, "The more Eucharist we receive, the more we will become like Jesus, so that on this earth we will have a foretaste of Heaven." He asked his parents to take him to all the places where Eucharistic miracles had occurred and two and a half years later, he had completed his project. In all, Carlo researched and documented over "Eucharistic miracles that occurred over the centuries in different countries around the world and have been acknowledged by the Church." He created a website which contains a virtual museum containing all his research and findings. In addition, he created panel presentations which have been displayed around the world. According to the introductory panel, "In the United States alone, thanks to assistance from the Knights of Columbus, The Cardinal Newman Society and The Real Presence Association and Education, with the support of Cardinal Raymond L. Burke, it has been hosted in thousands of parishes and more than 100 universities." The panels have been displayed on all five continents and have inspired many by their amazing photographs and beautiful stories.

He remains an inspiration, especially to teenagers who aren't sure whether they could be both holy and "normal" and individually unique. While he may have led a devout prayer life — he went to Mass everyday — Carlo was very much interested in being a teenager in the 21st century. While his interests were very broad, he also found time to volunteer for work with children and the elderly for, as he said, "Our aim has to be the infinite and not the finite. The Infinite is our homeland. We have always been expected in Heaven."

OMG (Oh My God for those unfamiliar with text shorthand)! The maturity and holiness expressed by such a young man is difficult to comprehend yet goes well beyond inspirational. It is truly awe-inspiring and deeply humbling. What inspiration and truth are the words of Carlo Acutis, a teenage computer prodigy and genuinely saintly human being. "Our aim has to be the infinite and not the finite. The Infinite is our homeland. We have always been expected in Heaven." Seldom have I read anything so profound. I cannot help but believe this: if each of us were to look deep into our souls and reflect on how near or far away we are in accepting the wisdom of those words, spoken by a teenage computer geek, we would see the world as it should be, a finite respite on the journey to our infinite homeland, where we are expected with eager anticipation. The finite is fleeting, the Infinite awaits.

The next stage in the canonization process is to send all the biographical works accumulated to Rome to be reviewed by the Congregation for the Causes of the Saints. If approved, the cause for Carlo Acutis will proceed and the Holy Father can declare him to be "venerable."

Sticks and Stones ...
And words can really hurt

Ever are such wondrous things which God has made for such good purpose; the hand of man has much abused. Never has there been a time so dark and cold and yet it is the same as yesteryear and before. The mind sees what the eyes cannot and yet the past is left forgotten, corrupted by the maggots of empty thoughts and selfishness. Sweet pleasant dreams of golden days are but dreams which never were, for man has better thoughts of paradise.

Jesus said "Let the one among you who is without sin be the first to throw a stone" (Jn 8:7) yet how little do we remember his words. We certainly pay small heed to them for we seldom consider ourselves sinners. We may not toss stones at one another or beat someone with a stick but then sticks and stones are not the only way pain can be inflicted upon another. An old adage, often used in a questionable attempt to persuade children to ignore taunts and teasing goes "sticks and stones may break my bones, but words will never hurt me." While perhaps true with respect to breaking bones, words can and often do inflict pain and cause suffering, even harsher or crueler than that which might result from stoning or lashing with a stick. The scars may last far longer, although unseen, hidden deep within, invisible to all but the one so cruelly scarred. Words can inflict mortal wounds, no less deadly than the stone or stick. And all too common, words are used to warp the mind, harden the heart, and kill the spirit, a tragedy so great, yet beyond the notice of all but God. The means of our own demise will not come from instruments constructed to forever still the hearts of men nor will it be by brutal forces hell bent on complete annihilation. No, it will be by our thoughts—or rather the abdication of our minds to think, to reason, and to pray— which will destroy what God has so wonderfully made.

God created all manner of creatures, big and small, yet only in man did he favor with an immortal soul, a mind so constructed for reasoned thought, free will to make independent choices, and the desire to know and love him. Throughout the course of human history, man has seldom used those gifts for their true purpose, which was for the glory and honor of God. Man's gift of mind, of independent and creative thought, has atrophied, is atrophying still, to the point where reason has either been lost or casually discarded, replaced by unreason, mindlessness, and selfish egocentric sensibilities. In short, we have lost or are rapidly losing the ability to think beyond our selves, to seek the truth no matter which direction the compass points.

We use words now as weapons: not to kill but to destroy, not to describe but to defame, not to love but to hate, not to hope but to despair, not to build up but to tear down. Fact has been replaced by opinion, objective truth has become subjective, rational thought has been displaced by the irrational, meaning no longer has meaning, life is not worth living, death is but the end, man has created god. The young especially, inculcated by progressive ideological views largely devoid of historical facts, ask why many of an older generation fail to understand and accept their own worldview. They cannot or are unwilling to admit their perspective is seriously flawed, based not on objective reality but on progressive utopian groupthink. They cannot see that which they have been taught may be untrue or some distortion of the truth. It is past time they learned the truth and the truth shall set them free. God gave each a mind to know the truth, so use it well.

God Descends to Man
So man can ascend to God

It is difficult to imagine a time without Christmas and yet we know once upon a time the world knew nothing of him, for far more of history has gone before than after. But there came a night when God condescended to become man, so we might ascend to him. How fortunate then are we to know and to have received the gift of Jesus, that most precious of gifts, God's only Son.

We live each year anew, enjoying the gifts of life and love and so much more, yet how seldom do we pause to kneel in gratitude for all we have and have received? Tradition says there will be mistletoe and presents beneath a tree, song and laughter with family and friends, cards and letters, phone calls and packages, cold mornings and snow, sleigh bells and warm fires, and stockings hung by the chimney with care. Memories of bright shiny packages, each tied with a bow, anticipating, wondering, what would they bestow. All this is good yet how we forget, without Jesus on Christmas, no Christmas we'd get. Each day is a new day, a pearl of great price; do we pause, do we pray, do we ever think twice, of the one gift he sent us, so precious and small, the greatest gift ever, given for all. There is not a gift greater than his, and yet we are wanting more every year, so this year for Christmas let us pause and reflect on all we have and never forget how much we are loved by the One who is Love, who came down from heaven on a night long ago to bring joy, hope, and Christmas for his children below.

May the joy and peace of our Lord Jesus Christ be with each and every one of you this Christmas and may Almighty God descend upon you and remain with you forever. Merry Christmas, everyone.

Angels We Have Heard
From the mouths of angels

We are familiar with the narrative from Luke of the nativity, the birth of Jesus and how circumstances resulted in him being wrapped in swaddling clothes and laid in a manger. We are also familiar with the shepherds to whom an angel of the Lord appeared proclaiming the good news that a savior had been born who is Christ and Lord. And then suddenly a multitude of heavenly host appeared with the angel praising God. Throughout ancient history, there are many instances of angels appearing, messengers of God, such as to Mary announcing to her she was to be the mother of the Son of God. We know God created angels, but we know little else concerning them. So, in order to find out more about angels, what better than to turn to a few of the smallest angels for some answers.

Why do angels wear halos?

Angel Olive, age 6: Everybody's got it all wrong. Angels don't wear halos anymore. I forget why, but scientists are working on it.

How are angels created?

Angel Matthew, age 6: It's not easy to become an angel! First, you die. Then you go to Heaven, and then there's still the flight training to go through. And then you got to agree to wear those angel clothes.

Do Angels work?

Angel Mitchell, age 7: Angels work for God and watch over kids when God has to go do something else.

Is that what guardian angels do?

Angel Henry, age 8: My guardian angel helps me with math, but he's not much good for science.

What do angels eat?

Angel Jack, age 6: Angels don't eat, but they drink milk from Holy Cows!!!

Do angels talk?

Angel Daniel, age 9: Angels talk all the way while they're flying you up to heaven. The main subject is where you went wrong before you got dead.

Do angels ever get angry?

Angel Reagan, age 10: When an angel gets mad, he takes a deep breath and counts to ten. And when he lets out his breath again, somewhere there's a tornado.

Are angels busy all the time or do they ever get time off?

Angel Sara, age 6: Angels have a lot to do and they keep very busy. If you lose a tooth, an angel comes in through your window and leaves money under your pillow. Then when it gets cold, angels go south for the winter.

Where do angels live?

Angel Jared, age 8: Angels live in cloud houses made by God and his Son, who's a very good carpenter.

Are there boy and girl angels?

Angel Antonio, age 9: All angels are girls because they gotta wear dresses and boys didn't go for it.

Have you ever met or seen an angel?

Angel Ashley, age 9: My angel is my grandma who died last year. She got a big head start on helping me while she was still down here on earth.

Do angels watch over animals?

Angel Vicki, age 8: Some of the angels are in charge of helping heal sick animals and pets. And if they don't make the animals get better, they help the child get over it.

What don't you understand about angels?

Angel Sarah, age 7: What I don't get about angels is why, when someone is in love, they shoot arrows at them.

Your Journey of Faith
To be young and Catholic

Christmas awakens the somnolent soul from dreams of hope for a resurgent faith. While the world seems to endlessly wallow in manmade quagmires of hatred and violence, death and despair, materialism and secularism, hope grows at times in the most unlikely of places. Recently, in the aftermath of a shooting of a 14-year old knife-wielding high school student, another student from the same high school spoke to fellow students in his AP English class. Here is a portion of his speech:

> ...our generation is stagnant; we're attracted to selling ourselves short and lowballing our goals like metal to a magnet. We are OK with kind of wanting to succeed, kind of putting

in effort, kind of caring for each other, kind of being nice and, from my understanding, this means you will kind of live.

Have we really become this society? This bitter, rude, illogical generation that takes the definition of indecency to a new level. Each battle has its own devils but in our situation are we the serpent that feeds Adam and Eve from the tree? We must address this issue not from the root but from the seed, we were raised this way, watching shows where the cue to laugh was at an insult. ...

I myself am guilty, not for taking these actions but being a bystander, if you are not part of the solution you are part of the problem. I task the bystanders to become involved, to put an end to this virus. We will create a generation where there is no tolerance for such words. There are some who are bulletproof to such terms, but there are those who feel that at school and online it is hunting season and they are birds. ... To those birds, do not go gentle into that good night, for you only need to fly higher, elevate your mind to where barrages of insulting bullets do not dare climb. To the shooter of insults, the killer of dreams, the murderer of self-esteem, are you paid to be rude? Do you feel dominant taking these inhuman, primitive actions? It is 2016 and the idea of dominance is obsolete, that ideology is no more useful than flies on meat. We are not paid to be rude so we might as well be nice. It is easier to respect and have manners in life.

...we must begin with breeding positivity instead of making matters worse. When you join this battle "do not fear, for I am with you" (Isaiah 41:10). In order to create a kind positive life, we must learn to be kind and positive towards each other.[132]

An article written for the National Catholic Register points to a growing number of college students whose journey of faith has continued despite the often-anti-Christian secular environment. One young woman, Aurora Griffin, "was on a mission — a Catholic mission — while at Harvard University."

The author of the recently released *How I Stayed Catholic at Harvard* was Rhodes Scholar and *magna cum laude*, Phi Beta Kappa graduate of the Ivy League. During her time at Harvard, she wrote for *The Harvard Crimson*, served as president of the *Catholic Student Association* and took the lead in having the "black mass" canceled on campus. "For all of us, there are moments that come to define who we are in the public eye. Fighting the black mass was one of these for me, as was writing a pro-life op-ed in The Harvard Crimson."

Another young woman, Barbara Soares, who earned her undergraduate and master's degrees from Montclair University and her doctorate from Columbia University offered:

I've been a Catholic science major in secular institutions for most of my life, and I've had my share of challenges as both a student and researcher. Still, each challenge gave me the opportunity to attain a deeper understanding of my faith and, as such, ultimately made me a stronger defender of my faith.

---

[132] Victor Arriaga Medina, *Choose Kind*, Reno Gazette Journal, Dec. 11, 2016, 1E.

She offers this advice to Catholic students in challenging environments: "Keep growing. Take 10-15 minutes a day for a podcast, homily transcript or YouTube video to learn the rich history and vibrant life of the faith you profess. The more you know, the stronger your faith will grow in even the most secular environment. Don't ever stop learning about your faith.[133]

December 30, 2016

Doctrine of Progress
Just call it what it is—the Fall

The late great English writer and convert to Catholicism G. K. Chesterton was often referred to as the "prince of paradox." Time magazine once observed: "Whenever possible Chesterton made his points with popular sayings, proverbs, allegories—first carefully turning them inside out." One of his most enduring works *Orthodoxy* is at once entertaining, enlightening, yet at times difficult to decipher, but throughout there is much grist to grind.

> This startling swiftness with which popular systems turn oppressive is the third fact for which we shall ask our perfect theory of progress to allow. It must always be on the look out for every privilege being abused, for every working right becoming a wrong. In this matter I am entirely on the side of the revolutionists. They are really right to be always suspecting human institutions; they are right not to put their trust in princes nor in any child of man. The chieftain chosen to be the friend of the people becomes the enemy of the people; the newspaper started to tell the truth now exists to prevent the truth being told. Here, I say, I felt that I was really at last on the side of the revolutionary. And then I caught my breath again: for I remembered that I was once again on the side of the orthodox.

> Christianity spoke again and said: "I have always maintained that men were naturally backsliders; that human virtue tended of its own nature to rust or to rot; I have always said that human beings as such go wrong, especially happy human beings, especially proud and prosperous human beings. This eternal revolution, this suspicion sustained through centuries, you (being a vague modern) call the doctrine of progress. If you were a philosopher you would call it, as I do, the doctrine of original sin. You may call it the cosmic advance as much as you like; I call it what it is—the Fall."

Chesterton's point: progressive doctrine fails precisely for its unsustainable belief in the perfection of man; Christianity succeeds by its honest acknowledgment of man's fallibility.

---

[133] Kathryn Minaliak, To be Catholic at College: Advice for Sticking to the Faith in a Secular Environment, National Catholic Register, Dec. 11, 2016, 7

Futile Reform
Removing the detritus

Pope Emeritus Benedict XVI was and is, first and foremost, one of the greatest if not the greatest of theologians in our time. He has been described as "the main intellectual force in the Church" whose prolific writings in defense of traditional Catholic doctrine and values are unsurpassed in their theological understanding and insight. He has authored sixty-seven books, primarily under the name Joseph Cardinal Ratzinger, three encyclicals, and three apostolic exhortations. In *Called To Communion: Understanding the Church Today*, first published over twenty-five years ago, then Joseph Cardinal Ratzinger, Prefect of the Congregation for the Doctrine of the Faith, thoughtfully observed the rising antipathy and defensive reactions articulated by a vast majority of people. "The word Church and the reality it stands for have been discredited. It seems that even constant reform can hardly do much to change the situation. Or is it just that so far no one has discovered the kind of reform that could make of the Church a company worth belonging to?"[134] In answer to the question as to why the Church incurs the dislike of so many, even among the most faithful, he points to many diverse even contrary reasons.

> Some are unhappy because the Church has conformed too much to the standards of the world; others are angry that she is still very far from doing so. Most people have trouble with the Church because she is an institution like many others, which as such restricts my freedom. ... The thirst for freedom is the form in which the yearning for redemption and the feeling of unredemption and alienation make their voices heard today. The call for freedom demands an existence uncramped by prior givens that keep me from fully realizing myself and throw up external obstacles to my chosen path.

> The limits that the Church erects seem doubly burdensome because they reach into man's most personal and most intimate depths. For the Church's rules for ordering life are far more than a set of regulations to keep the shoulder-to-shoulder traffic of humanity as far as possible from collision. They inwardly affect my course in life, telling me how I am supposed to understand and shape my freedom. They demand of me decisions that cannot be made without painful renunciation. Is this not intended to deny us the sweetest fruits in the garden of life? Is not the way into the wide open closed by the restrictive confines of so many commandments and prohibitions? Is not thought kept from reaching its full stature just as much as the will is? Must not liberation consist in breaking out of such immature dependency? And would not the only real reform be to rid ourselves of the whole business?[135]

---

[134] Joseph Cardinal Ratzinger, *Called To Communion: Understanding the Church Today (Zur Gemeinshaft gerufen: Kirche heute verstehen)*, second edition by Herder, Frieburg im Breisgau, 1991, (San Francisco: Ignatius Press, 1996), 133-134.

[135] Joseph Cardinal Ratzinger, *Called To Communion*, 134-35.

What ultimately comes about is a fierce anger generated out of frustration because the Church is not as our dreams picture her to be and thus "a desperate attempt is undertaken to bring her into conformity with our wishes: to make her a place for every freedom, a space where we can move freed of our limits, an experiment in utopia, which, after all, must exist somewhere."[136] The most common response in answer to how such reform might achieve success is, "we are just beginning," stated with naïve arrogance by those who are convinced that previous generations failed to get it right. They now understand what must be done and despite any resistance to their views it must be begun. As these reformers see it, "The Church is not a democracy. She has not yet—so it seems—integrated into her constitution that basic patrimony of rights and freedoms elaborated by the Enlightenment that has since then been acknowledged as the basic rule for the political organization of communities."

> It thus appears as the most normal thing in the world to make up for lost time, which means first establishing once and for all this basic patrimony of structures of freedom. We must move—it is maintained—from the paternalistic Church to the community Church; no one must any longer remain a passive receiver of the gift of Christian existence. Rather, all should be active agents of it. The Church must no longer be fitted over us from above like a ready-made garment; no, we "make" the Church ourselves, and do so in constantly new ways. It thus finally becomes "our" Church, for which we are actively responsible. The passive yields to the active. The Church arises out of discussion, compromise and resolution. Debate brings out what can still be asked of people today, what can still be considered by common consent as faith or as ethical norms. New short formulas of faith are composed.[137]

Yet immediately questions arise. Who has the right to make decisions? What is the basis of the decision-making process? But an even more fundamental issue stands in protest against such a democratic agency.

> Everything that men make can also be undone again by others. Everything that has its origin in human likes can be disliked by others. Everything that one majority decides upon can be revoked by another majority. A Church based on human resolutions becomes a merely human church. It is reduced to the level of the makeable, of the obvious, of opinion. Opinion replaces faith. And in fact, in the self-made formulas of faith with which I am acquainted, the meaning of the words "I believe" never signifies anything beyond "we opine". Ultimately, the self-made church savors of the "self", which always has a bitter taste to the other self and just as soon reveals its petty insignificance. A self-made church is reduced to the empirical domain and thus, precisely as a dream, comes to nothing.[138]

What Cardinal Ratzinger concludes is this form of reform narrows the scope of reason and thus results in losing sight of the mystery that is Church. What is needed is not a constant remodel of the Church in accord to our tastes or self-invention; rather

---

[136] Joseph Cardinal Ratzinger, *Called To Communion*, 136.

[137] Joseph Cardinal Ratzinger, *Called To Communion*, 137.

[138] Joseph Cardinal Ratzinger, *Called To Communion*, 139-40.

what is needed is a clearing away, a removal of our subsidiary constructions in order that the pure light from above may shine. He explains what he means through the use of a metaphor borrowed from Michelangelo. "With the eye of the artist, Michelangelo already saw in the stone that lay before him the pure image that, hidden within, was simply waiting to be uncovered. The artist's only task—so it seemed to him—was to remove what covered the statue. Michelangelo considered the proper activity of the artist to be an act of uncovering, of releasing—not of making."[139] Saint Bonaventure offered a similar thought by stating the sculptor does not make anything, rather his work is "ablatio"—the removal of what is not really part of the sculpture. In this way, that is by means of *ablatio*, the *nobilis forma*—the noble form—takes shape.

> Rightly understood, this image contains the prototypical model of Church reform. The Church will constantly have need of human constructions to help her speak and act in the ear in which she finds herself. Ecclesiastical institutions and juridical organizations are not intrinsically evil; on the contrary, to a certain degree they are simply necessary and indispensable. But they become obsolete; they risk setting themselves up as the essence of the Church and thus prevent us from seeing through to what is truly essential. This is why they must always be dismantled again, like scaffolding that has outlived its necessity. Reform is ever-renewed *ablatio*—removal, whose purpose is to allow the *nobilis forma*, the countenance of the bride, and with it the Bridegroom himself, the living Lord, to appear. Such *ablatio*, such "negative theology", is a path to something wholly positive. This path alone allows the divine to penetrate and brings about *"congregation"*, which as both gathering and purification is that pure communion we all long for, where "I" is no longer pitted against "I" and self against self. Rather, the self-giving and self-abandonment that characterize love become the reciprocal reception of all that is good and pure. Thus, the world of the kindly father who reminds the jealous older son what the content of all freedom and the realization of utopia consist of becomes true for every man: "All that is mine is yours" (Lk 15:31; cf. Jn 17:10).[140]

What we need is, Cardinal Ratzinger believes, "not a more human, but a more divine Church; then she will also become truly human."

> And for this reason, everything man-made in the Church must recognize its own purely ancillary characters and leave the foreground to what truly matters.

> The freedom that we rightly expect from and in the Church is not achieved by introducing the principle of majority. This freedom does not rest on the fact that as many as possible prevail against as few as possible. Its basis is rather that no one may impose his own will on the others, since all know themselves to be bound to the word and will of the One who is our Lord and our freedom.[141]

It is the spiritual nature of the Church which gets covered up by all the administrative machinery constructed over time. The more we build the less place there is for the Divine. What is truly needed, in the Cardinal's opinion is "that we ought to begin an

---

[139] Joseph Cardinal Ratzinger, *Called To Communion*, 141.
[140] Joseph Cardinal Ratzinger, *Called To Communion*, 142-43.
[141] Joseph Cardinal Ratzinger, *Called To Communion*, 146.

unsparing examination of conscience on this point at all levels in the Church. On every level this would have to have very real consequences and would be bound to bring about an *ablatio* that would allow the true inherent form to reemerge and could restore to us in a wholly new way the feeling of freedom and of being at home."[142] It is important for us to understand the Church is not like worldly institutions or associations for it does not exist in order to constantly occupy us but to provide a path and to guide us into eternal life. This then moves us away from the general and objective to the personal, away from the removal of the unnecessary from the Church to a personal liberating removal of what keeps us from eternal life with God. "Indeed, it is hardly the case that we always and immediately see in the other the "noble form", the image of God that is inscribed in him. What first meets the eye is only the image of Adam, the image of man, who, though not totally corrupt, is nonetheless fallen. We see the crust of dust and filth that has overlaid the image. Thus, we all stand in need of the true sculptor who removes what distorts the image; we are in need of forgiveness, which is the heart of all true reform."[143] Cardinal Ratzinger then makes a crucial point, changing the conversation from the ecclesial to the personal; critical to fully understanding what is needed for a successful renewal of the Church.

> Here we have reached a very central point: I believe that the core of the spiritual crisis of our time has its basis in the obscuration of the grace of forgiveness. But let us first take note of the positive side of the present: morality is gradually coming back into favor. It is recognized, indeed, it has become evident, that all technical progress is questionable and, in the end, destructive when there is no corresponding moral advancement. It is recognized that there is no reform of man or of humanity without moral renewal. But the call for morality ultimately remains without effect, because the criteria are veiled in a fog of discussions. In fact, man cannot bear sheer morality, he cannot live by it: it becomes a "law" for him that provokes contradiction and engenders sin. For this reason, where forgiveness—true forgiveness guaranteed by authority—is not recognized or believed, morality must be cut down to size so that the conditions of sinful action can never actually occur for the individual. Today's discussion of morality is making great strides toward liberating man from guilt by precluding the occurrence of the conditions that make it possible. One is reminded of the mordant aphorism of Pascal: "*Ecce patres qui tollunt peccata mundi!*" (Behold the fathers who take away the sins of the world). According to these "moralists", guilt simply no longer exists.[144]

> It goes without saying, however, that this method of freeing the world from guilt is all too cheap. In their heart of hearts, those who have been liberated in this fashion know perfectly well that the whole experience is untrue; they know that there is sin, that they themselves are sinners and that there must be a real way to overcome sin.

An extensive footnote recalls an essay of A. Gorres, Schuld und Schuldgefuhle, in Internationale katholische Zeitschrift 13 (1984) which states: "Psychoanalysis has

---

[142] Joseph Cardinal Ratzinger, *Called To Communion*, 146-47.
[143] Joseph Cardinal Ratzinger, *Called To Communion*, 148.
[144] Joseph Cardinal Ratzinger, *Called To Communion*, 149-50.

found it difficult to admit that among other guilt feelings there are also some that can be traced back to real guilt. It cannot accept these data without embarrassment ... because its philosophy does not recognize freedom ... its determinism is the opium of the intellectuals. In the psychoanalytic mind, Sigmund Freud far surpassed the poor unenlightened Rabbi Jesus. He, in fact, could only forgive sins and still found it necessary to do so, whereas Sigmund Freud, the new Messiah from Vienna, did far more: he rid the intellectual world of sin and guilt."

> Nor indeed does Jesus call those who have already freed themselves and who therefore—as they think—have no need for him whatever; rather, he calls those who know themselves to be sinners and for this very reason are in need of him. Morality retains its seriousness only where there is forgiveness—real forgiveness ensured by authority; otherwise it lapses back into the pure empty conditional. But true forgiveness exists only when the "price", the "equivalent value", is paid, when guilt is atoned by suffering, when there is expiation. The circular link between morality, forgiveness and expiation cannot be forced apart at any point; when one element is missing, everything else is ruined. Whether or not man can find redemption depends on the undivided existence of this circle. In the Torah, the five books of Moses, these three elements are knotted together inseparably, and it is therefore impossible to follow the Enlightenment in excising from this core of the Old Testament canon an eternally valid moral law, while consigning the rest to past history. This moralistic manner of giving the Old Testament relevance for today is bound to fail; it was already the pith of the heresy of Pelagius, who has more followers today than appears at first glance.

> Jesus, on the other hand, fulfilled the whole law, not a portion of it, and thus renewed it from the ground up: he himself, who suffered the whole tale of guilt, is at once expiation and forgiveness and is therefore also the only reliable and perennially valid basis of our morality. It is impossible to detach morality from Christology, because it is impossible to separate it from expiation and forgiveness.

> In Christ, the whole law is fulfilled, and morality has thereby become a more concrete claim on us that it is now more possible to satisfy. From the core of faith, then, the way of renewal opens again and again for the individual, for the Church as a whole and for humanity.

> Forgiveness, together with its realization in me by way of penance and discipleship, is first of all the wholly personal center of all renewal. But because forgiveness touches the very core of the person, it gathers men together and is also the center of the renewal of the community. For when the dust and filth that disfigure God's image in me are removed, I thereby become similar to the other who is likewise God's image; above all I become similar to Christ, who is the image of God without qualification, the model according to which we have all been created.[145]

All too often our view of the Church is limited by what we see with human eyes. The Church is more than those who meet on Sundays to celebrate the Eucharist, more than the pope, bishops, priests, and deacons. The Church encompasses not only those

---

[145] Joseph Cardinal Ratzinger, *Called To Communion*, 148-53.

mentioned but reaches further—beyond the limits of death, for to her belong the communion of saints, all the unknown and unnamed, all men who believe in Christ. Those incapable of giving life, along with any accompanying pain and suffering meaning and value, hold a worldview that is good for nothing for it falls short precisely at the hour of the most serious crisis of existence.

> Those who have nothing to say about suffering except that we must fight against it are deceiving us. It is, of course, necessary to do everything one can to lessen the suffering of the innocent and to limit pain. But there is no human life without suffering, and he who is incapable of accepting suffering is refusing himself the purifications that alone allow us to reach maturity. …

> Life reaches farther than our biological existence. Where there is no longer anything worth dying for, even life itself is no longer worth living.[146]

January 06, 2017

Christ's Final Command
A disciple is more than a name

Pope Saint John Paul II in the second year of his pontificate issued his Apostolic Exhortation *Catechesi Tradendae*: "On Catechesis In Our Time".

> The Church has always considered catechesis one of her primary tasks, for, before Christ ascended to His Father after His resurrection, He gave the apostles a final command—to make disciples of all nations and to teach them to observe all that He had commanded. He thus entrusted them with the mission and power to proclaim to humanity what they had heard, what they had seen with their eyes, what they had looked upon and touched with their hands, concerning the Word of Life. He also entrusted them with the mission and power to explain with authority what He had taught them, His words and actions, His signs and commandments. And He gave them the Spirit to fulfill this mission.

> Very soon the name of catechesis was given to the whole of the efforts within the Church to make disciples, to help people to believe that Jesus is the Son of God, so that believing they might have life in His name, and to educate and instruct them in this life and thus build up the Body of Christ. The Church has not ceased to devote her energy to this task."[147]

The Catechism of the Catholic Church, quoting from that very same document, states: "Catechesis is an education in the faith of children, young people, and adults which includes especially the teaching of Christian doctrine imparted, generally

---

[146] Joseph Cardinal Ratzinger, *Called To Communion*, 155.
[147] Pope Saint John Paul II, *Apostolic Exhortation: Catechesi tradendae*, October 16, 1979, §1.

speaking, in an organic and systematic way, with the view to initiating the hearers into the fullness of Christian life."[148]

The importance of catechesis cannot be understated or ignored, yet that is precisely what we have done. We have become "Christians In Name Only" woefully ignorant of what Jesus taught. It is incumbent upon all Christians to know what it truly means to be a disciple. Let us resolve this year to become true disciples of Christ Jesus.

The Word of the Lord
Fulfilled in the hearing

Christians, and with greater respect, Catholics, often underappreciate or misunderstand the significance and importance of Scripture in the liturgy. This, I believe, is primarily due to a lack or absence of catechesis with respect to the whole of liturgy, but specifically when it relates to the reading of Scripture which is the Word of the Lord. Sacred Liturgy is seldom thought of much beyond what Catholics experience at Mass; it is the liturgy of the Eucharist which generally takes center stage. How else to explain those who consistently arrive sometime near the transition point between Word and Eucharist? After all, the liturgy of the Word is not an obligatory element in faithfully observing the Lord's day, is it? Jesus gave us the Eucharist in remembrance of him; he never said anything about listening to Scripture, did he? What many deem incidental to the liturgy, that is Scripture, is to the contrary, as essential as the Eucharistic rite; together, Scripture and Eucharist, form the sacrament of the liturgy.

> Scripture is for liturgy, and scripture is about liturgy. The liturgy, likewise, proclaims the scriptures even as it interprets and actualizes them. The unity of scripture and liturgy may be described as both material and formal.
>
> It is material in that the content of scripture is, to a great extent, concerned with the liturgy, and the content of the liturgy is drawn from scripture. Liturgy figures most prominently in salvation history's key moments — creation, the flood, the call of Abram, the exodus, and the founding of the kingdom of David. Scripture, for its part, figures most prominently in every aspect of the liturgy, in both the ritual words and ritual actions. This is most evident in the liturgy of the word, but also in the institution narrative and in many of the standard prayers. Scripture is, in this important sense, about liturgy, just as liturgy is about scripture.
>
> Their relationship is formal in that scripture took its final form — it was canonized — for the sake of liturgy, and the canon itself derived from liturgical tradition."[149]

The canon of Sacred Scripture, the texts included in the Old and New Testaments, are the direct result of its liturgical use. As one scholar observed: "That which is canon

---

[148] Catechism of the Catholic Church (CCC) §5, CT §18.
[149] Scott Hahn, *Letter and Spirit: From Written Text to Living Word in the Liturgy*, (The Crown Publishing Group; 1st edition, November 8, 2005).

comes to us from ancient communities of faith, not just from individuals. … The whole of the Bible, the sum as well as all its parts, comes to us out of the liturgical and instructional life of early believing communities."[150] The liturgical pattern found within Scripture is not a new or recent view. Both ancient rabbis and modern scholars have long agreed as to the liturgical character of the whole of Scripture. As Scott Hahn writes:

> The cosmos itself seems to follow a liturgical calendar. God created the world in six "days" for the sake of the seventh, the Sabbath, which he made holy (Gen 2:3). Thus, the first pages of the canonical scriptures set a sabbatical rhythm for all subsequent history. This divine model established the order for humanity: work was ordered to worship, labor to liturgy. Man subdued the earth in order to consecrate its fruits to God. From the beginning, then, God made time holy, and creation itself became a cosmic temple with Adam as its high priest.

> From the first two generations, then, the scriptures present mankind as liturgical by nature—*homo liturgicus*. …

> From Genesis to Revelation, the texts themselves demonstrate the formal unity of scripture and liturgy. Scripture is, by and large, about liturgy. Often, it is liturgy—or the culpable neglect of liturgy—that drives the biblical drama. Liturgy sustains the assembly of God's people—the *qahal*, the *ekklesia*, the church—and liturgy restores it when it falls."[151]

The scriptural canon was primarily determined for liturgical purposes, yet it was liturgical use that preceded and determined the canon. Although the Church finalized the New Testament canon at the councils of Hippo (393 a.d.) and Carthage (397 a.d. and 417 a.d.) and was subsequently ratified by Pope Damasus I, the Church had been celebrating the Eucharistic liturgy for more than three centuries. Early evidence proves Sacred Scripture had always played an important and key role in the liturgy. As Everett Ferguson points out: "The church did not have to wait until the end of the second century (and certainly not the fourth century) to know what books to read in church."[152] As Scott Hahn points out, "in an interesting historical turnabout, liturgical use became a primary criterion for compiling the canon that would officially limit the books deemed suitable for liturgical use. … Scripture is canonized for liturgy, and it is liturgy that canonizes scripture." It is incumbent upon us to acknowledge the importance Scripture played within the liturgical mission of Jesus. The question asked at the beginning as to whether Jesus ever called for the reading of scripture in a liturgical setting can be readily answered in the affirmative. One must only look to the Gospels to understand its importance. According to Luke, Jesus began his public ministry and announced his mission when he "went according to his custom into the synagogue on the Sabbath day. He stood up to read and was handed a scroll of the prophet Isaiah"

---

[150] James A. Sanders, *From Sacred Story to Sacred Text* (Philadelphia: Fortress, 1987), p. 162.
[151] Scott Hahn, *Letter and Spirit*.
[152] Everett Ferguson, "Factors Leading to the Selection and Closure of the New Testament Canon," in McDonald and Sanders, p. 296.

(Is 61:1-2; 58:6). After reading, he rolled up the scroll, "handed it back to the attendant and sat down, and the eyes of all in the synagogue looked intently at him. He said to them, 'Today this scripture passage is fulfilled in your hearing.'" (Lk 4:16-17, 20-21). Jesus was clearly following traditional Hebrew liturgical form, even preaching a homily, anticipating the objections that would be raised, defending his mission utilizing other Hebrew scriptures (1 Kgs 17 and 2 Kgs 5).

> The liturgy then as now was non-sacrificial. "It was a liturgy of the word—involving scriptural prayer, proclamation, and interpretation. Indeed, it is likely that the Christian liturgy of the word derived from this formative experience of the first-generation Christians, who were predominantly Jews.
>
> Biblical religion has always required the proclamation of God's word within the assembly of God's people. In the old covenant, that proclamation had always been public, communal, and liturgical. It remained so with the new covenant of Jesus Christ.
>
> Jesus' subsequent preaching placed a particular emphasis on the hearing of the word."[153]

Saint Paul confirms the importance of "hearing" in his Letter to the Romans: "So faith comes from what is heard, and what is heard comes by the preaching of Christ" (Rom 10:17). He asked the church in Galatia, "Did you receive the Spirit by works of the law, or by hearing with faith" (Gal 3:2)?

> In the liturgy, the people assemble to hear the terms of the law proclaimed, to bear witness to the oath, and to enact and renew the covenant. It involves more than just the republication of information—more than just "reading them their rights." It is a dialogue. The people hear the word of God and they respond in faith. Moses "took the book of the covenant, and read it in the hearing of the people; and they said, 'All that the Lord has spoken we will do, and we will be obedient'" (Ex 24:7). To put it in more familiar terms: the assembly hears the readings in every liturgy, and they respond with the creed and the Anaphora[154]—the oath and the offering of sacrifice.
>
> Implicit in every element of the process—proclamation, hearing, and response—is the divine authority of God's word. ... Men might violate their covenant oaths; but the "word of the Lord" stood as an ultimate and irrevocable authority—a divine speech act. "Let God be true though every man be false" (Rom 3:4).[155]

In third-century Alexandria the Christian theologian Origen urged the adoption of a very practical piety toward both Scripture and Eucharist:

> You who are accustomed to attending the divine mysteries know how, when you receive the body of the Lord, you guard it with all care and reverence lest any small part should

---

[153] Scott Hahn, *Letter and Spirit*.

[154] The *Anaphora* is the most solemn part of the Divine Liturgy, or the Holy Sacrifice of the Mass, during which the offerings of bread and wine are consecrated as the body and blood of Christ. This is the usual name for the part of the Liturgy in Greek-speaking Eastern Christianity. In western Christian traditions which have a comparable rite, the *Anaphora* is more often called the Eucharistic Prayer. When the Roman Rite of the Catholic Church had a single Eucharistic Prayer (between the Council of Trent and Vatican II) it was referred to as the Canon of the Mass.

[155] Scott Hahn, *Letter and Spirit*.

fall from it, lest any piece of the consecrated gift be lost. For you believe yourself guilty, and rightly so, if anything falls from there through your negligence. But if you are so careful to preserve his body, and rightly so, why do you think that there is less guilt to have neglected God's word than to have neglected his body?[156]

Subsequent the Reformation, apologetics have at times reduced all discussion of the liturgy to solely defending transubstantiation. Even Catholic apologists have emphasized—as unfortunate as it most assuredly is—the act of consecration while relegating scripture to a mostly incidental position.

> The word is the Lord's, but it is revealed to mankind. It must be written, but primarily so that it can be proclaimed "in the midst of the assembly" (Sir 15:5) in every generation. Theologian Jeremy Driscoll said it with startling simplicity: "The book is a means to an end." And the end, he explained, is "the presence of the living Word in the midst of the believing assembly, accomplishing and extending to that assembly what has been accomplished in concrete historical events." Put, by Driscoll, into even more lapidary terms: "Scripture is the announcement of the Word of God; liturgy is its actualization.[157]

Perhaps there is no better place to observe the importance and relationship between Scripture and liturgy than in Luke's account of the conversation that took place on the road to Emmaus (Lk 24:13-25). It is a familiar passage in which we hear how two disciples, on the day that Jesus rose from the dead, were walking toward a village, Emmaus, talking about all the things that had occurred. And, as Luke tells us, "it happened that while they were conversing and debating, Jesus himself drew near and walked with them, but their eyes were prevented from recognizing him" (Lk 24:15). Jesus questions them and elicits their account of the past several days, to which they conclude, "But we had hoped that he was the one to redeem Israel" (Lk 24:21). Jesus then admonishes them for their lack of faith: "Oh, how foolish you are! How slow of heart to believe all that the prophets spoke! Was it not necessary that the Messiah should suffer these things and enter into his glory" (Lk 24:25-26)? He then, beginning with Moses and all the prophets, interpreted all that was referred of him in the scriptures, replacing it with a thoroughgoing exegesis of his own. When they arrive at Emmaus, still unaware of who he was, the two disciples urge him to stay and dine with them and "it happened that, while he was with them at table, he took bread, said the blessing, broke it, and gave it to them. With that their eyes were opened, and they recognized him, but he vanished from their sight. Then they said to each other, "Were not our hearts burning within us while he spoke to us on the way and opened the scriptures to us" (Lk 24:32)? They returned to where the apostles were and "recounted what had taken place on the way and how he was made known to them in the breaking of the bread" (Lk 24:35).

Here we see the liturgy in its most familiar and essential form with scripture proclaimed and opened up, followed by the breaking of the bread. In the Emmaus

---

[156] Origin, *On Exodus* 13.3.
[157] Scott Hahn, *Letter and Spirit.*

encounter, the breaking of the bread, is referred to as a *koinonia*, a communion. This same term is found in Acts (2:42) to describe the church's eucharistic fellowship and it is used twice in 1 Corinthians (10:16) to describe the Christian's reception of the Eucharistic body and blood of Christ. Christians at liturgy receive a "participation in the blood of Christ," "a participation in the body of Christ," a share in his suffering, death, and resurrection. "The Liturgy consists of this participation of the members of Christ's mystical body in the mysteries which Christ, their Head, originally fulfilled."[158] "Do you not know," Paul writes, "that all of us who have been baptized into Christ Jesus were baptized into his death" (Rom 6:3)? "This is why every Eucharistic liturgy conforms to the pattern established at Emmaus: the opening of the scriptures followed by the breaking of the bread; the liturgy of the word followed by the liturgy of the Eucharist. The Mass, then, is the place *par excellence* of the scriptures' faithful reception. It is the place where, by grace and by habit, the scriptures are rendered most intelligible to the disciples and most potent to transform human lives."[159] No matter how far back one travels, in any Biblical religion (Jewish or Christian) the proclamation of God's word within the assembly has been both essential and required. In the ancient Jewish covenant, the proclamation of scripture was public, communal, and liturgical and it remained so with the new covenant of Jesus Christ.

> For both Jews and Christians, the scriptural texts, though historical in character, are not merely records of past events. The scriptures are intended to sweep the worshiper into their action. Liturgy is the privileged place of this "actualization" of God's word, because the liturgy is itself formed from the scriptures and by the scriptures. Scripture is, in this sense, for liturgy.

> All of scripture is intrinsically liturgical. Liturgy is like a golden thread that runs through the many pearls of salvation history and holds them together. Remember that the *oikonomia*, the divine economy, refers to all the acts by which God reveals himself and communicates his life. In the Old Testament, these acts often appear as liturgical acts — even when they take place in the midst of battles, family disputes, and the ordinary administration of a nation-state. The divine drama turns on ritual acts of worship, blessing, cursing, oath-swearing, fasting, penance, and, most significantly, sacrifice. In the New Testament, we discover that the liturgies of the Old Testament found typological fulfillment in the sacrifice of Christ. The New Testament reveals as well that Christ's unique sacrifice extends through time in the sacramental liturgy of the church."[160]

Modern Christianity has largely forgotten that Scripture is the word of God. Scripture is seldom read or heard outside of the liturgy for we no longer listen to his voice with any real sense of awe and wonder.

> [T]oday in large segments of the academy and even the Christian community, the Bible tends no longer to be read and studied as Scripture—a "word" spoken by God to a

---

[158] Danielou, *The Lord of History*, 259.

[159] Scott Hahn, *Letter and Spirit*.

[160] Scott Hahn, *Worship in the Word: Toward a Liturgical Hermeneutic*, St. Paul Center for Biblical Theology, Letter & Spirit I (2005): 101-136.

community that acknowledges this word as authoritative and normative for its life and worship. Instead it is read as "text," a literary and historical artifact bearing no more or less meaning or legitimacy than any other product of ancient civilization.

The consequences of this shift in biblical understanding and interpretation have been felt in every area of Catholic and Protestant faith and life—from doctrinal formulations and organizational structures to disciplines and worship.

Insofar as the canon of Scripture was established for use in the liturgy, and inasmuch as its content is "about" liturgy, it follows that we must engage Scripture liturgically if we are to interpret these texts according to the original authors' intentions and the life-situation of the believing community in which these texts were handed on.[161]

What ought to be abundantly clear is the essential and specific role Scripture plays in the liturgy. Those who question its value show little regard for the word of God by their own words and actions. To take lightly the efficacy of the liturgy of the Word, displayed through their habitual lateness at liturgical celebrations, is to disrespect and trivialize God's Word.

January 13, 2017

A Time of Conversion
Ordinary Time isn't so ordinary

Questions concerning the liturgical seasons almost always center on Ordinary Time. Ordinary Time officially begins on the day immediately following the Feast of the Baptism of the Lord.

The first Sunday of Advent marks the beginning of the liturgical year, and continues until the Christmas season which concludes with the Baptism of the Lord. Thus, Ordinary Time begins the following day, either on Monday or Tuesday, not on Sunday. The remainder of the week, however, is counted as the First Week in Ordinary Time, which means the following Sunday is the Second Sunday in Ordinary Time.

Ordinary Time is bifurcated, that is, it is interrupted for the duration of Lent and the Easter Season, resuming on the Monday immediately following Pentecost Sunday and concludes on the thirty-fourth Sunday (The Solemnity of Christ the King). Our bishops write:

Christmas Time and Easter Time highlight the central mysteries of the Paschal Mystery, namely, the incarnation, death on the cross, resurrection, and ascension of Jesus Christ, and the descent of the Holy Spirit at Pentecost. The Sundays and weeks of Ordinary

---

[161] Scott Hahn, *Letter and Spirit.*

Time, on the other hand, take us through the life of Christ. This is the time of conversion. This is living the life of Christ.

Ordinary Time is a time for growth and maturation, a time in which the mystery of Christ is called to penetrate ever more deeply into history until all things are finally caught up in Christ. The goal, toward which all of history is directed, is represented by the final Sunday in Ordinary Time, the Solemnity of Our Lord Jesus Christ, King of the Universe.

Ordinary Time offers us an extraordinary opportunity to grow and mature in our faith and in our relationship with Jesus Christ. Why not make it Extraordinary Time?

Once Upon a Dream
The music danced

Music is the voice of the soul singing praise to God. It is prayer with wings that are wont to lift the spirit beyond the bounds of earth to pierce the veil of heaven.

I was once asked whether I ever used contemplative prayer in my faith life. Like many, prayer was often perfunctory and rote, lacking of any meaningful purpose. To my reasoned mind, contemplation engendered raw and visceral visions of a small naked cell of foreboding emptiness and silence; nothing to break the endless monotony of catatonic staring at cold barren walls. So, I answered, without a second's thought, in the negative to such unpleasant thought. Yet, after but a moment to reflect, I realized the nightmarish image held no sway upon reality; contemplative prayer was far more than any thought or vision; it was and had been an integral part of my life although I had not recognized it as such. I came to realize that, rather than avoiding it, I had been devoting much of every day in contemplative prayer, at times as much as four hours throughout the day. How was that possible? Just thinking of it brings a smile, for I came to understand the music soothed my restless soul and purged all unholy thought from my mind. Whenever I would sit before the piano my soul would sing with such joy to God, as it dispelled all the ugliness, the hatred, bitterness, anger, vile and sinful thoughts from my mind, heart, and soul. Music envelops me, wrapping my entire self with a blanket so complete the light within my soul is captured there. I lose all thought of time and space and being to the notes that dance upon the keys; from where these notes arrive, I know not, except from where else but God.

Some of those who create the music we hear will tell you they compose it long before they hear it played; hearing every note so selfishly complete, from a place deep within, its playing is little more than afterthought. But then I cannot help but think of all the melodies denied to those who would await, quite eagerly I suppose, to hear them, but for the lack of ever putting note to paper. My soul cries out in melodies which can but be expressed by laying hands upon the instrument of my desire and teasing out what rests within, note on note until the song bursts forth, to find release from deep within. I hear the song, but hear it not, until it plays upon the keys. I cannot help but wonder why, but then again, I care little in the knowing, satisfied only that I hear the music and, in the moment, have no conscious thought of anything but God. Music plays upon my soul; it gives it wings to soar, if only for the briefest flight. I know not why nor do I care at all. It matters only the music moves me in unexpected ways. I never know where the muse will lead me yet I laugh at journey's end for it never is what was expected and yet it is precisely what it was meant to be. Is it not the same with life? We never know what is in store yet what awaits us in the end is precisely what God intended.

The music I write taunts and teases without respect for beat or measure. Music, to my wayward ear, should ebb and flow, as water flows down its courses, never forced to run a steady pace but to meander for a while until the moment when it cries for speed: a lively dash through narrow channels, down thundering chasms to calm still waters once again. Measured beat and cadenced note will seldom find a place to rest upon the score, for the music cannot sing with such hard shackles worn. The Spirit moves the fingers, breathing melody to life; my poor play denies what credit may come due, for the beauty of the music, of the song which God has so wonderfully inspired is of his making, none of mine. Whether what is written pleases all or some or none at all is of small concern for every note and nuanced beat comes from him with consummate love; he has, with perfect pitch, composed the song for each to play.

It is we who, like a child with wild abandon, beats with neither artistry nor skill upon the keys. We care not for the melody but the discordant noise we make from their pounding. We stubbornly refuse to play the music—the music which God has inscribed upon the soul—for we listen not to him but to the gods of our mortal base desires. We choose to contemplate our navel rather than meditate upon his score divine.

The music writ upon the soul plays soft and low and yet the world and all its noise are silenced by the whispered melody it evokes. Mindless beats and violent notes so amplified to turn the mind to vacuous mush can deny but for the moment the unceasing love song which still plays within. It cannot be silenced lest the heart is stilled from beating, though it can be lost, forgotten, remembered only by a passing thought so brief, not worth a mention. Yet the song plays on and on and forever, no matter whether ear is bent to hear it. There is no need for naked walls or empty rooms, silence will not increase the volume nor will darkness improve the sound. It is the measure of devotion, the immersion of the mind, and the loss of self-awareness gives the soul its voice. Such contemplation holds the soul beneath the surface, banished from the constant twists and turns of wind and wave and the tumult of a blasphemous world. In contemplation there is no silence, there is no noise, only music, a duet played by you and God. Why then do we deny ourselves the music writ upon the soul? Why are we reluctant to enter into communion with the Composer of our song? Why do so many refuse to listen to the sweet, sweet melody of a loving God?

The instrument upon which I hear his music is uniquely mine and mine alone. Every soul hears their song, written for the instrument which God has made. God writes the music, creates the instrument upon which to play the notes, yet he leaves the playing of it to the musician. We can choose to play what he has written or simply refuse to listen. Either choice, the music will forever play.

Once upon a dream the music danced. I know not from whence it came or where it wished to go, but only that it lingered long enough for the writing of it. I have no answers, only questions; God has no questions, only answers. There is great symmetry in that. Each moment of our lives plays a different tune; each sings a song far different than the last. So, it is with music. Thank God for that.

January 20, 2017

Doing the Right Thing
Always do what is good

We have heard the story many times: Jesus enters the synagogue and encounters a man with a withered hand. The Pharisees watch closely to see if he would dare cure the man on the Sabbath. Knowing what was in their hearts, Jesus invites the man to stand before them and asks if it is lawful to do good on the Sabbath rather than to do evil, to which they refuse to answer. Two things should be noted in this instance: Jesus looks at them "with anger" and then says to the man, "Stretch out your hand." Only one other time in the Gospels do we hear of Jesus getting angry (Mt 21:12). That in itself makes this noteworthy, it should inform us this is significant and to read this with care. The second thing to note is what Jesus does not do. Jesus takes no direct action nor does he physically touch the man: he simply asks him to stretch out his hand. And for asking the man to do something he could not do but now could, the Pharisees condemned Jesus for violating the Sabbath laws and they began to conspire to put him to death. Rather harsh judgment for simply requesting someone to stretch out his hand, don't you think?

Yet in many ways, there are many who act in like manner, even today. Consider: A motorist driving across the Golden Gate bridge sees a man about to commit suicide by jumping off the bridge. He stops his car in the middle of the bridge and is able to coax the man out of his suicidal jump. A policeman arrives, approaches the motorist and gives him a traffic ticket for illegally parking his vehicle on the bridge. What lesson can we learn from this? I believe Jesus would tell us doing good is always the right thing to do, no matter the consequences. Never do the right thing expecting a reward, for indeed you may be punished for doing so.

How Big Is My Church?
Bigger than you might think

What we envision as church is too small, for our minds deny the full nature of the Body of Christ. One of the first ordained deacons in the nascent church, protomartyr Stephen, at the climax of his trial, "full of the Holy Spirit, gazed into heaven and saw the glory of God, and Jesus standing at the right hand of God; and he said, 'Behold, I see the heavens opened, and the son of man standing at the right hand of God'" (Acts 7:55-56).

The vision which Stephen saw was strikingly similar to the views of the early Christian church. Those early Christians saw Christ as the high priest, standing at the right hand of God, in fulfillment of and officiating at the liturgy of the church. This was not a novelty developed by the early Christian churches, but rather a profound development of ancient Israel's understanding of divine worship.

> The people of Israel considered their earthly liturgy to be a divinely inspired imitation of heavenly worship. … The prophets expressed this belief in a mystical way, as they depicted the angels worshiping amid songs and trappings that were clearly recognizable from the Jerusalem temple (see Is 6 and Ezek 1). The hymns sung by the angels were the same songs the Levites sang before the earthly sanctuary.

> We find the idea in full flower at the time of Jesus Christ and expressed in the non-canonical books of Enoch and Jubilees and in the Dead Sea Scrolls. What the priests did in the temple sanctuary was an earthly imitation of what the angels did in heaven.

> None of this was mere pageantry. Both the heavenly and earthly liturgies had more than a ceremonial purpose. The angelic liturgy preserved a certain order not only in the courts of the Almighty, but in the entire universe. God had given over the governance of creation to his angels, and so the world itself was caught up in a cosmic liturgy: "Holy, holy, holy is the Lord of hosts; the whole earth is full of His glory" (Is 6:3). As Israel's priests performed their temple liturgy, they—like their counterparts in heaven—preserved and sanctified the order of the cosmos.[162]

Considering this ancient understanding and practice of an all-encompassing liturgy, the beauty and profundity of the petition found in the Lord's prayer "Thy will be done on earth as it is in heaven," offers new and greater insight, adding to our understanding of what we are praying. This view of a shared liturgy of heaven and earth has broader implications beyond the petition in the Lord's prayer. Both Christian and Jewish scholars have noted the evolving understanding of the unity of temporal and divine liturgies. As A. G. Martimort explains: "This singular interplay of earth and heaven is characteristic of the Christian liturgy. There are not two liturgies, any more than there are two Churches. Rather, as the same Church is a pilgrim on earth and

---

[162] Scott Hahn, Ph.D., *Letter and Spirit: From Written Text to Living Word in the Liturgy*, (The Crown Publishing Group; 1st edition, November 8, 2005).

triumphant in heaven, so the same liturgy is celebrated here below in figurative rites and without figures 'beyond the veil' in the heavenly sanctuary."[163] Erik Peterson, noting the historical and cosmological development that has taken place, highlighted in the Book of Revelation, writes, "We see clearly that the earthly Jerusalem with its temple worship has been the starting point for these ideas and images of primitive Christian literature; but the starting point has been left behind and it is no longer upon earth that Jerusalem is sought as a political power or centre of worship but in heaven, whither the eyes of all Christians are turned."[164] Rabbi Baruch Levine, in his commentary on Leviticus, has noted the Mass's continuity with the worship of Jerusalem's temple. Following the destruction of the temple in 70 A.D., Judaism moved their non-sacrificial worship to the synagogue; the liturgy of the Christian church took up the temple's sacrificial liturgy, in a renewed form. "Christian worship in the form of the traditional mass affords the devout an experience of sacrifice, of communion, and proclaims that God is present. The Christian church, then, is a temple."[165] Christ, in the liturgy of the new covenant now served as high priest of the liturgy in heaven and on earth—a liturgy led in the earthly church by his clergy, who "preside in the place of God."[166] This sense of angelic presence is particularly evident in early church liturgies.

> "The early Christians professed their belief in the angelic presence and power in the heavenly liturgy, the church's liturgy, and the "cosmic liturgy" of all creation. God had delegated both liturgical and cosmic ministries to the angels; but Christians now shared that liturgical and cosmic authority as they worshiped with the angels. Thus, the Book of Revelation shows liturgical action as directing human history.

> The doctrine of the angels, like the arm of God, has not been shortened over time; and it remains integral to every liturgy of the apostolic churches. In the Roman liturgy's prefaces, this theme is especially strong: "And so with all the choirs of angels in heaven, we proclaim your glory and join in their unending hymn of praise. ... Holy, Holy, Holy ..."

> Cardinal Ratzinger has noted that the New Testament's apocalyptic imagery is overwhelmingly liturgical, and the church's liturgical language is overwhelmingly apocalyptic. "The parousia is the highest intensification and fulfillment of the liturgy," he writes. "And the liturgy is parousia. ... Every Eucharist is parousia, the Lord's coming, and yet the Eucharist is even more truly the tensed yearning that He would reveal His hidden Glory."[167]

This heavenly-earthly liturgy is profoundly presented in the fourth-century Syriac *Liber Graduum*, or Book of Steps.

> Since we know that the body becomes a hidden temple and the heart a hidden altar for spiritual worship, let us be diligent in this public altar and before this public temple. ... For our Lord and his first and last preachers did not erect in vain the church and the altar

---

[163] A. G. Martimort, *The Church at Prayer*, (Collegeville, MN: Liturgical Press, 1992).
[164] Erik Peterson, *The Angels and the Liturgy* (New York: Herder and Herder, 1962), p. ix.
[165] Baruch Levine, *Leviticus* (Philadelphia: Jewish Publication Society, 1989), pp. xxxviii, 11.
[166] Ignatius of Antioch, *Magnesians* 6.1.
[167] Scott Hahn, Letter and Spirit.

and baptism, all of which are visible to physical eyes. It is through these visible things, however, that we shall be in these heavenly things, which are invisible to eyes of flesh, our bodies becoming temples and our hearts altars (Heb 11:3). Let us open [the door] and enter into this visible church with its priesthood and its worship. ... Then ... that heavenly church and spiritual altar will be revealed to us and we will sacrifice praise upon it through the prayer of our hearts and the supplication of our bodies while believing in this visible altar and this priesthood, which serves [the altar] true for us.

The church is much bigger than we think. For all God's creatures, on earth and in heaven, sing in eternal praise and glory to God.

January 27, 2017

For What it is Worth
Searching for happiness

There is, as all evidence does secure, an overabundance of unhappiness in the world these days, true happiness a rare commodity. The happy soul, embarrassed and uncomfortable admitting to owning such a pleasant state, diligently tries to suppress all that would give evidence to their good nature, so not to offend the unhappy multitude. It takes no genius to observe all the pain and suffering: self-inflicted wounds upon unhappy lives; of all who cry out in anguish—so often masked as hatred, anger, hopelessness and despair—railing against the futility of life itself. They search for answers and in finding none, lash out against the injustice of it all. The seventeenth-century mathematician and philosopher Blaise Pascal wrote: "All men seek happiness. This is without exception. Whatever different means they employ, they all tend to this end. ... This is the motive of every action of every man, even of those who hang themselves."[168] Such happiness of which Pascal writes is more than any superficial happiness which may be purchased or even the much more profound happiness of human love. What he speaks of is the desire to satisfy our deepest desires.

> All complain, princes and subjects, noblemen and commoners, old and young, strong and weak, learned and ignorant, healthy and sick, of all countries, all times, all ages, and all conditions. ... What is it, then, that this desire and this inability proclaim to us, but that there was once in man a true happiness of which there now remain to him only the mark and empty trace, which he in vain tries to fill from all his surroundings, seeking from things absent the comfort he does not receive from things present. ... But these are all inadequate, because the infinite abyss can only be filled by an infinite and immutable object, that is to say, by God himself.

---

[168] Blaise Pascal, *Pensees*, §425.

Our misanthropic tendency to seek happiness in anything that is not God is nothing new, of course; we have been at it since the dawn of time. For some unfathomable reason we are wont to find our own happiness rather than accepting the joy that can only be found in God. At its core, our unhappiness is rooted in how we perceive ourselves: are we real and truly made in the image and likeness of God, beings of infinite and inestimable value, or are we, as atheist biologist Francis Crick describes, merely a "vast assembly of nerve cells and their associated molecules,"[169] a biochemical machine worth only as much as the material of which we are composed? Those who deny, or think nothing of, the existence of God are inevitably want to pathetically satisfy their hunger and thirst for happiness in all manner of created things, even when the thing is a person, a biochemical machine of no intrinsic worth, as Saint Augustine admitted of himself.

> Late have I loved you, O Beauty ever ancient, ever new, late have I loved you! You were within me, but I was outside, and it was there that I searched for you. In my unloveliness I plunged into the lovely things which you created. You were with me, but I was not with you. Created things kept me from you; yet if they had not been in you they would have not been at all. You called, you shouted, and you broke through my deafness. You flashed, you shone, and you dispelled my blindness. You breathed your fragrance on me; I drew in breath and now I pant for you. I have tasted you, now I hunger and thirst for more. You touched me, and I burned for your peace.[170]

Augustine also stated this truth when he prayed, "Lord, you have made us for yourself, and our hearts are restless until they find their rest in you."

> [Kenneth Hensley asks]: If the atheist were correct that nothing exists but the natural order (no God or gods, no human souls, no spirits of any kind) and that you and I are in every aspect of our beings the products of nature—evolved within nature and therefore utterly "one with nature"—why have the vast majority of human beings throughout history believed in and desired to know and live forever in heaven with a God who doesn't exist?

> If there were no God, it seems it would be "natural" for us to not believe in God. ... If we human beings are as one with nature as an apple hanging from a tree, why do we seem so entirely not one with nature?

> Actually, it seems that what is "natural" for us is to believe in God. What seems "natural" for us is to believe that we've come from somewhere rather than from nowhere.[171]

The Catechism of the Catholic Church states at the very beginning: "The desire for God is written in the human heart, because man is created by God and for God; and God never ceases to draw man to himself. Only in God will he find the truth and

[169] Francis Crick, *The Astonishing Hypothesis: scientific search for the soul*, (Touchstone, 1995).
[170] Saint Augustine, *Confessions*, translated by Edward Bouverie Pusey, 401 A.D.
[171] Kenneth Hensley, *Made In His Image and Likeness: How I Talk to Atheists*, Catholic Answers Magazine, January-February 2017, p. 21.

happiness he never stops searching for."[172] Knowing God is etched into our very being. "Although man can forget God or reject him, He never ceases to call every man to seek him, so as to find life and happiness."[173] Perhaps those who forget God or reject him should give serious thought to what would be true if he was nothing more than a biological machine. For instance, what if the universe is, as well-known atheist Richard Dawkins insists—a universe in which there is "no design, no purpose, no evil, no good, nothing but blind pitiless indifference"?[174] These views of Crick and Dawkins—both unconsciously and implicitly—have increasingly and alarmingly become the dominate worldview. Few are those who would stop to consider the implications of such views for the meaning of life, for morality, for the value and dignity of the human person, for human rights, for self-consciousness, for free will. One implication of such a worldview can be vividly illustrated by answering a simple question: is the human person more valuable than a dog, a cat, a tree, or for that matter, a rock? This is not as preposterous a question as one might first intuit, for if there is no God, human beings are necessarily nothing more than biochemical machines, worth nothing beyond the matter of which they are composed. "In other words, we are either created in the image of carbon atoms—and therefore not worth much more than carbon—or we are created in the image of God and therefore infinitely valuable. Our secular, post-Judeo-Christian society has rendered human beings less significant than at any time in Western history."[175] Secular humanism, in its strident denial that human beings are made in the image and likeness of God, has led to the irrational equating of human beings with animals. In surveys over the course of thirty years "of asking high school and college students if they would first try to save their dog or a stranger, two-thirds have always voted against the person. They either don't know what they would do, or they actually vote for the dog. Many adults now vote similarly." What this sadly indicates is a steady erosion of religious moral and ethical norms and values with an increasing tendency toward making moral and ethical decisions based on the individual's emotions and feelings. Thus, since most feel more for their pet than they do for a stranger, two out of three of those surveyed choose to save the animal first. If humans are, as Crick contends, nothing more than a vast assembly of nerve cells and their associated molecules, then there is no reason for elevating human worth over that of an animal. And thus, we see programs such as "Holocaust on Your Plate" developed by the animal-rights group People for the Ethical Treatment of Animals (PETA) which contends there is no difference between barbequing chicken and burning Jews in the holocaust. This, of course, makes perfect sense when you consider a human and a chicken to be of equal worth. This secular-humanist reasoning is of course virulently antithetical to Christian values which place infinite value upon the human person. It is why, for so many, the human fetus is spoken of in terms so inhumanely vacant. To those who see little value

[172] Catechism of the Catholic Church §27.

[173] Catechism of the Catholic Church §30.

[174] Richard Dawkins, *River Out of Eden: A Darwinian View of Life*, (New York, NY, 1995), pp. 131-132.

[175] Dennis Prager, *Are Humans More Valuable Than Animals?*, PragerU.com

in human life, the fetus is but an amorphous clump of cellular mass, worthless, unless deemed otherwise by the mother. The next logical step in this dehumanizing morass of irrational insanity is of course to elevate environmental elements—trees, rivers, mountains, sage brush, air, icebergs, rocks, ad nauseam—to be infinitely more precious and valuable than the human person.

Where this has inevitably led is to a deeply entrenched narcissistic social consciousness where life holds little or no intrinsic value. Counterintuitive, as it first may appear, this has led to the uncompromising fabrication of an ever-increasing and seemingly endless production of rights, injustices, and all manner of *isms* (racism, ethnocentrism, feminism, xenophobia, fanaticism, radicalism, liberalism, conservatism, progressivism, socialism, communism, etc., etc.). Look deep and long into this self-centric abyss of self-idolatry and you will find … nothing of intrinsic or redemptive value, for if the human person is held to such mean and insignificant worth, of what possible value can their contrived issues be?

It is a sign of their great unhappiness which compels them to lend their voices to the discordant masses which object to most everything and yet nothing much at all. Their unhappy voices demand a hearing above the clamorous throng which denies their voice; no one ever listens but to their own for theirs is right, all the others, wrong. There is no God, nothing more than this drear time upon the earth, and so they search until they can no longer for a thing which eludes their grasp and disappoints their pleasure. They are nothing and to nothing they shall return. They live for the moment, not realizing that moment has already passed. The future holds a darkened lamp, illuminating nothing but the endless night which awaits with deadly silence their unhappy end. Is it any wonder when so many share such indignancy of plight that unhappiness abounds with such sour delight?

True happiness can never be obtained nor purchased where there is no value in its possession by one who is of such low opinion of their own intrinsic value. When man decides what price for life, another will demand a discount, bargaining ever lower, until life can neither be purchased nor given away. Only God can create a soul, only God can create us all. "The human person, created in the image of God, is a being at once corporeal and spiritual. Man, whole and entire, is therefore willed by God."[176] We are of infinite value in God's eyes, and only in him can we find true and everlasting happiness.

---

[176] Catechism of the Catholic Church §362.

Playing God
Editing what God has made

What Aldus Huxley envisioned life to be in the year 2540 AD when he penned *Brave New World* is far too quickly becoming reality, some 500 years before its time. Playing God has long been the dream of those who would improve upon what God has created. Considering our first parents bought into the fiction they could be like gods—just look what that got them—you would think man would have been disabused of such a notion, yet man continues undaunted in the quest to alter what God has made in his image and likeness. Of course, that is the consummate issue upon which human editors so adamantly deny: that there is a God, from whom we are imaged. Without God, man is, as mentioned elsewhere, nothing more than "a vast assembly of nerve cells and their associated molecules," (see *For What It Is Worth*) raw material available for manipulation and social engineering by those who propose to know better. "In recent years, threats to the dignity of human life, and to the very idea of human beings as creatures made in the image and likeness of God, have rapidly multiplied and taken new forms that read like the most fanciful science fiction. What used to sound like cinematic nightmares are now becoming reality,"[177] writes David A. Prentice, vice president and research director at the Charlotte Lozier Institute in Washington, D.C. Huxley's terrifying vision of a future where humans are concocted in hatcheries, engineered for specific social and productive qualities, was made ever more frightening in the 1999 science fiction film, *The Matrix*, where humans are enwombed from birth to death by sentient machines in order to harness their body heat and electrical activity as an energy source. Such humans live out their lives in a simulated reality, never realizing their lives are unreal. Although far from reality today—at least one would hope what we know is real and true—the truth is first steps have already been taken down the road which may well and truly lead to precisely such an end. Irrespective of the well-intentioned aims of these so-called "medical advances," such research and experiments ought to be properly considered dangerous, abusive, misguided, and most certainly unethical. As C. S. Lewis rightly warned in *The Abolition of Man*,

> [All] long-term exercises of power, especially in breeding, must mean the power of earlier generations over later ones. ... Each generation exercises power over its successors: and each, in so far as it modifies the environment bequeathed to it and rebels against tradition, resists and limits the power of its predecessors. This modifies the picture which is sometimes painted of a progressive emancipation from tradition and a progressive control of natural processes resulting in a continual increase of human power. In reality, of course, if any one age really attains, by eugenics and scientific education, the power to make its descendants what it pleases, all men who live after it are the patients of that power. They are weaker, not stronger: for though we may have put wonderful machines in their hands we have pre-ordained how they are to use them. ... The last men, far from

---

[177] David A. Prentice, Ph.D., *O Brave New World*, Columbia Magazine, February 2017, p. 21.

being the heirs of power, will be of all men most subject to the dead hand of the great planners and conditioners and will themselves exercise least power upon the future.[178]

The question which must be asked with all seriousness and deliberation is this: who among men should be bequeathed the decisive authority to sit in judgment of man, to decide what is an improvement or what should be altered to benefit humankind? In other words, who will be allowed to play God? What bothers most is the casualness with which human engineers, in the name of scientific progress, commoditize human life. With each and every experiment numerous lives are destroyed. "Human life becomes a commodity to be constructed based on desired 'features.'" The 2008 Vatican document *Dignitas Personae* on bioethical questions noted, "In the hypothesis of gene therapy on the embryo, it needs to be added that this only takes place in the context of *in vitro* fertilization and thus runs up against all ethical objections to such procedures. For these reasons, therefore, it must be stated that, in its current state, germ line cell therapy in all its forms is morally illicit" (§26). The document continued by stating, "Finally, it must also be noted that in the attempt to create **a new type of human being** one can recognize **an ideological element** in which man tries to take the place of his Creator" (§27, emphasis in the original). Dr. Prentice points out that scientists are continually pushing the frontiers of science and ethics.

> Scientists have now created artificial mouse eggs, starting with just a bit of the rodent's skin. The process began with an ethical technique — creation of induced pluripotent stem (iPS) cells, which look and act like embryonic stem cells but do not involve the destruction of an embryo. These cells were formed by adding a few genes to a normal skin cell, reprogramming it as if reprogramming a computer. Next, specific proteins were added to the iPS cells, stimulating them to form immature egg cells in the laboratory. Finally, the immature eggs were incubated with fetal tissue, which matured the eggs. Some of these, when fertilized with mouse sperm, produced born mice.

> While it is unlikely that humans will be born via artificial eggs anytime soon (the artificial mouse eggs produced mostly abnormal animals, with a successful birth rate of less than 1 percent), some scientists see this as having potential for large-scale human experiments. This goal of mass production of laboratory-generated human beings is completely against the foundational principles of human dignity. It treats human life as a manufactured commodity, not as something of inherent worth."[179]

Human embryos constructed—how unsettling it is to write such a term—in the laboratory are a reality and scientists are pushing the envelope in developing artificial wombs to provide a means of full gestation calling to mind the hatcheries in *Brave New World*. Even more unsettling are the attempts being made to engineer chimeras, creatures created from elements of two or more species by combining animal and human DNA. Heretofore completely fictional, scientists in the United States, funded by the

---

[178] C. S. Lewis, *The Abolition of Man*, from The Complete C. S. Lewis Signature Classics (New York, NY, HarperCollins, 2002), pp. 719-720.
[179] David A. Prentice, *O Brave New World*, p. 21-22.

National Institutes of Health (NIH), are creating human-animal chimeras today, going well-beyond ethical boundaries. While there are licit reasons for some of the ongoing research and experimentation, there are clearly ethical and moral boundaries which *must* never be crossed. The difficulty lies with the question previously asked: who decides, who gets to play God?

Food for the Soul
Hunger satisfied, a meal complete

Whenever we come together to celebrate the liturgy we do so in prayer and thanksgiving for what we are about to receive. The liturgy is in every sense a healthy meal, in which we are fed full and sanctifying food, guaranteed to fill our souls with grace. Each time we come before the table of the Lord, what is placed before us is a meal complete, carefully prepared to provide a balance of four essential food groups, each necessary for proper nourishment of the soul. Our souls, while incorporeal and immortal, still require nourishment in order to be found pleasing to God. Thus, we must feed and care for our spiritual selves just as we do for our physical bodies.

At the *West Coast Biblical Studies Conference* last weekend, John Bergsma, Professor of Theology at the Franciscan University of Steubenville, spoke, in part, of how we as members of the Body of Christ share in a full spiritual meal at every Mass. He outlined the four "food groups" which we partake with every liturgical sacrifice:

1. We receive apostolic teaching which fills our thoughts with God's love,

2. We feed our hearts by offering a portion of what we have received from God,

3. We satisfy our hunger for Christ's salvific death and resurrection in the breaking of the bread, and

4. We offer our prayers and petitions in thanksgiving to our heavenly Father for all the gifts we have received.

One thought, in addition to these "food groups", we are nourished by the music that fills our minds, hearts, and souls with joyful song in praise to God for all we have received and are about to receive. Let us always be well-nourished by the love of Jesus Christ.

On Holy Ground
Know that the Lord is near

When Moses came to Horeb, the mountain of God, and spied a bush which was burning yet was not consumed, he was curious to discover why the bush was not consumed. As he approached, God called out from the bush to Moses and said, "Do not come near; put off your shoes from your feet, for the place on which you are standing is holy ground." And Moses hid his face, for he was afraid to look at God (Ex 3:1-6). In the final chapters of the Book of Exodus (37-40), Moses is instructed by God to build the Ark of the Covenant, the Table for the Bread of the Presence, the Lampstand, the Altar of Incense, the Altar of Burnt Offering, the Court of the Tabernacle, and various vestments, oils and incense. The Tabernacle was where the Ark was placed, screened by a veil, which only the high priest could approach, and then only once a year.

> So Moses finished the work. Then the cloud covered the tent of meeting, and the glory of the Lord filled the tabernacle. And Moses was not able to enter the tent of meeting, because the cloud abode upon it, and the glory of the Lord filled the tabernacle. Throughout all their journeys, whenever the cloud was taken up from over the tabernacle, the people of Israel would go onward; but if the cloud was not taken up, then they did not go onward till the day that it was taken up. For throughout all their journeys the cloud of the Lord was upon the tabernacle by day, and fire was in it by night, in the sight of all the house of Israel" (Ex 40:33-38).

Throughout Scripture and for nearly two millennia of Church history, the Tabernacle and the space surrounding it has been considered "holy ground," the place where God was most visibly present, where, like Moses, man knelt in great awe and reverence, and with fear of the Lord. That disposition toward revering the presence of Christ in the Tabernacle resting within the Sanctuary in the house of God seems to have faded away, lost in the panoply of social exigencies and a steady deterioration in the belief and devotion toward our Creator God. We often tend to forget ourselves whenever we are in the holy presence of God, wishing to socialize with friends and fellow disciples in Christ, but are such actions appropriate? There are many who wish to take the opportunity before, during, and after Mass to silently and devoutly pray yet find it difficult to do so with so many conversations breaking the sacred silence on holy ground. Robert Cardinal Sarah has observed this tendency and agrees with those who complain of the noisy disruption. "Many Catholics rightly complain about the absence of silence in … the celebration of our Roman liturgy. It is … important, therefore, to recall the meaning of silence as a Christian ascetical value, and therefore as a necessary condition for deep, contemplative prayer, without forgetting the fact that times of silence are officially prescribed during the celebration of the Holy Eucharist, so as to highlight the importance of silence for a high-quality liturgical renewal."[180]

---

[180] Robert Cardinal Sarah, *Silence in the Liturgy*, *L'Osservatore Romano*, January 30, 2016.

General norms of the Catholic Church provide guidance and explanation for the necessity of silence. Before Mass there should be a general atmosphere of silence. This does not exclude a quiet word of greeting, a nod of recognition or a friendly handshake among parishioners. What should be avoided is the steadily rising hum of multiple conversations in the pews, often on frivolous themes, interrupted only by the announcement the celebration is about to begin. When this happens, the result is that while the body and the voice are ostensibly raised in prayer, the mind tarries on the theme of conversation. In contrast, an overall spirit of silence allows for an easy transition from the world to the celebration of the mystery.

The General Instruction of the Roman Missal, in No. 45, states: "Sacred silence also, as part of the celebration, is to be observed at the designated times. Its purpose, however, depends on the time it occurs in each part of the celebration. ... Even before the celebration itself, it is commendable that silence to be observed in the church, in the sacristy, in the vesting room, and in adjacent areas, so that all may dispose themselves to carry out the sacred action in a devout and fitting manner." After Mass, the most charitable approach is to quietly leave the main body of the Church so as to facilitate the recollection of those who wish to extend their personal thanksgiving for Communion. This quiet is similar to the situation before Mass as it does not exclude a friendly greeting. But actual conversation should not begin until outside. Silence is an important component of the Liturgy as well.

> All parishes should allow for silence in the church as soon as one enters into it, for to enter into a Catholic Church is to pull back the door into heaven itself. But alas, too many churches are more and more like meeting places of gossip and idle chit-chat before Mass. Yet most priests fail to address the issue of silence in their churches. To speak up—even politely—to people in the parish is to be met with consternation and a look of bewilderment as well as the typical response that "Mass hasn't started yet" or "Mass is over." They fail to give any acknowledgment that Jesus is still present in the reserved Eucharist. Thus, Mass is often reduced to somewhat of a show. On the door to the Monastery of the Sisters of the Precious Blood in Manchester, NH is a sign which says, "For the sake of Jesus present in the tabernacle kindly maintain silence in this place."
>
> In the Old Testament the (minor) prophet, Habakkuk declared to the people of ancient Israel in his oracle of the same name: "the LORD is in his holy temple; silence before him, all the earth." The prophet Zephaniah likewise calls for silence: "Silence in the presence of the Lord God! Yes, the LORD has prepared a sacrifice…". If these two prophets called for silence before the presence of God how much more should we, the people of the New Testament, be silent before Jesus present in the tabernacle—Body, Blood, Soul & Divinity."[181]
>
> Our modern world is starved of silence and Holy Mass should be a privileged moment to escape the hustle and bustle of daily life and, through worship and participation in

---

[181] Cynthia Trainque, *On The Importance of Silence in the Liturgy*, catholicexchange.com, June 29, 2016.

Christ's eternal sacrifice, become capable of giving an eternal value to these same daily and transitory activities.

To help achieve this, we should foment by all available means the spirit of attentive and active silence in our celebrations and refrain from importing the world's clamor and clatter into their midst.[182]

To be silent is to breathe in quiet moments. You cannot breathe in and speak at the same time. To speak, you must breathe out, thus, breaking the silence. You must be silent in order to breathe in the Breath of God. You must be silent to hear His Voice.[183]

February 10, 2017

The Genius of a Mind
Life is still worth living

Perhaps it is nothing more than whispered thought floating on a breeze or memory's lingering scent which is wont to tease forgetfulness. There is, of course, no way of knowing where or how or whence such idle thought or distant memory should tantalize, and yet, from slumber it awakens, demanding much of one's attention. Few are they who issue thought so profound they transcend the passing of the years or command man's briefest mental exercise. Most are long forgotten, dying stillborn before the tongue can flutter and the lips can separate. But those who make lasting memories are as precious jewels, which shine, not in shadow or in darkness, but only by the light of day. The genius of a mind, all but now a distant memory, unknown and unremembered by those who care not for what belongs to yesterday, such genius cries out in anguish the need to be recalled and yet again considered, to neither be dismissed nor tossed away. For though years have flown since once his sonorous voice, with wit and laughter did fill the air, the echo of his words still ring of truths which the world has long denied yet so sorely needs today. The world, it feels, is growing colder, dark shadows hold the light at bay. From thoughtless minds, the Nietzschean throng cries out in anger and in hate: "God is dead," "Live long and prosper." But no one listens anymore.

We ought to remind ourselves despite all the ugliness, hatred, anger, bitterness, strife, and evil that abounds, "Life is worth living." For those who have yet to abandon their minds to vacant mindlessness and self-desire, dare to read what once was spoken by a man so blessed by God, Venerable Archbishop Fulton J. Sheen (1895-1979).

---

[182] Father Edward McNamarq, *Sounds of Silience*, (Rome: A ZENIT Daily Dispatch, January 20, 2004).
[183] Charles Lanham, *The Voices of God*, (Reno, NV: Deacon's Corner Publishing, 2014), 12.

On God:

The need for God never disappears. Those who deny the existence of water are still thirsty. And those who deny God still want him in their craving for beauty and love and peace, which he alone is.

If the new crime be, to believe in God, let us all be criminals.

God does not frown on your complaint. Did not His Mother in the Temple ask: 'Son why hast Thou done so to us?' And did not Christ on the Cross complain: 'My God why has Thou abandoned Me?' If the Son asked the Father, and the Mother, the Son —why should not you? But let your wails be to God, and not to man. And at end of your sweet com-plaining prayer you will say: "Father into Thy Hands I commend my spirit." They who complain to others never see God's purposes. They who complain to God find that their passion, like Christ's turns into compassion.

God love you! That is the way I shall conclude my broadcasts, and that is the way I shall begin them today. I want the first word on the air of this New Year to be God. It is God who makes us happy. It is Love which makes old things new. It is you who count the years in terms of God's abiding love. Combining all three we have "God love you," which is but another way of saying "Happy New Year".

God leaves each one free to reject his infusion of love—for gifts cease to be gifts if they are forced on us. God respects our freedom of will; he did not even enter into this human order of ours without consulting a woman. So neither does he elevate us to partake of his divine nature without our free consent.

On Jesus Christ:

It is so hard to admit that one is a sinner; it is so hard to climb the hill of Calvary and kneel beneath a cross and ask for pardon, forgiveness. Certainly, it is hard. But it is harder to hang there.

They who have not the Spirit call him a great man, a teacher, a master, but to see Him as the Lord of heaven and earth as the Son of the Living God, comes only through the Holy Spirit.

All of a sudden the world has become filled with a race of people called the "I am not". Our Divine Lord seven times said "I am" e.g. "I am the good Shepherd". 70x7 these peo-ple say "I am not" e.g. "I am not a believer because." Their words tell how empty they are and how they hunger for the Eucharistic Bread that makes us one. They talk as if they were disappointed in love — and everyone is who has only the world to love. That is why they warn everyone against falling in love with Christ's Mystical Body. Like a man who missed the boat, they tell others never to go to sea for a rest. They admit their thirst, but they do not want others to drink.

A little boy who had been to Sunday School told his father that he learned that God the Father and Son were equal. The father said: "That is ridiculous. I am your father; you are my son. I existed a long time before you." "No," said the boy, "you did not begin to be a father until I began to be a son." At Christmas, He Who was eternally generated by the Father is generated in time, in the womb of a virgin Mary. The Son of God then becomes the Son of Man. As the word which I speak to you is not different because I give it breath and sound, so neither is the Word of the Son of God changed because He takes on a human nature like ours in all things except sin. "The Word became flesh and dwelt amongst us."

On Faith:

Judge the Catholic Church not by those who barely live by its spirit, but by the example of those who live closest to it.

In vain will the world seek for equality until it has seen men through the eyes of faith. Faith teaches that all men, however poor, or ignorant, or crippled, however maimed, ugly, or degraded they may be, all bear within themselves the image of God, and have been bought by the precious blood of Jesus Christ. As this truth is forgotten, men are valued only because of what they can do, not because of what they are.

Those who love God do not protest, whatever He may ask of them, nor doubt His kindness when He sends them difficult hours. A sick person takes medicine without asking the physician to justify its bitter taste because the patient trusts the doctor's knowledge; so the soul that has sufficient faith accepts all the events of life as gifts of God in the serene assurance that God knows best.

On Morality:

Why is it that the world has confessed its inability to inculcate virtue in the young? Very simply because it has not correlated morality to any love nobler than self-love. Things fulfill their proper role only when integrated into a larger whole. Most lives are like doors without hinges, or sleeves without coats, or bows without violins; that is unrelated to wholes or purposes which give them meaning.

Moral principles do not depend on a majority vote. Wrong is wrong. Even if everybody is wrong. Right is right. Even if nobody is right.

The first direct, human limitation of infant life in the history of Christianity took place in the village of Bethlehem through an infant-controller whose name was Herod. The prevention of infant life was simultaneously an attack upon Divinity in the person of God made man, Jesus Christ our Lord. No one strikes at birth who does not simultaneously strike at God, for birth is earth's reflection of the Son's eternal generation.

The root principle of birth-control is unsound. It is a glorification of the means and a contempt of the end; it says that the pleasure which is a means to the procreation of children is good, but the children themselves are no good. In other words, to be logical, the philosophy of birth-control would commit us to a world in which trees were always blooming but never giving fruit, a world full of signposts that were leading nowhere. In this cosmos every tree would be a barren fig tree and for that reason would have upon it the curse of God.

On Love:

If love craves a cross—even God's true love is sacrificial. That is why courtship is characterized by gift-giving—a surrender of what one has. In marriage this sacrificial love should deepen by a surrender of what one has. Because too many measure their love for one another by the pleasure which the other gives, they are in reality not in love, but in the swamps of selfishness. Our poor, frail human souls at best are like jangled strings, made toneless by self-love; and not until we tighten them with self-discipline can we attune them to those harmonies that come from God, wherein each, having given to the other hostage of its heart, finds himself free in the glorious liberty of the children of God. Peace first came to the world when the Wise Men discovered a family. And the dawn of peace will come again when other wise men return to homes where they see the human family of father, mother, and children, as the reverse order of the Holy Family: a Child, a Mother, and a Father."

On Knowledge:

Intellectual knowledge is not the one thing necessary. Not all the PhD's are saints, and all the ignorant are not demons. Indeed, a certain type of education may simply turn a man from a stupid egotist into a clever egotist and, of the two, the former has a better chance of salvation.

How many universities in our land founded as religious institutions for the propagation of a particular Christian creed, today adhere to the creeds they were found to propagate?

On Human Nature:

The less we think we are, the more good we do ... reducing themselves to zero they leave room for infinity, where those who think themselves infinite, God leaves with their little zero.

The simple words "thank you" will always stand out as a refutation of determinism, for they imply that something which was done could possibly have been left undone.

Bad temper is an indication of a man's character; every man can be judged by the things which make him mad.

If you do not live what you believe, you will end up believing what you live. Believe the incredible and you can do the impossible.

Courtesy is not condescension of a superior to an inferior, or a patronizing interest in another's affairs. It is the homage of the heart to the sacredness of human worth.

Contentment is not an innate virtue. It is acquired through great resolution and diligence in conquering unruly desire; hence it is an art which few study.

Emptiness as regards the self, is balanced by compassion for others. The less stress on the ego, the more care there is for neighbor. At the moment St. Francis emptied himself of his possession, he made himself free for compassion.

From a material point of view, we are worth so little. The content of a human body is equivalent to as much sugar as there is in two lumps, as much oil as there is in seven bars of soap, as much phosphorus as there is in 2200 matches, and as much magnesium as it takes to develop a photograph. In all, the human body, chemically, is worth a little less than two dollars—So why should any mortal Spirit be proud? But spiritually we are worth more than the universe.

Once our helplessness is rendered up to the power of God, life changes and we become less and less the victims of our moods. Instead of letting the world determine our state of mind, we determine the state of the soul with which the world is to be faced. The earth carries its atmosphere with it as it revolves about the sun; so can the soul carry the atmosphere of God with it in disregard of turbulent events in the world outside.

It used to be that the most popular biographies were the lives of good men for the sake of imitation, rather than scandals for the sake of making ourselves believe we are more virtuous.

God does not love us because we are loveable of and by ourselves, but because he has put his own love into us. He does not even wait for us to love; his own love perfects us. Letting it do this, with no resistance, no holding back for fear of what our egotism must give up, is the one way to the peace that the world can neither give nor take away.

We always make the fatal mistake of thinking that it is what we do that matters, when really what matters is what we let God do to us. God sent the angel to Mary, not to ask her to do something, but to let something be done. Since God is a better artisan than you, the more you abandon yourself to him, the happier he can make you.

No man discovers anything big unless he makes himself small.

You think you are having a good time, but time really is the greatest obstacle in the world to happiness, not only because it makes you take pleasures successively, but also because you are never really happy until you are unconscious of the passing of time. The more you look at the clock, the less happy you are. The more you enjoy yourself, the less conscious you are of the passing of time.

Sunlight is all about the house, but for sunlight to get in we must open the blinds. The physician of souls can cure, but we must know we are sick and must want to be cured. God Calls! We can pretend we do not hear, we can accept Him, or we can reject His voice. It is each person's inalienable right to decide

On Religion:

A religion that doesn't interfere with the secular order will soon discover that the secular order will not refrain from interfering with it.

A few decades ago, nobody believed in the confession of sins except the Church. Today everyone believes in confession — with this difference: some believe in confessing their own sins; others believe in confessing other people's sins. The popularity of psychoanalysis has nearly convinced every one of the necessity of some kind of confession for peace of mind. This is another instance of how the world, which threw Christian truths into the wastebasket in the nineteenth century, is pulling them out in isolated secularized form in the twentieth century, meanwhile deluding itself into believing that it has made a great discovery. The world found it could not get along without some release for its inner unhappiness. Once it had rejected confession and denied both God and guilt, it had to find a substitute.

Humanism has been defined as "the endeavor to keep the best spiritual values of religion while surrendering any theological interpretation of the universe." In its broadest sense it is an endeavor to have Christianity without Christ, godliness without God, and Christian hope without the promise of another life.

I don't want my life to be mine, I want it to be Christ's. The more ego there is, the less there is of Christ.

A man can join any other movement, group, or cult without provoking hostile comment from his neighbors and friends; he can even found some esoteric sun cult of his own and be tolerated as a citizen exercising his legitimate freedom and satisfying his own religious needs. But as soon as anyone joins the Catholic Church, hatred, opposition appear.

The greatest love story of all time is contained in a tiny white host.

Neither theological knowledge nor social action alone is enough to keep us in love with Christ unless both are proceeded by a personal encounter with Him. Theological insights are gained not only from between two covers of a book, but from two bent knees before an altar. The Holy Hour becomes like an oxygen tank to revive the breath of the Holy Spirit in the midst of the foul and fetid atmosphere of the world.

The mark of the true Church is that it will never get on well with the passing moods of the world.

On Truth:

It is easy to find truth; it is hard to face it and still harder to follow it. The only people who ever arrive at a knowledge of God are those who, when the door is opened, accept that truth and shoulder the responsibilities it brings. It requires more courage than brains to learn to know God. God is the most obvious fact of human experience, but accepting him is one of the most arduous.

Christian love bears evil, but it does not tolerate it. It does penance for the sins of others, but it is not broadminded about sin. REAL LOVE involves real hatred: whoever has lost the power of moral indignation and the urge to drive the sellers from the temples has also lost a living fervent love of Truth.

The examination of one's own conscience is the hardest of all revolutions to begin and only saints have the courage to do it.

The Spirit Denied
That which defines us

What becomes of those who hold no value for another, whose lives are measured, not by the exceptional, but by the banal and mundane, who deny the existence of that which makes each of us uniquely human? Those who hold the prevailing secular worldview of man as a product of natural evolution, absent any ineffable attributes such as spirit, reason, intellect, and conscience must necessarily move to diminish and denigrate the dignity of the human person. That which defines us as human, absent from all other living creatures, is the unity of body and soul created in the image of God. Our bodies are animated by our spiritual souls, intended by God to become temples of the Spirit.

Though made of body and soul, man is one. Through his bodily composition he gathers to himself the elements of the material world; thus they reach their crown through him, and through him raise their voice in free praise of the Creator. For this reason man is not allowed to despise his bodily life, rather he is obliged to regard his body as good and honorable since God has created it and will raise it up on the last day. Nevertheless, wounded by sin, man experiences rebellious stirrings in his body. But the very dignity of man postulates that man glorify God in his body and forbid it to serve the evil inclinations of his heart.[184]

The unity of soul and body is so profound that one has to consider the soul to be the "form" of the body: i.e., it is because of its spiritual soul that the body made of matter becomes a living, human body; spirit and matter, in man, are not two natures united, but rather their union forms a single nature.[185]

Examples of the precipitous decline in ethical and moral norms within major social and cultural groups are far too numerous to mention. However, one recent example should be sufficient to give evidence of the dismal and abhorrent moral morass in which we find ourselves now slogging. A recent survey, funded by Dallas-based dating service Match, conducted by Research Now found nearly half (48%) of Millennials have had sex "before" a first date. A biological anthropologist and chief scientific advisor to Match, who helped develop the survey notes, "We have a real misunderstanding of Millennials. ...they are very career-oriented, so sex before the first date could be a 'sex interview,' where they want to know if they want to spend time with this person." Have we really sunk that low? Really? Sex has been reduced to an interview, utilizing performance as a means of evaluating likeability? That is beyond bizarre, beyond immoral, beyond rational understanding. But wait! There's more! A licensed clinical social worker and certified sex therapist says, "In many ways sex has become a less intimate part of dating. With dating apps making it easier than ever to hop in bed, now the intimate part can oftentimes be introducing a partner to friends and family. We used to think of sex as you crossed the line now you are in an intimate zone, but now sex is almost a given and it's not the intimate part. The intimate part is getting to know someone and going on a date."[186]

Precisely how anyone can define intimacy as "getting to know someone and going on a date" is simply mind-boggling. The most beautiful, loving act designed by God has been diminished to nothing more than an item on a checklist designed to determine how well one may like another. Is it any wonder why so many see nothing immoral or sinful anymore? The moral decay lies rotting all around us, its stench revolting. Sex has been demoted to the trivial and unimportant. What is now far more important is the phone. "Singles don't like people who have a cracked phone or those who use a

---

[184] *Gaudium et Spes*: Pastoral Constitution of the Church in the Modern World, §14.

[185] Catechism of the Catholic Church §365.

[186] Mary Bowerman, *Sex before first date OK, but a cracked phone? Think again*, Reno Gazette Journal, February 6, 2017, B01

clicking sound when typing." Now those are real turnoffs and absolute relationship killers, don't you know? Really?

Objections Noted
Tone it down, please!

Following last week's essay, *On Holy Ground,* as expected, several readers opined, both in support or not, and their words were inciteful, gracious, and welcome. In response to one who suggested it might have been better to have said, "tone it down, please" I responded, in part, thus:

Thanks for writing. While I share similar feelings with some of what you have to say concerning who we are as a people and our desire to socialize and love one another, I must, with all due respect, disagree with you on a number of points.

Yes, we are not in a seminary or convent and yes we are perhaps as you write "sinners, irreverent, improper, gauche, and debauched bunch group of attendees ('irritating, rude, offensive', et al)" but we are nevertheless in the presence of God in His temple. One does not need to be a seminarian, clergy, or religious to recognize and give due reverence to Almighty God and his Son, Jesus Christ our Lord. It seems to me one of the biggest challenges we face as members of the Body of Christ and his Church today is the serious and prevailing lack of reverence and awe we display whenever we enter into His presence. If you have ever been present in a courtroom you will recognize how solemn and silent the room becomes whenever the judge is seated behind the bench. Those in the courtroom are not asked to simply tone it down please, but to be silent. How much more so should we be whenever we find ourselves in God's presence? Those who find themselves facing judgment in the courtroom generally act with decorum, whether guilty or innocent, and should they insist on not acting thusly are summarily removed from the courtroom while their trial continues without them. Again, should not similar rules of etiquette and decorum be applied when before our Lord God, the final judge of the universe? The Church is a place where we come together as a community to worship and to give praise and glory to the One who made us. It is not a bawdy house, brew pub, dance hall, or social club. If, and when, we enter the house of God with the understanding it is other than a place of worship, we make a very public affirmation it is we who are of greater importance than our Creator God.

When we "come in off the streets" as you wrote, and enter the narthex, we have yet to enter the church proper and therefore brief social conversations may and can occur as long as they are conducted quietly and with deference to those who have entered further into the nave of the church. Traditionally, the narthex, while considered a part of the church building, has not been considered part of the church proper, and therefore quiet conversation is permitted. But once you enter the church proper you are in the presence of our Lord God, on Holy Ground, and God commands all our respect, honor, and reverence. We all, and I include myself here, need to be reminded from time to time of the reason we come to church and the One with whom we truly come to worship, to praise, and to give thanks for all we have received. We come indeed because we are sinners, broken people in desperate need of God's forgiveness and mercy. We come to be filled with God's grace and love. We come to be fed through the body and blood of our Lord, Jesus Christ, so we can be healed. If we come for any other purpose, we have come to the wrong house.

So, to paraphrase: "I say parishioners: …silence please! Bow your heads and pray for God's mercy, for you are in His Holy Presence! Blessing be upon us for more reverence to God our Father, Son, and Holy Spirit." Peace be with you. Amen.

February 17, 2017

The KISS Principle
The efficacy of simplicity

Sometimes the best answer is the simplest; not necessarily the most complete nor the most satisfactory, just the most appropriate and thus the best response.

Not that long ago, I picked up a book, written by Father Robert J. Spitzer, of whom I have both met and have sincere admiration. Having read numerous books on the existence of God, I was very eager to read Father Spitzer's book, *New Proofs for the Existence of God: Contributions of Contemporary Physics and Philosophy*. Sadly, I have yet to finish reading the book, although I have managed to digest, with serious difficulty, perhaps a third of it. It is heavy, heavy, heavy stuff, indeed.

Case in point, there is a postscript to Part One with the quite unimposing title of: *Inflationary Cosmology and the String Multiverse* by Bruce L. Gordon, Ph.D. The second sentence really says it all: "We begin by noting that the Borde-Vilenkin past-incompleteness theorem for inflationary universes has been strengthened, and will discuss the significance of this fact for various pre-big-bang inflationary scenarios in string cosmology, including landscape and cyclic ekpyrotic models."[187] And no, I have not a clue what the learned doctor was attempting to say.

Now admittedly, I should note Father Spitzer is intellectually far beyond the genius of most, having taught graduate courses on faith and reason, metaphysics, philosophy of God, and philosophy of science at Georgetown, Gonzaga, Seattle, and St. Louis universities. He was president of Gonzaga University for eleven years and now serves as

---

[187] Robert J. Spitzer, SJ, *New Proofs for the Existence of God: Contributions of Contemporary Physics and Philosophy*, (Eerdmans, June 29, 2010, 319 pages), 75.

the president of the Magis Center of Reason and Faith and the Spitzer Center. He has produced two television series for EWTN and received a Templeton Grant for teaching physics and metaphysics. So, one must concede Father Spitzer has more than a few brain cells swirling around within that space between his ears. But that does not guarantee easy reading, in fact, I would suggest much the opposite. Which is unfortunate for we mere mortals, that is all the rest of us, for what he writes is of great importance to all believers, not just to the academic elite.

Yet, my intent here is neither to promote nor denigrate Father Spitzer or his book, but rather to consider the benefits of the KISS principle, specifically as it relates to faith and God. For those who might be unfamiliar with the KISS principle, let me explain. KISS, in this particular instance is an acronym which stands for "Keep It Simple Stupid", a rather obvious, mildly pejorative phrase, with an equally obvious meaning. While I must confess to having been the recipient of just such an admonition on countless occasions, to which I must, in all candor, hopelessly plead GUILTY, albeit with mitigating factors. What those mitigating factors are specifically will have to be set aside for a later time. Here, I wish to focus on the "efficacy of simplicity" when dealing with matters of faith.

Once upon a time, a very long time ago, I attended a small Catholic parochial school, taught by holy Dominican Sisters (encased from head to toe in habits of black and white) watched over by an elderly (in my youthful mind, ancient) Irish Monsignor. Religion was seriously taught, primarily from the Baltimore Catechism, and woe to the one who could not respond with inerrant accuracy, word for precise word from its pages. The Baltimore Catechism was then, to most American Catholics, as much or more the Bible as the Bible itself. It was what Catholics were taught and what they believed. And it was simple to read and to understand. Was it comprehensive? No. Did it answer all the questions concerning God? No. Was it appropriate for all ages? Arguably so, in as much as everyone could read and understand it. Was it outdated? Again, one could argue that was the case as it was first published in 1885 upon orders of the Third Plenary Council of Baltimore and approved by John Cardinal McCloskey, then Archbishop of New York. The original intent was to provide a uniform textbook of Christian doctrine for all Catholics. The first edition was largely the work of a single priest, Father Januarius De Concilio, written over a period of ten days. It was significantly revised in the latter part of the twentieth century into four volumes, each targeting a specific age group. This revision involved hundreds of theologians, scholars and teachers and took years to review and edit. Did it contain doctrinal or dogmatic errors? No. While there was some initial criticism, reviews were overwhelmingly positive, and it quickly became the Catechism adopted and taught in virtually every Catholic parochial school in the U.S.

So why do we no longer teach from the Baltimore Catechism? Simply put, because it has been completely updated and replaced by the Catechism of the Catholic Church, a monumental and beautifully composed work first proposed by the Extraordinary

Assembly of the Synod of Bishops convened by Pope Saint John Paul II in 1985. In 1986, Pope Saint John Paul II then composed a commission of 12 bishops and cardinals, under the direction of Joseph Cardinal Ratzinger to begin this enormous project which labored over the next decade to produce a Catechism with over 900 pages (English edition.)

Is it better? Arguably, and in many respects, yes. It is certainly more comprehensive, making extensive use of material from ancient sources, early church writers, as well as papal encyclicals, council documents, and other church papers. Is it simple to read and to understand? No. Its intentional audiences are clergy, scholars, and theologians, not adult laity or children. For those less acquainted or prepared for the profound theological treatises from the likes of Augustine and Aquinas, there are other "simplified" editions: the *Youcat* for youth as well as the United States Catholic Catechism for Adults, although regrettably, even with their simplification they fall short in their approach to simple catechesis, lacking anything approaching the simplicity and directness of the Baltimore Catechism.

While the Baltimore Catechism has largely fallen into disuse, it remains an excellent resource for young children. After all, if it was good enough for your grandparents, it ought to be good enough for your children. Currently, there are two versions available: The official version written by the U.S. Bishops at the Third Plenary Council of Baltimore and the St. Joseph version adapted for smaller children. The Baltimore Catechism is divided into individual lessons with a definition of terms at the start of each. Each section is then divided into a brief question and answer format which makes for quick reading and quick apprehension. Included in the back are standard Catholic prayers and hymns children should learn. The Baltimore Catechism is divided into No. 1, 2, 3, and 4 which are available individually or in a complete set. The numbers are intended for grade-level appropriateness for elementary, middle, and high school, respectively, with the last one ideal for educators. The second version is The New Saint Joseph Baltimore Catechism. It is based on the Baltimore Catechism but revised with the addition of lots of pictures, large print, and easy-to-understand language and presentation that's more attractive to children. It also includes discussion questions, T/F, fill-in-the-blanks, bible reading passages, projects, and prayers after each section. In the back are the Holy Rosary, Stations of the Cross, Catholic Prayers including the Mass, and a dictionary of terms. This is divided into No. 1 and 2, for elementary and middle school respectively.

For those of us who grew up learning our faith from the Baltimore Catechism, the question and answer format still rings in our heads, even though a half-century or more separates now from then:

Q. *Who made the world?*
A. God made the world.

Q. *Who is God?*
A. God is the Creator of heaven and earth, and of all things.

Q. *What is man?*
A. Man is a creature composed of body and soul, and made to the image and likeness of God.

Q. *Why did God make you?*
A. God made me to know Him, to love Him, and to serve Him in this world, and to be happy with Him forever in the next.

Q. *What must we do to save our souls?*
A. To save our souls, we must worship God by faith, hope, and charity; that is, we must believe in Him, hope in Him, and love Him with all our heart.

Simple? Yes. Understandable? Yes. Theologically sound? Yes. Memorable? Absolutely! If you have any doubts, just ask anyone who was catechized in a Catholic parochial school prior to the 60s or 70s. No doubt, most, when asked "Why did God make you?" will, with little or no difficulty, respond with the correct answer.

Too often, these days, we look for and expect too much, too deep, too complex, too profound, too complete, too big an answer to the questions that arise. In some ways, I suppose, this is the direct result of the availability of unlimited—or so it would appear—easy access to information delivered through the Internet. Have a question? Just ask Google or Bing or Alexa or Siri. We no longer have to exert much effort to obtain answers to our questions. Unfortunately, the quality, accuracy, even the truth of the answers is too often questionable. Of course, to further compound the problem, the majority of our children today are educated in public schools, completely devoid of even a mention of religion, faith, or heaven-forbid, God. This has not always been the case, although many would and do claim this to be so. Fifty years ago, God had yet to be denied mention within the hallowed halls of public education; every child stood with hand upon the heart to recite the pledge of allegiance with "one nation, under God" in every classroom, every morning; priests and nuns were allowed, even encouraged to teach religion in the public schools, although generally after regular school hours, as were other denominations or faiths. Students were taught history without the necessity for some anonymous panel to first excise any and all mention of God, faith, or religious events, lest anyone be offended, stigmatized, or traumatized by the mere mention of the name of God.

What elevates this principle—the efficacy of simplicity or KISS—to more than a passing thought is, in part I suppose, the direct result of my ongoing graduate studies in Biblical Theology. What has become abundantly clear to this poor student is while there is much to learn of our faith, of the church, of who we are and who made us, theologians in large measure suffer with great difficulty to see the forest for the trees. Even that is often much too granular, for they are often so engrossed in the minutiae they cannot see the leaf for the stem. Simply put, they spend far too much time study-ing a single snowflake they lose sight of the gathering storm threatening to bury them.

Case in point: Saint Thomas Aquinas, an Italian Dominican priest and Doctor of the Church is considered to be one of the Catholic Church's greatest philosophers and the-ologians. His best-known work, *Summa Theologiae*, is a brief but unfinished 3,500-page instructional guide (i.e. Catechism) for beginners. Aquinas conceived the *Summa* as a work suited to beginning students: "Because the Master of Catholic Truth ought not only to teach the proficient, but also to instruct beginners (according to the Apostle: As unto little ones in Christ, I gave you milk to drink, not meat — 1 Cor. 3:1, 2), we purpose in this book to treat of whatever belongs to the Christian Religion, in such a way as may tend to the instruction of beginners."[188] As learned and esteemed as Aquinas most assuredly was, I would humbly suggest this beloved saint missed the mark for pro-ducing an instruction guide for beginners. To highlight the wide disparity in writing styles between the *Summa* and the Baltimore Catechism, here Aquinas responds to the question as to whether in Holy Scripture a word may have several senses:

> I answer that, The author of Holy Writ is God, in whose power it is to signify His mean-ing, not by words only (as man also can do), but also by things themselves. So, whereas in every other science things are signified by words, this science has the property, that the things signified by the words have themselves also a signification. Therefore that first signification whereby words signify things belongs to the first sense, the historical or literal. That signification whereby things signified by words have themselves also a sig-nification is called the spiritual sense, which is based on the literal, and presupposes it. Now this spiritual sense has a threefold division. For as the Apostle says (Heb. 10:1) the Old Law is a figure of the New Law, and Dionysius says (Cœl. Hier. i) the New Law itself is a figure of future glory. Again, in the New Law, whatever our Head has done is a type of what we ought to do. Therefore, so far as the things of the Old Law signify the things of the New Law, there is the allegorical sense; so far as the things done in Christ, or so far as the things which signify Christ, are types of what we ought to do, there is the moral sense. But so far as they signify what relates to eternal glory, there is the anagogical sense. Since the literal sense is that which the author intends, and since the author of Holy Writ is God, Who by one act comprehends all things by His intellect, it is not unfitting, as Augustine says (Confess. xii), if, even according to the literal sense, one word in Holy Writ should have several senses."[189]

Now perhaps his response is in some measure less difficult to understand than one might find reading Father Spitzer's book, yet it still belies the simplicity necessary for instructing beginners.

As well-intentioned as our catechists and religious educators may be in inculcating our children with the knowledge of the Catholic faith, far too many are growing up knowing little if anything about their faith. The fault however does not rest with our

---

[188] St. Thomas Aquinas, *Summa Theologiae, I Prologue.*
[189] St. Thomas Aquinas, *Summa Theologiae, I q.1 a.10 resp..*

catechists and religious educators but must be placed squarely upon the shoulders of parents of latchkey children who have little or no time in their busy lives nor, all too often, the inclination to instruct or communicate the tenets of the faith to their children. Historically, the current generation of parents were raised in much the same environment, with an absence of catechesis often accompanied by poor church attendance, thus resulting in a repeating pattern of religious illiteracy. Simply put, "What we've got here is failure to communicate"[190] the essentials of our faith, either by word or deed, in language sufficiently simple and clear enough for our young to grasp. The efficacy of simplicity is evident, but it must be taught, early and often, with sincerity and faith.

A Shell of Christianity
Those willing to die for their faith

We who live in affluent Western cultures find little in common with the less sophisticated, less educated, less advantaged peoples of the world. Collectively, we pay little attention to those in whom we consider to be our cultural inferiors. Clearly not what Christ demands of us. Our self-absorption and cultural secularism skew our worldview, ultimately resulting in a superficial and callous view of our own Christianity.

In an opinion piece written for the February 2017 Columbia magazine, Supreme Knight Carl A. Anderson wrote of Martin Scorsese's recent film, *Silence*, about two Jesuit missionaries who travel to Japan during the terrible 17th-century persecution of Christians there. It is an article worth reading for it pointedly raises several disturbing questions, questions which we who are fortunate enough to live in a time and place relatively free of harsh and deadly persecution and martyrdom should take seriously and dig deep within our own consciences to discern and understand. The film based upon the 1966 novel of the same name written by the late Japanese Catholic author Shusaku Endo, "raises profound questions regarding the challenge to Christian faith in the midst of suffering and a hostile culture. The most obvious is suggested in the film's title: How are we to understand the silence of God amid great suffering and evil?"[191]

In a lengthy (1:07.46) roundtable forum filmed at John Paul the Great Catholic University in Escondido, California, four professors discuss the book and the movie and offer their unique and insightful observations on what the author Endo and film director Scorsese have portrayed. As Doctor Tom Harmon observes, the central theme for both is Apostasy, that the Japanese authorities have discovered martyrdom doesn't actually do much to stamp out the Christian community. One of the ways the authorities undermine the Christian faith is the public renunciation of the faith by the

---

[190] A quotation from the 1967 film *Cool Hand Luke*
[191] Carl A. Anderson, *The Future of the Faith*, Columbia magazine, February 2017, p. 3.

Japanese peasants and the missionary priests by stepping on an image of Jesus Christ or one of the Saints, especially the Virgin Mary. The central figure, Father Rodriguez is told to step on the image of Christ or one or more of the peasants will suffer crucifixion.[192] Further on in his article, Carl Anderson writes:

> During one of the film's highpoints there is an exchange between two Jesuits missionaries. The younger Jesuit asserts that Christianity is universally true—if it is not true in every culture, then it cannot be true for any. But the older one replies that Christianity cannot take root in Japan.

> The reality is, however, that thousands of Japanese had become Christians and endured horrible torture and death rather than renounce their faith. But to this fact, the older Jesuit claims that these Japanese martyrs do not really understand the faith; they embrace a mere shell of Christianity.

> There is something deeply troubling about this scene, where the sophisticated, highly educated Westerner rationalizes his abandonment of Christianity, while "wretched" Japanese peasants willingly give their lives for their faith.

> In many places in the West today, the light of Christian faith is diminishing, while throughout much of the rest of the world Christianity is growing stronger. This is especially true in Asia, Africa and the Middle East, where many Christians are being persecuted and killed because of their faith.

With so many of our poorer, less-privileged, less sophisticated brothers and sister enduring persecution and martyrdom for their faith, should not we be asking ourselves whether we have the strength of faith to endure the same? Let us pray for so great a faith.

February 24, 2017

What Love is This
Is it love ... enough?

Two questions, only two. And no, I do not care to hear the answers, for such thoughts are far too personal to share, and yet, please consider them with all the

---

[192] John Paul the Great Catholic University Faculty Roundtable Discussion: Silence, February 3, 2017, https://www.youtube.com/watch?v=iJUoefcUWVc moderated by Michael Barber, Ph.D., Chair of the Department of Theology, joined by Father Andrew Younan, a Chaldean Priest from Iraq and Professor of Philosophy, Christopher Riley, Ph.D, Professor of Film and Screenwriting, and Thomas Harmon, Ph.D. Professor of Theology & Culture.

gravitas they require. Answer then, with deliberateness and grave concern, in silent stillness hear what speaks within your heart.

A song first sung sixty-two years ago in 1955 begins:

> *Love and marriage, love and marriage.*
> *They go together like a horse and carriage.*
> *This I tell you, brother,*
> *you can't have one without the other.*

These lyrics sound "nice" yet somehow evoke a sentiment lacking a thing essential; there is no feeling of permanence or deep emotional commitment, no sense of unity or oneness with another. This leads to the first question which I ask of every couple with whom I meet to prepare for marriage:

What *love* is this which you express?

Love too easily trips the tongue; it is too often but a blithe response to some pleasant experience. In the case of two persons "in love," what they believe love is seldom reaches the lofty heights demanded of a life-long commitment to one another. Youthful inexperience denies love beyond their passion, for that is what love is, don't you see, and that leads to the second question:

Is it love … enough?

Perhaps, yet no flame can burn hot for eternity. What happens when passion wanes, when love no longer boils but simmers low? Without the heat of passion's breath, will such love be enough to warm the heart? If not, what then the union in sweet passion's name?

And of God too oft forsaken, thus marriage vows too oft forgotten. Passion lasts but for the moment, love will last forevermore.

Rude Awakening
From peaceful slumber

Noticeably absent these days from public discourse, social commentary, or didactive pedagogy is an awareness of and recognition for the essentiality of a strong moral code. Morality is a topic studiously avoided for the simple reason any discussion of it necessarily raises uncomfortable questions and inconvenient challenges to many of our social norms, behavioral modalities, and perceptions of reality. We are no longer guided by principles of right or wrong, good or evil but rather by our basest desires and our "feelings", what feels good, or what is our "right." We have managed to remove "sin" and "immorality" from our lexicon; we have become amoralists, living only for ourselves and our own interests, nothing more. Even those who most earnestly desire to live a "moral" life, a good life, have on too many occasions succumbed to the enticements laid before them. The secular, relativist vacuum which has managed to suck every mote of morality from our consciousness is principally to blame for the high level of moral decay in which we find ourselves mired. But each of us also shares in the increasing rot and decay in which we now wallow for all too quickly and easily we find ourselves closing the door on our consciences whenever we find it convenient to do so. The problem is largely one of coating ourselves with Vaseline so we can slide past hard moral choices without suffering pangs of guilt or shame, without remorse. Instead of choosing what we know to be objectively and morally good, we rationalize the evil we do by degree: it's just a little white lie; it's ok to steal food if you are really hungry; it's not really a human being.

Intrinsic evil is, by definition, naturally evil because the act itself is absolutely contrary to reason, to nature, and to God. Such evil can never be considered good for it is not the opposite of good but rather the absence of good. Because good cannot be both good and the absence of good (or evil,) an evil act can never be considered a good act. For instance, a truth by its nature is true and thus is good while a lie, by its nature, is false, as the intent is to deceive or hide the truth and thus is intrinsically evil because it is intrinsically untrue and deceptive. Popes have written numerous encyclicals concerning intrinsic evil.

> But no reason, however grave, may be put forward by which anything intrinsically against nature may become conformable to nature and morally good ... No difficulty can arise that justifies the putting aside of the law of God which forbids all acts intrinsically evil.[193]

> ... it is never lawful, even for the gravest reasons, to do evil that good may come of it — in other words, to intend directly something which of its very nature contradicts the moral order, and which must therefore be judged unworthy of man, even though the intention is to protect or promote the welfare of an individual, of a family or of society in general.[194]

To demand a "do over," to demand the right to choose to avoid or to eliminate the consequences of a prior choice would be the height of hubris and the epitome of chutzpah. It would also be irresponsible and immoral. Should a person's first choice be an immoral one, any attempt to avoid the consequences of such a choice would only serve to compound the immorality of the first. It is precisely the principle underlying the idiom "two wrongs don't make a right." Without stepping too deeply into the morass euphemistically salved as "pro-choice" let us focus our attention on a choice seldom considered, a choice rooted in the immorality so prevalent today, choosing sexual intercourse, not out of love or for procreation but for the mere self-gratifying pleasure. The consequences of indulging in such hedonistic delights are evident in the genocidal numbers of elective abortions performed every single day. No matter what color you wish to paint it, two immoral choices will never make a moral one.

---

[193] Pope Pius XI, *Casti Cannubii.*
[194] Pope Paul VI, *Humanae Vitae*, §14.

When life begins has now been well established to be at the moment of conception yet those who would disagree will argue it is irrelevant for they claim it is not when life begins that is of any importance but rather when a life becomes a person. The mental gymnastics used by some to define personhood are truly mind-boggling, abhorrent, decidedly immoral, and definitively intrinsically evil. In one instance, two bioethicists, in a well-respected journal laid claim to this astounding bit of logical legerdemain: "By showing that (1) both fetuses and newborns do not have the same moral status as actual persons, (2) the fact that both are potential persons is morally irrelevant, and (3) adoption is not always in the best interest of actual people, the authors argue that what we call 'after-birth abortion' (killing a newborn) should be permissible in all cases where abortion is."[195] The authors went further to define a newborn as any infant under the age of four! My first reaction upon reading this piece of *unctuous vomitus* was to immediately and involuntarily disgorge the contents of my stomach. Inexplicably, far too many ascribe to this particularly grotesque point of view.

After a particularly difficult night I woke with a somewhat more pleasant thought, thinking of the experience shared by each of us yet remembered by none, of that time when the entire universe which we know is confined to our mother's womb. Although our mind and body may be incapable of cognitive thought or understanding, in those earliest moments of our lives, the soul, created and installed by God at the moment of conception, comes into existence fully formed.

> *A long, long time ago,*
> *much before I knew*
> *of larger things,*
> *I slept and*
> *then I*
> *dreamt.*
>
> *I knew nothing beyond*
> *the inviting womb*
> *where I began*
> *to grow and*
> *grow and*
> *grow.*
>
> *When I heard soft murmurs*
> *of sweet lullabies,*
> *I felt somehow,*
> *the music*
> *was for*
> *me.*

---

[195] . Giubilini & F. Minerva, "*After-birth abortion: why should the baby live?*", Journal of Medical Ethics, March 2012.

It was a pleasant time
floating without care
or worry there
not knowing;
growing
so.

What began so empty
over time grew small;
it left small space
to float or
even
move.

Yet I would often stretch
my limbs and against
the shrinking walls
would attempt
to make
room.

For the most part I slept
and dreamed pleasantly
it seemed to me
even though
nothing's
left.

A time came when I woke
with some urgency
knowing, sensing
something strange,
something
new.

My warm, inviting home
with waves of action
was suddenly
compelling
me to
leave.

Yet, I did resist it.
What, I did not know,
yet I feared it,
for it was
squeezing
me.

It was so difficult
to resist the force
compelling me,
pushing me,
pulling
me.

I felt something touch me
and then suddenly
I was blinded
by a light
in my
eyes.

The world that I had known
for so long was gone,
there were no walls,
I could move
freely
now.

And then I felt it, pain!
It hurt so I cried,
the noise I heard
came from me,
from my
mouth.

So rudely awakened
from peaceful slumber
with sensations
new and so
I was
born.[196]

---

[196] Charles R. Lanham, *Echoes of Love: Effervescent Memories*, (Reno, NV: Deacon's Corner Publishing, 2015), 75-87.

Walking Away
Who or what is God's rival

Listening to Bishop Paul Tighe last weekend at the Los Angeles Religious Education Congress, I was struck by a question he posed: "What or who is God's chief rival for your heart?" It is certainly a timely and an important question, one for each of us to reflect upon as we enter this season of Lent. Jesus asked his disciples "But who do you say that I am?" to which Peter replied, "You are the Christ, the Son of the living God" (Mt 16:15). If asked, how would you respond? Would it be the same, bearing in mind as Christians we regularly profess him to be God, the only Son of the Father? How we see God, the Father, Son, and Spirit is of great spiritual importance, but of even greater importance is whether we have placed anything or anyone before him. Is there something or someone who contends for our heart, who comes between and before God?

> Jesus said to his disciples, "I am the bread of life; he who comes to me shall not hunger, and he who believes in me shall never thirst. ...Truly, truly, I say to you, unless you eat the flesh of the Son of Man and drink his blood, you have no life in you; he who eats my flesh and drinks my blood has eternal life, and I will raise him up on the last day." And many of his disciples found this too difficult to hear and they walked away, no longer willing to listen and to follow him (Jn 6:34-35, 53-54, 60, 66).

Walking away from God is all too easy, for there are many temptations, each a rival for God's love. Here's another thought from last weekend: "If I don't want the Eucharist then I don't want Jesus." When we place other things or other people before and above God, when we desire other than the Eucharist we are most assuredly walking away, turning our backs away from no greater love.

Keep Them from Idols
Teaching idolatry in our schools

W. Ross Blackburn, rector of Christ the King, an Anglican Fellowship in Boone, North Carolina offered well-considered advice on the education of children (Touchstone: March/April 2017, *Keep Them From Idols*, 31-37) in which he posits it takes generations of fidelity to God to insure faithful servants.

> The Scriptures understand that we are largely a product of our generations, and therefore put great weight on generational faithfulness, particularly passing on the knowledge of God to future generations. This is nowhere clearer than in the Shema of Deuteronomy 6:4-9. ...

The Shema begins as follows: Hear, O Israel: The Lord our God, the Lord is one. You shall love the Lord your God with all your heart and with all your soul and with all your might (Deut. 6:4-5)

Israel's life is to be lived out in all areas as a practical response to God, who redeemed her and called her to himself. It has a bearing on, among other things, worship, one's economic life, one's sexual relationships, one's understanding of justice, and as we shall see, the raising of one's children. ... Nothing in Israel's life fell outside this command to love God, for all of life was an expression of this primary call.

Blackburn adds while this portion of the Shema is largely uncontroversial with the Christian community, what follows is, as he states, "nothing less than a philosophy of education."

And these words that I command you today shall be on your heart. You shall teach them diligently to your children and shall talk to them when you sit in your house, and when you walk by the way, and when you lie down, and when you rise. You shall bind them as a sign on your hand, and they shall be as frontlets between your eyes. You shall write them on the doorposts of your house and on your gates. (Deut. 6:6-9)

What Blackburn writes next is key.

At least three matters are worth noting. First, the command assumes that education is chiefly about God, in the implication that loving God and following his commands is the most important thing that a child can learn. Second, it establishes the parents as responsible for raising children to love God. Finally, it calls for such an education to be carried on in the course of life.

This is but an introduction to what Blackburn suggests are practical guidelines to ongoing, life-long education of our children. He firmly believes, as do I, "education is chiefly about God. If that sounds strange, it is because we have understood education to be a different endeavor than raising children to know God. Yet Deuteronomy implies an educated child is not, in the first place, a child who has acquired skills or information, but rather one who knows and loves God." Speaking on the modern educational premise of "not-God," a premise axiomatic in our public, and much of our private, education, he writes:

[T]o see this, one need only recognize that teaching, "In the beginning, God created the heavens and the earth" is forbidden, while the equally radical notion that God did not create the heavens and the earth is taught as scientific truth....The idea that God has anything to do with the natural world, or historical movements, or mathematics, is effectively sidelined in the name of "neutrality".

Yet this supposed neutrality is in fact a very bold statement that it is possible—even appropriate—to understand the world apart from God. In other words, underneath such a philosophy is a sturdy metaphysical commitment that is just as "religious" as any religious perspective it might seek to sideline. In effect, the prevailing philosophy of education has institutionalized Psalm 14:1: "The fool says in his heart, there is no God."

The extent to which any educational system is built upon the premise of not-God, whether explicitly or implicitly, is the extent to which that educational system has become idolatrous. And it is so by definition. Which brings us back to the First Commandment.

Blackburn recalls a comment made earlier in the year on a political commentary website concerning the alarming dissolution of the family in the U.S., and the consequent effects on raising children.

> I think there are all sorts of traditional, social ways of taking care of kids, and of taking care of your parents, and as those things evaporate the real problem is we are not yet efficiently replacing them with state-based solutions. (Bloomberg.com/news/videos/2015-02-23/the-global-flight-from-the-family-eberstadt)

> [His response]: "The comment is revealing, for it locates the problem not in the dissolution of families, but rather in the lack of state-based alternatives, clearly implying that the family is irrelevant as long as the state picks up the responsibility of raising and educating children. While obviously the words of one commentator, the Church does well to pay attention here, for our culture is moving decidedly in the direction of offering our children to the state. Political initiatives such as universal publicly funded pre-school make clear that there are many in our world who believe the state should take the lead in raising children, and who have the political power to see it done.

Blackburn concludes his article with four broad suggestions.

> First, let us take seriously that the call to love God is countercultural, sometimes even in the Church. Loving God should be practically discernible, positively and negatively, in the life of the Church, and in the families within the Church.

> Second, let us recognize the home as the primary context of education, and the call of parents to educate and disciple their children. Education is far more than imparting information. It is chiefly about forming Christian character and judgment, teaching children to love God in all of life. Yet much of our current practice, allowing secular education to be undertaken by the schools and religious education by Sunday schools or youth groups, in effect suggests that education is best carried out by experts that can impart secular or religious information. The effect is to sideline parents, who are often deeply involved in neither.

> Third, let us remember that teaching children to love God means that education is firmly grounded in the cross of Christ. Why is the cross of Christ so crucial? The cross reveals God most completely. We only love God insofar as we know who he has revealed himself to be in Christ and what he has done for us in Christ. Correspondingly, because man is made in the image of God, it follows we cannot know ourselves apart from knowing God, and it is folly to seek to understand the nature and movements of man if we don't know who man is. Man is not only the image of God, but as Christ is the most complete revelation of God, man is the image of Christ. And he is therefore the image of Christ crucified. The call to Jesus' disciples, therefore, is to 'love one another, as I have loved you' (Jn 13:34). And what is the purpose of education, if not to love God and learn to serve one another because we love him?

Finally, we need to see the connection between the family and the witness of the Church. As evident throughout Scriptures, the witness of the Church is chiefly manifest in her presence, even before her proclamation, for the witness of God's people rests on who we are before what we do.

This is but a brief summarization of the complete article. It is well worth reading the entire article and I encourage readers to do so by visiting Touchstone's website at touchstonemag.com. To find the article click on THE NEW ISSUE block, then *Keep Them from Idols* under Features.

March 10, 2017

Under Construction
For the love of knowing

This is personal, but hopefully, it will be at least marginally useful to a few. Last September I voluntarily matriculated at John Paul the Great Catholic University, with the express intent of obtaining a graduate degree in Biblical Theology. Now for some, attending graduate school may be "no big thing," but when one is fast approaching seven decades on this grand green globe, some have seriously questioned the state of my mental faculties. To those I say, "Fair enough." I admit to on occasion having been accused of having a few screws loose, so I am not at all offended or taken aback by their concerns for my mental health. But I do find myself often concerned about the mental well-being of others. And no, I am not claiming I am the only sane person living in a global insane asylum. No, No, and No! So please, call me crazy, but believe me when I tell you, there is a method to my madness. What worries is the seeming disinclination of so many to know, really and truly know anything beyond a tight circumscribed set of data and even then, for some, that is more than they are wont to know. And, this is incredibly important, knowing is not the same as learning or wisdom, although to know a thing you must first learn of it, and wisdom only comes when you use what you know wisely. Knowledge does not necessarily come with a college degree; such higher education may open heretofore unknown vistas but then, little more, for unless the mind is receptive and open to accepting new ideas, with flexibility and alacrity, knowledge can never fill the mind. Perhaps an analogy will help illustrate. Imagine trying to fill a jar (mind) with a liquid (knowledge) … with the lid in place, tightly sealing it. No matter how fast or hard you pour (educate) nothing will alter what is inside that closed jar (mind) unless and until the lid is removed. Then and only then, when the jar (mind) is wide open to receive, can the jar be filled.

The mind is a wondrous creation, uniquely human in its ability to reason; the rational mind is God's gift, it is what, above all else, differentiates man from all other creatures. Yet there are those who would deny such distinctiveness, who, all too eagerly at times, deny any possibility of ontological discontinuity between humans and other animals. Stephen M. Barr, professor of physics at the University of Delaware and author of *The Believing Scientist: Essays on Science and Religion*, in his review of the book *Why Only Us: Language and Evolution* by Berwick and Chomsky notes:

> Only humans are made in the image of God and have immortal souls endowed with the spiritual powers of rationality and freedom. This does not admit of degrees: One either has an immortal soul or one does not. The discontinuity must therefore be historical as well as ontological. In our lineage there must have been a first creature or set of creatures who were human in the theological sense, but whose immediate progenitors were not.

> This seems to fly in the face of evolutionary biology. Evolution occurs gradually, by the accumulation of genetic changes that spread through populations. New species do not appear at a single stroke, in one generation; there was not a "first cat" whose parents were non-cats. There is no contradiction with theology, however. Biological speciation is indeed a gradual process, but in the traditional Christian view, the conferring of a spiritual soul upon human beings is not a biological process at all. It is quite consistent to suppose that a long, slow evolutionary development led to the emergence of an interbreeding population of "anatomically modern humans," as paleo-archeologists call them, and that when the time was ripe, God chose to raise one, several, or all members of that population to the spiritual level of rationality and freedom.[197]

Barr reminds of the 2004 Vatican document *"Communion and Stewardship: Human Persons Created in the Image of God,"* under the authorization of then Joseph Cardinal Ratzinger: "Catholic theology affirms that the emergence of the first members of the human species (whether as individuals or in populations) represents an event that is not susceptible of a purely natural explanation and which can appropriately be attributed to divine intervention. Acting indirectly through causal chains operating from the beginning of cosmic history, God prepared the way for what Pope John Paul II has called 'an ontological leap … the moment of transition to the spiritual.'" Modern secular thought, of course, objects to any notion of human exceptionalism. Since Copernicus, science has eschewed anthropocentrism[198] in any form, contributing to what Stephen Jay Gould called "the dethronement of man."

> A more promising approach to finding the beginnings of human rationality may lie with the study of language. This is paradoxical, perhaps, in that spoken language leaves no fossils or artifacts. One can, however, investigate the neural machinery of language, the genetic basis of that machinery, and the deep underlying structures of language itself.

---

[197] Stephen M. Barr, *First Words*, First Things (April 2017), 61-63.

[198] **Anthropocentrism** (/ˌænθroʊpoʊˈsɛntrɪzəm/, from Greek Ancient Greek: ἄνθρωπος, *ánthrōpos*, "human being"; and Ancient Greek: κέντρον, *kéntron*, "center") is the belief that human beings are the most important entity in the universe. Anthropocentrism interprets or regards the world in terms of human values and experiences.

This is the avenue pursued in the remarkable new book *Why Only Us* by Robert C. Berwick and Noam Chomsky. … Using an array of sophisticated arguments based on discoveries in linguistics, neuroscience, genetics, computer science, evolutionary theory, and studies of animal communication, they develop a set of hypotheses about the nature and origins of human language, which will (if they hold up) have far-reaching implications. … [They] argue that only human beings have language. It is not that there are other animals possessing it in germ or to a slight degree; no other animals, they insist, possess it at all. The language capacity arose very suddenly, they say, likely in a single member of the species *Homo sapiens*, as a consequence of a very few fortuitous and unlikely genetic mutations.

What Berwick and Chomsky have observed is a radical dissimilarity between all animal communication systems and human language. Animals communicate simply and linearly whereas human language—and here it gets highly technical in its description—involves the capacity to generate, by a recursive procedure, an unlimited number of hierarchically structured sentences. The authors provide an example to illustrate this: "Birds that fly instinctively swim." As they explain it, the adverb "instinctively" can modify either "fly" or "swim," that is, the sentence can be read "Birds that fly instinctively—swim" or "Birds that fly—instinctively swim." The resulting ambiguity is obvious. But there is no ambiguity in the sentence "Instinctively birds that fly swim." As the authors note, here "instinctively" must modify "swim" despite its greater linear distance. There is much more, of course, but this ought to be sufficient to answer at the very least the question of whether there is an ontological discontinuity between humans and other animals. Berwick and Chomsky arrive, on purely empirical grounds, at the conclusion there is. All animals communicate, but only humans are rational; and for Berwick and Chomsky, human language is primarily an instrument of rationality. Barr concludes, "They present powerful arguments that this astonishing instrument arose just once and quite suddenly in evolutionary history—indeed, most likely in just one member of *Homo sapiens*, or at most a few. At the biological level, this involved a sudden upgrade of our mental machinery, and Berwick and Chomsky's theories of this are both more plausible than competing theories and more consistent with data from a variety of disciplines. But they recognize that more than machinery is involved. The basic contents and meanings, the deep-lying elements of human thought—"word-like but not words"—were somehow there, mysteriously, in the beginning."

Elsewhere, I happened upon this gem—admittedly taken completely out of context but apropos nonetheless: "I learned from the experience, in the end, that all vanity is vanity, all lust is lust, and all excess is excess, no matter what the objects of one's desire."[199] Why apropos, you may well ask? It is so for no other reason that it returns us to the beginning. Why I decided to embark on a rigorous graduate course of study at my somewhat advanced age, it may be argued, may be nothing more than simple

---

[199] David Bentley Hart, *From a Vanished Library*, First Things (April 2017), 28.

vanity. But then, I think not, for as I stated before, there is method to my madness, which I will now endeavor to explain. God made us in his image and likeness and breathed life—a soul—into each of us, along with the gift of reason, the ability to think, to know and to love him. He expects us to use—to the best of our ability—his gift for good and to never stop, until we see him face-to-face in heaven. Each has been given a variety of gifts and no one is void of any gift. We are called by God to make the most of what we have, no matter how great or how small.

> It is said that every apparently new thing has always been with us. Alas, this doesn't seem to be the case. The industrial revolution, science as a replacement for religion, and the phenomenon of the wonderful and limitless increase in money (without a similar increase in its material equivalent) have given rise to a new mentality, one that finds it increasingly difficult to perceive the fusion of spirit and matter, the spiritual content of reality that those who lived in the preindustrial world across thousands of years took for granted. The forces that determine our lives have become invisible. None of them has found an aesthetic representation. In a time that is overloaded with images, they have lost the power to take form, with the result that the powers that govern our lives have an intangible, indeed, a demonic quality. Along with the inability to create images that made even the portrait of an individual a problem for the twentieth century, our contemporaries have lost the experience of reality. For reality is always first seized in a heightened form that is pregnant with meaning.[200]

What is perhaps the gravest sin is to waste the mind, to leave it fallow, stupefying one's mind by feeding it what amounts to nothing more than mental junk food or worse, nothing at all. The vacuous disregard for the mind is a rapidly growing epidemic, fueled by the insatiable lust for empty pleasures, absent any spiritual or moral ground upon which one can kneel in humble gratitude for the gifts we have been given. We each have the freedom to choose, to choose whether to strive to make the most of, through dedication and utmost effort, the gifts God has given us, or not. Either way, it is entirely up to us; God gave us the gifts, it is up to us to fully employ them. This past quarter has been at times overwhelming, often difficult, stressful, challenging, too near the breaking, but ... oh, the now knowing of the new; the unexpected turns, the heights and depths of learning, of understanding what I did not know before. And the friends I found among the pages, pages, pages, and the endless pages I read: those I will remember and remember well and long. Why, you ask? To feed my mind, to now know more than I knew then, to use the limits of what I have been given for the glory of the One of whom I owe everything I am and hope to be.

---

[200] Martin Mosebach, Return to Form, First Things (April 2017), 42.

March 17, 2017

The Rising Son
Looking toward the East

When Christ comes to us in the Eucharist, it is both a proclamation and a supplication. We conclude the Eucharistic prayer with both: "When we eat this Bread and drink this Cup, we proclaim your Death, O Lord until you come again." We acknowledge and affirm the Lord Jesus is present, in the here and now, and is the One who is yet to come. As Catholics, our faith calls us to believe at the moment of consecration, what was before no longer remains. What was mere bread and wine has now become the mystical body and blood of our Lord Jesus Christ.

"When the ancient Israelite prayed, he turned towards the Jerusalem temple. In this way, he linked his prayer to the salvation history which united God with Israel and was focused and made present in the temple. He prayed to the God who willed to be glorified in that temple, and in doing so, integrated his prayer with Israel's law of faith, the order established by God himself."[201] The earliest Christians—who were almost entirely Jews—turned, not toward the temple, but to the East to pray, toward the rising sun. This orientation symbolized Christ who had risen from the dark night of death into the glory of the Father and who now reigns over all. The cosmos thus became a sign of Christ and wherever the Christian community met they would trace the cross on the east wall of their worship space in order to properly orient themselves in prayer to the risen Lord. The rising sun also signifies the returning Christ, he who promises to come again in glory. The image of the rising sun represents the intimate relationship between faith in the resurrection and the desire and hope for the parousia. "The two are one in the figure of the Lord who has already returned as the risen One, continues to return in the Eucharist, and so remains he who is to come, the hope of the world.... This cross was understood as a sign of the returning Son of Man, and also as a threat of eschatological punishment."[202]

Here we must pause to offer a brief but necessary explanation. Having just completed a course carrying the cryptic title *"Ecclesiology and Eschatology,"* of which I not only had no knowledge but could not pronounce, I can only assume others may not know what is meant by the word. "For centuries eschatology was content to lead a quiet life as the final chapter of theology where it was dubbed 'the doctrine of the last things.' But in our own time, with the historical process in crisis, eschatology has moved into the very center of the theological state. Some twenty years ago, Hans Urs

---

[201] Joseph Cardinal Ratzinger, *Eschatology: Death and Eternal Life*, (Washington, D.C.: The Catholic University of America Press, 1988), 6; trans. Michael Waldstein, 1; originally published in German under the title *Eschatologie—Tod und ewiges Leben* (Regensburg: Friedrich Pustet Verlag, 1977).
[202] Joseph Cardinal Ratzinger, *Eschatology: Death and Eternal Life*, 7.

von Balthasar called it the 'storm-zone' of contemporary theology. Today it appears to dominate the entire theological landscape."

It is important, when trying to discern the meaning of eschatology to begin with Jesus Christ, to look to the Lord. "Eschatology's meaning and driving force depend upon the power of this waiting on Christ, not on temporal expectation of the world's end or transformation, no matter of what kind." To emphasize the importance and the centrality of Christ in any discussion of eschatology, Ratzinger argues, "The truly constant factor is Christology. It is upon the integrity of Christology that the integrity of all the rest depends, and not the other way around." The central question concerning eschatology revolves around the essential character of the message of Jesus Christ. Yet, before one can hope to make inroads into understanding the eschatological nature of his message, we must first admit and acknowledge the fundamental nature of human life: man was created in the image and likeness of God, with the capacity to know and love his Creator, with a mortal body and an immortal soul.[203]

> The God who made the world and everything in it, being Lord of heaven and earth, does not live in shrines made by man, nor is he served by human hands, as though he needed anything, since he himself gives to all men life and breath and everything. And he made from one every nation of men to live on all the face of the earth, having determined allotted periods and the boundaries of their habitation, that they should seek God, in the hope that they might feel after him and find him. Yet he is not far from each one of us, for "In him we live and move and have our being"; as even some of your poets have said, "For we are indeed his offspring" (Acts 17:24-28).

"All men are therefore called to the one and the same goal, namely God Himself."[204] It is this innate calling of the heart toward a relationship with God that makes a human being immortal; it is what is embedded deep into man's very being, it comes from our immortal soul. The soul is a gift from God; "given to man to be his very own possession. That is what is meant by creation, and what Thomas [Aquinas] means when he says that immortality belongs to man by nature."[205] Ratzinger asks how it is possible for human beings to live in a fashion that goes counter to their own essence: closed off from, rather than open to, the rest of being. Since, from the very beginning, man has seemingly wanted to generate his own immortality.

> He would like to fabricate it out of his own stuff: *non omnis moriar*, not everything about me will perish. The *monumentum aere perennius*, the achievements I bequeath, these will immortalize a part of me. But in this attempt to manufacture eternity, the vessel of man must, at the last, founder. What endures after one is not oneself. Man falls headlong into the unreal, yielding up his life to unreality, to death.

---

[203] Joseph Cardinal Ratzinger, *Eschatology: Death and Eternal Life*, 11.
[204] Pope Paul VI, *Gaudium et Spes*, Pastoral Constitution of the Church in the Modern World, 24 §1.
[205] Joseph Cardinal Ratzinger, *Eschatology: Death and Eternal Life*, 155.

An existence in which man tries to divinize himself, to become "like a god" in his auton- omy, independence and self-sufficiency, turns into a Sheol-existence, a being in nothingness, a shadow-life on the fringe of real living.[206]

Faith in God and in his promise of eternal life with him is thus the essential first step in eschatological understanding. Jesus Christ, God made man, is the tree of life whence we receive the food of immortality. In addition, the hope in the eschatological resurrection of the body, that Christian belief in the unity and inestimable value of the whole person, body and soul, as it journeys toward eternal life with Jesus Christ and the expectation of seeing God face-to-face provides the impetus to take the next step. Ratzinger once again observes "part of the Christian idea of immortality is fellowship with other human beings. Man is not engaged in a solitary dialogue with God. He does not enter an eternity with God which belongs to him alone…. It takes place, therefore, within the 'body of Christ,' in that communion with the Son which makes it possible for us to call becoming a son with the Son, and this must mean in turn by becoming one with all those others who seek the Father."[207] As we are all members of the Body of Christ, that is the Church, it is reasonable to ask, as does Schönborn, "The Church is where Christ is. How then would it be possible for her not to be primarily in heaven, where Christ is?"[208] The Apostle Paul reminds us of this frequently.

> If then you have been raised with Christ, seek the things that are above, where Christ is, seated at the right hand of God. Set your minds on things that are above, not on things that are on earth. For you have died, and your life hid with Christ in God. When Christ who is our life appears, then you also will appear with him in glory (Col 4:1-4).

> So we are always of good courage; we know that while we are at home in the body we are away from the Lord, for we walk by faith, not by sight. We are of good courage, and we would rather be away from the body and at home with the Lord. So whether we are at home or away, we make it our aim to please him. For we must all appear before the judgment seat of Christ, so that each one may receive good or evil, according to what he has done in the body (2 Cor 5:6-10).

> But our commonwealth is in heaven, and from it we await a Savior, the Lord Jesus Christ, who will change our lowly body to be like his glorious body, by the power which enables him even to subject all things to himself (Phil 3:20-21).

> So then you are no longer strangers and sojourners, but you are fellow citizens with the saints and members of the household of God, built upon the foundation of the apostles and prophets, Christ Jesus himself being the cornerstone, in whom the whole structure is joined together and grows into a holy temple in the Lord; in whom you also are built into it for a dwelling place of God in the Spirit (Eph 2:19-22).

---

[206] Joseph Cardinal Ratzinger, *Eschatology: Death and Eternal Life*, 156.
[207] Joseph Cardinal Ratzinger, *Eschatology: Death and Eternal Life*, 159.
[208] Christoph Cardinal Schönborn, O.P., "*The Kingdom of God and the Heavenly-Earthly Church*," Letter & Spirit 2 (2006): 217; 221.

Saint Augustine asks: "Who is the city of God, if not the holy Church?"[209] Are they one and the same? Augustine then answers his own question: "Thus, the Church is already now the kingdom of Christ and the kingdom of heaven."[210]

"We do not believe that one can refuse to identify the Church and the kingdom. We have two concepts here, but only one single reality. The Church is the kingdom; the kingdom is the Church. The concept of 'kingdom' refers to eschatology. But it is precisely with Jesus that eschatology, which belongs above all to the qualitative order, has broken into time. From the time of Christ onward, the whole Church has entered the end time; she is eschatological."[211] What Schönborn argues, and I believe rightly so, is this: "If the Church is essentially heavenly, since she is 'there where Christ is,' if she is his body, and it is 'not only the believers who are alive today that belong' to this body 'but also those who have lived before us, and those who will come after us until the end of time,' then it is not possible to grasp a reason not to identify the Church and the kingdom of God."[212]

Catholic eschatology is inextricably grounded in the age-to-come and its presence in the here and now. The pilgrim Church, that is, the Church on earth, is always and at the same time, united with the Church in heaven. It will attain full perfection only in the glory of heaven, "at the time for establishing all that God spoke by the mouth of his holy prophets from of old" (Acts 3:21). Then will the Pilgrim Church, the whole of mankind, be perfectly reestablished in Jesus Christ as it is written "For he has made known to us in all wisdom and insight the mystery of his will, according to his purpose which he set forth in Christ as a plan for the fullness of time, to unite all things in him, things in heaven and things on earth" (Eph 1:9-10). Jesus, in speaking of his impending death, resurrection, and glorification, said, "when I am lifted up from the earth, I will draw all men to myself (John 12:32). This should not, however, be construed as a portent of the last days, any more so in that his ascension denotes his absence. Christ is always present, just as he told his disciples, "I am with you always, to the close of the age" (Matthew 28:20). As Ratzinger explains, "What this means is that the Christian hope is not some news item about tomorrow or the day after tomorrow. ... Hope is now personalized. Its focus is not space and time, the question of 'Where?' and 'When?,' but relationship with Christ's person and longing for him to come close."[213]

It is important to consider the image of the disciples (the apostles, the entire community of believers in Jesus, and Mary, the mother of Jesus) gathered in the upper

---

[209] Augustine, *The City of God*, Bk. 16, chap. 2, in *A Select Library of the Nicene and Post-Nicene Fathers of the Christian Church*, vol. 2, ed. Philip Schaff (Grand Rapids, MI: Eerdmans, 1977), 310.

[210] The City of God, Bk. 20 chap 9, in A Select Library of the Nicene and Post-Nicene Fathers, 429.

[211] Christoph Cardinal Schönborn, O.P., "*The Kingdom of God and the Heavenly-Earthly Church*," Letter & Spirit 2 (2006): 223; Cardinal Charles Journet, *L'Eglise du Verbe Incarnè*, 2: 997, n. 1; compare 60-91 and *Nova et Vetera* 38 (1963), 307-10.

[212] Christoph Cardinal Schönborn, O.P., "*The Kingdom of God and the Heavenly-Earthly Church*," Letter & Spirit 2 (2006): 223.

[213] Joseph Cardinal Ratzinger, *Eschatology: Death and Eternal Life*, 8.

room, united in prayer (Acts 1:12-14), "as the context in which the Church is born; the Eleven, who are listed by name; Mary, the women and the brethren—it is a genuine *qahal*, a covenant assembly with diverse orders, which is at the same time a mirror of the entire new people."[214] The primitive church is clearly depicted—as noted in Acts 2—by the early converts' adherence to the teaching of the apostles—previewing apostolic succession and of the official witness entrusted to the successors of the apostles, to the community—in the breaking of the bread and to the prayers. This is validated by Jesus when he says, "All authority in heaven and on earth has been given to me. Go therefore and make disciples of all nations, baptizing them in the name of the Father and of the Son and of the Holy Spirit, teaching them to observe all that I have commanded you" (Mt 28:18-20).

At Pentecost, Ratzinger observes, "at the moment of her birth, the Church was already catholic, already a world Church." Thus, there was never a local church from which, over time, other local churches were established. What is true is quite the opposite, "what first exists is the one Church, the Church that speaks in all tongues—the *ecclesia universalis*; she then generates Church in the most diverse locales, which nonetheless are all always embodiments of the one and only Church. The temporal and ontological priority lies with the universal Church; a Church that was not catholic would not even have ecclesial reality."[215]

This recognition of an eschatological Christ is deeply rooted in the messianic hopes of the people of Israel. In Zechariah we read: "I will pour out on the house of David and the inhabitants of Jerusalem a spirt of compassion and supplication, so that, when they look on him whom they have pierced, they shall mourn for him, as one mourns for an only child, and weep bitterly over him, as one weeps over a first-born" (Zech 12:10). Further on the prophet says, "On that day there shall be a fountain opened for the house of David and the inhabitants of Jerusalem to cleanse them from sin and uncleanness" (Zech 13:1). This will later be restated in the Revelation to John: "Behold, he is coming with the clouds, and every eye will see him, every one who pierced him; and all tribes of the earth will wail on account of him" (Rev 1:7). In Daniel, we find a description of he who would reign over the whole kingdom of God: "and behold, with the clouds of heaven there came one like a son of man, and he came to the Ancient of Days and was presented before him. And to him was given dominion and glory and kingdom, that all peoples, nations, and languages should serve him; his dominion is an everlasting dominion, which shall not pass away, and his kingdom one that shall not be destroyed" (Dan 7:13-14). The "Son of Man" was a messianic reference, thus for first century Jews, whenever Jesus referred to himself as the "Son of Man"— found 84 times throughout the New Testament—they heard him clearly claim to be

---

[214] Joseph Cardinal Ratzinger, *Called to Communion: Understanding the Church Today* (San Francisco: Ignatius Press, 1996), 41; trans. Adrian Walker; originally published in German under the title *Zur Gemeinschaft gerufen: Kirche heute verstehen*, second edition, (Freiburg im Briesgau: Herder, 1991).
[215] Joseph Cardinal Ratzinger, *Called to Communion*, 44.

the Messiah, the one who is to come. Thus, the meaning and driving force of Catholic Eschatology rests entirely and powerfully in the waiting on Christ and not on any expectation of a coming end time. At the Last Supper, by his Davidic kingship and divine authority, Jesus said to the Apostles: "as my Father appointed a kingdom for me, so do I appoint for you that you may eat and drink at my table in my kingdom, and sit on thrones judging the twelve tribes of Israel."(Lk 29-30). The Apostles were thus granted authority to rule as vice-regents over the *ekklēsia*, the universal church, the kingdom of David, the new Jerusalem. This kingdom over which Christ now reigns forever is both heavenly and earthly, as Peter proclaims: "This Jesus God raised up, and of that we all are witnesses. Being therefore exalted at the right hand of God, and having received from the Father the promise of the Holy Spirit, he has poured out this which you see and hear" (Acts 2:32-33).

There is a strong tendency among scholars and exegetes to inflict modern biases on ancient Jewish texts, thus, by failing to establish proper context, they often misinterpret what was intended. This is especially true in understanding the kingdom in the context of the Last Supper. "Jesus not only saw the Kingdom as an eschatological reality. He also saw it as a messianic kingdom, an international kingdom, and a heavenly kingdom. Moreover, when Jesus' teachings about the banquet are juxtaposed with his words and deeds in the Upper Room, together they also suggest that Jesus saw himself and his disciples as participating in the heavenly kingdom and anticipating the eschatological kingdom precisely by means of the liturgy of the Last Supper."[216] A banquet or feast, whether eschatological or covenantal, was both familiar and common practice in ancient Judaism. There are many passages in Jewish Scriptures from which one can ascertain the frequency and importance of a banquet. Pitre observes "When we turn outside the Old Testament to early Jewish literature such as the Dead Sea Scrolls and the pseudepigraphal works, we find that expectation of the messianic banquet is even more pronounced. By far the most explicit witness is found in the Dead Sea Scroll known as the Rule of the Congregation." Pitre then turns to the pseudepigrapha *1 Enoch* which "describes the age of salvation as a time when the righteous will be allowed to dine in the heavenly Temple on the fruit of the Tree of Life. ... Later in the same book, the future banquet is described again. But this time it is explicitly messianic." Jesus' teaching in the gospels concerning the eschatological banquet can be found most explicitly in Matthew 8:11-12 and Luke 13:28-29.

Let us remember, whenever we come together in prayer, to look to the East, for there we will surely see the rising Son of God.

---

[216] Brant Pitre, "The "Ransom for Many," the New Exodus, and the End of the Exile: Redemption as the Restoration of All Israel (Mark 10:35-45," Letter & Spirit 1 (2005): 52.

Turn Down the Lights
Extinguishing the conscience

There is a growing sentiment among many that Pope (Emeritus) Benedict XVI should be, after his death, declared a Doctor of the Church. Few would disagree the gentle, humble, self-effacing man born Joseph Ratzinger on Holy Saturday, April 16, 1927 has been a brilliant theologian and a prodigious writer. Just 35 years old at the outset of the Second Vatican Council, then Father Joseph Ratzinger served as a *peritus*, or expert theological consultant to Cardinal Frings of Cologne and was an important and respected voice throughout the four sessions of the Council.

Now, as he approaches his ninth decade, a new book, *Benedict XVI Last Testament* in his own words, written by Peter Seewald in an interview format, Pope Benedict speaks candidly of his life as a theologian, a priest, bishop, cardinal, and pope. It is an amazing read, revealing the depths of his humility and devotion to God and Church. There is so much that can be said, but two quotes should be enough to illustrate.

Asked: "So when you stand before the Almighty, what will you say to him?" he responded: "I will plead with him to show leniency towards my wretchedness." Elsewhere he opines "The real problem at this moment of our history, is that God is disappearing from the human horizon." He emphasizes the real crisis confronting the Catholic Church is not a scarcity of priests, nor even declining membership; it is a dwindling faith. The neglect of God and the extinguishment of Christian conscience are at the root of the crisis. The consequence is lukewarm worship, watered-down liturgy, neglect of missions, and an uncertain, quavering voice on the great moral dilemmas of our time. Such an indictment should give Catholics everywhere pause. His voice, like Aquinas, is too important to ignore.

A Ship of Fools Redux
Still lost and sinking fast

Arguably, the debate concerning the existence of God has been waging for a very long time, and no doubt the battle will continue into the far distant future. Perhaps it may even go on until the end of time itself when, irrespective of which side of the argument you reside, it will be resolved without the necessity for further debate. Rest assured, eventually the answer to the question will become perfectly obvious to everyone. What is obvious is that a large majority find themselves holding to a belief in a Divine Presence, the Source of all that exists, and the Creator of us all. Those who do not hold to such a belief are decidedly in the minority. What is difficult to determine with any precision or accuracy is the population of those who proclaim a belief in God but find the matter largely irrelevant within the conduct of their daily lives. Assuredly and equally unfortunate, their numbers are both significant and growing. It is important to note the preponderance of the population will readily admit to believing in God; that is and never has been at issue. Pope Emeritus Benedict XVI explained this with remarkable insight when he wrote it is "not as though God had been denied—not on your life! He simply was not needed in regard to the 'reality' that mankind had to deal with. God had nothing to do. Has not Christian consciousness acquiesced to a great extent—without being aware of it—in the attitude that faith in God is something subjective, which belongs in the private realm and not in the common activities of public life where, in order to be able to get along, we all have to behave now *etsi Deus non daretur* (as if there were no God)."[217]

God has no relevance to man, or so man proclaims, for man no longer believes in absolutes. "Absolute truth belongs only to one class of humans—the class of absolute fools."[218] So claimed Ashley Montagu, evolutionist and humanist. Montagu makes it clear that, at best, truth is relative—and anyone who states differently is to be categorized as a fool. Sir Julian Huxley agreed: "We must now be prepared to abandon the god hypothesis and its corollaries like divine revelation or unchanging truths, and to change over from a supernatural to a naturalistic view of human destiny."[219] This ever-increasing, or so it would appear, attitude of "supreme self-sufficiency," the burning desire to cut ourselves loose from the apron strings of God, is inexplicable yet it has clearly taken root and continues to grow at an alarming rate. The late paleontologist of Harvard, George Gaylord Simpson wrote: "Man stands alone in the universe, a unique product of a long, unconscious, impersonal, material process with unique understanding and potentialities. These he owes to no one but himself, and it is to himself that he is responsible. He is not the creature of uncontrollable and undeterminable forces but is his own master. He can and must decide and manage his own destiny."[220] There are two premises underlying these arguments for man's self-sufficiency: first, there are no absolute truths—the best that can be argued is all truth is relative; second, the truth about God is relative. Thus, the conclusion: those who believe in God are fools. This "logical" statement is patently illogical and verifiably false, yet few would attempt to voice a counterargument for fear of being forever characterized a fool.

What then must be said? Let us begin by looking at the claim there is no absolute truth, that all truth is relative. Is that true? If it is true that all truth is relative, then doesn't that necessarily argue it must be absolutely true and if it is absolutely true, then it cannot be relatively true? But let us dig deeper. Relativism is the philosophical

---

[217] Joseph Cardinal Ratzinger, *Introduction to Christianity*, (San Francisco, CA: Ignatius Press, November 30, 2004).

[218] Ashley Montagu, The Atlanta Journal and Constitution, p. 4-C, July 26, 1981.

[219] Julian Huxley, Fortune Magazine, February 1965.

[220] George Gaylord Simpson, *Life of the Past* (New Haven, CT: Yale University Press, 1953).

position that all points of view are equally valid, and all truth is relative to the individual. Here we can categorize relativism into three groups[221]:

1. **Cognitive relativism (truth)**—affirms all truth is relative, meaning no system of truth is more valid than another one, and there is no objective standard of truth. This thus denies there is a God of absolute truth.

2. **Moral/Ethical relativism**—all morality and ethics are relative to the social group within which they are constructed

3. **Situational relativism**—ethics (right and wrong) are dependent upon the situation.

The philosophy of relativism has become pervasive within our culture and society. Absolute truth has been abandoned and God has been rejected. The notions of right and wrong, good and evil have been relativized, left to the whims of the individual. It has become a plague of pandemic proportions. This plague of moral relativism has infected us, weakening our intrinsic moral norms, encouraging what were once considered moral wrongs ("sin" and "evil") to now be accepted as relative goods. Anyone who dares speak out against moral relativism and its "anything goes" philosophy is instantly labeled an intolerant bigot. The blatant hypocrisy of this is lost on those who profess all points of view are true. What moral relativism means is all points of view are true except those views that profess and teach moral absolutes, an absolute God, or absolute right and wrong. If morality and ethics are relative, then "right" and "wrong" are reduced to opinion. If there are no moral absolutes, no absolute God, no absolute truth then there can be no moral facts, only moral opinion. In a secular world, there can only be opinions about morality; they may be either personal or societal opinions, but only opinions. Even atheist philosophers acknowledge without God, there can be no objective morality.

Let us pause to clarify what we mean when we use the word "secular." Secular is an adjective denoting attitudes, activities, or other things that have no religious or spiritual basis; contrasted with sacred. In the context of this essay, it will generally be associated with humanism (secular humanism,) a worldview that the entire universe and all life are the result of random coincidence. The secularist contends the universe created itself and random chemicals just happily combined to form a single-celled lifeform which mutated over billions of years into the incredible array of life found on earth today. To the secularist, we are nothing more than an advanced animal, or a chance combination of chemicals. There is no God, no absolutes. There is only unhappy coincidence.

Now nothing said so far should be construed to mean if you don't believe in God, you aren't a good person. Christians hold no singular claim to goodness. There are good and moral atheists, just as there are Christians who are immoral and evil. Their

---

[221] Matt Slick, *What is relativism?*, Christian Apologetics and Research Ministry

existence has nothing to do with whether there is a God. The existence of God only ensures good and evil objectively exist and are not merely opinions. Without God, there are no moral absolutes, what we are left with is moral relativism — morality relative to the individual or society (please note this must, by definition, be reduced to individual opinion.) Without God, "good" and "evil" are reduced to nothing more than "I like" and "I don't like." If there is no God, the statement "Murder is evil" is the moral equivalent to "I don't like murder." There are, of course, those who would argue moral absolutes are not necessary. They would argue people refrain from murder because they don't wish to be murdered. That opinion is nothing more than wishful thinking. No doubt, Hitler, Stalin, and Mao were averse to being murdered, yet their personal aversion didn't prevent them from murdering hundreds of millions of people. God has no relevance to man, or so man proclaims. Without God there is nothing and no one to establish an objective moral code or to elevate the respect due for every human life. We are living in a society, and in a world, where God has been declared irrelevant, where there is no absolute truth and therefore all truth is both subjective and relative, and where one lives by a self-imposed, ego-centric moral code. Take but a cursory look around and you will see the countless vacuous minions who have so fully subscribed to such a self-absorbed, self-immolating, amoral, narcissistic culture.

In an allegorical tale perhaps best known as the *Ship of Fools*, Plato describes a vessel populated by deranged, frivolous, or oblivious passengers aboard a ship without a pilot. They are completely ignorant of where they are going and care nothing for the circumstances of their fellow passengers or for themselves. What is most disconcerting is how Plato's prescient philosophical musings fall far too close to the current cultural lineation to provide us with any small comfort.

Those who find no relevance for God are like the fool who built his house on sand. Without a foundation constructed upon the solid rock of God's law, a fool's house, his life, and those who built likewise, will be lost to the vagaries and fickleness of the slightest breeze or the mildest weather.

This attitude dismisses and discards God to the trash heap of irrelevance carries with it implications and ramifications often not immediately apparent or readily realized. Removing God from the *Calculus of Relevance* eradicates the foundational underpinnings for moral behavior. If man, absent God, decides what is right or wrong, good or bad, true or false, then morality becomes the plaything of subjective argument and personal relevancy. What subsequently is elevated to greater importance, what is deemed most relevant is neither God nor His commandments upon which we are obliged to adhere, but that which we decide is right for us, what is of personal relevance, the moral code which we choose to define and follow. There are no absolutes, no objective moral code upon which one is forced to conduct one's self. I choose, I decide. I win, you lose. I'm right, you're wrong. I'm good, you're bad. I live, you die. Please take careful note of the fact the central tenet upon which life (or more specifically, life other than one's own) is now subjectively focused is on "I" which quite clearly dismisses the inconsequential existence that is not "I". Only "I" am relevant, all else is of no great import, entering the conscious mind only to the extent it is relative to the all-important "I".

It does not take much effort to see how deeply ingrained this subjective, relativistic misanthropy has enveloped and ensconced itself within the very fabric and timbre of our lives. The dehumanization and devaluation of human life is both glaringly and publicly evident in the unfathomable volume of judicially legal – although objectively and morally unjust and illegitimate—terminations (killings) exercised through acts of abortions, euthanasia, and assisted suicides, the horrendous acts of barbarism, terrorism, and genocide perpetrated on a global scale, and the widespread and growing pandemic created by the pornography, sex and slave trade industries. Perhaps nothing exemplifies the devaluation of human life more than those who ascribe to the thinking of radical environmentalism, specifically to that of animal rights activism, which espouses to a form of cosmological egalitarianism. This egalitarianism has an instinctive distaste for hierarchical ordering and especially for assigning value within the natural world in accordance with increasing levels of complexity, organization, and awareness.

> Traditional taxonomy divides living organisms into plant and animal kingdoms and then describes and ranks them from lesser to greater, with its high termination in man. This way of doing things accorded with philosophy and theology that assigned value in accordance with a universal principle—"you are worth more than many sparrows." Egalitarianism, however, with its attendant prejudices against not only value assignment, but the very acknowledgement of hierarchy, radically destabilizes any institution in which it is allowed free rein.

> Touching those of natural science, it leads to the inability to consider human populations more important than those of other animals, turns endangered species lists into religious litanies, and allows university teachers to propose that the death of much of the human race on behalf of the biosphere might not be all that bad. Linnaeus would not be proud."[222]

What this egalitarian view emphasizes is humans are no more valuable than a dog or a cat or even a tree. The God-centric understanding of man created in his image and likeness, and thus of infinite value has been replaced by the secular humanistic and relativistic views that devalue the worth of the human person. Their reasoning: since there is no God, human beings are only material beings—and worth nothing beyond the matter of which they are composed. The result: over the past 30 years, when high school and college students have been asked if they would first try to save their dog or a stranger, two-thirds have always voted against the person. PETA, the animal rights

---

[222] S. M. Hutchens, *Quodlibet: Man on the Level*, Touchstone: A Journal of Mere Christianity, March/April 2017, 5.

group, argues there is no difference between the barbecuing of chickens in America and the burning of Jews in the Holocaust.

What makes this so terribly appalling is we appear to have lost the ability or desire to be horrified by any of it at all. We have become dead to life; overwhelmed by the realization so much of mankind has declared both God and His creation to be irrelevant. We have largely and in a very real sense abdicated our rational minds to unthinking, mindless groupthink, all while having an unreasoning compulsion to "just get along" with that thousand-pound gorilla standing menacingly before us. Man's inhumanity has supplanted and suborned any vestiges of that humanity which has been gifted to him by God. Without God—the Father, Son, and Holy Spirit—at its core, life as we understand it, becomes nothing more than an amorphous existence, without meaning or purpose. And if one's epistemology holds life is irrelevant then it necessarily follows the value of all life is worth little or nothing at all. If life holds no value, then assuredly love is lost as well, for love can only embrace that which it holds most dear. To love and to be loved presupposes and requires an existence worthy of love, both human and divine. Here we may finally deduce that essential element which has been so blatantly and quite surgically excised from the calculus, and that is the relevance and essential presence of God. God is the purest and ultimate form of love, for He is Love. God created us out of love and loves all His creation without condition or qualification. God's love for us preordains our value, for love of a nullity is irrational, it is absolute nonsense which makes no sense at all. God is the essential Element, the Constant upon which all life is derived. Remove God from the calculus and nothing remains, absolutely nothing. God does matter. God is relevant. It is only the foolish who would dare declare otherwise.

March 31, 2017

The Essence of Being
Death cannot touch the spirit

Jesus does not deliver us from dying, but he does deliver us from death. It is the very nature of our being that does demand such an unwelcome rest; the cessation to all we've come to know, and yet, in dying, life continues unabated, different and transformed. The uncaring grip of death cannot touch the spirit; it holds no lien upon the soul, for the spirit is immune from death's untimely finitude. Death touches none but hearts still beating, carving deep, weeping wounds which deny surcease of pain so dark, the ache of missing so unbearable.

Yet, as difficult as it may be to accept, let us always remember this: the spirit takes no part in dying; the one who once danced and sang, laughed and cried, lived and loved, so full of life, still remains among the living. This is what Jesus promised. This is what we must believe. Dying is a part of living. We are born, we live, and then we die. But dying plays no role in being, for in becoming we are forever, never to be nevermore. The essence of our being is the spirit, the body but a shell in which the spirit grows for a time. When Jesus said he was the resurrection and the life he did not mean the restoration of a corpse to life but rather a transformation to a new life.

Like the caterpillar—an ungainly worm now called to crawl upon the ground—who, in dying conquers death; to be reborn, transformed into the free-spirited butterfly, so too are we, in our dying, so wonderfully reborn and transformed.

Those, who now live so transformed, are always with us. They never leave us in their dying; their whispered voices linger long if we would but listen to the heart.

Ad Hominem
Losing the argument

Sandwiched among the thoughts and ramblings was this sentence: "They chose to ignore the truth before their eyes *ad hominem*, by attacking the character of Jesus." No doubt many heard or read it with but passing interest, a fleeting flickering itch too brief to scratch. While the phrase *ad hominem* was indeed quite deliberately put, its infrequent usage and uncommon language (Latin) in all likelihood did little to enhance the intended flavor of the statement.

Whether one is participating in a formal debate or simply having a substantive argument, it has become the standard gambit, whenever logic and facts fail to support one's position, to engage in *argumentum ad hominem* or *ad hominem* for short. The phrase *ad hominem* is Latin meaning "to the man" or "to the person" and is used to describe a logical fallacy in which an argument is rebutted by attacking the character, motive or other attributes of the person making the argument or a group associated with the argument, rather than attacking the substance of the argument itself. Attacking an opponent's character or personal traits in order to discredit and/or undermine their position allows one to do so without having to actually engage in the substance of it. Unfortunately, this logical fallacy, while never truly winning an argument, too often succeeds in deflecting the listener and the debaters from the substance of the issue under debate. It is a fallacious form of argument which has become the standard method in much of the current societal, cultural, political, and religious discourse.

It is easy and disconcertingly common to find examples of this: just turn to any talk show where two opposing points of view are presented. Listen carefully to each side in the debate and inevitably one side or both will turn away from arguing substance to character assassination. What should be a serious discussion on a substantive issue all too quickly descends to emotional mischaracterizations, vitriolic diatribes, and unreasoned childish temper-tantrums. The importance of the issue be damned.

Let us return to last week's gospel to see a near perfect example of *argumentum ad hominem*: Jesus heals a man born blind, a miraculous event, by all accounts. Those who knew the man, even those who were present when he gained his sight, something he had been denied since birth, refused to believe what they had seen with their own eyes. They had visible, hands-on proof of it but could not accept what they knew to be true. Blinded to the facts as they were, they did not attack Jesus *ad hominem*, ... But, most assuredly, the Pharisees did. The Pharisees, after questioning the man's parents and the man himself, attacked the character of the man born blind — "You were born totally in sin, and are you trying to teach us" (Jn 9:34)? — and Jesus as well — "This man is not from God, because he does not keep the Sabbath"(Jn 9:16). Notice the blatant deflection from the facts, the careful avoidance of any engagement in ascertaining the truth simply in order to retain their pompous self-importance and hypocritical self-righteous piety.

Of course, *ad hominem* attacks run amok and rampant throughout our public and political discourse, so much so that it has become the *de facto* norm in virtually all discussions, whether substantive or inconsequential. No longer possible, reasoned debate and real argumentation have been tossed aside, relegated to the dung heap of reason and rationality. "Real argumentation isn't raising your voice, gesticulating wildly, and picking up the other fellow by the lapels when he doesn't agree with you. Real argumentation is the calm, rational, reasonable discussion of differences. And differences there are. In *Rerum Novarum* (1891) Pope Leo XIII said there is nothing so valuable as viewing the world as it really is, and that includes a frank acknowledgment of differences. Only if differences are acknowledged can they be overcome or, if not overcome, at least put into perspective."[223]

Thus, one should never argue to win, rather, argue to explain. No one can ever truly win an argument; for truth is not a game to be won or lost. As Jesus said, "If you continue in my word, you are truly my disciples, and you will know the truth, and the truth will make you free" (Jn 8:31-32). Truth has a marvelous way of taking care of itself; once implanted in the mind, it will germinate and grow, and the mind will neither be able to resist nor get rid of it. Yet, for the truth to be explained, it must first be understood and accepted by those who are called to convey it to others. For Catholics, that is the task of every Catholic, clerical and lay, because we are all called to evangelize, to spread the good news, to tell the truth about our faith. But, as Pilate asked, "What is truth" (Jn 18:38)? It is incumbent upon all the faithful to know the truth and to explain it, and yet while "the harvest is plentiful, the laborers are few" (Lk 10:2). In a way, this is both an issue and an opportunity. Far too many priests and religious take

---

[223] Karl Keating, *Argue to Explain, Not to Win*, Catholic Answers Magazine, March-April 2017, 8.

a dim view toward a learned laity under the false belief only they can adequately and accurately proclaim the truth. Somehow that sounds pharisaically familiar.

> The folks in the pews want to learn about their Faith and want to see it defended. They'd love to do the defending themselves, if only someone would teach them how. Church "professionals" shy away from apologetics. They say it's uncharitable or divisive or unecumenical—and it can be, if done wrongly.

> When done the right way, apologetics can do more than anything else to bring us closer to "Bible Christians," who have been almost untouched by the endless committee meetings of mainline ecumenism. Those committees often seem to do their best to avoid any of the issues that people actually are interested in, and they often give outsiders the impression we have no grounds for our beliefs.

Beyond knowing the truth lies a more fundamental issue and that is knowing how to explain it, not with a polemical, strident approach vis-a-vis character assassination, i.e. *argumentum ad hominem*, but by calm, deliberative, reasoned argumentation. While *ad hominem* debates will most assuredly continue for the foreseeable future, perhaps it is time for people of faith to consider an alternative, "a still more excellent way…. When I was a child, I spoke like a child, I thought like a child, I reasoned like a child; when I became a man, I gave up childish ways…. Now I know in part; then I shall understand fully, even as I have been fully understood" (1 Cor 12:31; 13:11-12). Perhaps: "Let him who is without sin among you be the first to throw a stone" (Jn 8:7).

On the Transcendent
Being outside our own

What so provokes the mind are thoughts which lie unknowable, not subject to empirical discovery or disproof. It is the transcendent nature of God which so utterly frustrates those who are of a mind to know all there is to know. In their unknowing the unknowable they are thus reduced to exhibiting a childlike hubris in their pronouncements, especially on questions for which empirical scientific methods are undeniably impotent. We are a curious species indeed, constantly seeking answers to questions, only to discover ever more questions to be resolved. It is an endless agonizing futile quest—to seek full understanding—yet we doggedly persist. The more the mysteries of the universe unfold, the greater the largesse of our own pathetic ignorance.

A thought is what precisely? What proof can be reproducibly constructed to determine its existence? What shape, what color, what are the dimensions of pure whimsy;

how long will it persist? Does thought exist or is it but a figment, a brief interlude of neurons synapsing. Perhaps there is empirical proof thought exists, yet without such proof should we suggest there is no thought? How drear the thought of such thought-lessness. Such devoted energy to disprove what common sense concludes.

Beyond ourselves there must exist, in fashion beyond our knowing, "being", without form or matter, without time or place, without beginning, without ending, beyond our understanding. Such "being" outside our own must be none other than our God.

Dead or Alive
No longer your own

A war is raging. The enormity of the loss in human lives is staggering. Mankind, God's greatest creation, is being irredeemably expunged from the annals of history by none other than man himself. Such apocalyptic thoughts may, at first blush, sound unduly pessimistic, the ravings of a madman, yet alarmingly neither is the case. Contraception, compulsory and voluntary sterilization, abortion, euthanasia, assisted suicide, suicide, murder, assassination, execution, genocide, global jihad, ethnic cleansing, religious persecution and martyrdom, the list is long and terrifying; all methods and means devised by man to prevent and/or end human life.

We are and have become our own worst enemy. Our genius at annihilating our own species consequently knows no bounds. In this endeavor to commit total and complete suicide we stand alone among all other living creatures. The question is why? Why the apparent urgent need to eradicate ourselves from the earth? Why do we hate ourselves so much?

We used to hear of the indomitable human spirit, the unquenchable quest for great achievement despite obstacles and hardships. Man's capacity for greatness was boundless, limited only by his own doubts and fears. The human mind envisioned great ideas, looked to the stars, and eagerly and confidently reached out and made them his own. Yet, in his heart, man always knew there was one greater than himself, God, to whom man owed everything, including life itself. Life was precious, life was of inestimable value because it was from God, of God, and for God. God loved life and so did man. Yet, over time, as man grew in knowledge and conceit, God faded from their hearts and minds. Man declared: "God is dead," thus turning inward, dependent now only on himself for justification and valuation. Life was good until it was not. Self-worth held forth no value beyond the self. No medium of exchange now existed for which one might barter for one's life. Upon the ledger, life was now a debit not a credit, a liability not an asset. Life no longer was one's own but the mere possession of a faceless, sciolistic other, pretender to the throne of knowledge and the well-informed. And so, the war against the worthless masses did begin.

Lest we consider all this hyperbole—which it most assuredly is not—let us turn to what we know is true and telling: the proportion of reproductive age married women who use a modern or traditional contraceptive method rose from 55% to 63% between 1990 and 2010.[224] Between 1971 and 1977, China forced more than thirty million sterilizations of men and women. A 2014 report by the World Health Organization referenced ongoing targeted sterilization practices against specific population groups, including: women living in countries with coercive population control policies, people with disabilities (including intellectual disabilities), intersex and transgender persons. Since the beginning of 2017, the number of abortions performed worldwide has exceeded 11.2 Million and counting. Globally since 1980 over 1.45 Billion deaths have been the direct result of abortion. Around the globe, a growing number of countries have instituted policies promoting "medically assisted" suicide. In 2016, Canadian lawmakers passed legislation legalizing the practice nationwide. Doctors and nurses in Ontario are under enormous pressure to either perform assisted suicides or refer the patient to a willing physician. A similar law is in place in Vermont. Other states within the United States which have legalized physician-assisted suicide include California, Oregon, Washington, and Montana. Other states are currently in the process of enacting such legislation. The 2017 Nevada legislature currently has before it, SB 261, which would permit physician-assisted suicide.[225] Many countries around the world have legalized not only physician-assisted suicide, but euthanasia as well—the intentional killing of one person by another. According to Alex Schadenberg, executive director of the Euthanasia Prevention Coalition, "You have this new attitude that it's OK for a doctor to kill a patient just because they are suffering. But suffering is part of the human condition. The question is how do we, as a society, deal with those who are going through a difficult time in their life?" Colombia, Switzerland and Luxembourg now allow euthanasia. Legalized euthanasia in the Netherlands has been allowed since 1984. Today the government is pushing to expand euthanasia beyond those who are sick or dying, to encompass those who merely think their "life is complete." In 2004, in the Netherlands, a Catholic nun was euthanized against her will by a doctor who argued that his patient was dying of cancer and was hindered by her religious beliefs from making the best decision—so he made it for her. Belgium, with its liberal euthanasia laws, euthanizes mentally ill patients without their consent. It also allows terminally ill children to request euthanasia. Over 130 Million people were murdered by Mao Zedong, Joseph Stalin, and Adolf Hitler. Another 30 Million by others including Pol Pot, Kim Ilsung, Saddam Hussein, Sukarno, Mullah Omar, Benito Mussolini, Idi Amin, Ho Chi Minh, Hafez Bashar Alassad, Ayatollah Ruhollah Khomeini, Robert Mugabe, and General Augusto Pinochet.

---

[224] Alkema L. et al., National, regional, and global rates and trends in contraceptive prevalence and unmet need for family planning between 1990 and 2015: a systematic and comprehensive analysis, Lancet, 2013, 381 (9878): 1642-1652.
[225] SB 261 was not passed into law.

Tragically, the list is woefully incomplete and inadequate, lacking the emotional impact it should in order to truly show man's inhumanity toward man. Consider the case of Stephanie Packer, a 34-year old mother of four, suffering from scleroderma, a terminal autoimmune disease attacking her lungs. "One week after California's physician-assisted suicide law went into effect June 9, 2016, the Packers encountered a major hurdle when Stephanie received a disturbing letter from her health insurance company. Stephanie was told her doctor-recommended chemotherapy treatment that the company previously promised was now being denied. However, she was later informed that her plan would cover a lethal dose of suicide pills — at the incredibly low cost of $1.20."[226] Upon learning of Stephanie's plight, a reporter friend set out to cover the story and asked the insurance company for comment, which they declined. The next morning Stephanie received a phone call from the insurance company informing her that the chemotherapy drug was once again approved. Unfortunately, cases similar to Stephanie Packer's too often fail to capture the attention they so richly deserve. And, when they do, the overwhelming response is often brutally unkind and dreadfully dishonest. In early 2015, three years after her diagnosis at the age of 29, Stephanie took her story of life public, speaking joyfully of her choice to live and enjoy what remaining time she had with her family. "Stephanie's outspokenness soon brought her to the attention of the national media. NPR, CNN, The Washington Post and other news outlets covered her story, and one media executive told her that her story had sent their ratings 'through the roof.'" As we have come to expect, there were those who hated her message of hope, love and life. Her husband, Brian, received death threats and as Stephanie recalls, "They just ate us alive after that. It was just comment after comment of nasty stuff. People told me that I should just off myself and that they feel bad for my kids."

On the day before the assisted suicide bill went into effect in California, Archbishop Jose H. Gomez of Los Angeles reflected on its disastrous and devastating consequences. "The logic of assisted suicide leads inevitably to the government and corporate administrators essentially deciding which lives are worth saving and caring for and who would be better off dead. The criteria for such decisions will always be arbitrary and the process will always mean the strong and powerful deciding the fate of those who are weak and less influential in society. This is the beginning of tyranny." On November 2, 2016, the Washington, D.C. city council voted 11 to 2 to legalize assisted suicide. Cardinal Timothy M. Dolan, archbishop of New York and chairman of the U.S. Bishops' Committee on Pro-Life Activities, noted this was the most extreme assisted suicide legislation in the United States. "It goes beyond assisted suicide by allowing third parties to administer the lethal drugs, opening the door even further to coercion and abuse. Every suicide is tragic, whether someone is young or old, healthy or sick. But the legalization of doctor-assisted suicide creates two classes of people:

---

[226] Clara Fox, *Stephanie's Fight to Live*, Columbia Magazine, January 2017, 16.

those whose suicides are to be prevented at any cost and those whose suicides are deemed a positive good."

What follows has been excerpted from an editorial in Columbia Magazine. What the editor, Alton J. Pelowski writes is profoundly on point and thus the bulk of it is reproduced here.

> On October 7, 1979, during his first visit to the United States as Pope, Saint John Paul II celebrated Sunday Mass on the National Mall in Washington, D.C. He took the opportunity to reflect in his homily on the dignity of human life. "I do not hesitate to proclaim before you and before the world that all human life — from the moment of conception and through all subsequent states — is sacred, because human life is created in the image and likeness of God. Nothing surpasses the greatness or dignity of the human person.... All human beings ought to value every person for his or her uniqueness as a creature of God, called to be a brother or sister of Christ."
>
> Nearly four decades later, in an increasingly divided world, these words serve as an important reminder that our common humanity transcends any cultural, racial or political differences. The Declaration of Independence expresses this in the assertion "that all men are created equal, that they are endowed by their Creator with certain unalienable rights." Yet, from a spiritual perspective, we are called not simply to coexist peacefully, but also to see our relationships with our neighbors as integral to who we are.
>
> In his message for the World Day of Peace Jan. 1, 2016, Pope Francis put it this way: "Personal dignity and interpersonal relationships are what constitutes us as human beings whom God willed to create in his own image and likeness. As creatures endowed with inalienable dignity, we are related to all our brothers and sisters, for whom we are responsible and with whom we act in solidarity. Lacking this relationship, we would be less human."[227]

Over the past fifty years our society, our nation has literally been transformed. We are no longer "One nation under God, with liberty and justice for all" but today a nation of egoistic amoralists seeking happiness for me, myself, and I. Since the sixties, we have seen the steady proliferation of rights as defined by man and the casual dismissal of those rights heretofore granted only by our Creator. The right to life, liberty, and the *pursuit* of happiness have given way to the right to choose, the right to work, the right to a living wage, the right to own a home, the right to a college education, the right to healthcare, the right to a same-sex marriage, the right to kill oneself, the right to be happy, and so on and on and on. These so-called rights all have a few things in common: they are creations of man and therefore transitory, subject to the whims of their creators, they elevate the few at the expense of the many, and they enthrone man as master of his domain. In all actuality, these societal and moral changes are nothing new; such tectonic shifts have been occurring since the very beginning. Adam and Eve chose to determine for themselves whether what God had forbidden was really evil or whether he was simply playing them for suckers. What is important to understand is

---

[227] Alton J. Pelowski, *Our Common Humanity*, Columbia Magazine, December 2016, 2.

the fall did not occur because they discovered the meaning of evil; the fall occurred because they did evil, they disobeyed God. They came to know evil by experiencing evil and becoming evil. And so, it began and so it continues today. Underlying the fall is this question: "Why would man, created by God and happy in the Garden of Eden, wish to commit such a flagrant act of disobedience?" Even one so universally revered as Saint Augustine had difficulty in providing an adequate response to that question. Saint Anselm however did provide at least one reasoned explanation in his dialogue *"On the Fall of the Devil"* where he argues angels, like humans, have two motivations for doing anything. The first motivation is self-interest or happiness which basically means doing what benefits you, what makes you happy. The second motivation is justice or morality which means doing what God wants you to do. It is difficult to conceive of any action or decision we might make not motivated in some way by either the desire to be happy or the desire to do what is right.

It is imperative we occasionally remind ourselves the God who created us chose to give us Free Will which means we are free to choose what is moral and right, that is, what God wants us to do, or to choose what we believe will make us happy. I am free to choose my way or God's way and if I choose my way, I can rest assured God will do nothing to prevent me from doing whatever I desire. Choosing self-interest or happiness over justice or morality requires—to paraphrase and skewer John the Baptist—for God to decrease while I increase. As we diminish our reliance on God and ignore our relationship with our Creator, we find ourselves in the devil's embrace, desiring only that which serves our own self-interest. We become addicted to achieving happiness and like any addict achieving that "happiness high" becomes all that matters. Nothing else, no one and certainly no God matters or holds any greater value. Sadly, few are entirely immune to this paradigm shift; it is simply a matter of the degree upon which we find ourselves tilting. So many, and I must include myself here, escaped from the supposed confines of a world created and ruled by God to live as gods in a world ruled by men. And we are now reaping exactly what we have sowed.

The value of a single life has plummeted from the lofty heights of beyond measure to the abyssal depths of nothingness. The unborn, the old, the infirm, the weak, the disabled, the nonconforming, and the unwanted are considered fodder for the flames, dismissed as burdens, their elimination for the greater good. All that matters is what is in one's self-interest, what makes one happy, nothing more. The devil is a cunning creature who knows our weaknesses and our faults. He strokes our egos and entices us with all manner of delights; and he is winning. We can fight against abortion, the death penalty, euthanasia, same-sex marriage, co-habitation, divorce, poverty, and any other injustice or moral wrong but we will not win the war against the devil until we take up the fight in defense of God. As long as we believe in the primacy of man, the devil wins and we lose. It is far past time for the devil to lose and for God to win. Each of us needs to once again acknowledge the return of the King to his heavenly throne, to his rightful place above all his creation. The King reigns supreme but we are his voices. We must elevate our voices so those who deny the King his rightful place may no longer be heard above our joyful song. It is well past time for us to step down from our self-deluded pedestals and to kneel before our God in humble obeisance to his glory. We are not gods. God loves each of us as if we are the only one. Death is the devil's domain; life belongs to God. Life is a gift from God and through him alone life is sustained. Jesus told us exactly what we must do. "You shall love the Lord, your God, with all your heart, with all your soul, and with all your mind. You shall love your neighbor as yourself." Love God. Love your neighbor. Love the life within you.

April 14, 2017

In Shadowed Footsteps
All the way to Calvary

Jesus told his disciples, "If any man would come after me, let him deny himself and take up his cross and follow me. For whoever would save his life will lose it, and whoever loses his life for my sake will find it. For what will it profit a man, if he gains the whole world and forfeits his life? Or what shall a man give in return for his life" (Mt 16:24-26)? This passage stands as a stark reminder of what is demanded of each of us if we are to be true disciples of Christ. The cross we carry seldom leaves a lasting mark, and yet, we bear it with begrudging indifference, bemoaning the injustice, the unfairness of it all. We do not heed the weight of it if it is light and easy; no burden seems too heavy until raw chafing wounds appear. And yet, we dare not look to the crosses borne by others lest we discover how small our own.

We walk in the shadowed footsteps of Christ crucified. Yet, we must reflect: do we love enough to follow him all the way to Calvary? Are we willing to take up a cross so mean as his; willing to lose everything, including life itself, for the sake of him? Few are tested so severe; too easily do we wear our faith with such banal insouciance. A moment's prayer on bended knee for those who, with their dying breath did crown him king. The Coptic Christians, martyrs this Palm Sunday last, have borne too long without complaint, a cross no one should have to bear. And yet, they walked in shadowed footsteps, all the way to Calvary. What will be asked of each of us? What cross awaits for us to bear? There is a cross for each to bear which must be carried through life's struggles, pains and sorrows in shadowed footsteps, all the way to Calvary.

No Act Condemned
Who am I to judge?

What death ensued this recent Palm Sunday in Egypt by most accounts was both horrifying and tragic. "The Islamic State claimed responsibility for two terrorist attacks on Coptic Orthodox churches in the Egyptian Nile Delta town of Tanta and the coastal city of Alexandria that killed at least 44 people during crowded Palm Sunday services, the latest in a string of attacks against the Christian minorities in the majority-Muslim country."

> ... the history of the church has always been one of suffering as waves of governments and competing religions have taken advantage of its people who are usually living as minorities. That history has continued in recent years.
>
> Attackers struck a Coptic church in Cairo in December, killing 25 people. In 2015, the Islamic State released a video purporting to show the beheading of 21 Coptic Christians who had been kidnapped in Libya. And on New Year's Day 2011, a bombing at a Coptic church in Alexandria, Egypt, killed 21 people."[228]

Terrorism is not new. Indeed, it is almost as old as humanity itself. Pilate offered the Jews a choice between Jesus and Barabbas, a known terrorist, and they chose the terrorist. It is the global reach and escalating nightmarish violence of today's terrorism which differentiates then from now. Yet terrorism is just one manifestation of and the inevitable endgame of the philosophy of relativism best expressed by Frederick Nietzsche "You have your way; I have my way. As for the right way, it does not exist."

A dozen years ago, then Joseph Cardinal Ratzinger, on the eve of his election to the papacy, speaking to the conclave of cardinals warned of the spread of a worldview which fervently espoused a *dictatorship of relativism*. "Today, having a clear faith based on the Creed of the Church is often labeled as fundamentalism. Whereas relativism, that is, letting oneself be "tossed here and there, carried about by every wind of doctrine," seems the only attitude that can cope with modern times. We are building a dictatorship of relativism that does not recognize anything as definitive and whose ultimate goal consists solely of one's own ego and desires." I have written before about relativism, but too often when topics of philosophy, ontology, theology, metaphysics and other ologies are even briefly mentioned, the eyes glaze over and the mind quickly wanders to more pleasant, congenial thoughts. But there are times when such esoteric matters are of so grave concern and of paramount importance, as in this instance, all should well attend. Relativism is not bad or evil *per se*. The height of a man relative to a giraffe is neither good nor bad, nor is it right or wrong; it is merely a generally true comparative observation. What Cardinal Ratzinger was describing wasn't that form of relativism. He was speaking specifically of moral relativism. Moral relativism, as a

---

[228] Russell Shaw, *Seek to escape the dictatorship of relativism*, Our Sunday Visitor, April 9-15, 5.

general theory, states truth and moral values are not absolute but are relative to the persons or groups who hold them. There are no objective truths, only personal opinion as to what is true. It is the belief that morality does not relate to any absolute principles of right and wrong, but "good" and "bad" are dependent on culture and circumstance. Such a philosophy is commonly expressed by people who, when faced with deciding whether something is right or wrong, will refuse to make a choice, saying something akin to "It all depends on what you believe," or "If you think it's right, it's right for you." What this boils down to is for the moral relativist, morality is nothing more than personal opinion. Moral relativism operates on the premise that no action, no matter how heinous, is never strictly wrong. You will hear the relativist advancing the argument: "I personally don't approve of abortion, but for others, it might be the right thing to do." Moral relativism comes in two flavors: subjective and cultural. Subjective relativism holds that everyone develops their own moral code and then looks for a group who share their own values and ideals. Cultural relativism holds if the people of a given culture firmly believe what they are doing is right, then it is right for them (i.e. cannibalism or human sacrifice.) The cultural relativist will often logically argue by means of a faulty syllogism:

- Group A believes abortion kills a human being

- Group B believes abortion removes an unwanted mass of tissue

- Therefore, abortion is neither objectively right nor objectively wrong. It is merely a matter of opinion that varies from culture to culture.

A syllogism is a type of logical argument in which one uses deductive reasoning to arrive at a conclusion based on two or more propositions that must be true. The fault in the relativist argument above is twofold:

1. The propositions are predicated not on objective, provable truths but on belief which is subjective. If one were to reduce the propositions to "abortion kills a human being" and "abortion removes a mass of tissue" both arguably could be asserted to be true, but,

2. The conclusion has no relation to the propositions, whether one or both of them are true. The relativist in a sense ignores the propositions and pulls the conclusion out of thin air. Neither proposition states the rightness or wrongness of abortion, rather both describe a point of view, a cultural bias or opinion as to what abortion accomplishes.

Modern anthropology has muddied the waters significantly by positing certain basic human goods like knowledge, friendship, play, religion, health or life are recognized and cherished within every culture but in different ways. What remains true is relativism has played a major role in culture war disputes concerning such issues as abortion, euthanasia, same-sex marriage, gender identification, or immigration. Multiculturalism, diversity, and tolerance also require a society based on a relativistic moral code. This same moral reasoning now dominates the popular culture of the sec-ularized west. Morality has become a matter of personal feeling "rather than judgments of objective truth." Sociologist Alan Wolfe has concluded in this relativistic worldview, the Ten Commandments have been subordinated to an all-encompassing 11th commandment: "Thou shalt not judge." To judge the choice of another as wrong or bad is arrogance on your part—a moral judgment in and of itself, but who's judging.

So, what precisely is wrong with moral relativism? First, in a fundamental and prac-tical way, all actions are permissible, not subject to criticism or challenge, since nothing can be adjudged intrinsically and morally wrong. Thus, anything goes, and nothing can be denied. Terrorists who believe in killing those who do not believe as they do: who are we to judge? They are only doing what they believe is right. The inescapable conclusion which can be made is our contemporary culture is, and has been for quite some time, on a relentless crusade to thoroughly emasculate objective truth, the hall-mark of humanity. "Over the span of life, the Word can be tested time and time again and its truths will stand tall as our culture's fascination with the subjective proves itself to be hollow and false."[229] Ravi Zacharias elsewhere writes, "Any message that threat-ens our autonomy is automatically rejected no matter what it is. For that very reason, centuries after Jesus, we have become the impoverished inheritors of a culture that understands neither law nor grace, where absolutes are debunked as the gasp of an antiquated thought pattern, and forgiveness is branded a beggar's refuge. It is not at all surprising that in Toynbee's study of history we are the first of 21 civilizations to attempt "civility" without a moral point of reference. To compound this further, we have come to these conclusions through a process that only causes us to sink deeper into the abyss of nihilism, where life has lost all meaning."[230] The problem for those who follow the moral relativist' creed—who are almost always secular humanists who either reject God outright or find small use for God—is they have no good answer to this two-part question: Is there anything wrong with anything (and why?) The re-nowned Catholic philosopher Michael Novak writing for National Review provides further insights on Cardinal Ratzinger's sermon on relativism.

> In today's liberal democracies, Ratzinger has observed, the move to atheism is not, as it was in the 19th century, a move toward the objective world of the scientific rationalist. That was the "modern" way, and it is now being rejected, in favor of a new "post-mod-ern" way. The new way is not toward objectivity, but toward subjectivism; not toward truth as its criterion, but toward power. This, Ratzinger fears, is a move back toward the justification of murder in the name of "tolerance" and subjective choice.

> Along with that move, he has observed (haven't we all?), comes a dictatorial impulse, to treat anyone who has a different view as "intolerant." For instance, those (on the "reli-gious right") who hold that there are truths worth dying for, and objective goods to be

---

[229] Ravi Zacharias, *On Relativism*.
[230] Ravi Zacharias, *Biblical Authority and Cultural Relativism*, rzim.org, October 15, 1993.

pursued and objective evils to be avoided, are now held to be "intolerant" fundamentalists, guilty of "discrimination."

In other words, the new dictatorial impulse declares that the only view permissible among reasonable people is the view that all subjective choices are equally valid. It declares, further, that anyone who claims that there are objective truths and objective goods and evils is "intolerant." Such persons are expelled from the community, or at minimum re-educated. That is to say, all Catholics and others like them must be converted to relativism or else sent into cultural re-training camps.

On the basis of relativism, however, no culture can long defend itself or justify its own values. If everything is relative, even tolerance is only a subjective choice, not an objective mandatory value. Ironically, though, what post-moderns call "tolerance" is actually radically intolerant of any view contrary to its own.

No great, inspiring culture of the future can be built upon the moral principle of relativism. For at its bottom such a culture holds that nothing is better than anything else, and that all things are in themselves meaningless. Except for the fragments of faith (in progress, in compassion, in conscience, in hope) to which it still clings, illegitimately, such a culture teaches every one of its children that life is a tale told by an idiot, signifying nothing.[231]

The lure of moral relativism, especially among the elite class—those firmly ensconced within the ivied halls of academia in particular—is neither recent nor new. Charles Dickens made note of this philosophical predilection mid-nineteenth century. "The American elite is almost beyond redemption. ... Moral relativism has set in so deeply that the gilded classes have become incapable of discerning right from wrong. Everything can be explained away, especially by journalists. Life is one great moral mush-sophistry washed down with Chardonnay. The ordinary citizens, thank goodness, still adhere to absolutes. ... It is they who have saved the republic from creeping degradation while their 'betters" were derelict."[232] America is by no means alone in its descent into the morass of moral relativism. *Der Spiegel*, a German weekly news magazine, in an interview with Geert Wilders, a leading member of the Dutch Parliament and outspoken critic of the growing Islamic cultural encroachment throughout Europe, asked Wilders what he had against Islam. His response:

Europe's greatest problem—not just today, but already for decades now—is cultural relativism. This has led to a situation today where Europeans no longer know what they should be proud of and who they really are—because a so-called liberal and leftist-imposed concept says that all cultures are the same.... It has to do with what is described by the wonderful German word *Leitkultur*, which means "dominant" or "guiding" culture. I think that we should be proud that our culture is better than Islamic culture, for instance. Anyone who says this is not a racist, Nazi or xenophobe. Those are labels that have been put on many people in the Netherlands, Germany and England—just because

---

[231] Michael Novak, *Culture in Crisis*, National Review, April 19, 2005.
[232] Charles Dickens, Dealings with the Firm of Dombey and Son: Wholesale, Retail and for Exportation, (London, U.K.: Bradbury & Evans, 1948).

we believe that Islam is a totalitarian and violent ideology. More of an ideology than a religion, comparable to communism and fascism. Islam threatens our freedom.[233]

Perhaps no more salient voice can be heard on the radical and existential threat for which moral relativism represents than the Catholic philosopher, Peter Kreeft. Admitting that for fallen humanity, moral practice has always been difficult, he submits

... at least there was always the lighthouse of moral principles, no matter how stormy the sea of moral practice got. But today, with the majority of our mind-molders, in formal education, or informal education—that is, media—the light is gone. Morality is a fog of feelings. That is why to them, as Chesterton said, "Morality is always dreadfully complicated to a man who has lost all his principles." Principles mean moral absolutes. Unchanging rocks beneath the changing waves of feelings and practices. Moral relativism is a philosophy that denies moral absolutes.

The philosophy that has extinguished the light in the minds of our teachers, and then their students, and eventually, if not reversed, will extinguish our whole civilization.

How important is this issue? After all, it's just philosophy, and philosophy is just ideas. But ideas have consequences. Sometimes these consequences are as momentous as a holocaust, or a Hiroshima. Sometimes even more momentous. Philosophy is just thought, but sow a thought, reap an act; sow an act, reap a habit; sow a habit, reap a character; sow a character reap a destiny. This is just as true for societies as it is for individuals.

How important is the issue? The issue of moral relativism is merely the single most important issue of our age, for no society in all of human history has ever survived without rejecting [such a] philosophy... There has never been a society of relativists. Therefore, our society will do one of three things: either disprove one of the most universally established laws of all history; or repent of its relativism and survive; or persist in its relativism and perish.

How important is the issue? C.S. Lewis says, in The Poison of Subjectivism, that relativism 'will certainly end our species and damn our souls.' Please remember that Oxonians are not given to exaggeration. Why does he say 'damn our souls?' Because Lewis is a Christian, and he does not disagree with the fundamental teaching of his master, Christ, and all the prophets in the Jewish tradition, that salvation presupposes repentance, and repentance presupposes an objectively real moral law. Moral relativism eliminates that law, thus trivializes repentance, thus imperils salvation.[234]

This issue, moral relativism, should in no way be considered to engender a liberal-conservative, left-right divide, for it transcends politics; it is far too important to be buried and trampled by the power elite. As Nobel Peace Prize-winner and Iranian jurist and activist, Shirin Ebadi, in an interview with Helen Thomas in 2004 for The Progressive clearly stated:

The idea of cultural relativism is nothing but an excuse to violate human rights. Human rights is the fruit of various civilizations. I know of no civilization that tolerates or justifies

---

[233] Der Spiegel Interview with Geert Wilders, *Merkel is Afraid*, November 09, 2010.
[234] Peter Kreeft, *A Refutation of Moral Relativism*, CatholicCulture.org.

violence, terrorism, or injustice. There is no civilization that justifies the killing of innocent people. Those who are invoking cultural relativism are really using that as an excuse
for violating human rights and to put a cultural mask on the face of what they're doing.
They argue that cultural relativism prevents us from implementing human rights. This
is nothing but an excuse. Human rights is a universal standard. It is a component of every
religion and every civilization.[235]

In the first chapter of Saint Paul's letter to the Romans, we find the argument for
the existence of the natural law.

> For the wrath of God is revealed from heaven against all ungodliness and wickedness of
> men who by their wickedness suppress the truth. For what can be known about God is
> plain to them, because God has shown it to them. Ever since the creation of the world his
> invisible nature, namely, his eternal power and deity, has been clearly perceived in the
> things that have been made. So they are without excuse; for although they knew God
> they did not honor him as God or give thanks to him, but they became futile in their
> thinking and their senseless minds were darkened. Claiming to be wise, they became
> fools, and exchanged the glory of the immortal God for images resembling mortal man
> or birds or animals or reptiles.

> Therefore, God gave them up in the lusts of their hearts to impurity, to the dishonoring
> of their bodies among themselves, because they exchanged the truth about God for a lie
> and worshiped and served the creature rather than the Creator, who is blessed for ever!
> Amen. (Rom 1:18-25).

The issue of moral relativism is not just a Catholic problem. It is an issue transcend-
ing denominational boundaries. LDS Elder D. Todd Christofferson spoke of the need
for Christians to defend their faith against moral relativism. "We need strong Christians who can persevere against hardship, who can sustain hope through tragedy, who
can lift others by their example and their compassion, and who can consistently overcome temptations. We need strong Christians who can make important things happen
by their faith and who can defend the truth of Jesus Christ against moral relativism
and militant atheism."[236] Nevertheless, for Catholics, the Church has been over the centuries a consistent voice, in developing its doctrine on relativism, insisting Catholics
should form their consciences in light of objective moral truth—truth they have a duty
to seek and accept. The Catechism of the Catholic Church clearly summarizes the illicit
nature of moral relativism.

> **1756** It is therefore an error to judge the morality of human acts by considering only the
> intention that inspires them or the circumstances (environment, social pressure, duress
> or emergency, etc.) which supply their context. There are acts which, in and of them-
> selves, independently of circumstances and intentions, are always gravely illicit by
> reason of their object; such as blasphemy and perjury, murder and adultery. One may
> not do evil so that good may result from it.

---

[235] Helen Thomas Interview, The Progressive, September 1, 2014.
[236] D. Todd Christofferson, "*The Power of Covenants*," Ensign, May 2009, pp. 19-23.

1798 A well-formed conscience is upright and truthful. It formulates its judgments according to reason, in conformity with the true good willed by the wisdom of the Creator. Everyone must avail himself of the means to form his conscience.

Relativism represents a threat to fundamental freedoms and the intrinsic value and dignity of human life; it further represents a serious problem with regard to the law. In his Encyclical, *Evangelium Vitae*, On the Value and Inviolability of Human Life, Pope Saint John Paul II directly and explicitly faulted relativism underlying laws that violate human life.

> At the basis of all these tendencies lies the ethical relativism which characterize much of present-day culture. There are those who consider such relativism an essential condition of democracy, inasmuch as it alone is held to guarantee tolerance, mutual respect between people and acceptance of the decisions of the majority, whereas moral norms considered to be objective and binding are held to lead to authoritarianism and intolerance.

> But it is precisely the issue of respect for life which shows what misunderstandings and contradictions, accompanied by terrible practical consequences, are concealed in this position.

> It is true that history has known cases where crimes have been committed in the name of "truth". But equally grave crimes and radical denials of freedom have also been committed and are still being committed in the name of "ethical relativism". When a parliamentary or social majority decrees that it is legal, at least under certain conditions, to kill unborn human life, is it not really making a "tyrannical" decision with regard to the weakest and most defenseless of human beings? Everyone's conscience rightly rejects those crimes against humanity of which our century has had such sad experience. But would these crimes cease to be crimes if, instead of being committed by unscrupulous tyrants, they were legitimated by popular consensus?[237]

In his earlier Encyclical, *Veritas Splendor*, John Paul explicitly cautioned against

> ... the risk of an alliance between democracy and ethical relativism, which would remove any sure moral reference point from political and social life, and on a deeper level make the acknowledgement of truth impossible. Indeed, if there is no ultimate truth to guide and direct political activity, then ideas and convictions can easily be manipulated for reasons of power. As history demonstrates, a democracy without values easily turns into open or thinly disguised totalitarianism.[238]

An underlying principle, seldom if ever publicly conceded by those who espouse to a relativist philosophy is human life—whether young, old, or somewhere within the boundaries that define living—is ultimately meaningless and succinctly terminal. Without meaning or something beyond this material existence, life holds no intrinsic value. Thus, having no true meaning or value beyond the sum of the component parts

---

[237] Pope Saint John Paul II, Encyclical Letter: Evangelium Vitae, March 25, 1995, §70.
[238] Pope Saint John Paul II, *Encyclical Letter: Veritas Splendor*, August 6, 1993, §101.

that make up the physical body, your value as a human being becomes both subjective and relative, completely subject to the opinion and personal valuation of another.

The Cross We Bear
Suffering uninterrupted

There is a cross bespoke for each, tailored to specifications so exacting as to test the soul: no more, no less, but to precisely measure the forbearance, the endurance of the soul. Each born into this world will bear their cross from birth until … well that depends on how well it is carried.

I was reminded of this during Easter Vigil when we knelt while the litany of the saints was sung. A childhood fall managed to permanently compress my lower spine which has led to a lifetime of recurring pain when nerves are pinched between too close vertebra. Coupled with aging knees which no longer care to bend and the moments it took to sing the litany quickly became excruciatingly painful. So much so I found myself requiring the strong arms of two much younger men to return me to an upright position. What this brief experience brought to mind after some reflection is but a small reminder. No matter the pain, no matter the loss, no matter the suffering we encounter throughout our lives we always have the option to accept it or to complain about it. We can look at it as a test of our fortitude, of our willingness to suffer short-term pain for long-term (i.e. eternal) happiness or we can look at it as a short-term indicator of far more excruciating eternity of suffering and pain.

The pain which I experienced was truly excruciating but only for a moment or two. The thought of suffering such pain uninterrupted forever reminded me it was only a test. It was only a test, but a test, nevertheless. A test which gave me pause to reconsider whether I have been carrying my cross without complaint or trying to offload its burden onto someone else. Jesus carried his cross without complaint and rose in glory. Should not we do the same?

For Want of Argument
The lost art of controversy

Over eight decades ago, Venerable Fulton J. Sheen lamented of the lost art of argument. Not argumentation—the often near-maniacal *ad hominem* rants of the irrationally close-minded—but deliberative, well-considered thought-provoking controversy.

Once there were lost islands, but most of them have been found; once there were lost causes, but many of them have been retrieved; but there is one lost art that has not been definitely recovered, and without which no civilization can long survive, and that is the art of controversy. The hardest thing to find in the world today is an argument. Because so few are thinking, naturally there are found but few to argue. Prejudice there is in abundance and sentiment too, for these things are born of enthusiasms without the pain of labor. Thinking, on the contrary, is a difficult task; it is the hardest work a man can do — that is perhaps why so few indulge in it. Thought-saving devices have been invented that rival labor-saving devices in their ingenuity. Fine-sounding phrases like "Life is bigger than logic," or "Progress is the spirit of the age," go rattling by us like express trains, carrying the burden of those who are too lazy to think for themselves.

Not even philosophers argue today; they only explain away. A book full of bad logic, advocating all manner of moral laxity, is not refuted by critics; it is merely called "bold, honest, and fearless." Even those periodicals which pride themselves upon their open-mindedness on all questions are far from practicing the lost art of controversy. Their pages contain no controversies, but only presentations of points of view; these never rise to the level of abstract thought in which argument clashes with argument like steel with steel, but rather they content themselves with the personal reflections of one who has lost his faith, writing against the sanctity of marriage, and of another who has kept his faith, writing in favor of it. Both sides are shooting off firecrackers, making all the noise of an intellectual warfare and creating the illusion of conflict, but it is only a sham battle in which there are no casualties; there are plenty of explosions, but never an exploded argument.

What is most disturbing, to my mind, based on all observable evidence, is the complacency which permeates those who should know better.

There has sprung up a disturbing indifference to truth, and a tendency to regard the useful as the true, and the impractical as the false. The man who can make up his mind when proofs are presented to him is looked upon as a bigot, and the man who ignores proofs and the search for truth is looked upon as broadminded and tolerant.

Another evidence of this same disrespect for rational foundations is the general readiness of the modern mind to accept a statement because of the literary way in which it is couched, or because of the popularity of the one who says it, rather than for the reasons behind the statement. In this sense, it is unfortunate that some men who think poorly can write so well. [239]

What immediately comes to mind is the precipitous descent from the heights of rational thought and constructive argument to the nadir of mob-rule and double-think which has of late become the norm on campuses of "higher" education. Once considered a sanctuary, "a place set aside for a holy purpose, not be reduced to the practicalities of daily life, must less to political utility," the university was then the locus for rational inquiry, conversation, and argument; a tranquil island where truth was pursued for its own sake. Anthony Esolen asks, and answers a crucial question.

---

[239] Fulton J. Sheen PhD, DD, LLD, *Old Errors and New Labels*, (New York: Century Co., 1931)

What happens when you deface the campus with political demonstrations? You serve notice to all students and faculty that will and force, not reason, should dominate. You do not begin a discussion. You end it, or you ensure that no reasoned discussion will take place to begin with. You imply a threat of force against anyone who should dare, within class or without, to differ from what you have set down as what all right-thinking human beings must accept.

How destructive is this? There are sins, and there are sins. The pitcher who fails to keep himself in good condition serves up a cripple pitch, and the batter deposits it into the bleachers. The priest lets his mind wander and disappoints his parishioners by his inattention. The professor cobbles together an article from two or three sources but never bothers to consult the most important. These sinners fail by deficiency.

That is not the case with the mob. The pitcher "cuts" the ball on his belt buckle to make his pitch dance, hiding his violation from the umpire. The professor, giving way to partisan inclination, tweaks the results of one of his sources, and raids another which he does not name. These sinners cheat, but their hypocrisy still recognizes, at least in theory, the good wherein they participate.

The batter runs the bases backwards. The professor takes a bullhorn and marches around campus, crying out, "Death to Patriarchy!" The priest interrupts the procession to dance with a man in drag, and to give hosts of the Eucharist to a clown, to juggle. Here we have something worse than the poor show, or the cheat. We have the spoilsport, the travesty, the sacrilege. We do not have a bad baseball game. We have no game at all. We do not have a slipshod religious procession. We have no religious procession. And we do not have a college, a sacred space set aside for the sake of truth. We have a tremendously expensive vacant lot for use by political mobs.[240]

Esolen earlier described a Corpus Christi procession where the priest solemnly carries the monstrance, while worshippers sing *Pange Lingua*.

The procession embraces young and old, men and women, made one in their common worship of the Lord who gave himself up for their salvation. They neither efface nor flaunt their individuality, nor slay it upon the altar of lust and violence. They forget it, … That does not mean that the worshipers warp or stifle their capacity to reason. As song is language straining upward, raised to its heights and even beyond, so reason refined of error and aimed toward the highest of its objects trembles upon the threshold of faith.

I assume that no sane person would have his financial blood drawn down to the dregs to support a vacant lot trampled by mobs. The public does have an interest in the sacred space of the college, and in its protection. Though the irony may be lost on our secular contemporaries, who seem to believe that the true university sprang like Athena full-grown from the head of a doper at Berkeley fifty-odd years ago, we may end up owing the survival of reason and its sanctuary to Christians, who invented the institution in the first place.

---

[240] Anthony Esolen, *Editorial: Campus Descent*, Touchstone Magazine, Volume 30, Number 3, May/June 2017, 3-4.

May owe—if professors, students, and administrators of Christian colleges remember what they are. For at my college right now, that Corpus Christi procession I imagined was forbidden, on the grounds that it might be "divisive," but political demonstrations enjoy official sanction and approval.

Returning to the observation that thinking is a difficult task which may explain why so few indulge in it, along with the current dismal and shameful state of our institutions of higher education, reminds me of a recent article in the local newspaper, which tragically relates. The article reported on the ongoing battle between the governor and the local school board over funding for a program signed into law two years ago with the heart-rending title *"Read By Grade 3"*. Neither the specifics of the program nor the arguments pro and con are germane here. What is germane but neither asked nor answered is of far greater importance and is indicative of what the Venerable Archbishop indicated when he wrote "Fine-sounding phrases … go rattling by us like express trains, carrying the burden of those who are too lazy to think for themselves." Digest, if you will, for a moment: *"Read By Grade 3"* While not oblivious to the challenges some children might face, the notion any child, by age nine, cannot read is simply beyond the pale. As a teacher, a parent, and a grandparent I have to ask what are these children being taught and how are they expected to learn if they cannot read competently by the third grade. Given this tragic inability to read at grade level or at all, it is easy to understand why the average reading level for Americans is no higher than grade 8. The ability to read is fundamental to learning; no other skill is as important or so essential. Yet, it would seem, our schools are incapable, unwilling, or negligent in teaching such an important and fundamental skill to our children. No doubt this view will raise some controversy and argument, to which I will only say, bring it on, provide reasoned argument, not diatribe or insult.

To be completely fair, the fault for the abject failure to teach our children to read does not rest solely upon the poor shoulders of those who teach in our schools. For just as teachers teach, parents parent and are therefore equally as responsible for their children's education and just as culpable when their children fail to learn. It matters little, in the end, as to who is at fault. For in the truest sense, we all are to blame for this mess we have made for ourselves. Each of us shares by some measure in the ever-deepening quagmire in which we now find ourselves sinking. We have sunk so low it is difficult to see a path that can leads us again to solid ground. But we must if we are to survive as a civilization. What is crucially important to comprehend is we have truly become a society of illiterates, a civilization lacking in the fundamental and necessary skills to think reasonably and rationally. We have lost the artistry of argument and controversy, no longer capable of expressing ourselves with clarity of thought and reasoned argument. Our Smartphones have surpassed us in smarts, relieving us of the drear onerous task of thinking for ourselves. And so, we have abrogated our responsibility to discern fact from fiction, truth from falsehood; for in all honesty, we simply no longer care to know it. Thus, campuses no longer attempt to educate, rather they protest and pontificate, and provide over-priced safe havens for indulgent, over-sensitized snow-flakes who are not inclined to think beyond their self-centeredness. Students now attend colleges and university to postpone life, not to discover it. Far too many are willing to disengage their minds, to accept as logical the infinite number of answers to the simple formula of two plus two. The fact there is one and only one true answer is of no consequence to such poor minds, for as Archbishop Sheen so sagely observed: "To some minds, of course, the startling will always appear to be the profound. It is easier to get the attention of the press when one says, as Ibsen did, that 'two and two make five,' than to be orthodox and say that two and two make four."

The lost art of controversy—here intended in its truest meaning—is, as quoted at the beginning, one without which no civilization can long survive. The Venerable Archbishop recognized the symptoms over eighty years ago, but few felt the need to listen; either that or they cared not enough to seek remedy for the affliction. It requires no stethoscope to hear the rales; now so loud we can no longer ignore its notice of civilization's impending demise. And yet, I have no answers, only questions. What is needed most is wisdom, yet of late wisdom appears in such short supply. So, shall we pray to God for wisdom, a thing we should have done long before?

The book of Job is the first of the wisdom books of the Old Testament. Here is what one writer offered which I found both useful and wise:

> So, what kind of wisdom are we supposed to get from it? We normally think of the wise person as the one with answers—but that is precisely what Job is not given. In Job, the wise person is the one who trusts God even when the answers are not clear. The wise person is the one who does not presume to know those answers and glibly apply them to the one who is suffering (like Job's friends did). The wise person is the one who questions God but accepts that not all of his questions will be answered in this life. What we get from Job, then, is not just certain bits of wisdom, but a new definition of wisdom itself. Wisdom is not just having answers but having the humility to respond properly when you don't.[241]

> *God, grant me the serenity*
> *to accept the things*
> *I cannot change,*
> *Courage to change*
> *the things I can,*
> *and Wisdom to know*
> *the difference. Amen.*

---

[241] Donald T. Williams, *Wise Without Answers*, Touchstone Magazine, Volume 30, Number 3, May/June 2017, 4.

The Power of Silence
Against the Dictatorship of Noise

Robert Cardinal Sarah, the prefect of the Congregation for Divine Worship and the Discipline of the Sacraments, is the co-author of *The Power of Silence: Against the Dictatorship of Noise*. In an interview for the National Catholic Register (April 16-29, 2017) Cardinal Sarah spoke of "the silence of Easter" which he likened to "a profound silence, an immense peace and a pure taste in the soul. It is the taste of heaven, away from all disordered excitement."

> I am struck always by the homily of Bishop Melito of Sardis in the office of Readings on Easter Saturday as the Church Universal awaits the great vigil of Easter: "Something strange is happening—there is a great silence on earth today, a great silence and stillness. The whole earth keeps silence because the King is asleep. The earth trembled and is still because God has fallen asleep in the flesh, and he has raised up all who have slept ever since the world began. God has died in the flesh, and hell trembles in fear."

> It is imperative for us to rediscover the Easter we celebrate in each of our Eucharists. We must rediscover the urgency and importance of celebrating the Eucharist in silence: the silence of Easter.

> Paschal vision does not consist in a rapture of the spirit; it is the silent discovery of God. If only the Mass could be, each morning, what it was on Golgotha and on Easter morning! Remember that the Resurrection of Christ itself on Easter morning was seen by no one and was made in silence. The sound of Christ's resurrection is not one of trumpet blasts and cymbal crashes, but, like the Introit chant of Easter morning, is a tranquil, mystical ascent from death to life.

> Easter marks the triumph of life over death, the victory of Christ's silence over the great roar of hatred and falsehood.

The Cardinal had much more to offer in his interview, but this struck a chord, something to meditate and to reflect on. We too often forget the importance of silence in the "celebration" of the Eucharist. We forget the Paschal mystery does not demand or call for a "rapture of the spirit" made so by the "joyful noise" of trumpet blasts and crashing cymbals. We forget only in silence can we truly discover God's presence.

> When you speak in a low voice, only people who are silent around you can hear you. God is a discreet lover — he is a silent and humble lover —and does not want to impose himself upon our freedom.

> In coming silently into this world, he wanted to show that his relationships with us were to be free. He didn't want to crush us like a dictator; but on the contrary, he wanted to make us free from the slavery of sin and from the tyranny of the devil. To do so, he acted humbly, the exact opposite to the pride of Satan.

There is great wisdom in his words, wisdom which we all should take into the silence of our hearts.

April 28, 2017

For Better or Worse
Forever means no matter what

As an extremely fortunate man now on the threshold of a half-century of marriage to a living saint—she must be to have put up with me for so long—I must admit to something many may find either difficult to accept or believe. There is no such thing as happy ever after. It does not exist, it never has, and never will. So, if you are wont to believe in fairy tales, please make every effort to dissuade yourself of such ill-considered thoughts. Marriage is forever and while there will be many wonderful, fantastic, incredible, beautiful, marvelous moments, there will unquestionably be moments of difficulties, doubt, pain and loss. Marriage is the sacramental union of two lives and although living itself can be the source of great joy and bliss, it has the tendency to frequently be messy and occasionally unpleasant. Yet, there is a special beauty that only manifests itself whenever a soul finds itself in the presence of a soulmate. It is a beauty that dwells below the surface, hidden deep within, until encouraged by love, it finds the desire and the courage to take wing and fly above the clouds. Beauty such as this can only bloom when nourished by forever love, which over time, is heard in whispers, memories, and echoes of love. Love is often complicated, messy, and poorly understood by those who believe they are love's masters. What is often taken to be love is seldom love at all but rather infatuation or a desire for intimacy coupled with passion. We live in an age where casual hookups and one-night stands have replaced intentional long-lasting relationships built upon authentic mutual self-giving love. The love necessary to endure forever is never easy to discover and even more difficult to describe. I have long believed such perfect love may best have been described by Saint Paul in First Corinthians 13:4-8:

> *Love is patient,*
> *love is kind.*
>
> *It is not jealous,*
> *love is not pompous,*
> *it is not inflated,*
> *it is not rude,*
> *it does not seek its own interest,*
> *it is not quick-tempered,*
> *it does not brood over injury,*
> *it does not rejoice over wrongdoing*
> *but rejoices with the truth.*
>
> *It bears all things,*
> *believes all things,*

hopes all things,
endures all things.

Love never fails.

If I have learned anything at all from forty-nine years[242] of being in love with my love it is that love must be nourished and sustained for it to endure. That, in and of itself, demands hard work and dedicated devotion. Love is never easy nor is it free or cheaply purchased. You must pay dearly for forever love. To love one another you must first like one another, respect one another, trust one another, be proud of one another. These are the minimums; you must always strive to do more. You must be of a mind that just as one cannot live without a heart or a brain, your spouse is even more essential to your well-being, to life itself. There is perfect truth in this: when you wed you become one flesh, no longer two but one. For myself, I have always been inordinately proud of my wife who I know is much smarter than I and far more capable. She is simply irreplaceable to me, as I firmly trust I am to her. It is our love that became one so many years ago and it is our love that binds us still.

When you marry, you love yourself and become one body, one spirit. Just as parts of your bodies are irreplaceable, so must you be to each other. No one should interpret what I have said as a proclamation of a perfect and saccharine relationship borne without occasional strife, discord, or hardships for that would seriously misrepresent the case. No, any marriage is destined to be apportioned its share of good times and bad times; that is simply part of life. Yet, just as you would not suggest amputating a limb should some portion of it cause you pain, neither should you discard that portion of yourself when inevitably unbridled passion wanes and youthful beauty fades. Our culture, biased and skewed by much of the popular media, has long promoted the notion that intimate relationships are physically noisy affairs, filled with perspiration and passion. Like magic, this image of intimacy is nothing but a pale illusion and a false dream. True intimacy is much deeper and far more complex.

Wanting More
It is enough to know we love

Oh how we once did soar with grace
to lofty heights above the clouds,
and we did fly too near the sun
and thus our hearts did melt
from the torrid heat of our desire
while our descent from heaven's gate
left us wanting, wanting more.

---

[242] The years continue flowing by and we are now fifty-two years on the way to forever together.

Once upon a time, so long ago,
across a crowded room we met,
and talked and talked and talked
and talked of many things, and yet,
we could not fill our souls with knowing
all that was the other, for it merely
left us wanting, wanting more.

The days of yesterday have slipped away
all but forgotten among the boxes
filled with "what might have been-s"
and "what was never meant to be-s".
But there were moments, oh such moments
when joyous gifts thrice surprised and
left us wanting, wanting more.

Do you ponder as I wonder
when the knowing of the other
was enough to simply be
in quiet presence, nothing more?
When did we soar beyond the sun
into cathedral silence, knowing nothing
left us wanting, wanting more?

It does not matter why or wherefore,
it is enough to know we love
the other more beyond the telling,
beyond the heat of passion's breath,
beyond the knowing of the other.
It is enough to love, my love,
forever wanting, wanting more.

Love whispers soft and low such
sweet music from the heart and
every note and measured beat
sings with such perfect harmony
a melody so pure the soul cries out
in sublime and joyful agony
echoes of love, wanting more.

Source and Summit
Rediscovering the presence of God

Do you feel the presence of God during the celebration of the liturgy? Do you believe you are in the presence of the divine?

> For the liturgy, "through which the work of our redemption is accomplished," most of all in the divine sacrifice of the Eucharist, is the outstanding means whereby the faithful may express in their lives, and manifest to others, the mystery of Christ and the real nature of the true Church. It is of the essence of the Church that she be both human and divine, visible and yet invisibly equipped, eager to act and yet intent on contemplation, present in this world and yet not at home in it; and she is all these things in such wise that in her the human is directed and subordinated to the divine, the visible likewise to the invisible, action to contemplation, and this present world to that city yet to come, which we seek.[243]

Robert Cardinal Sarah, prefect of the Congregation for Divine Worship and the Discipline of the Sacraments, is often of the same mind as Pope Emeritus Benedict XVI, especially when it comes to the celebration of the liturgy. Both believe the Church is facing a serious crisis and too many leaders in the Church have underestimated the danger. In the preface to the newly released Russian edition of the *Opera Omnia* (complete works) of Benedict XVI / Ratzinger, Benedict writes "it becomes ever clearer that the existence of the Church lives on the just celebration of the liturgy, and that the Church is in danger when the primacy of God does not appear anymore in the liturgy, and therefore in life. ... The deepest cause of the crisis that has subverted the Church is located in the effacing of the priority of God in the liturgy. In the conscience of the men of today, the things of God—and with this the liturgy—do not appear urgent, in fact. There is urgency for every possible thing. The things of God do not ever seem urgent. ... If God is no longer important, the criteria to establish what is important are changed. Man, by setting God aside, submits his own self to constraints that render him a slave to material forces and that are therefore opposed to his dignity."

In his introductory address to a German conference on the sacred liturgy, Cardinal Sarah noted:

> The serious crisis of faith, not only at the level of the Christian faithful but also and especially among many priests and bishops, has made us incapable of understanding the Eucharistic liturgy as a sacrifice, as identical to the act performed once and for all by Jesus Christ, making present the Sacrifice of the Cross in a non-bloody manner, throughout the Church, through different ages, places and nations. There is often a sacrilegious tendency to reduce the Holy Mass to a simple convivial meal, the celebration of a profane feast, the community's celebration of itself, or even worse, a terrible diversion from the anguish of a life that no longer has meaning or from the fear of meeting God face to face, because

---

[243] Pope Paul VI, Second Vatican Council, *Sacrosanctum Concilium, Constitution of the Sacred Liturgy*, December 4, 1963, § 2.

His glance unveils and obliges us to look truly and unflinchingly at the ugliness of our interior life. But the Holy Mass is not a diversion. It is the living sacrifice of Christ who died on the cross to free us from sin and death, for the purpose of revealing the love and the glory of God the Father. Many Catholics do not know that the final purpose of every liturgical celebration is the glory and adoration of God, the salvation and sanctification of human beings, since in the liturgy 'God is perfectly glorified and men are sanctified' (Sacrosanctum Concilium, n. 7). Most of the faithful—including priests and bishops—do not know this teaching of the Council. Just as they do not know that the true worshippers of God are not those who reform the liturgy according to their own ideas and creativity, to make it something pleasing to the world, but rather those who reform the world in depth with the Gospel so as to allow it access to a liturgy that is the reflection of the liturgy that is celebrated from all eternity in the heavenly Jerusalem. As Benedict XVI often emphasized, at the root of the liturgy is adoration, and therefore God. Hence it is necessary to recognize that the serious, profound crisis that has affected the liturgy and the Church itself since the Council is due to the fact that its CENTER is no longer God and the adoration of Him, but rather men and their alleged ability to "do" something to keep themselves busy during the Eucharistic celebrations. Even today, a significant number of Church leaders underestimate the serious crisis that the Church is going through: relativism in doctrinal, moral and disciplinary teaching, grave abuses, the desacralization and trivialization of the Sacred Liturgy, a merely social and horizontal view of the Church's mission.

[Cardinal Sarah adds, with pointed emphasis that] "the first to have abandoned her Christian roots and past is indisputably the post-conciliar Catholic Church. Some episcopal conferences even refuse to translate faithfully the original Latin text of the Roman Missal. Some claim that each local Church can translate the Roman Missal, not according to the sacred heritage of the Church, following the methods and principles indicated by Liturgiam authenticam, but according to the fantasies, ideologies and cultural expressions which, they say, can be understood and accepted by the people. But the people desire to be initiated into the sacred language of God. The Gospel and revelation themselves are "reinterpreted", "contextualized" and adapted to decadent Western culture. ...

Many refuse to face up to the Church's work of self-destruction through the deliberate demolition of her doctrinal, liturgical, moral and pastoral foundations. While more and more voices of high-ranking prelates stubbornly affirm obvious doctrinal, moral and liturgical errors that have been condemned a hundred times and work to demolish the little faith remaining in the people of God, ... [244]

Cardinal Ratzinger earlier acknowledged as much. "What the Popes and the Council Fathers were expecting was a new Catholic unity, and instead one has encountered a dissension which—to use the words of Paul VI—seems to have passed over from self-criticism to self-destruction. There had been the expectation of a new enthusiasm, and instead too often it has ended in boredom and discouragement. There had been the expectation of a step forward, and instead one found oneself facing a progressive

---

[244] Robert Cardinal Sarah, Introductory Message, Colloquium *"The Source of the Future"* ("Quelle der Zukunft") on the occasion of the 10th anniversary of the publication of the Motu proprio *Summorum Pontificum* by Pope Benedict XVI, March 29, 2017.

process of decadence that to a large measure has been unfolding under the sign of a summons to a presumed 'spirit of the Council' and by so doing has actually and increasingly discredited it."[245] One observable critique, mentioned by the Fathers of the Council, is that before men can come to the liturgy they must be called to faith and to conversion. This is of utmost importance, for as the Apostle wrote: "How then are they to call upon him in whom they have not yet believed? But how are they to believe him whom they have not heard? And how are they to hear if no one preaches? And how are men to preach unless they be sent" (Rom 10:13-15)? Here it is important to reiterate what the Council declared in *Sacrosanctum Concilium*:

> ... the liturgy is the summit toward which the activity of the Church is directed; at the same time, it is the font from which all her power flows. For the aim and object of apostolic works is that all who are made sons of God by faith and baptism should come together to praise God in the midst of his Church, to take part in the sacrifice, and to eat the Lord's supper.

> But in order that the liturgy may be able to produce its full effects, it is necessary that the faithful come to it with proper dispositions, that their minds should be attuned to their voices, and that they should cooperate with divine grace lest they receive it in vain. Pastors of souls must therefore realize that, when the liturgy is celebrated, something more is required than the mere observation of the laws governing valid and licit celebration; it is their duty also to ensure that the faithful take part fully aware of what they are doing, actively engaged in the rite, and enriched by its effects. [246]

The liturgy should bring us face to face with God in a personal relationship of intense intimacy. It should plunge us into the innermost life of the Most Holy Trinity. Pope Benedict XVI, in his letter which accompanied his *Motu proprio Summorum Pontificum* observed:

> Immediately after the Second Vatican Council it was presumed that requests for the use of the 1962 Missal would be limited to the older generation which had grown up with it, but in the meantime it has clearly been demonstrated that young persons too have discovered this liturgical form, felt its attraction and found in it a form of encounter with the Mystery of the Most Holy Eucharist, particularly suited to them.

> [As Cardinal Sarah observes]: Indeed, the Eucharist is not a sort of "dinner among friends", a convivial meal of the community, but rather a sacred Mystery, the great Mystery of our faith, the celebration of the Redemption accomplished by Our Lord Jesus Christ, the commemoration of the death of Jesus on the cross to free us from our sins. It is therefore appropriate to celebrate Holy Mass with the beauty and fervor of the saintly Curé of Ars, of Padre Pio or Saint Josemaría, and this is the *sine qua non* condition for arriving at a liturgical reconciliation "by the high road", if I may put it that way. I vehemently refuse therefore to waste our time pitting one liturgy against another, or the Missal of Saint Pius V against that of Blessed Paul VI. Rather, it is a question of entering

---

[245] Joseph Ratzinger and Vittorio Messori, *The Ratzinger Report: An exclusive interview on the state of the Church*, translated by Salvator Attanasio and Graham Harrison (San Francisco: Ignatius Press, 1985), 29-30.
[246] Sacrosanctum Concilium, Constitution of the Sacred Liturgy, § 10-11.

into the great silence of the liturgy, by allowing ourselves to be enriched by all the liturgical forms, whether they are Latin or Eastern. Indeed, without this mystical dimension of silence and without a contemplative spirit, the liturgy will remain an occasion for hateful divisions, ideological confrontations and the public humiliation of the weak by those who claim to hold some authority, instead of being the place of our unity and communion in the Lord. Thus, instead of being an occasion for confronting and hating each other, the liturgy should bring us all together to unity in the faith and to the true knowledge of the Son of God, to mature manhood, to the measure of the stature of the fullness of Christ... and, by living in the truth of love, we will grow into Christ so as to be raised up in all things to Him who is the Head (cf. Eph 4:13-15).

... The sense of the sacred that imbues and irrigates the rites of the Church is the inseparable correlative of the liturgy. Now in recent decades, many, many of the faithful have been ill-treated or profoundly troubled by celebrations marked with a superficial, devastating subjectivism, to the point where they did not recognize their *Heimat*, their common home, whereas the youngest among them had never known it! How many have tiptoed away, particularly the least significant and the poorest among them!

Cardinal Ratzinger, long before the publication of *Summorum Pontificum*, had observed the crisis in the Church and therefore the crisis of the weakening of the faith has come in large measure from the way in which we have treated the liturgy. Cardinal Sarah suggests three possible paths for the renewal (not reform) of the liturgy: Silence, Adoration, and Formation. "In silence, a human being gains his nobility and his grandeur only if he is on his knees in order to hear and adore God. For my part, I know that all the great moments of my day are found in the incomparable hours that I spend on my knees in darkness before the Most Blessed Sacrament.... and finally, immersion in the liturgy, in the deep mystery of God."

May 05, 2017

From a Mirror
What is wrong with us

Many a Sunday afternoon, while comfortably seated but a few feet from the water's edge on the north shore of Lake Tahoe, my eyes have looked south across the crystal clear waters at the surrounding mountains and considered just how close to heaven we were at that moment. It was always in those moments when I felt the intimate presence of God; it was as if every breath of air was saturated, filled with the sweet essence of his being. How small and insignificant we are in comparison; the magnificence of the mountains and the lake are testimony to his power and creative genius. And yet, God created it all for us out of love.

We are his beloved children, he made us in his image and likeness, he gave us the universe for our domain, all we could ever possibly want or enjoy. Like spoiled rich kids, we have blown it, wasted it, squandered every bit of our inheritance. Not once, mind you, but repeatedly; it is as if we are incapable of any true feelings of gratitude for all we have been given. There are great gobs of ugliness and depravity in this world, far too much, and yet we too quickly throw up our hands and give up; after all what can any one person do to resolve any of this mess? Well, here is a thought: Nothing is going to change until you and I figure out what is wrong with the person we see staring back at us in the mirror.

Looking at the night sky, there is an awesome beauty in the sight of countless stars kept silently in place by a God who knows what he is doing. And yet, I cannot help but imagine him looking down on us, his beloved creation who has steadfastly cheated on him—adulterers we are—and yet he remains hopelessly in love, wanting nothing more than for us to love him back.

Falling Silent
Let your conscience be your guide

So much to read, so little time. Here I must confess a thing. There are moments when discordant, disjunctive thoughts threaten to overwhelm; hope of assimilation tossed by ill-winds which blow no good. There is connective tissue which, like dark matter, defies direct observation, yet patient diligence will discern the truth. So, patience, dear reader. Forgive the wandering contrivances of my mind for there is no straight and narrow road upon which to travel.

Headline: In Uganda, child sacrifices frighteningly too common: Ritual killings persist despite efforts to curtail (Tonny Onyulo Special for USA Today, Monday, May 1, 2017).

It's been a year since Cynthia Misanya found the dismembered body of her 10-year-old daughter, Jane, in a pit under an outhouse." A wealthy business man and neighbor was subsequently arrested and admitted using the girl as a human sacrifice in a witchcraft ritual to bring him good fortune. When Jane was found, almost every body part was missing. Tragically, in Uganda and elsewhere, this horrific practice is all too common. As many as 29 human sacrifices, primarily of children, are reported each year.

Headline: Mentally Ill Woman Euthanized in Canada (Wesley J. Smith, National Review, April 25, 2017). Smith wrote how he had expected Canada to one day allow euthanasia as a "treatment" for serious mental illness only to discover the future had met the past: a 58-year-old mentally ill woman had been euthanized because she was suffering. He concludes: She was suffering! … That's the logic. So let's quit pretending that assisted suicide will ever remain solely for the terminally ill—once society accepts the premise that killing can be a proper remedy to suffering ... Canada is following the path trod by Belgium and the Netherlands. (Mark my words, euthanasia conjoined with organ harvesting within a few years.)

Headline: Oregon Bill Legalizes Starving Dementia Patients (Church Militant, Portland, Ore, Bradley Eli, M.Div., Ma.Th. April 28, 2017).

A bill in Oregon's senate is crafted to allow mentally ill patients to be starved to death. Current Oregon law mandates that healthcare providers give food and water to all conscious patients, who can receive it naturally such as by spoon feeding. SB 494, which is currently in the Senate Judiciary Committee, would remove this mandate for patients suffering from dementia and other mental illnesses.

The bill would allow for the starvation and dehydration of such patients at the request of a legal guardian or by third parties if guardianship was lacking.

Headline: What Palm Sunday Means to Egypt's Copts (Samuel Tadros, The Atlantic, April 12, 2017).

At Saint George Church, a Coptic church in Tanta, Egypt, the deacons were finishing the final vowels in Evlogimenos (the Hosanna to the King of Israel), when the bomb exploded, leaving 28 worshipers dead and many others wounded. Shortly afterwards, a suicide bomber, failing to enter Saint Mark's Cathedral in Alexandria, where the Coptic Pope was leading the liturgy, detonated his bomb outside the church, leaving 17 people dead.

There is more, of course, but there is only so much one might ingest without roiling the stomach. In his encyclical *Evangelium vitae*, Pope Saint John Paul II wrote: "To claim the right to abortion, infanticide and euthanasia, and to recognize that right in law, means to attribute to human freedom a perverse and evil significance: that of an absolute power over others and against others" (§ 20). Alexis de Tocqueville feared a democracy without religious constraints—what he called its power to kill souls and prepare citizens for servitude[247]—which is arguably precisely where we find ourselves today. He "saw the strength of American society, the force that kept the tyrannical logic of democracy in creative check, was the prevalence and intensity of religious belief. ... Religion moderates democracy because it appeals to an authority higher than democracy itself."[248] Archbishop Charles Chaput writes that modern technology has driven our democratic society in unforeseen directions. The state has taken on elements of a market model that requires the growth of government as a service provider. "The short-term needs and wants of voters begin to displace long-term purpose and planning. In effect, democracy becomes an expression of consumer preference shaped and led by a technology-competent managerial class. It has plenty of room for personal

---

[247] Alexis de Tocqueville, *Democracy in America*, translated and edited by Harvey C. Mansfield and Delba Winthrop (Chicago: University of Chicago Press, 2000), 418.

[248] Alexis de Tocqueville, *Democracy in America*

'values.' But it has very little space for appeals to higher moral authority or shared meaning."[249] In the Old Testament, following the Exodus, Joshua lead the people of Israel into the Promised Land "and all that generation also were gathered to their fathers; and there arose another generation after them, who did not know the Lord or the work which he had done for Israel" (Judges 2:10). Each generation leaves a legacy for those that follow.

> But the biggest failure of so many people of my (baby boomer) generation, including parents, teachers, and leaders in the church, has been our failure to pass along our faith in a compelling way to the generation now taking our place.

> The reason the Christian faith doesn't matter to so many of our young people is that—too often—it didn't really matter to us. Not enough to shape our lives. Not enough for us to suffer for it. As Catholic Christians, we may have come to a point today where we feel like foreigners in our own country—"strangers in a strange land," in the beautiful English of the King James Bible (Ex 2:22). But the deeper problem in America isn't that we believers are "foreigners." It's that our children and grandchildren aren't.[250]

On a deeper level, what we are now realizing is the rapid erosion—and in many cases—a complete loss of conscience, of a rational morality. As Cardinal Ratzinger rightly pointed out in an address in 1991: "When there is no God, there is not morality and, in fact no mankind either." His words are reminiscent of the Fathers of the Second Vatican Council: "For without the Creator, the creature would disappear. … When God is forgotten … the creature itself becomes unintelligible" (Gaudium et Spes, § 36). Ratzinger argues our understanding of conscience has become distorted, tortured and bent by the hands of those who have no desire to know truth.

> Conscience appears here not as a window through which one can see outward to that common truth that founds and sustains us all, and so makes possible through the common recognition of truth the community of wants and responsibilities. Conscience here does not mean man's openness to the ground of his being, the power of perception for what is highest and most essential. Rather, it appears as subjectivity's protective shell, into which man can escape and there hide from reality.

> … conscience does not open the way to the redemptive road to truth—which either does not exist or, if it does, is too demanding. It is the faculty that dispenses with truth. It thereby becomes the justification for subjectivity, which would not like to have itself called into question. Similarly, it becomes the justification for social conformity. As mediating value between the different subjectivities, social conformity is intended to make living together possible. The obligation to seek the truth terminates, as do any doubts about the general inclination of society and what it has become accustomed to. Being convinced of oneself, as well as conforming to others, is sufficient. Man is reduced to his

---

[249] Charles J. Chaput, Archbishop, *Strangers in a Strange Land: Living the Catholic Faith in a Post-Christian World*, (Henry Holt and Co., February 21, 2017), 5-6.

[250] Charles J. Chaput, Archbishop, *Strangers in a Strange Land*, 6.

superficial conviction, and the less depth he has, the better for him. ... Firm, subjective conviction and the lack of doubts and scruples that follow from it do not justify man.[251]

According to psychologist Albert Gorres the feeling of guilt, the capacity to recognize guilt, belongs essentially to the spiritual make-up of man. This feeling of guilt disturbs the false calm of conscience. Those who are incapable of perceiving guilt are, in his words, spiritually ill, "a living corpse, a dramatic character's mask. ... Monsters, among other brutes, are the ones without guilt feelings. Perhaps Hitler did not have any, or Himmler, or Stalin. Maybe Mafia bosses do not have any guilt feelings either, or maybe their remains are just well hidden in the cellar. Even aborted guilt feelings.... All men need guilt feelings."[252] Cardinal Ratzinger adds, "No longer seeing one's guilt, the falling silent of conscience in so many areas is an even more dangerous sickness of the soul than the guilt that one still recognizes as such. He who no longer notices that killing is a sin has fallen farther than the one who still recognizes the shamefulness of his actions, because the former is further removed from the truth and conversion."[253] We have been numbing our consciences, desensitizing ourselves of guilt by subjective tranquilization. Perhaps the bitterest example of this enormous devastation of the human spirit comes from those liberated from Marxist systems in Eastern Europe. They speak of a blunting of the moral sense, of the loss of capacity for mercy, and how human feelings were forsaken. An entire generation was lost for the good, lost for humane deeds.

> Error, the 'erring' conscience, is only at first convenient. But then the silencing of conscience leads to moral danger, if one does not work against it. ... the identification of conscience with superficial consciousness, the reduction of man to his subjectivity, does not liberate but enslaves. It makes us totally dependent on the prevailing opinions and debases these with every passing day. Whoever equates conscience with superficial conviction identifies conscience with a pseudo-rational certainty, a certainty that in fact has been woven from self-righteousness, conformity, and lethargy. Conscience is degraded to a mechanism for rationalization, while it should represent the transparency of the subject for the divine, and thus constitute the dignity and greatness of man.[254]

How ought we understand "conscience"? This is not a mere academic question. By now, it should be coming clear: we redefined what it means to be moral. Cardinal Ratzinger—borrowing a position first coined by Robert Spaemann—contends: "Conscience is an organ, not an oracle."

> It is an organ because it is something that for us is a given, which belongs to our essence, and not something that has been made outside of us. But because it is an organ, it requires growth, training and practice. I find the comparison that Spaemann makes with speech is very fitting in this case. Why do we speak? We speak because we have learned to speak

---

[251] Joseph Cardinal Ratzinger, *On Conscience*, (San Francisco: Ignatius Press, 2007), 16.

[252] Alfred Gorres, " *Schuld und Schuldgefahle*," in Internationale katholische Zeitschrift "*Communio*" 13 (1984): 434, as cited in Ratzinger, *On Conscience*, 18.

[253] Joseph Cardinal Ratzinger, *On Conscience*, 18-19.

[254] Joseph Cardinal Ratzinger, *On Conscience*, 21-22.

from our parents. We speak the language that they taught us, although we realize there are other languages, which we cannot speak or understand. The person who has never learned to speak is mute. And yet language is not an external conditioning that we have internalized, but rather something that is properly internal to us. It is formed from outside, but this formation responds to the given of our own nature: that we can express ourselves in language.

Man is as such a speaking essence, but he becomes so only insofar as he learns speech from others. In this way we encounter the fundamental notion of what it means to be a man: Man is a being who needs the help of others to become what he is in himself. We see this...once again in conscience.

Man is in himself a being who has an organ of internal knowledge about good and evil. But for it to become what it is, it needs the help of others. Conscience requires formation and education. It can be stunted, it can be stamped out, it can be falsified so that it can only speak in a stunted or distorted way. The silence of conscience can become a deadly sickness for an entire civilization.[255]

When man separates himself from God, no longer acknowledging that his existence depends on the love and mercy of a creator, he abandons all that is precisely moral in the strictest sense. This is necessarily so, for when man recognizes nothing but what he has himself made, any sense of morality becomes subject to personal whim.

In the last analysis, the language of being, the language of nature, is identical with the language of conscience. But in order to hear that language, it is necessary, as with all language, to practice it. The organ for this, however, has become deadened in our technical world.[256]

The irony of the present moment is that the same tools we use to pick apart and understand the natural world, we now use against ourselves. We're the specimens of our own tinkering, the objects of our social and physical sciences. In the process, we've lost two things. We've lost our ability to see anything sacred or unique in what it means to be human. And we've lost our capacity to believe in anything that we can't measure with our tools. As a result we're haunted by the worry that none of our actions really has any larger purpose.

The post-Christian developed world runs not on beliefs but on pragmatism and desire. In effect—for too many people—the appetite for comfort and security has replaced conviction. In the United States, our political institutions haven't changed. Nor have the words we use to talk about rights, laws, and ideals. But they no longer have the same content. We're a culture of self-absorbed consumers who use noise and distractions to manage our lack of shared meaning. What that produces in us is a drugged heart—a heart neither restless for God nor able to love and empathize with others.[257]

There is, of course, nothing new under the sun, what is now has been before. It is but sad irony to realize man's divine obsession, his desire to be as gods, can only be

[255] Joseph Cardinal Ratzinger, *On Conscience*, 61-62.
[256] Joseph Cardinal Ratzinger, *On Conscience*, 67.
[257] Chaput, Strangers in a Strange Land, 11.

attained through practiced self-annihilation. In *City of God*, Augustine describes the Romans of the Late Empire. "This is their concern: that every man be able to increase his wealth so as to supply his daily prodigalities, so that the powerful may subject the weak for their own purposes. Let the poor court the rich for a living so that under their protection they may enjoy a sluggish tranquility; and let the rich abuse the poor as their dependents, to minister to their pride. Let the people applaud not those who protect their interests, but those who provide them with pleasure. Let no severe duty be commanded, let no impurity be forbidden … In his own affairs let everyone with impunity do what he will."[258] Two millennia and all too little has changed. How chilling it is to consider those public servants who so gratuitously help poor people kill their own children by providing "legal" low or no cost abortions on demand. Return and reread the headlines: consider how willing and eager those in power are to ease suffering by their tender mercies and unselfish altruism in formulating a "final solution" to the unbearable agonies of living. How commendable and compassionate. We are guilty yet we own no guilt. We share our humanity yet despise all but the self. We love ourselves and hate our neighbor. We save the trees and kill our children. We believe in fairy tales yet deny the existence of God. Once there was a comic character, a possum named Pogo who did opine, "We have met the enemy and he is us." Each sordid tale an empty lie, void of truth, no guilt or shame to wound the soul. We care not for neighbor. We care not for God. We care but for the god which we have made. It is lonely being god, when god is all alone.

May 12, 2017

Loved into Being
Not of our own making

All that exists was brought into being by pure uncaused love. Our impoverished minds have neither the power nor the capacity to comprehend such love—anymore a painting can appreciate the artist, or a song might acknowledge the composer. Such incomprehensible, undeserved beauty—an unearned gift of love—this magnificent expression of timeless, unbounded love denies the intellect even as it touches and lifts the spirit. All God has created is inherently good; it exists because it pleases Him to bring such pleasure to those whom He has created. It is for us—beneficiaries of His largesse—to acknowledge the goodness of His gifts and to show our gratitude through faithful stewardship and unending worship.

---

[258] Saint Augustine of Hippo, *City of God*, Book II, Chapter 20.

Modern man finds this unacceptable, an insult to our vanity. Such beauty proves of realities and truths beyond man's own command. It proves the insubstantialities of the human mind, the insignificance of man against the infinitude of God. It reminds of dependence where independence is preferred; the power to control: a narcotic, a faithless drug to sooth and salve man's fragile ego. What bitter irony when power craved by so many accumulates to the few; the powerless moved not by greed or power but by necessity and fear. The power of man is nothing to that of God, and yet we choose to bow not to His power but to our own.

Man has not the power of creation; such power is beyond our poor genius. It is, to borrow a common euphemism, simply above our pay grade. And yet, we are wont to deny such powerlessness. For to acknowledge the smallness of our nature would be to lay assault upon our hubristic egos, requiring we grant unconditional dependence to a higher power.

May 26, 2017

A Right Order to Love
God at the center

There is a right order to love. Likewise, there is a wrong order which is rather a sordid, all-consuming disorder of that which we call love. The more I come to having God at the center of my being, of my life, the more I am able to love others. It feels a bit odd how that works. Jesus said the greatest commandment was to love God with all your heart, and with all your mind, and with all your soul. I cannot help but wonder how many of us—and I am speaking mainly of myself here—hear those words and say we love God, but … not with anything close to all our hearts, minds, and souls. Rather, I believe we too often love God absentmindedly, much as an afterthought or only when we happen to need something from him. What I find most interesting is the more I place God at the center, the less I revere myself. That is as it should be but so seldom is it perceived as so.

Too often, the order of love which Jesus taught—that is: God, neighbor as self — is reversed, ordered to self, neighbor, and only then toward God. What strikes me is when we love ourselves more than neighbor or God, we can never truly love at all, for true love demands an unselfish giving of oneself, while self-love is selfish, engendering only the desire to be loved, not to love. What I have come to realize is when God is the center of our being—when the order of our love is as it should be, that is, God, neighbor, self — then in loving God, in giving all of one's self to him, his love is reflected through us toward our neighbors and in turn reflected back upon one's self. When we love God above all else, we inoculate ourselves against "the slings and arrows of outrageous fortune" thrown our way; it becomes easy to turn the other cheek and through his mercy, to forgive.

Mirror, Mirror ...
Made in our image only better

What is to become of man? Only God knows the answer although, to be sure, there are those who, given sufficient license, would presume to know as much. Increasingly, shrill voices carried aloft on antinomian winds, have effectively silenced dissenting voices. The voices of the few, or the one, now carry the day; the many have been struck dumb by the riotous, irrational din of those who would be gods; for there are no other gods but them. The worrisome question which, like some poor stuttering fool, cannot escape the tongue with any coherent speech, dies without a hearing; it matters not, for no one is listening. We have become reflections, images of our own making. Like Narcissus we have fallen in love with our own reflection. We stare into the mirror and ask, "Mirror, mirror on the wall, who's the fairest of them all," and never once dispute the answer.

Archbishop Charles J. Chaput recently wrote "religion only works its influence on democracy if people really believe what it teaches. Nobody believes in God just because it's socially useful. To put it in Catholic terms, Christianity is worthless as a leaven in society unless people actually believe in Jesus Christ, follow the Gospel, love the Church, and act like real disciples. If they don't, then religion is just another form of self-medication. And unfortunately, that's how many of us live out our Baptism."[259] Further on, he reflects on Tocqueville's fear concerning democracy without religious constraints—what Tocqueville called its power to kill souls and prepare citizens for servitude—and suggests that "is arguably where we find ourselves today."

> The political impact of new technologies has been massive. They shape the nature of our reasoning and our discourse. They've moved us away from a public square tempered by logic, debate, and reflection based on the printed word, to a visual and sensory one, emotionally charged and spontaneous.

> The credibility of a liberal democracy depends on its power to give people security and freedom — with "freedom" measured largely by the number of choices within each person's private control. The goal of modern technology is to expand those choices by subduing the natural world; to put nature at the service of society in general, and individual consumers in particular. As a result, modern democracy isn't just 'open' to modern technology; it now depends on it. The two can't be separated.

---

[259] Charles J. Chaput, Archbishop of Philadelphia, *Strangers in a Strange Land: Living the Catholic Faith in a Post-Christian World*, (Henry Holt and Co., February 21, 2017), 5.

As the progress of democracy and technology go hand in hand, the political influence of polling, focus groups, behavioral experts, and market research grows. The state gradually takes on elements of a market model that requires the growth of government as a service provider. The short-term needs and wants of voters begin to displace long-term purpose and planning. In effect, democracy becomes an expression of consumer preference shaped and led by a technology-competent managerial class. It has plenty of room for personal 'values.' But it has very little space for appeals to higher moral authority or shared meaning. ...

Private beliefs make no public demands; and if they do, those demands can easily be ignored or pushed to the margins.[260]

Here then, Archbishop Chaput states what should be obvious. "The irony of the present moment is that the same tools we use to pick apart and understand the natural world, we now use against ourselves. We're the specimens of our own tinkering, the objects of our social and physical sciences. In the process, we've lost two things. We've lost our ability to see anything sacred or unique in what it means to be human. And we've lost our capacity to believe in anything that we can't measure with our tools.[261] Social and cultural norms have been turned on their heads. No longer is man a creature of God, made in his own image and likeness. No longer is man bound by the stultifying limitations of the past or the strictures of a God-given natural moral code. No. Man is now of his own making and will bow to only himself. Of course, what has just been said most assuredly will offend by its presumption of gender. Perhaps "it" would somehow soften the devastating assault to the heart and ameliorate the naked effrontery such harsh, uncaring verbiage impinges upon those with such tender sensibilities. The slippery slope upon which we are sliding denies escape or turning back; we are now passive, compliant residents in an asylum under management by those rightly adjudicated certifiably mad. Recent reports do indict with Orwellian precession the narcissistic affairs of the heart. Tradition is under assault, besieged by a secular, narcissistic culture whose mindless, unreasoned goal is the repudiation of objective truth. While the assaults have come from many fronts, two forces dominate the societal and cultural landscapes: the assault on traditional family values and the assault on what it means to be human. "In the Christian tradition, marriage has historically been understood as a lifelong, conjugal covenant between a man and a woman, a union of love that involves the giving of oneself to God and to others. Today the institution of marriage, which has flourished not only among Christians but across many religious traditions of the world, is being challenged from many angles and by many practices. Until quite recently, these were all regarded as inimical to human flourishing in society."[262] In June 2015, the U.S. Supreme Court, in Obergefell v. Hodges, struck down the nation's understanding of marriage and in doing so effectually changed the meaning

---

[260] Charles J. Chaput, *Strangers in a Strange Land*, 5.

[261] Charles J. Chaput, *Strangers in a Strange Land*, 6.

[262] Timothy George, *Same-Self Marriage*, First Things, November 17, 2014.

of family, eradicating the need for the natural relationships—husband and wife, mother and father—at the core of the institution of marriage and family.

> With Obergefell, marriage and family no longer precede and limit the state as humanity's basic social units grounded in nature. Instead, **they now mean what the state says they mean.** (*emphasis added*) And that suggests deeper problems, because in redefining marriage and the family, the state implicitly claims the authority to define what is and isn't properly human. Buried in Obergefell is the premise that who we are, how we mate, and with whom we mate are purely matters of personal choice and social contract. Biology is raw material. Gender is fluid. Both are free of any larger truth that might limit our actions. And the consequences of that premise will impact every aspect of our shared political, economic, and social life. Why so? Benedict XVI explained it simply and well: '[The] question of the family is not just about a particular social construct, but about man himself—about what he is and what it takes to be authentically human … When such commitment is repudiated, the key figures of human existence likewise vanish: father, mother, child—essential elements of the experience of being human are lost.'

> People who hold a classic understanding of sexuality, marriage, and family have gone in just twenty years from pillars of mainstream conviction to the media equivalent of racists and bigots.[263]

Less than two years after Obergefell, the steep slippery slope has become vertiginous. Nothing is taboo, nothing is illicit, anything is permissible; such practices as same-sex marriages, polygamy, incest, polyamorous relationships are "normal"; moral objections are hate crimes.

In Greek mythology, Narcissus was a handsome young man with whom all the beautiful young women fell in love. But he spurned their affection in favor of his own attractive self. While walking through the forest, he knelt to drink at a clear pool of water and was so enthralled by his own beauty he instantly fell in love with himself. He drowned grasping for his own reflection. Like Narcissus, we have become enthralled by our own image, by our self-declared godhood. We have become so enamored with the self, some have turned to Sologamy, the marriage of one to one's own self. Take Nadine Schweigert, a thirty-six-year-old-woman from Fargo, North Dakota. In front of some forty of her closest friends, she said to herself, "I, Nadine, promise to enjoy inhabiting my own life and to relish a lifelong love affair with my beautiful self."

> In some ways same-self marriage is the logical outgrowth of what cultural critic Christopher Lasch described in his 1979 bestseller "*The Culture of Narcissism*". Lasch, building on Sigmund Freud's classic essay "*On Narcissism*" of 1916, applied the term to the sense of grandiosity and excessive self-love that seem to mark not only psychologically disordered individuals but post-sixties American society as a whole.

> Lasch died twenty years ago at age sixty-one. He was not a religious believer, but he understood well how the values, beliefs, and practices of the larger culture would issue

---

[263] Charles J. Chaput, *Strangers in a Strange Land*, 2.

in "the narcissism epidemic," ... Narcissism is more than modern rugged individualism gone to seed. At its heart is a spiritual disorder, what Martin Luther (borrowing a phrase from Augustine) described as *incurvatus in se*, "twisted back into one's self."[264]

In Lasch's own words, he clearly foresaw, back in the seventies, what the future portended. "The best hope of emotional maturity, then, appears to lie in a recognition of our need for and dependence on people who nevertheless remain separate from ourselves and refuse to submit to our whims. It lies in a recognition of others not as projections of our own desires but as independent beings with desires of their own. More broadly, it lies in acceptance of our limits. The world does not exist merely to satisfy our own desires; it is a world in which we can find pleasure and meaning, once we understand that others too have a right to those goods. Psychoanalysis confirms the ancient religious insight that the only way to achieve happiness is to accept limitations in the spirit of gratitude and contrition instead of attempting to annul those limitations or bitterly resenting them."[265] Obviously, we are confused. We neither know who we are, nor what we are, nor why we are; on occasion we have no clear idea when or where we are. We have become mentally constipated, incapable of moving a single thought beyond self-induced delusions and fantasies, incapable of perceiving reality. And yet, we stand high upon the stage proclaiming, "Look at me, I am god, king of the universe!" What hubristic nonsense. We have come to the altar of scientific advancement and we bow in obeisance to man's omnipotence.

Aldous Huxley's vision of the future of mankind appears terrifyingly prescient, albeit half-a-millennia earlier than he foresaw in 1932. Huxley's *Brave New World* anticipated developments in reproductive technology, sleep-learning, psychological manipulation, and classical conditioning. Huxley's dystopian science fiction novel, published during the heyday of eugenics, envisioned a world where everyone is a clone, the product of a process which takes a single fertilized egg, arrests the development, and then forces it to bud or split, creating up to ninety-six viable embryos, which in turn create ninety-six identical twins. Human fetuses are conditioned through a carefully designed regime of chemical, thermal and other environmental stimuli in order to optimize the fetus' later role in society. A more recent example is the movie The Matrix, where human bodies are kept in an amniotic fluid as living batteries to power the machines which now control the world. So much for early twentieth-century science fiction and the far distant future. The past and the future have coalesced into the present, at least in part, but what is real today is both alarming and horrifying.

NextNature.net (NNN), an organization currently investigating the relation between technology and biological reproduction, has published a timeline which will ostensibly "function as an incubator for medical, cultural and technological

---

[264] Timothy George, *Same-Self Marriage*.

[265] Christopher Lasch, *The Culture of Narcissism: American Life in an Age of Diminishing Expectations*, (W. W. Norton & Company; Revised edition, May 17, 1971).

developments in relation to the artificial womb."[266] The stated goal of the NNN project "is to develop thought-provoking scenarios that facilitate a ***much-needed*** (??? *emphasis added*) discussion about the way technology radically alters our attitude towards reproduction, gender, relationships and love in the 21st century." Henrick-Jan Grievink, writing for NNN, placidly and with disturbing equanimity observes, "Humanity is facing the disconnection between biological reproduction and the body, facilitated by the emerging technology of the Artificial Womb. Envisioned in bleak science fiction scenarios many times in the past, this technology is about to become a reality in our present. But how will it affect our culture—and how should that new culture be designed? If birds lay eggs, why shouldn't humans do that, too?"[267] To his credit, Grievink recognizes there is a potential dark side to ectogenesis.

> Ectogenesis holds the potential to disconnect biological reproduction from the female body. … it is difficult not to see a bleak side to this: another precious (for some even holy) domain of life under the control of technology, instantly marketable and leading to further commodification of bodies and ultimately, human breeding factories in totalitarian regimes.

> However, there might also be a liberating, emancipatory side to this technology; the artificial womb can easily be imagined for medical reasons, to help reducing infant mortality rates. But simultaneously it might become the ultimate feminist dream that once and for all creates a level playing field for men and women, as well as gay, queer or transgender couples. We can only wait for the day three people in a polyamorous relationship will have their own baby — AND take equal responsibility for her/his upbringing.

As horrifying as this might be for those who still hold onto at least a shred of their humanity, who still believe life is sacred and holy, that we are creations of God and not the manufacture of man, there is still more vomitus to digest. While Grievink pines for the day a child might be conceived in a polyamorous relationship, his pining is a dollar late and three pennies short. In a case of "been there, done that," three men, a polyamorous "throuple" living in Nova Scotia, Canada, two years ago, with the help of one of the men's sister who was used as a surrogate, conceived three children together. Unfortunately, there have been others thus conceived.

But wait! There's more! That artificial womb...is no longer the mere subject of futuristic science fiction. As far back as four years ago, scientists at Juntendo University in Tokyo developed a practice called EUFI, *extrauterine fetal incubation*. In EUFI, goat fetuses had catheters threaded through the large vessels in the umbilical cord which then supplied the fetuses with oxygenated blood, while suspended in incubators that contained artificial amniotic fluid heated to body temperature. Within the past year, an artificial womb was used to bring a premature lamb, born at the equivalent of 23

---

[266] NextNature.net, *Artificial Womb: the Timeline*, https:nextnature.net/people/67788, January 5, 2017.
[267] NextNature.net, *Ectogenesis, Artificial Womb, Human Egg*, https:nextnature.net/people/hendrik-jan-grievink/, January 5, 2017.

weeks in a human gestational period, to term. "The artificial womb, or 'biobag' in this case, imitates the environment of a womb: dark, sterile and with controlled tempera-ture. The biobag is filled with synthetic amniotic fluids in which the lamb fetus submerges. The lamb's umbilical cord is connected to sources of oxygen and nutrition. With the support of circulation, the lamb develops till the premature organs are ready to take the outside world. This method has been proven to be extremely effective so far. The lamb exhibited normal development in any aspect, compared to a 'normal' lamb."[268] What's next? Humans of course. Although Alan Flake, the doctor behind the artificial womb experiment has adamantly argued: "I don't want this to be visualized as humans hanging on the walls in bags. This is not how this device will work or look," it is impossible to look at the artificial womb, the plastic "biobag" with tubes going in and out and not have precisely just such a vision.

What is lacking in all this is any thought of what it means to be human, a being made in the image and likeness of God. We have lost the ability to comprehend the inestimable value of human life. "As a result," notes Archbishop Chaput, "we're haunted by the worry that none of our actions really has any larger purpose.

> The post-Christian developed world runs not on beliefs but on pragmatism and desire. In effect—for too many people—the appetite for comfort and security has replaced con-viction. In the United States, our political institutions haven't changed. Nor have the words we use to talk about rights, laws, and ideals. But they no longer have the same content. We're a culture of self-absorbed consumers who use noise and distractions to manage our lack of shared meaning. What that produces in us is a drugged heart—a heart neither restless for God nor able to love and empathize with others.

> In his monumental work, *City of God*, "Augustine argues that when Adam sinned against God, creation fell with him. Nature, including human nature, is now crippled by evil. Sin infects all human endeavors. Man, by his own efforts can't be perfected. For Augustine, Rome is a new Babylon and the symbol of earthly power for every generation. But Rome is merely the material face of another, deeper reality. In the mind of Augustine, every inhabitant of our world actually belongs to one of two invisible cities that will commingle until the end of time—the City of Man, consisting of the distracted, the confused, the indifferent, and the wicked, and the City of God made up of God's pilgrim people on earth. In Augustine's words, "The two cities have been formed by two loves; the earthly city by the love of self, even to the contempt of God; the heavenly by the love of God, even to the contempt of self. The former, in a word, glories in itself, the latter in the Lord. For the one seeks glory from men; but the greatest glory of the other is God, the witness of conscience."[269]

---

[268] NextNature.net, *2017—Artificial Womb Incubates Fetal Lamb*, https:nextnature.net/people/elle-zhan-wei/, January 5, 2017.
[269] Charles J. Chaput, *Strangers in a Strange Land*, 12-13.

Chaput then asks whether an African bishop now dead for nearly sixteen hundred years has anything useful to offer to American Christians who live is a very different world and suggests Augustine might well answer this way:

> First, he would say that we don't in fact live in such a different world. Many of the details of daily life have changed — our tools, memories, and expectations; our frames of thought and our command of nature. But the human condition is the same. We're born; we grow; we die. We ask what our lives mean. We wonder whether any larger purpose guides the world, and why the people we love age and weaken and then pass on. Beauty still pierces our hearts. Hurting the poor and the weak still shames us. Augustine's two cities are still with us. And in their essentials, they're still very much the same.

> Second, Augustine would remind us that as long as the City of God and the City of Man are commingled, 'we [believers] also enjoy the peace of Babylon.' In other words, the temporal peace and security provide by the state allow us to sojourn, imperfectly but more or less unmolested, toward heaven. Therefore Christians have a duty to pray for earthly rulers. And when possible, we should help to make the structures of this world as good as they can be.

> Which raises the issue of politics. Augustine's attitude toward politics was a mixture of deep skepticism and a sense of moral obligation. For Augustine, sin infects even the best human motives. No political part is pure. No political order, no matter how seemingly good, can ever constitute a just society.... Public office can be an honorable Christian vocation. But any Christian involvement in politics needs to be ruled by modest expectations and a spirit of humility. Success will always be limited. No legal system will ever be fully just.

> Third and finally: If the key sin of the nineteenth and early twentieth centuries was an overweening pride in human progress, Augustine might say that the key sins of the twenty-first century — at least, in much of the developed world — are cynicism and despair. Not the brand of despair we see in the panic or severe depression that drives some persons to suicide. Rather, Augustine would mean the kind of despair that's really a subtle inversion of pride. He'd mean the icy, embittered vanity that defies reality and truth, despite its own failures, and that comes from the mouth of Satan in Milton's Paradise Lost: 'The mind is its own place, and in itself can make a heaven of hell, a hell of heaven.' As Satan puts it, better to rule in hell than serve in heaven.[270]

Despite evidence to the contrary — evidence so obvious even the least-informed would be hard pressed to deny — "stubborn refusal to see anything beyond the horizon of this earthly life fills the air the developed world now breathes." We are witness to the decline in the dignity of the human person and perhaps ultimately, as C. S. Lewis suggested, in "the abolition of man." What Grievink observed, "of life under the control of technology, instantly marketable and leading to further commodification of bodies and ultimately, human breeding factories," exists, in varying forms, today, and has been well documented and attested for nearly twenty years.

---

[270] Charles J. Chaput, *Strangers in a Strange Land*, 13-15.

Back in 2000, Chris Wallace, then with ABC, revealed on 20/20 a "hidden camera investigation has found a thriving industry, in which aborted fetuses women donate to help medical research are being marketed for hundreds — even thousands of dollars." According to Matthew Balan, a news analyst at Media Research Center, in a report originally written for the Media Research Center, Planned Parenthood has been selling body parts from aborted babies for at least fifteen years (Balan reported this two years ago.) He wrote, in August 2015: "The main target of the ABC investigation, Dr. Miles Jones, 'over lobster bisque and roast duck...explained the business of selling human fetuses'—echoing the first Center for Medical Progress video, where Planned Parenthood's senior director of medical service, Dr. Deborah Nucatola, ate a salad and sipped on wine while discussing the sale of fetal body parts." He reminds us "back in 2000, National Right to Life reported that Planned Parenthood actually 'supported the harvesting of baby parts for research' and had at least one clinic that helped supply aborted babies to firms featured in Wallace's 20/20 report."[271]

The devaluation of the human person, no matter the age or physical condition, is *prima facie* evidence of a society, a nation, and a world gone mad. The global trafficking in human life for purposes of forced labor alone now generates an estimated $150 billion in profits annually. This estimate does not include the profits generated by the exploitation of the 4.5 million victims of human sex trafficking.

While, at least for now, human breeding factories remain in the domain of fiction, the reality is the human body is now viewed as raw material, a marketable commodity, which, to paraphrase a well-known commercial for Doritos-brand chips: "Take all you want, we can always make more." Americans in particular have been a consumer society for a long time. Our most important social and economic activities are centered on acquiring and consuming things. News of the latest widget, the smartest gadget, the fastest, sexiest, most glamorous, bestous, mostus, biggest, latest, greatest: they enthrall and entice us. We live to buy and buy again and again. We will absolutely die without the latest thing. What is new is instantly old. What was the best—blink and it becomes the worst. What is in vogue one minute is garbage the next. So, it should come as no surprise much the same holds true for the human person. The current demand for insurance to cover the "reproductive health" of women is a prime example of our disposable consumer society. Of course, "reproductive health" is the code phrase for either preventing new life via contraceptive drugs and devices or medical procedures such as tubal ligation, or in killing unborn life through the use of abortifacients or surgical abortion. No matter how pleasant the euphemism, the truth is savage and murderous; all done solely for convenience or inconvenience, depending on one's perspective. The human person, outside of one's own selfish interests, no longer is of any

---

[271] Matthew Balan, Planned Parenthood Has Been Selling Body Parts From Aborted Babies For At Least Fifteen Years, August 2015.

value. Thus, we continue to see increasing demands for the legal means to terminate life, whether at the behest of the person (assisted suicide) or not (euthanasia).

Oh, for the love of God!

Charles (Chuck) R. Lanham was ordained into the Permanent Diaconate September 17, 2011. It has been a long and often tortuous road.

Deacon Chuck continues to serve the parish of Saint Albert the Great Catholic Community of the Diocese of Reno, Nevada. He is the Director of Adult Faith Formation and Homebound Ministries for the parish, conducts frequent adult faith formation workshops, and is a regular homilist. He also serves as the bulletin editor and manages the parish website.

He has written over a 1,000 weekly essays on theology, faith, morals, teachings of the magisterium and the Catholic Church meant to illuminate, illustrate, and catechize. All his reflections, homilies, and commentaries are posted and available https://deaconscorner.org. Comments are always welcome and appreciated.

Deacon Chuck is the author of two previous books: **The Voices of God: hearing God in the silence** which offers the reader insights into how to hear God's voice through the noise surrounds that us. **Echoes of Love: Effervescent Memories** contains prose and verse and speaks to the heart of love.

Happily married to Janet for fifty-two years, they have two daughters and five grandchildren.

He holds undergraduate degrees in History & Political Science, and Business Administration, and a graduate degree in Computer Science. He is a Vietnam Veteran, serving in the U.S. Army for nine years. He has worked at several large computer hardware and software companies, and as an entrepreneur founded three startup companies. He is the author of numerous technical papers and books and shares a patent for a remote monitoring device.

He lives in Reno, Nevada, just minutes away from the shores of Lake Tahoe, where he is convinced that you cannot get much closer to heaven than there.

He regularly speaks to groups of all ages and sizes and would welcome the opportunity to speak to your group.

If you would like to be placed on a mailing list for future books or would like to have him speak to your group, email:

Deacon.Chuck@deaconscorner.org.

www.ingramcontent.com/pod-product-compliance
Lightning Source LLC
Chambersburg PA
CBHW081416090426

42738CB00017B/3387